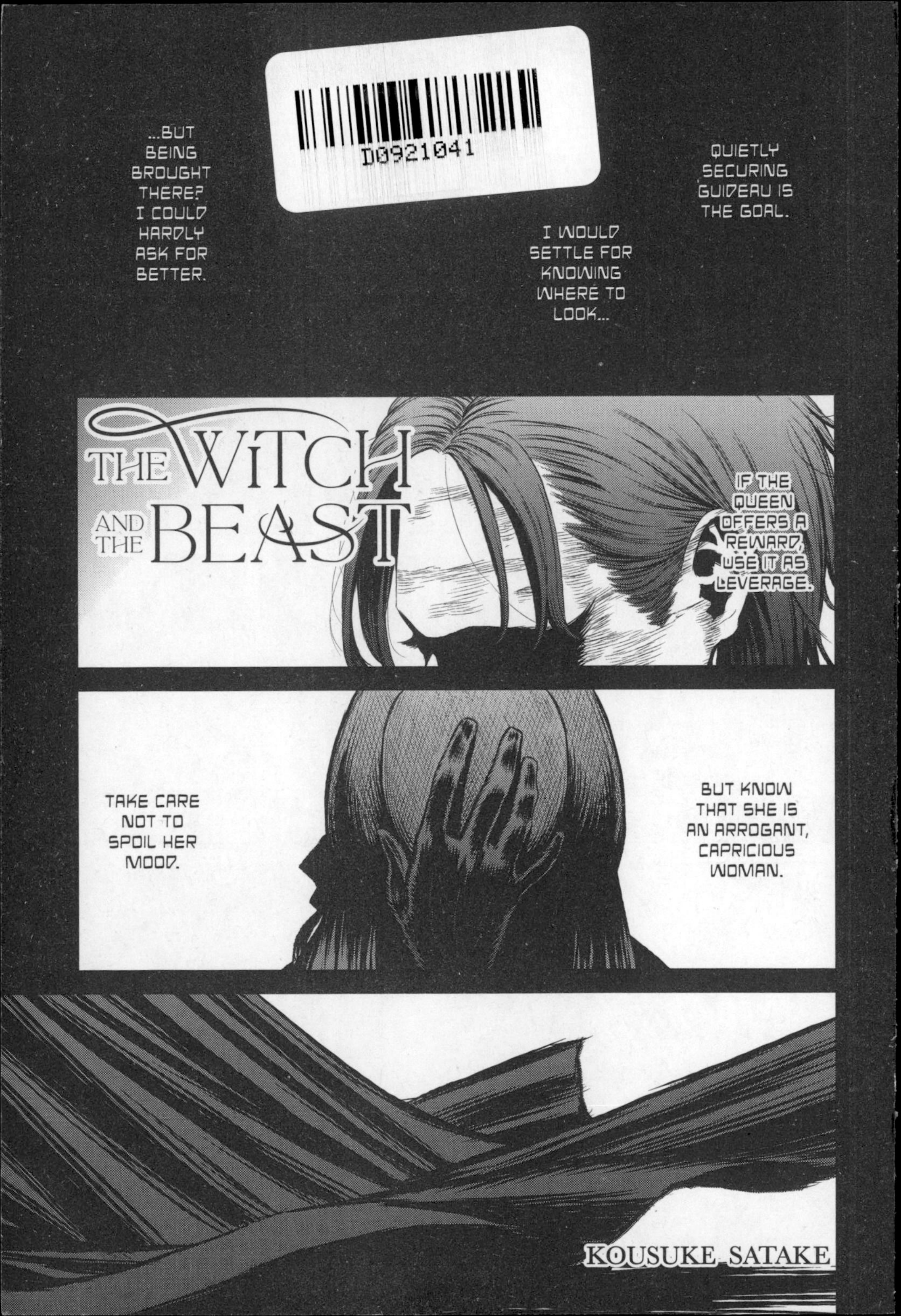
QUIETLY SECURING GUIDEAU IS THE GOAL.
I WOULD SETTLE FOR KNOWING WHERE TO LOOK...
...BUT BEING BROUGHT THERE? I COULD HARDLY ASK FOR BETTER.
THE WITCH AND THE BEAST
IF THE QUEEN OFFERS A REWARD, USE IT AS LEVERAGE.
BUT KNOW THAT SHE IS AN ARROGANT, CAPRICIOUS WOMAN.
TAKE CARE NOT TO SPOIL HER MOOD.
KOUSUKE SATAKE

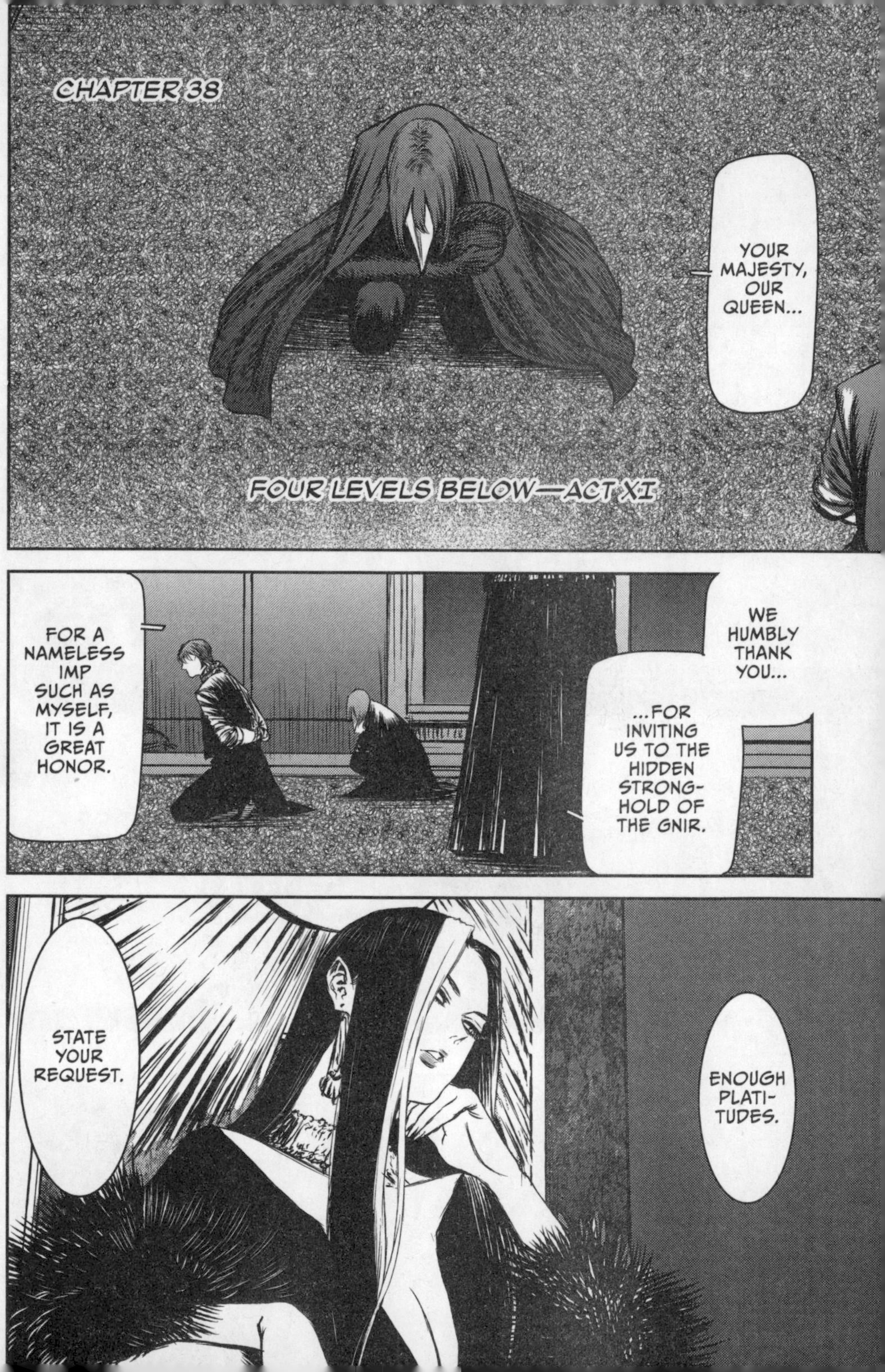
CHAPTER 38
YOUR MAJESTY, OUR QUEEN...
FOUR LEVELS BELOW—ACT XI
WE HUMBLY THANK YOU...
...FOR INVITING US TO THE HIDDEN STRONGHOLD OF THE GNIR.
FOR A NAMELESS IMP SUCH AS MYSELF, IT IS A GREAT HONOR.
ENOUGH PLATITUDES.
STATE YOUR REQUEST.

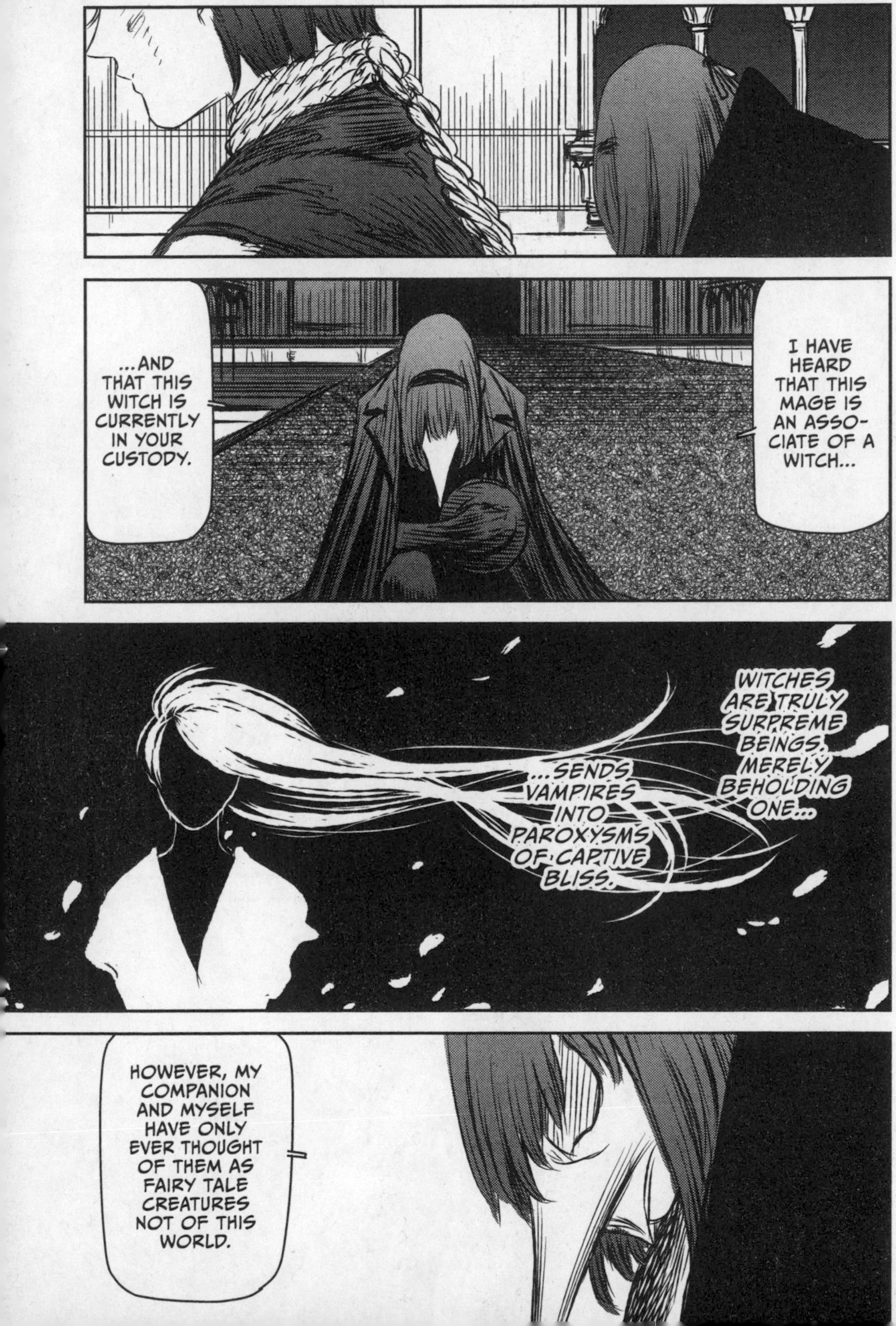
I HAVE HEARD THAT THIS MAGE IS AN ASSOCIATE OF A WITCH...
...AND THAT THIS WITCH IS CURRENTLY IN YOUR CUSTODY.
WITCHES ARE TRULY SUPREME BEINGS. MERELY BEHOLDING ONE...
...SENDS VAMPIRES INTO PAROXYSMS OF CAPTIVE BLISS.
HOWEVER, MY COMPANION AND MYSELF HAVE ONLY EVER THOUGHT OF THEM AS FAIRY TALE CREATURES NOT OF THIS WORLD.

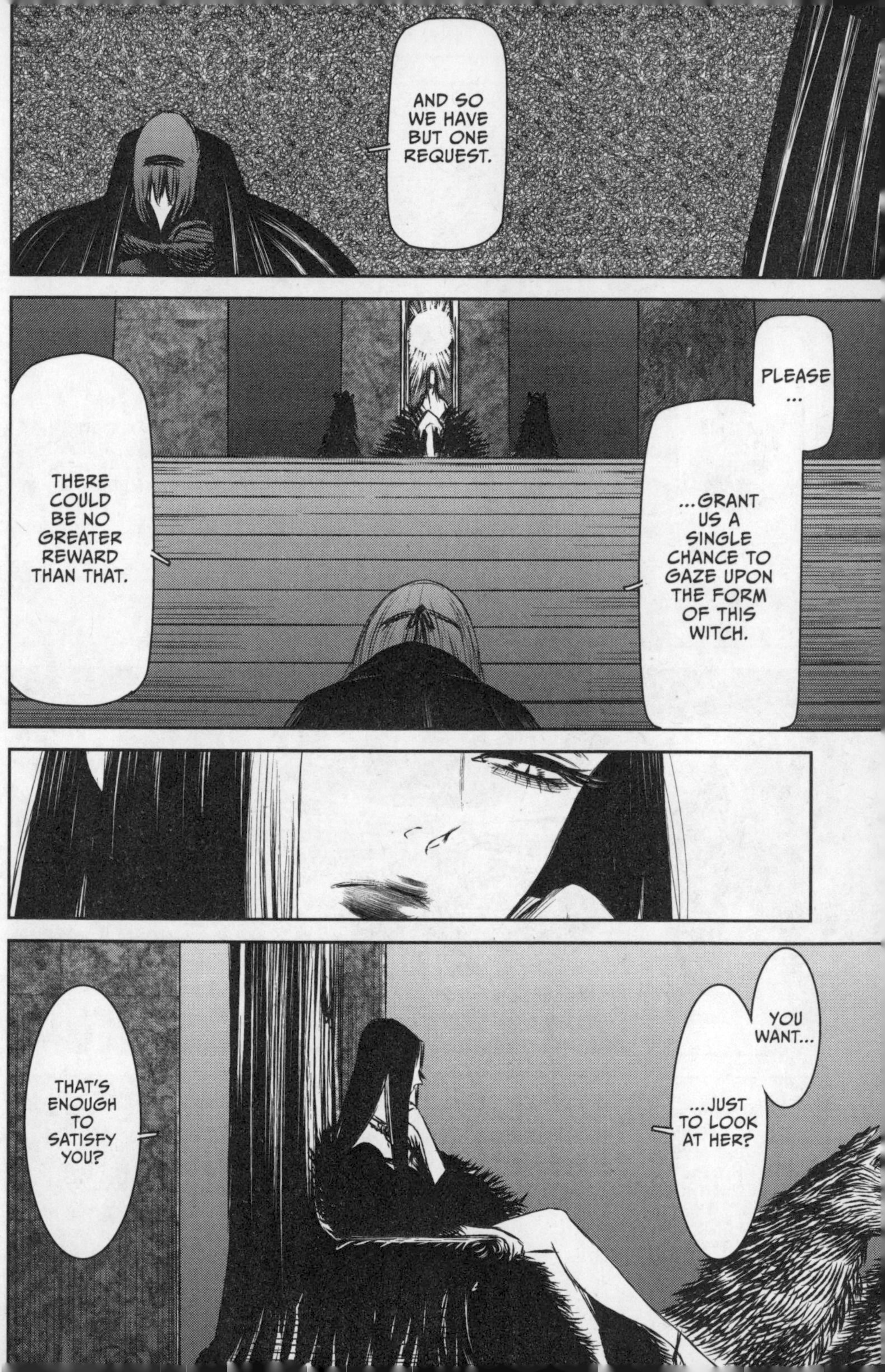
AND SO WE HAVE BUT ONE REQUEST.
PLEASE ...
...GRANT US A SINGLE CHANCE TO GAZE UPON THE FORM OF THIS WITCH.
THERE COULD BE NO GREATER REWARD THAN THAT.
YOU WANT...
...JUST TO LOOK AT HER?
THAT'S ENOUGH TO SATISFY YOU?

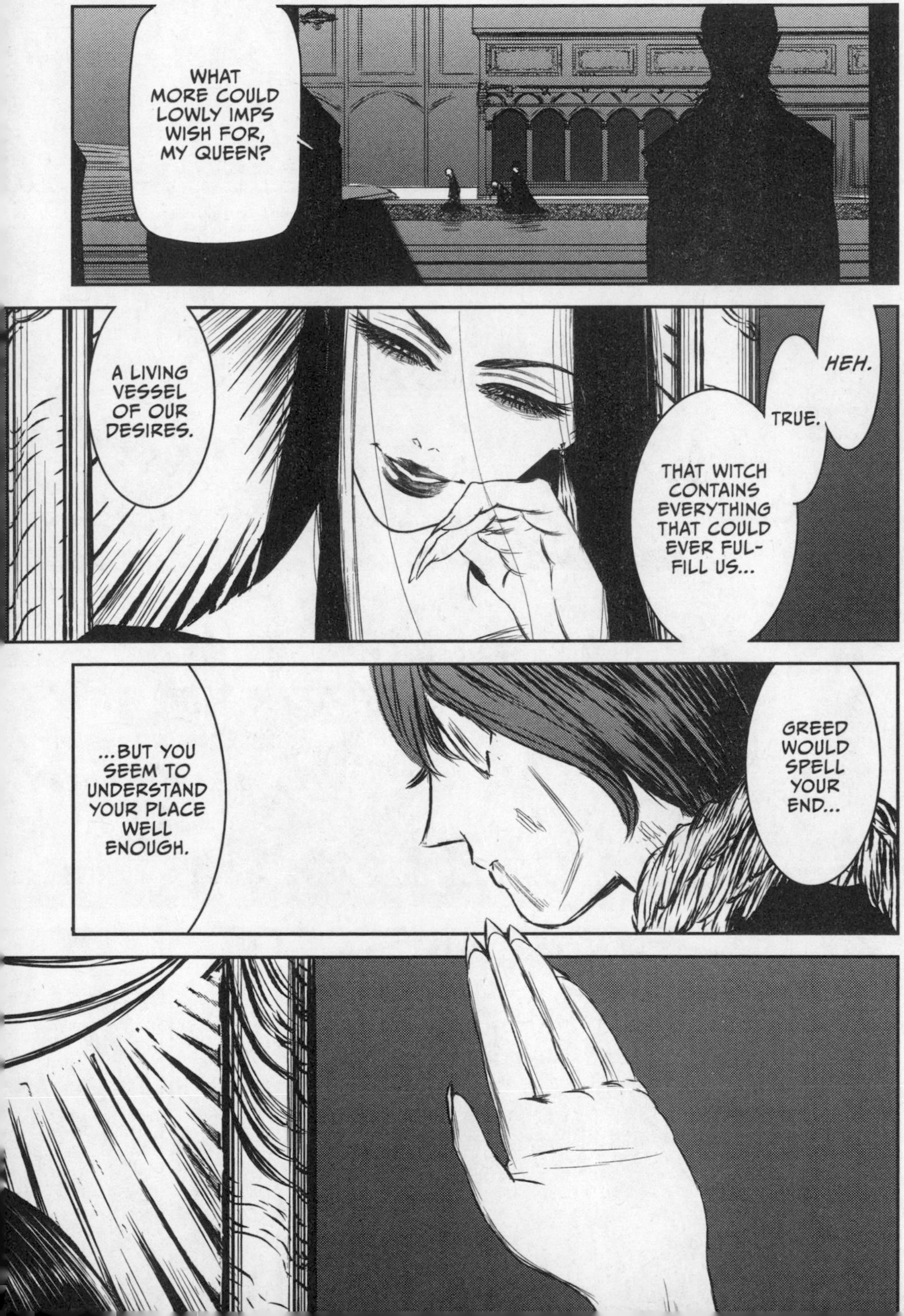
WHAT MORE COULD LOWLY IMPS WISH FOR, MY QUEEN?
HEH.
TRUE.
THAT WITCH CONTAINS EVERYTHING THAT COULD EVER FUL-FILL US...
A LIVING VESSEL OF OUR DESIRES.
GREED WOULD SPELL YOUR END...
...BUT YOU SEEM TO UNDERSTAND YOUR PLACE WELL ENOUGH.

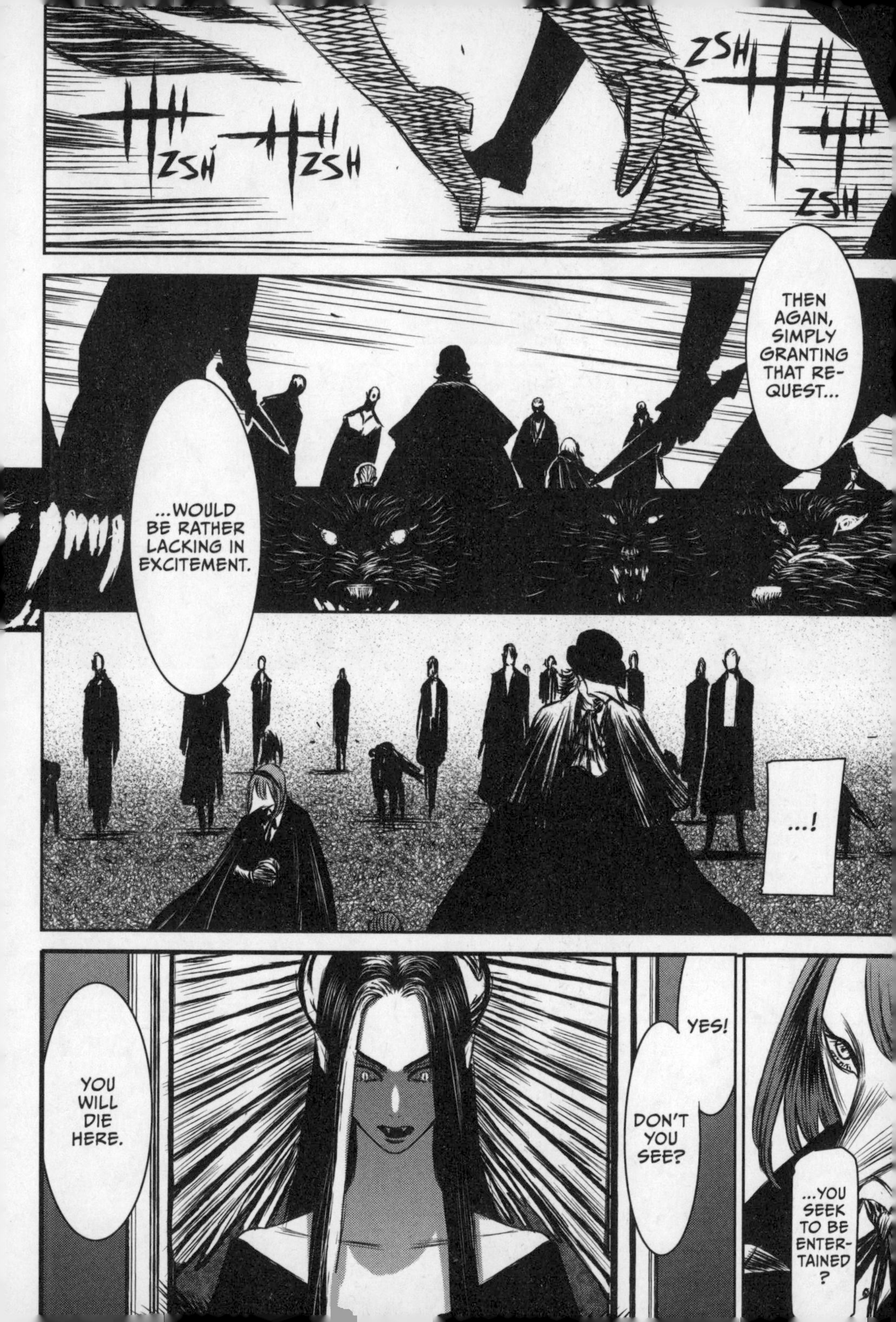
ZSH
ZSH
ZSH
ZSH
THEN AGAIN, SIMPLY GRANTING THAT RE-QUEST...
...WOULD BE RATHER LACKING IN EXCITEMENT.
...!
...YOU SEEK TO BE ENTER-TAINED?
YES!
DON'T YOU SEE?
YOU WILL DIE HERE.

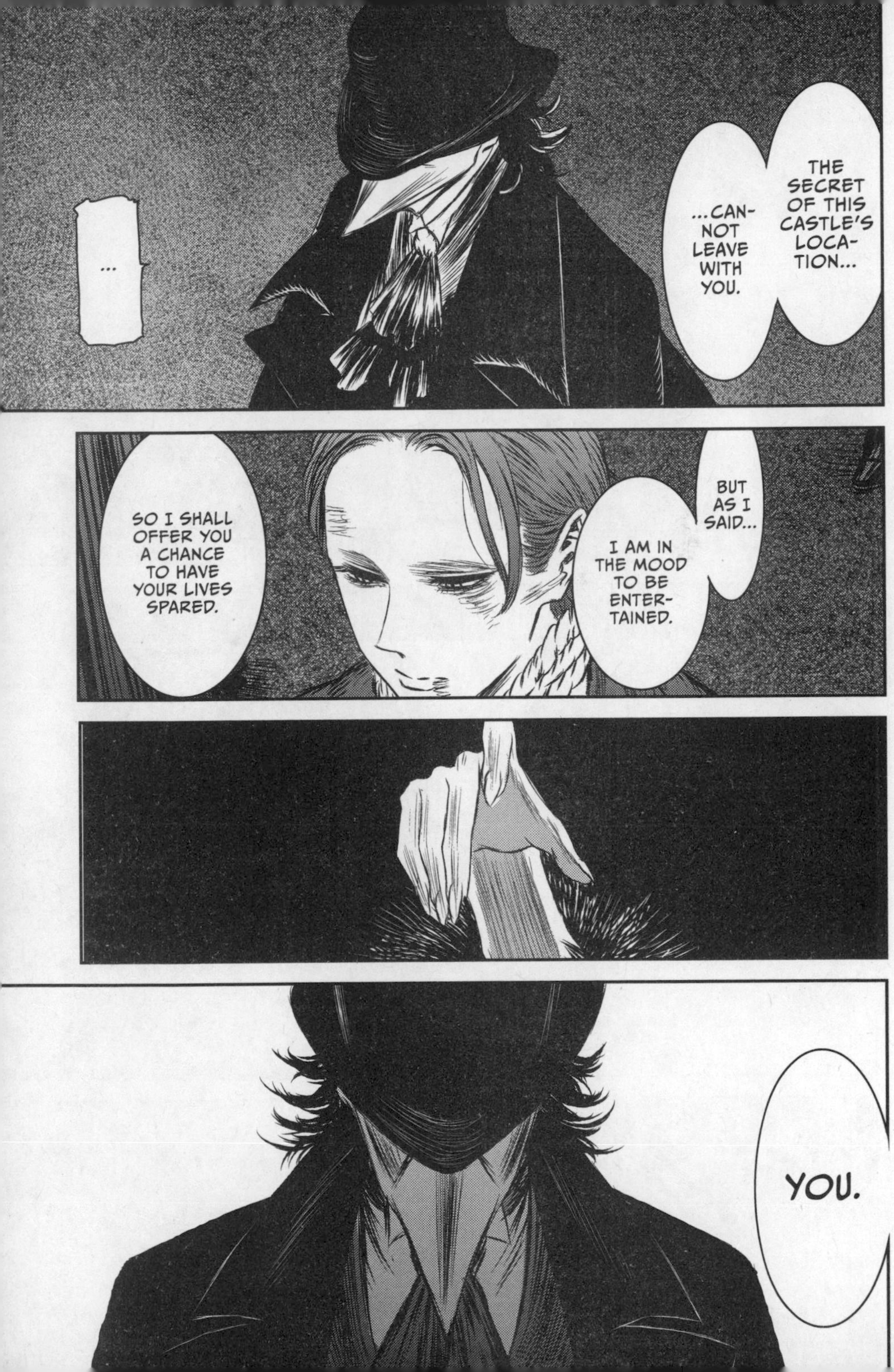
THE SECRET OF THIS CASTLE'S LOCATION...
...CANNOT LEAVE WITH YOU.
...
BUT AS I SAID...
I AM IN THE MOOD TO BE ENTERTAINED.
SO I SHALL OFFER YOU A CHANCE TO HAVE YOUR LIVES SPARED.
YOU.

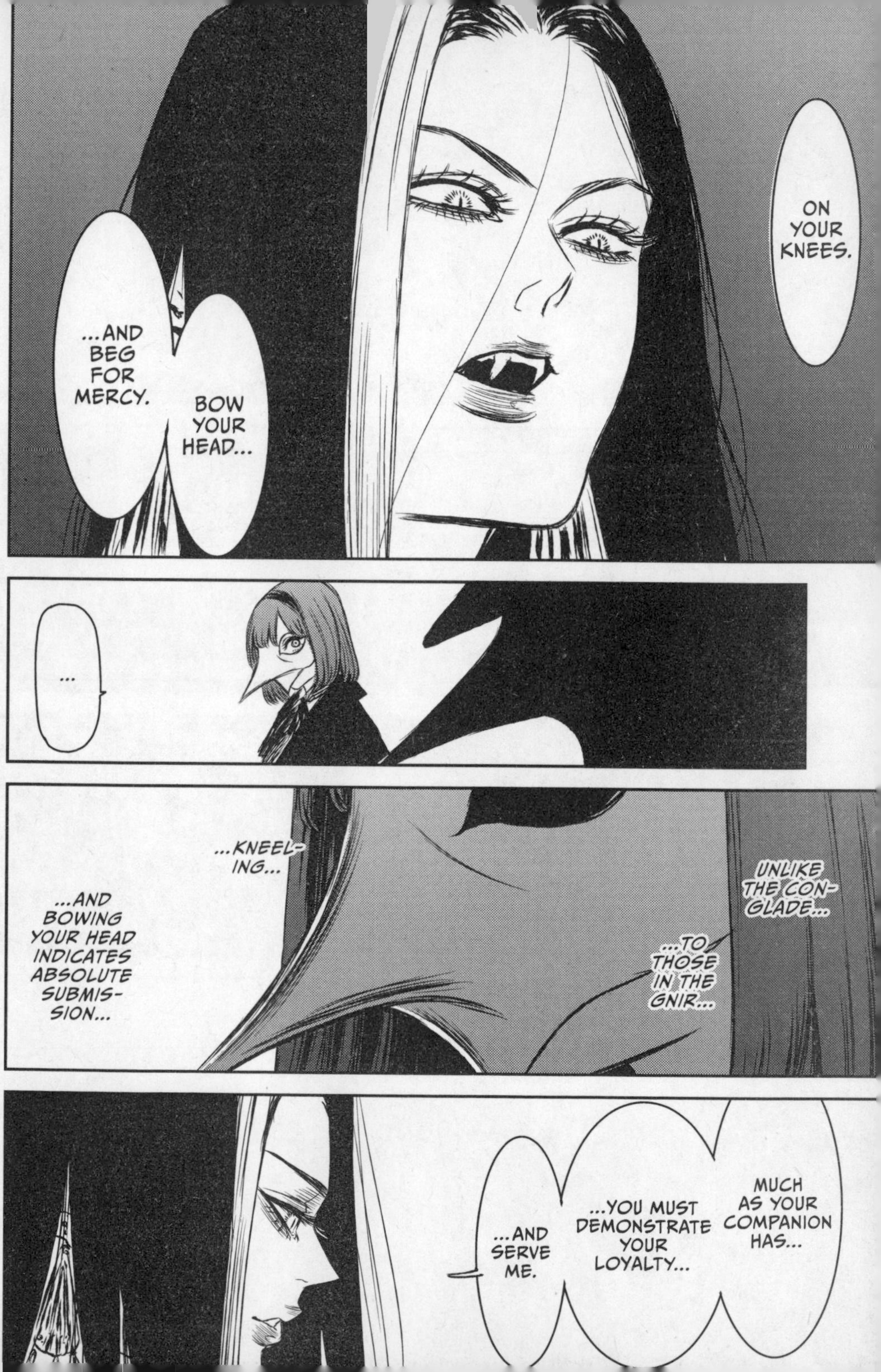
ON YOUR KNEES.
BOW YOUR HEAD...
...AND BEG FOR MERCY.
...
UNLIKE THE CON-GLADE...
...TO THOSE IN THE GNIR...
...KNEEL-ING...
...AND BOWING YOUR HEAD INDICATES ABSOLUTE SUBMIS-SION...
MUCH AS YOUR COMPANION HAS...
...YOU MUST DEMONSTRATE YOUR LOYALTY...
...AND SERVE ME.

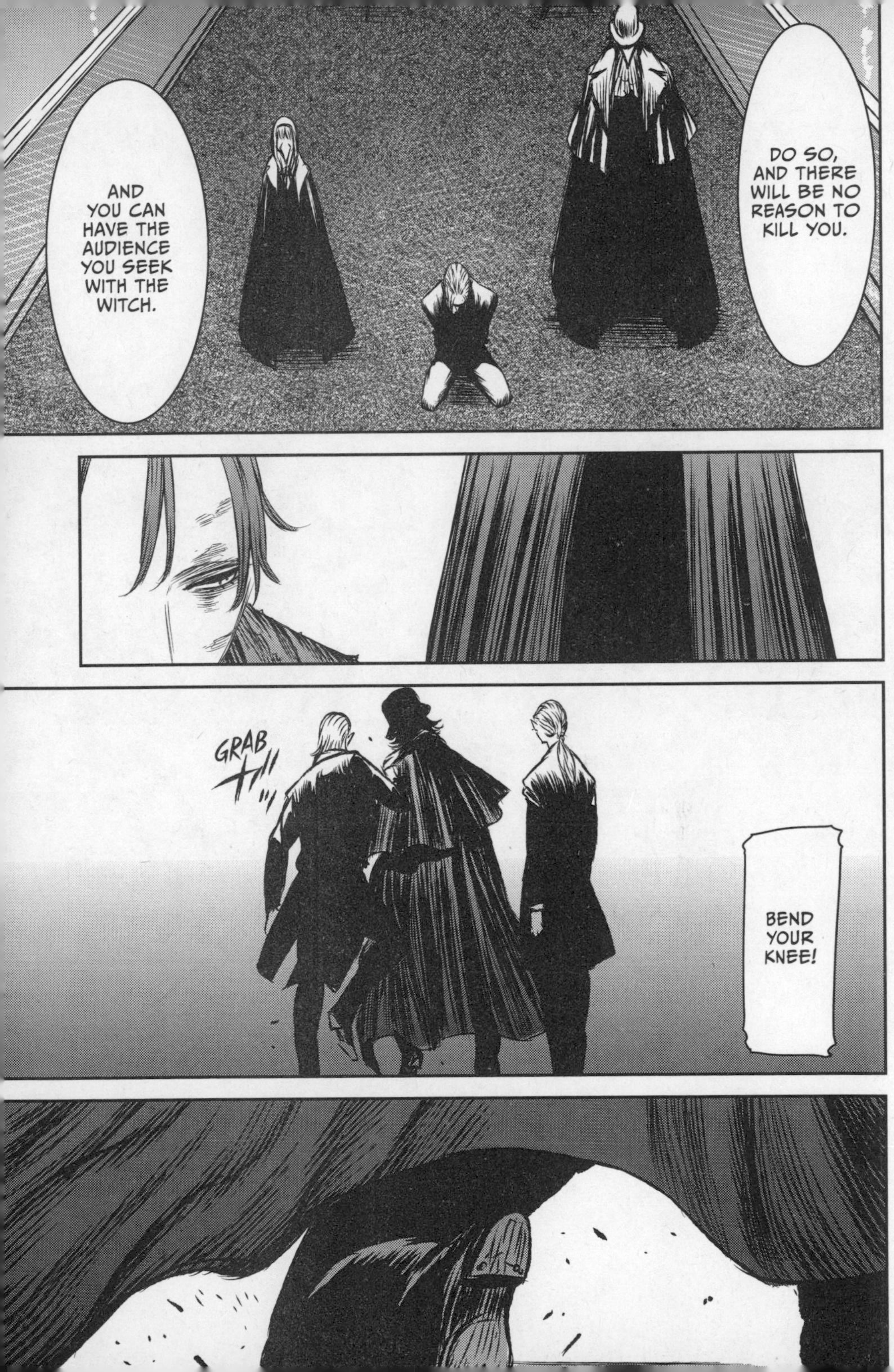
DO SO, AND THERE WILL BE NO REASON TO KILL YOU.
AND YOU CAN HAVE THE AUDIENCE YOU SEEK WITH THE WITCH.
GRAB
BEND YOUR KNEE!

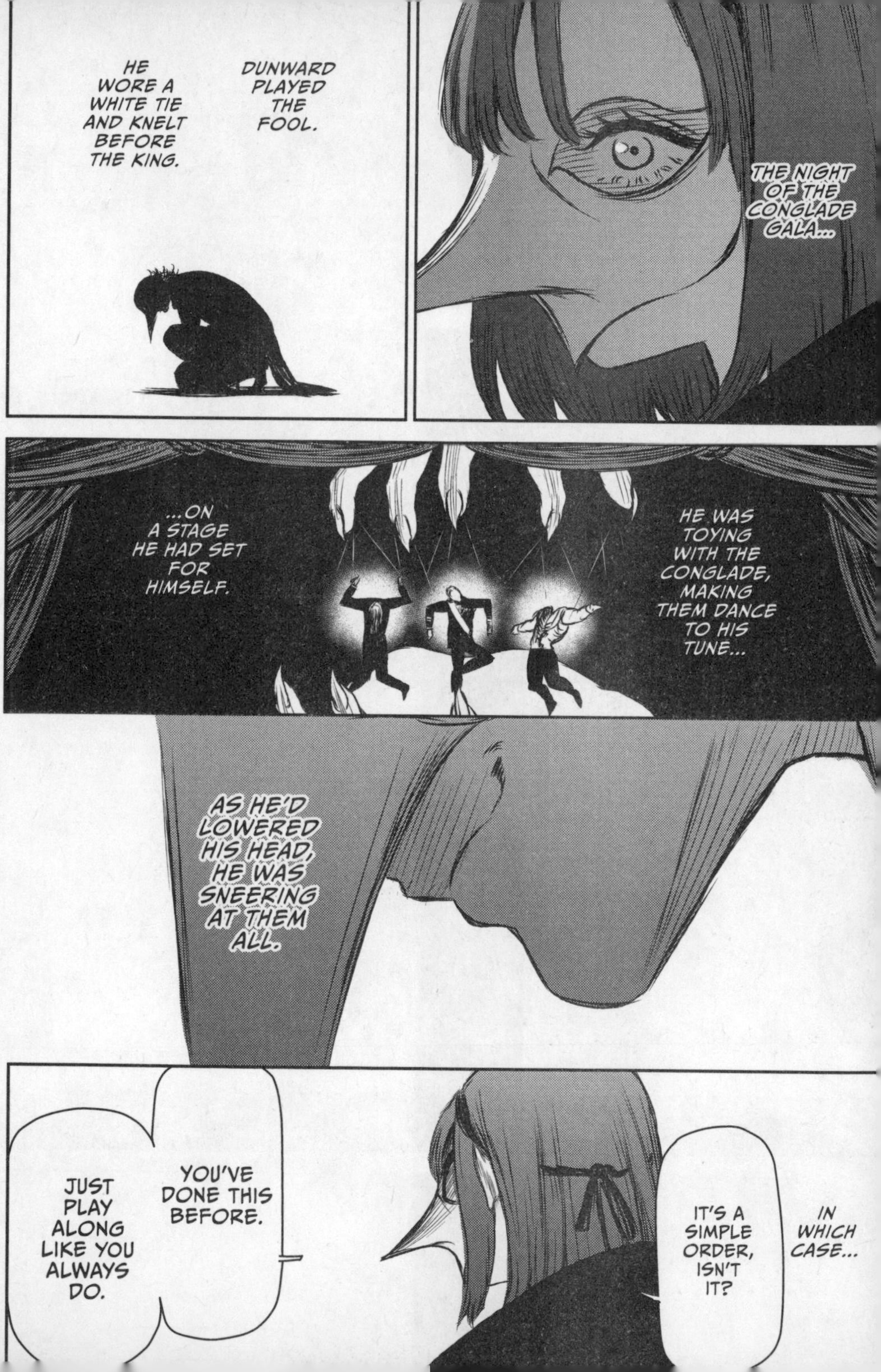
THE NIGHT OF THE CONGLADE GALA...
DUNWARD PLAYED THE FOOL.
HE WORE A WHITE TIE AND KNELT BEFORE THE KING.
HE WAS TOYING WITH THE CONGLADE, MAKING THEM DANCE TO HIS TUNE...
...ON A STAGE HE HAD SET FOR HIMSELF.
AS HE'D LOWERED HIS HEAD, HE WAS SNEERING AT THEM ALL.
IN WHICH CASE...
IT'S A SIMPLE ORDER, ISN'T IT?
YOU'VE DONE THIS BEFORE.
JUST PLAY ALONG LIKE YOU ALWAYS DO.

...JUST ANOTHER STAGE YOU'VE SET FOR YOUR-SELF?

IS THIS NOT...

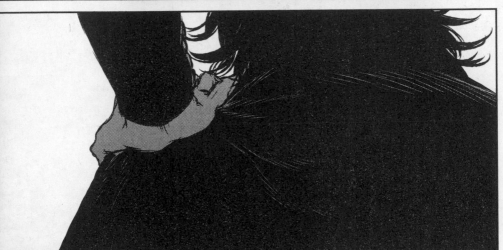

A "STAGE"...?

...

HEH HEH...

YOU'RE EXACTLY RIGHT...

YES, INDEED.

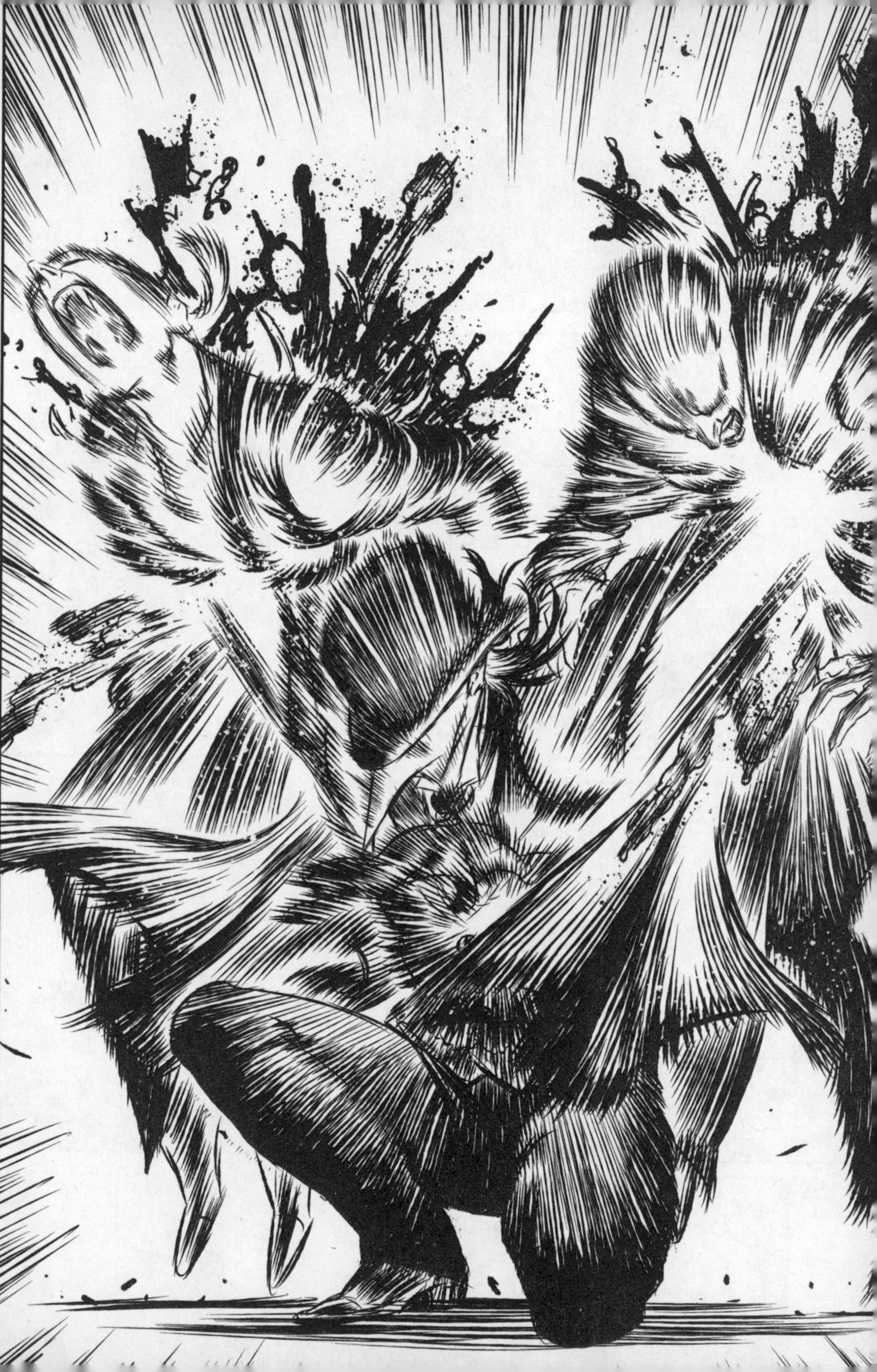

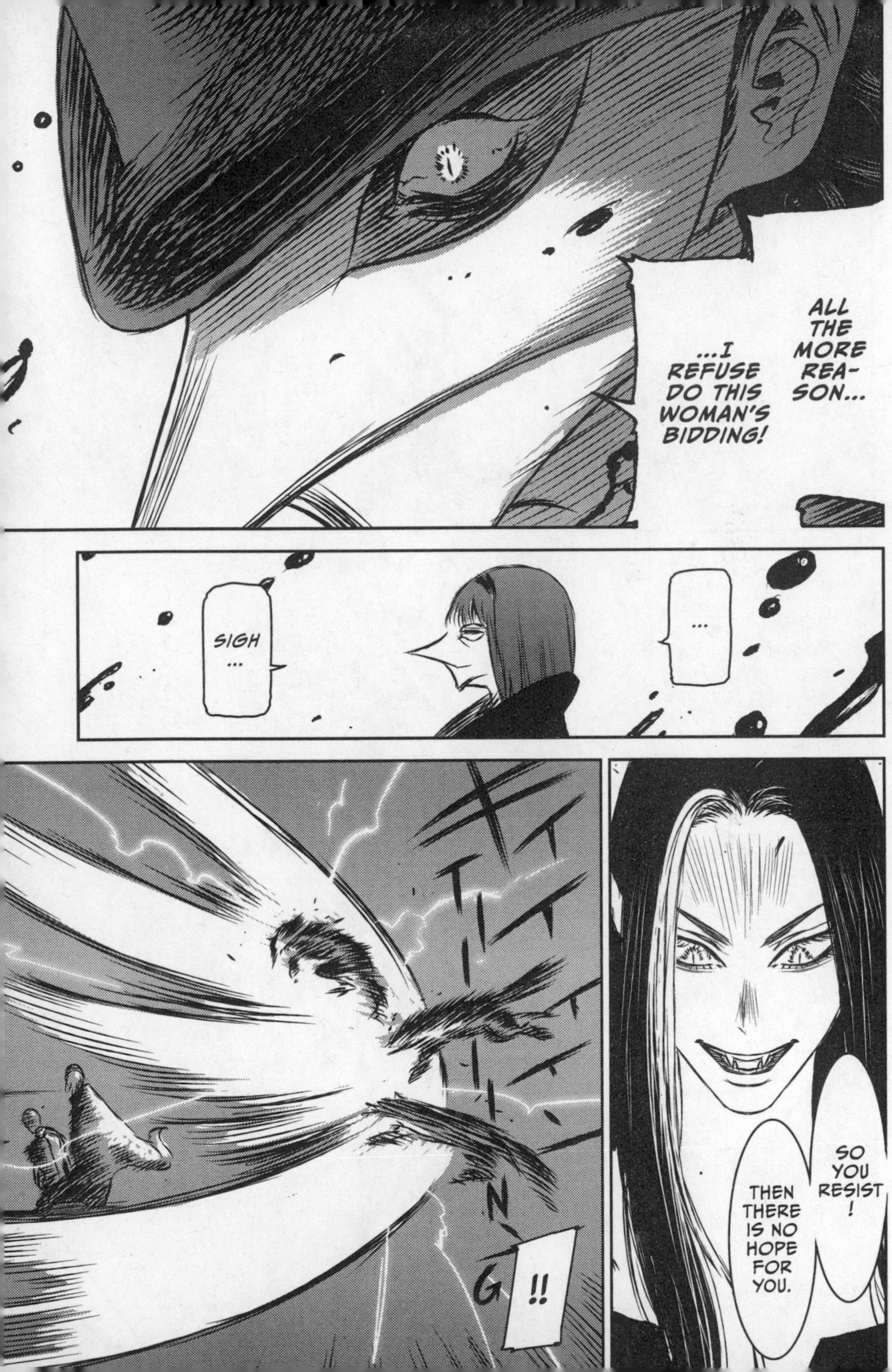
ALL THE MORE REASON...
...I REFUSE DO THIS WOMAN'S BIDDING!
...
SIGH ...
SO YOU RESIST!
THEN THERE IS NO HOPE FOR YOU.
!!

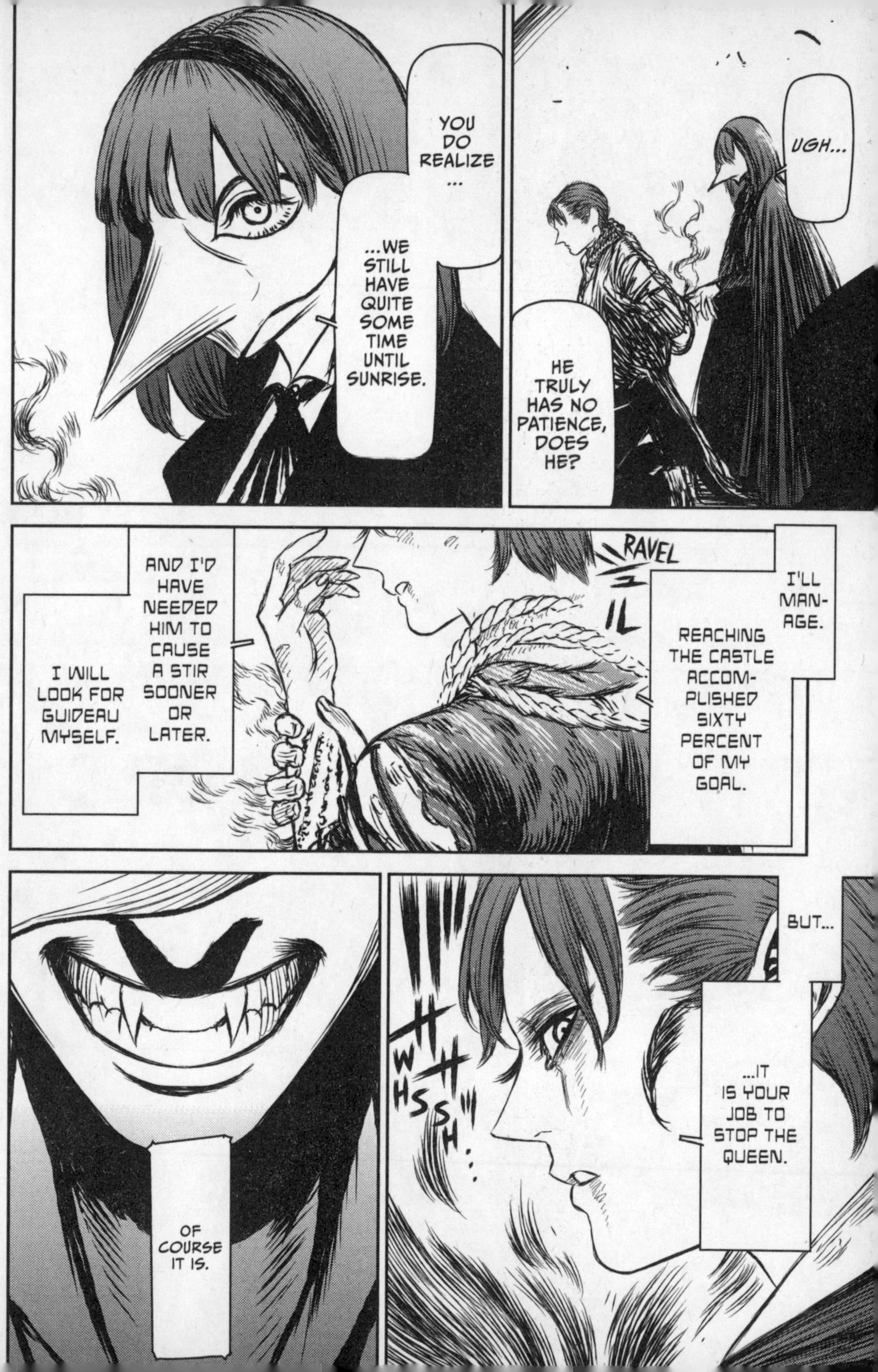
UGH...
HE TRULY HAS NO PATIENCE, DOES HE?
YOU DO REALIZE ...
...WE STILL HAVE QUITE SOME TIME UNTIL SUNRISE.
I'LL MAN-AGE.
REACHING THE CASTLE ACCOM-PLISHED SIXTY PERCENT OF MY GOAL.
AND I'D HAVE NEEDED HIM TO CAUSE A STIR SOONER OR LATER.
I WILL LOOK FOR GUIDEAU MYSELF.
WHSSH...
BUT...
...IT IS YOUR JOB TO STOP THE QUEEN.
OF COURSE IT IS.

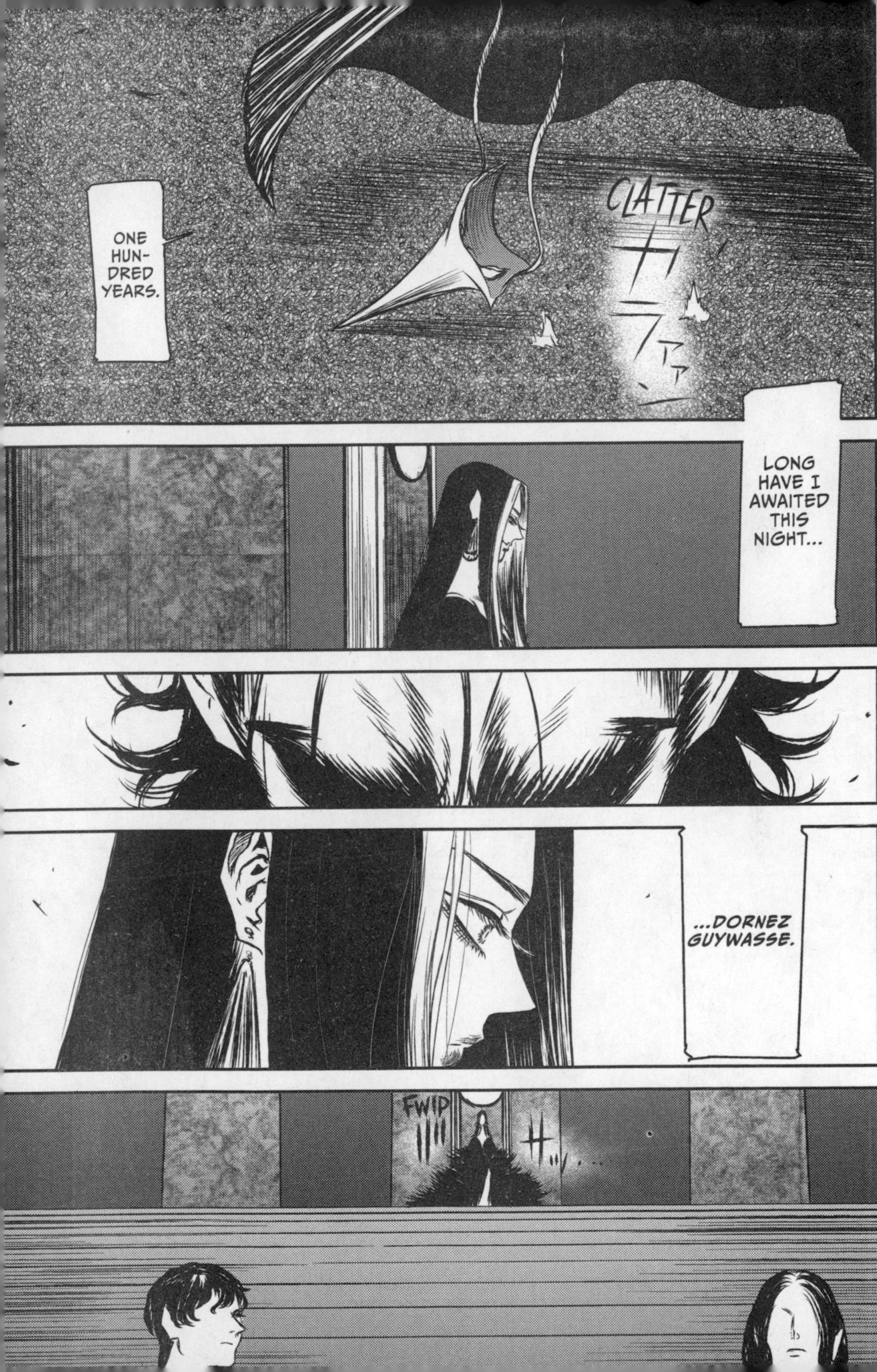
CLATTER
ONE HUN-DRED YEARS.
LONG HAVE I AWAITED THIS NIGHT...
...DORNEZ GUYWASSE.
FWIP

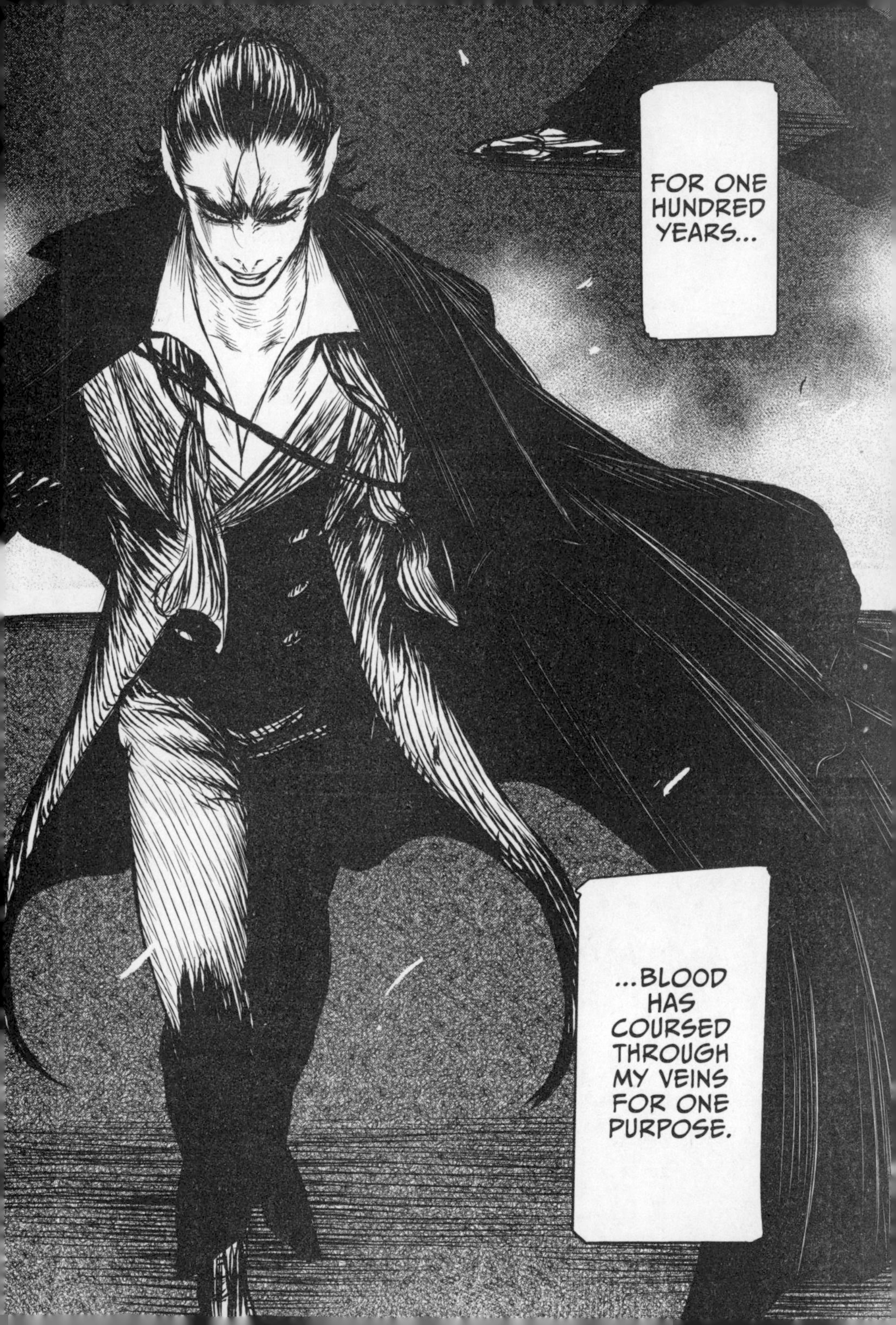
FOR ONE HUNDRED YEARS...
...BLOOD HAS COURSED THROUGH MY VEINS FOR ONE PURPOSE.

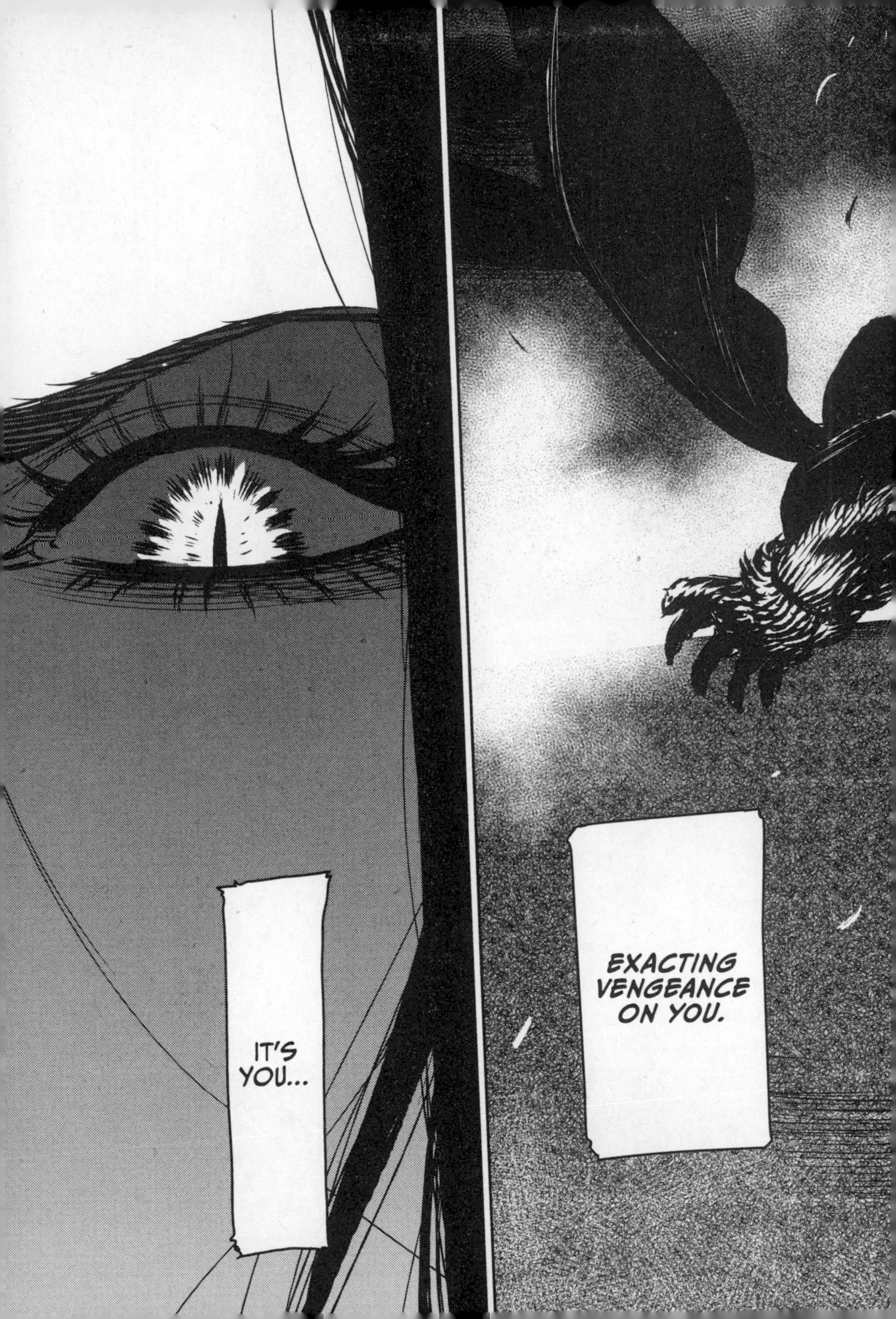
EXACTING VENGEANCE ON YOU.
IT'S YOU...

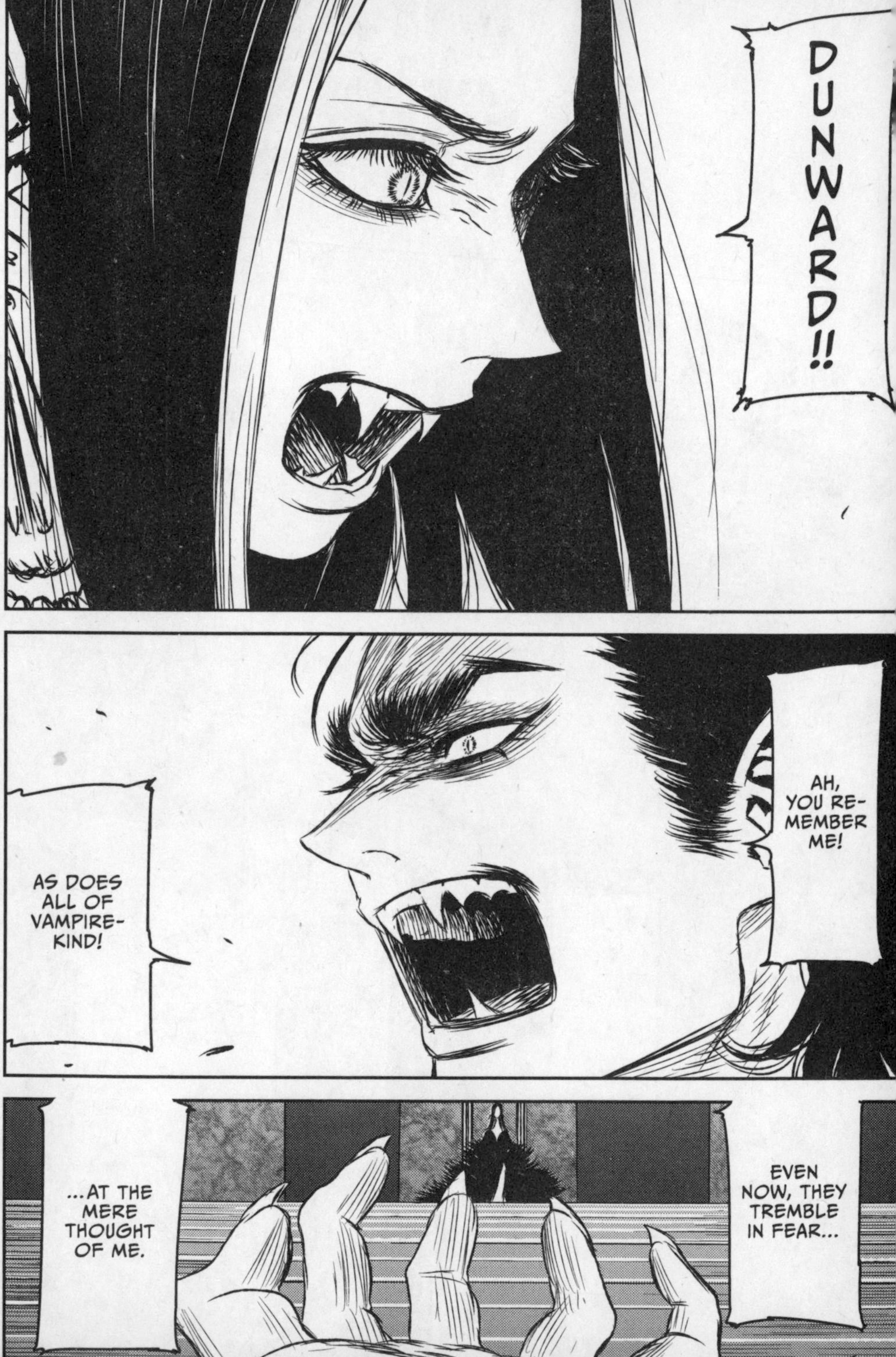
DUNWARD!!
AH, YOU RE-MEMBER ME!
AS DOES ALL OF VAMPIRE-KIND!
EVEN NOW, THEY TREMBLE IN FEAR...
...AT THE MERE THOUGHT OF ME.

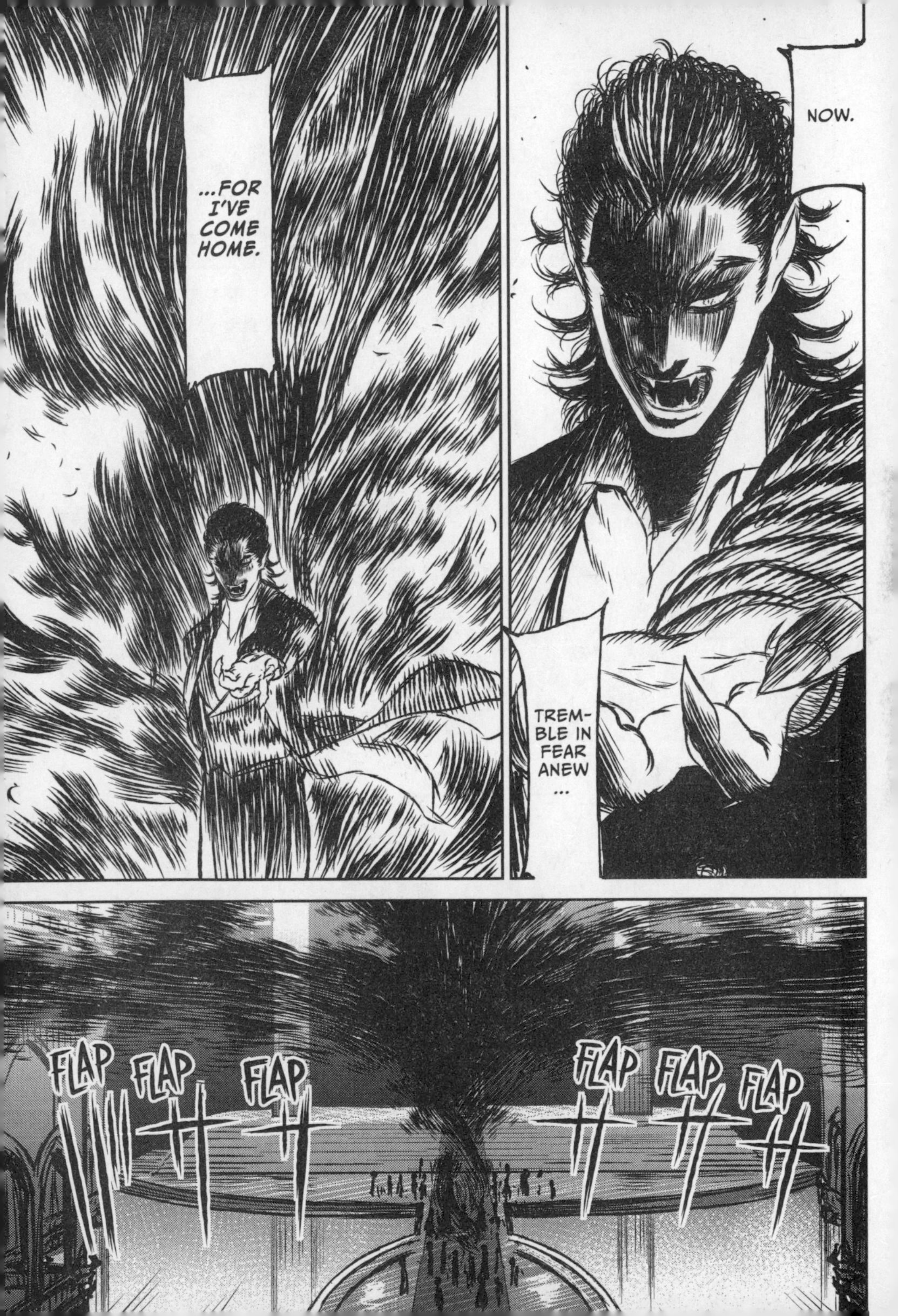
NOW.
TREM-BLE IN FEAR ANEW ...
...FOR I'VE COME HOME.
FLAP FLAP FLAP
FLAP FLAP FLAP

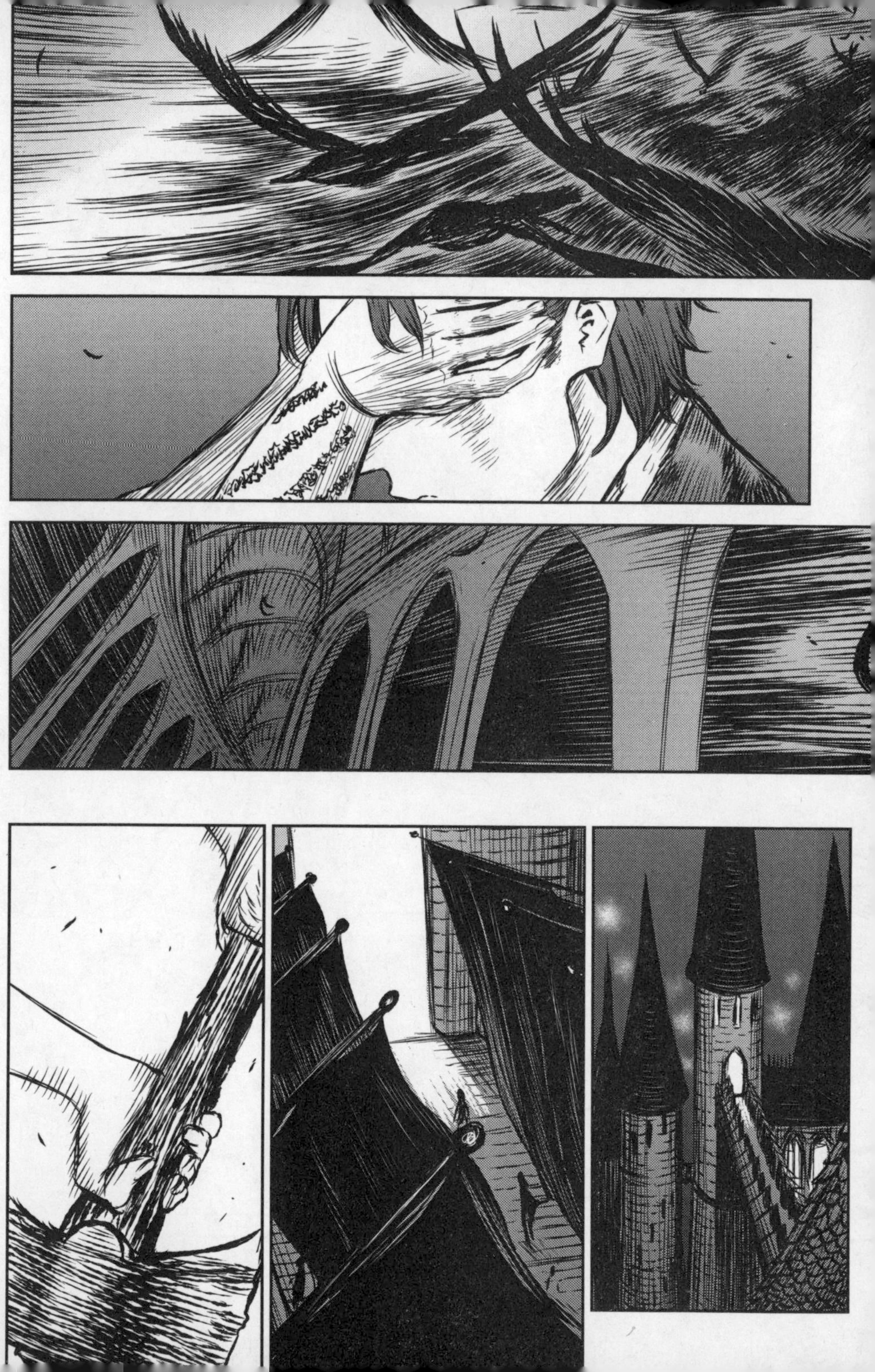

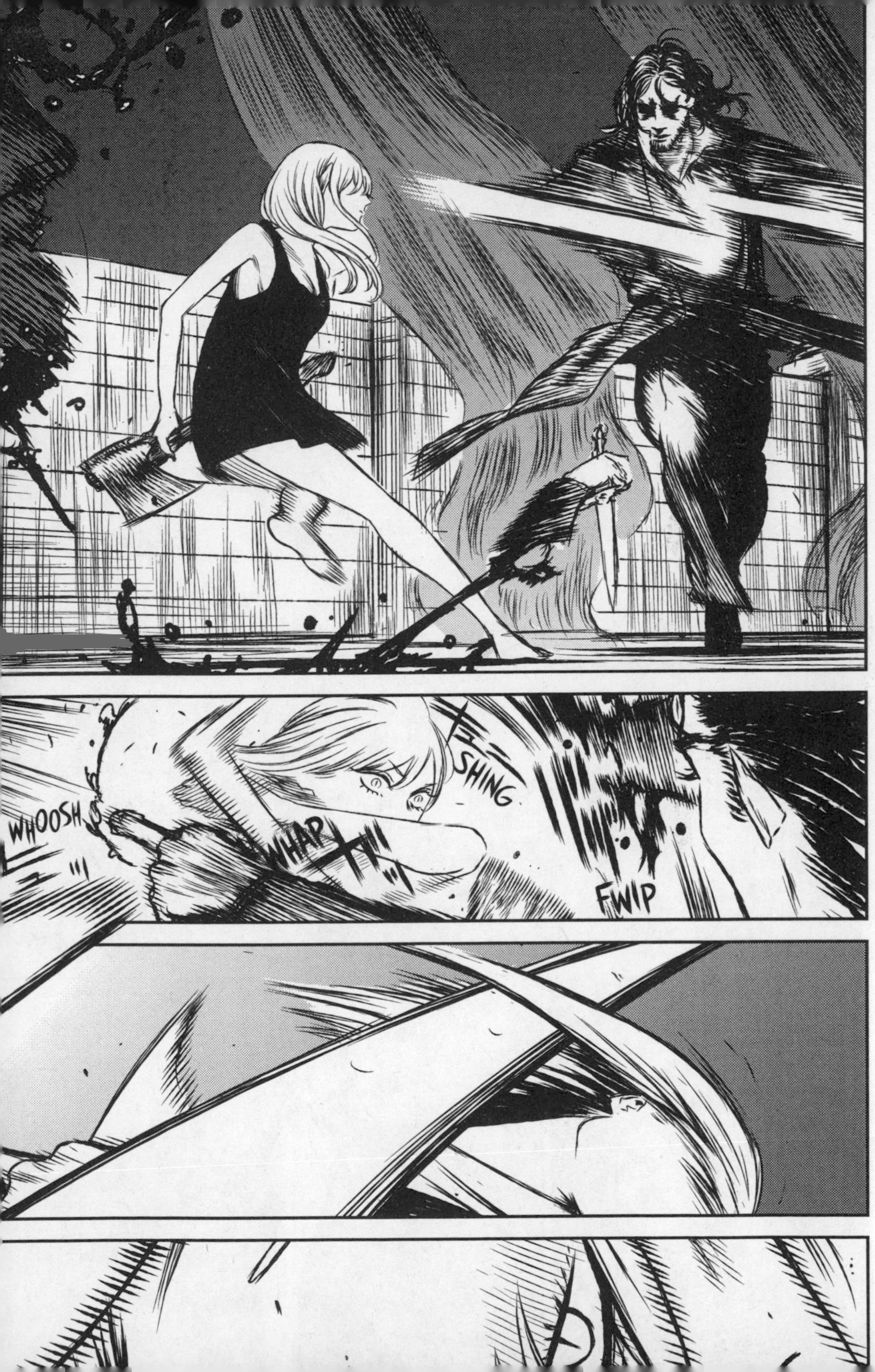
SHING
FWIP
WHAP
WHOOSH

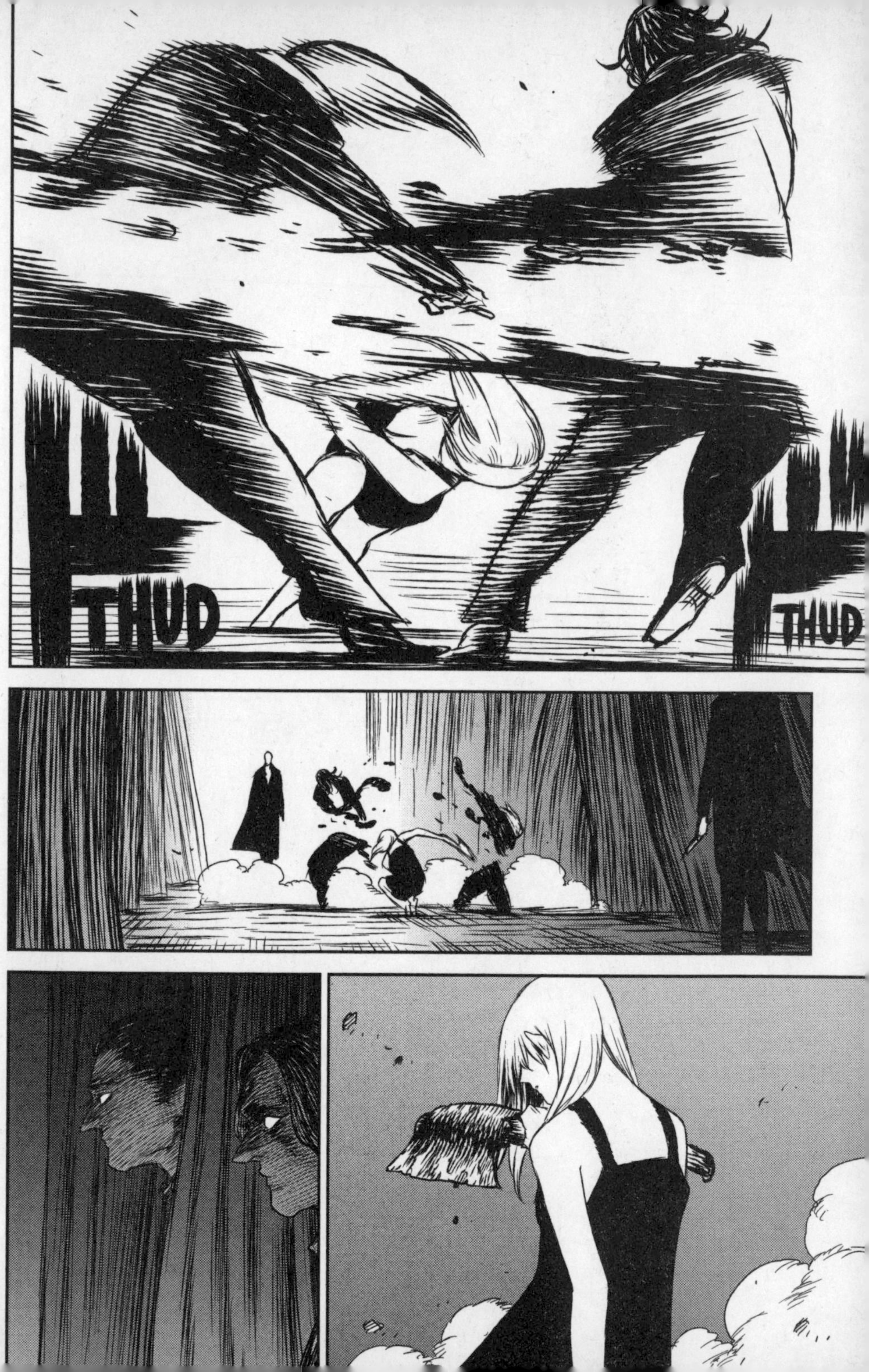
THUD
THUD

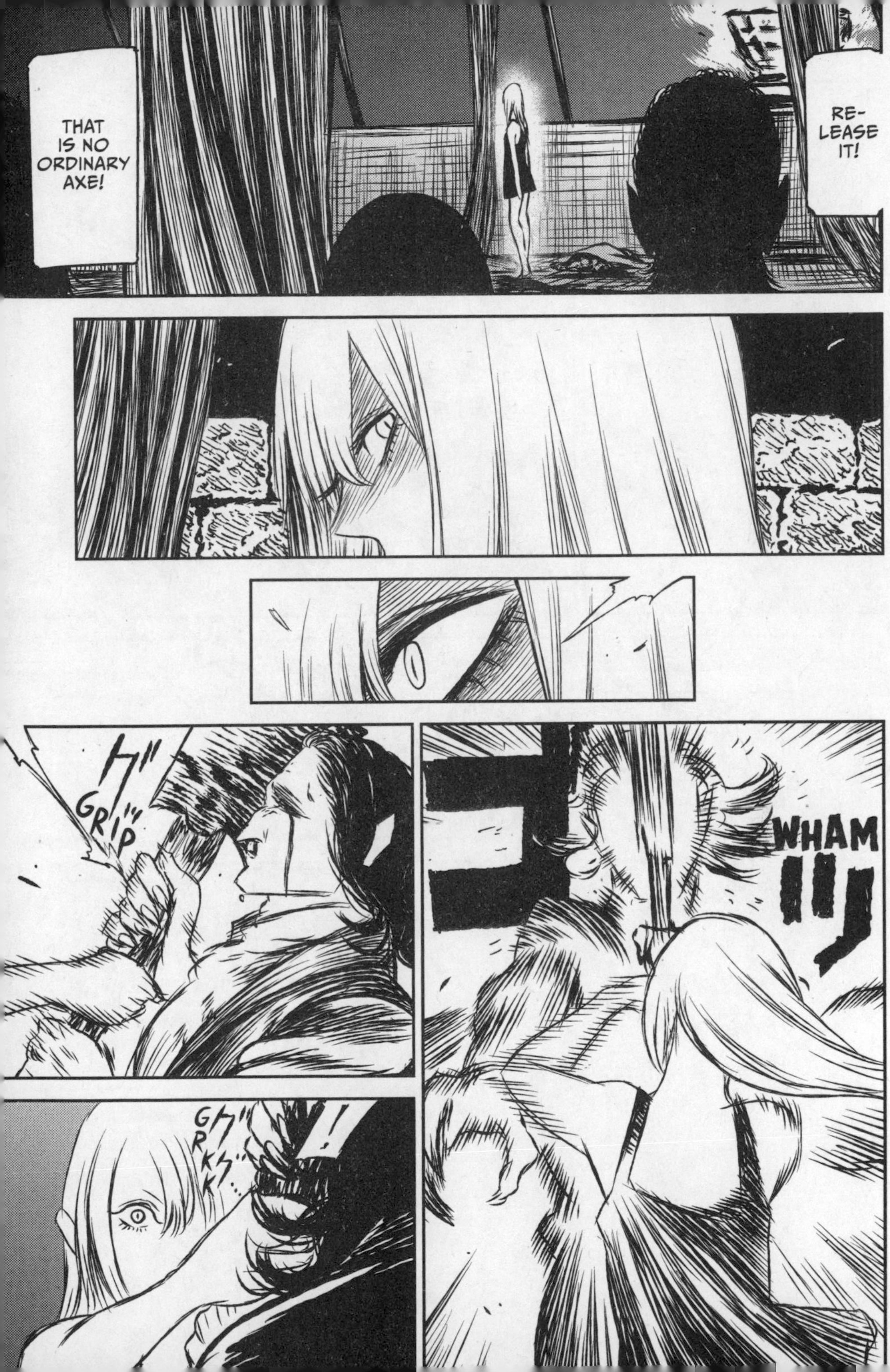
RE-LEASE IT!
THAT IS NO ORDINARY AXE!
WHAM
GRIP

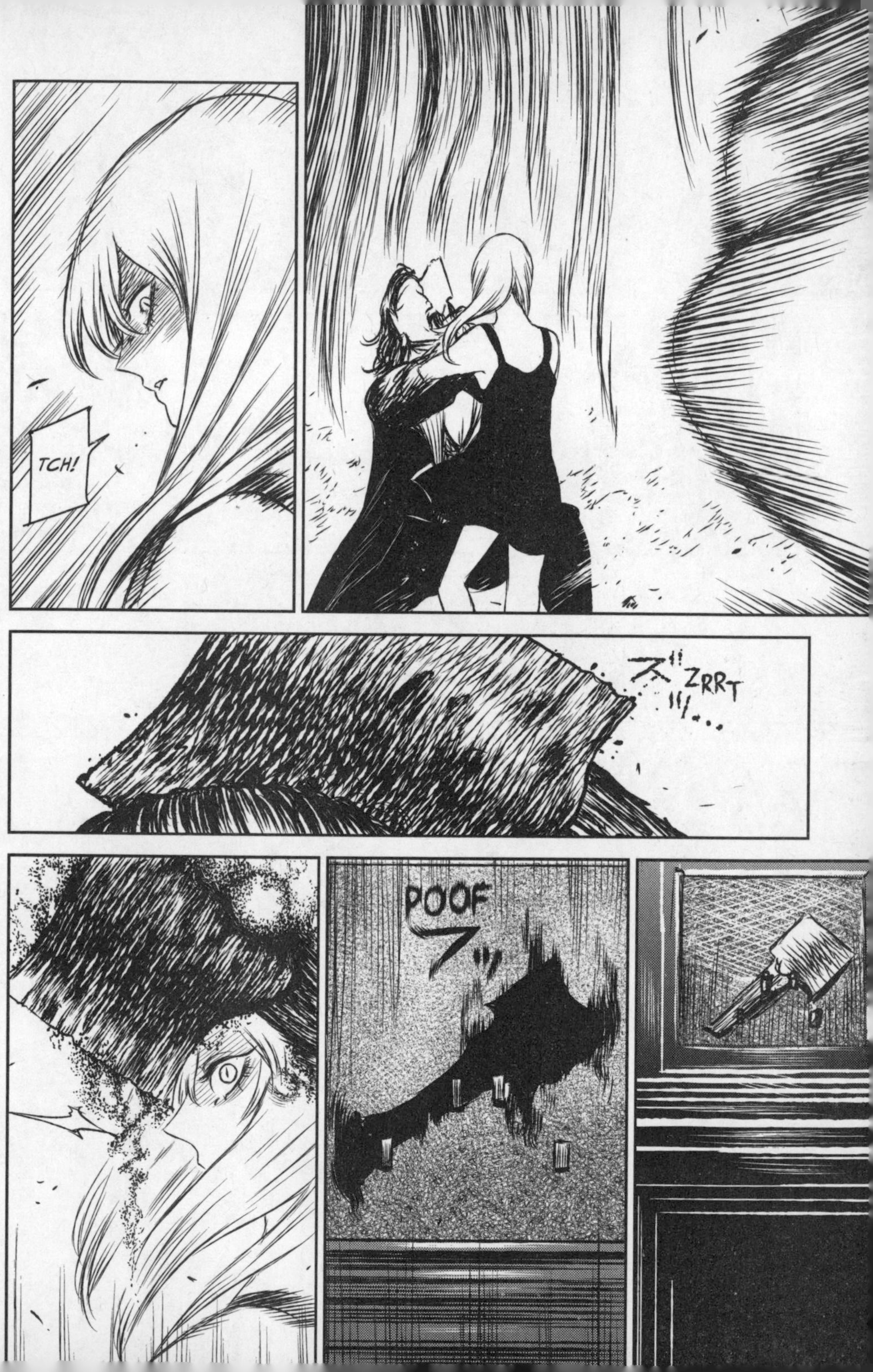
TCH!
ZRRT
POOF

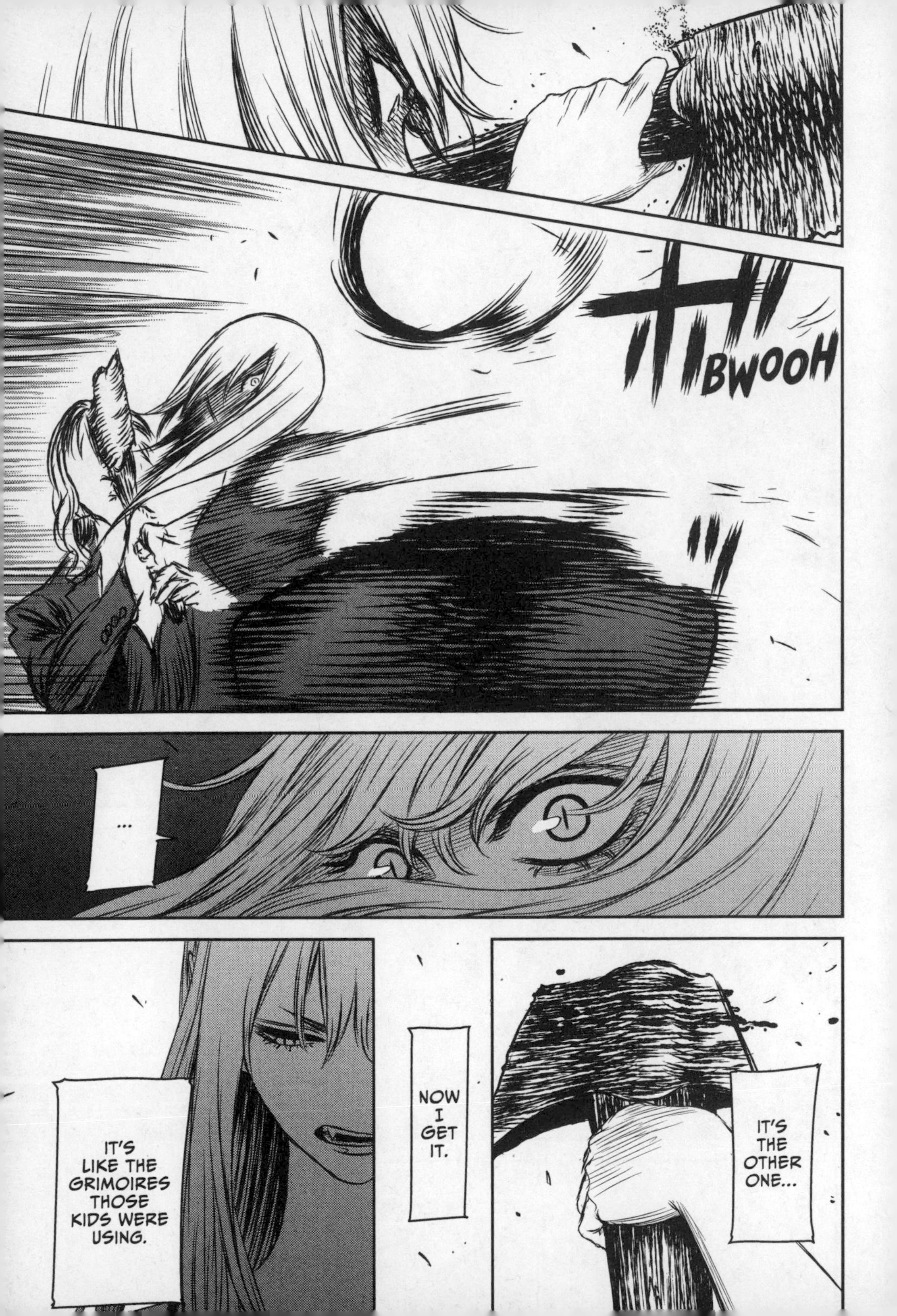
BWOOH
...
IT'S THE OTHER ONE...
NOW I GET IT.
IT'S LIKE THE GRIMOIRES THOSE KIDS WERE USING.

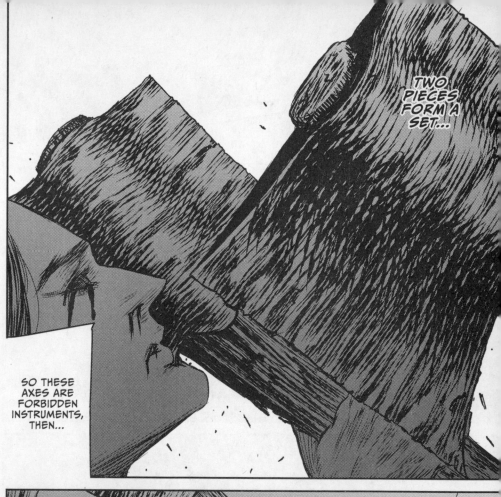

TWO PIECES FORM A SET...

SO THESE AXES ARE FORBIDDEN INSTRUMENTS, THEN...

ゴ
キ
ュ

GLUG.

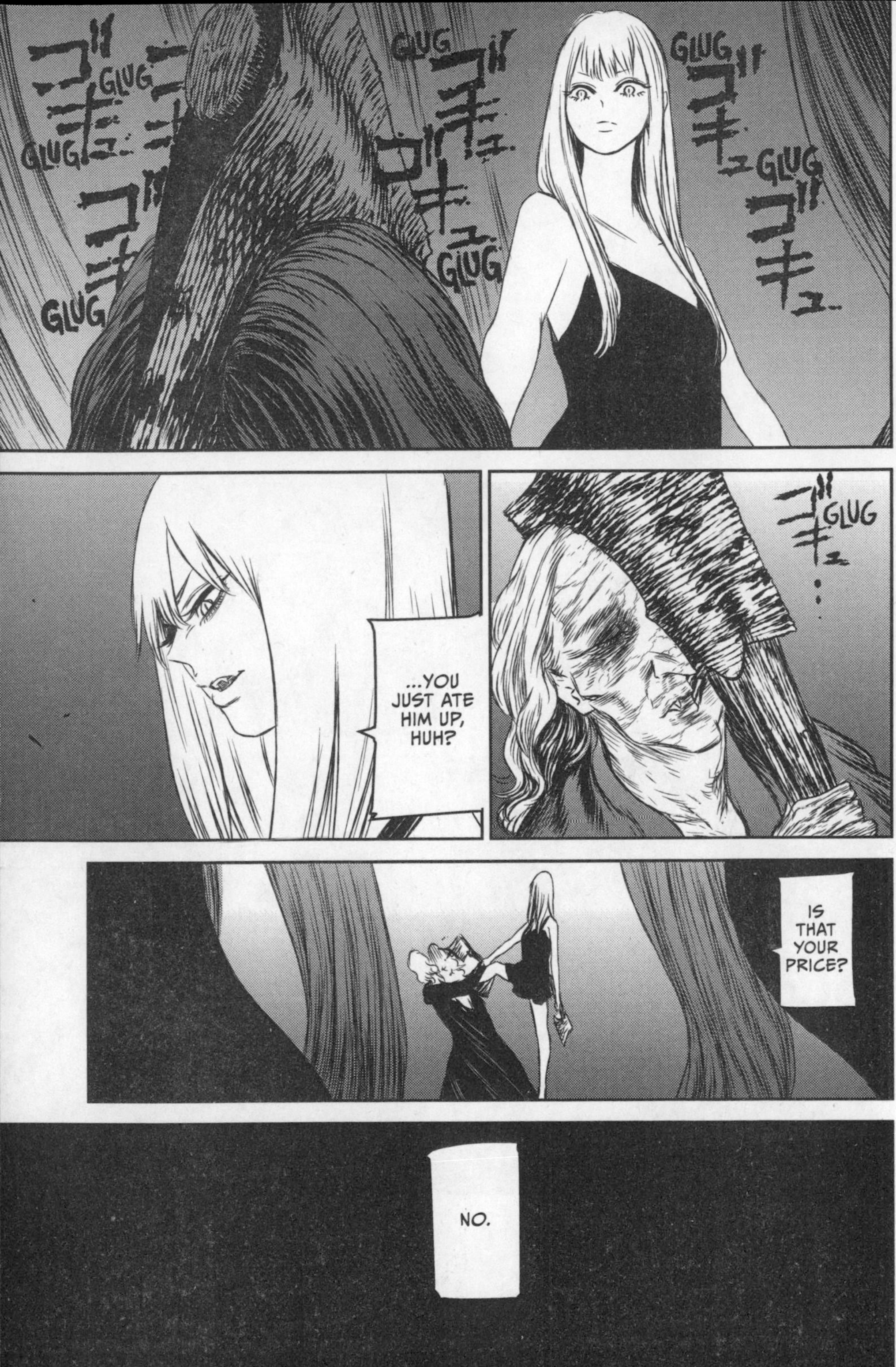
GLUG
GLUG
GLUG
GLUG
GLUG
GLUG
GLUG
...YOU JUST ATE HIM UP, HUH?
IS THAT YOUR PRICE?
NO.

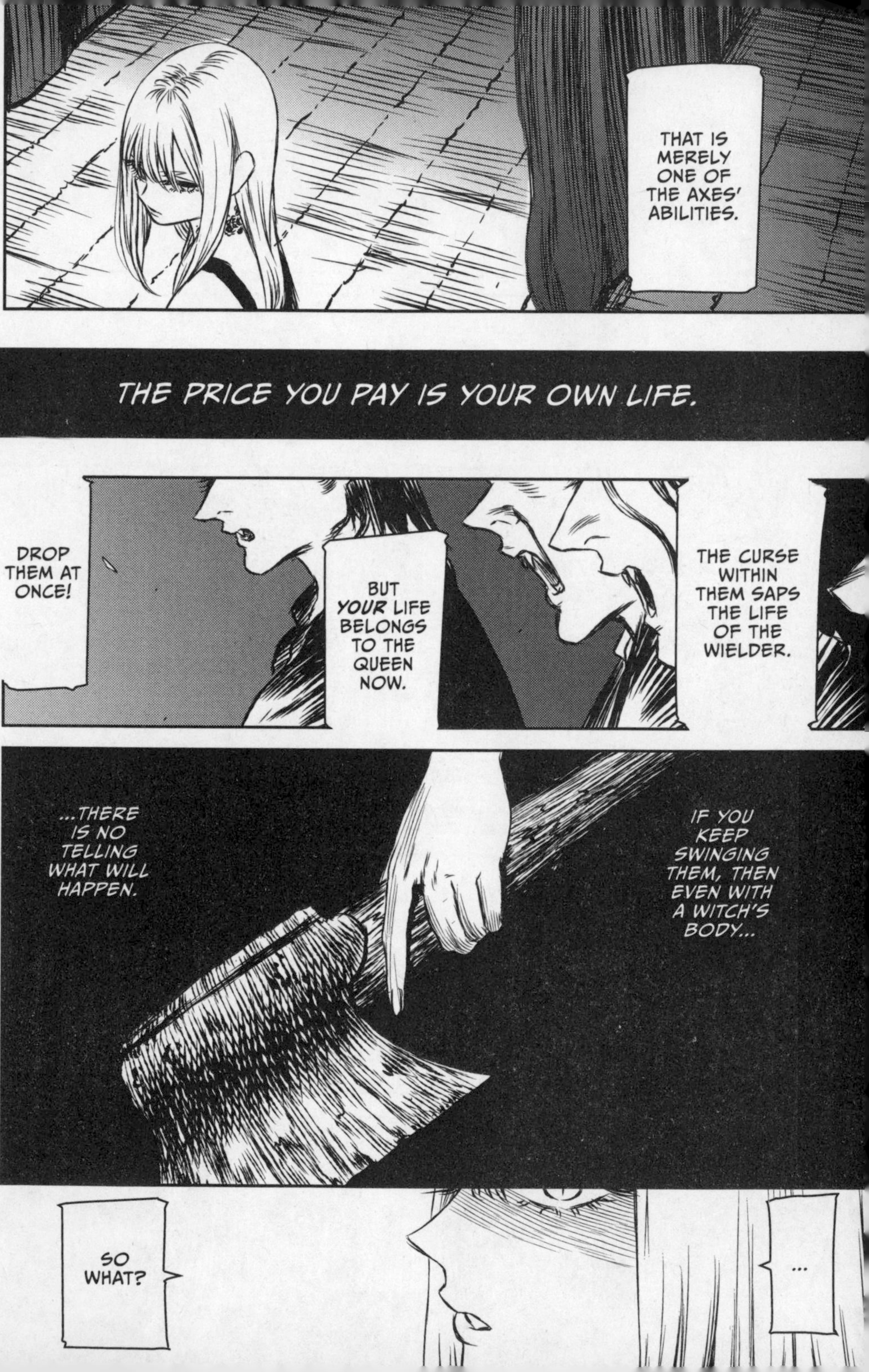
THAT IS MERELY ONE OF THE AXES' ABILITIES.
THE PRICE YOU PAY IS YOUR OWN LIFE.
THE CURSE WITHIN THEM SAPS THE LIFE OF THE WIELDER.
BUT YOUR LIFE BELONGS TO THE QUEEN NOW.
DROP THEM AT ONCE!
IF YOU KEEP SWINGING THEM, THEN EVEN WITH A WITCH'S BODY...
...THERE IS NO TELLING WHAT WILL HAPPEN.
...
SO WHAT?

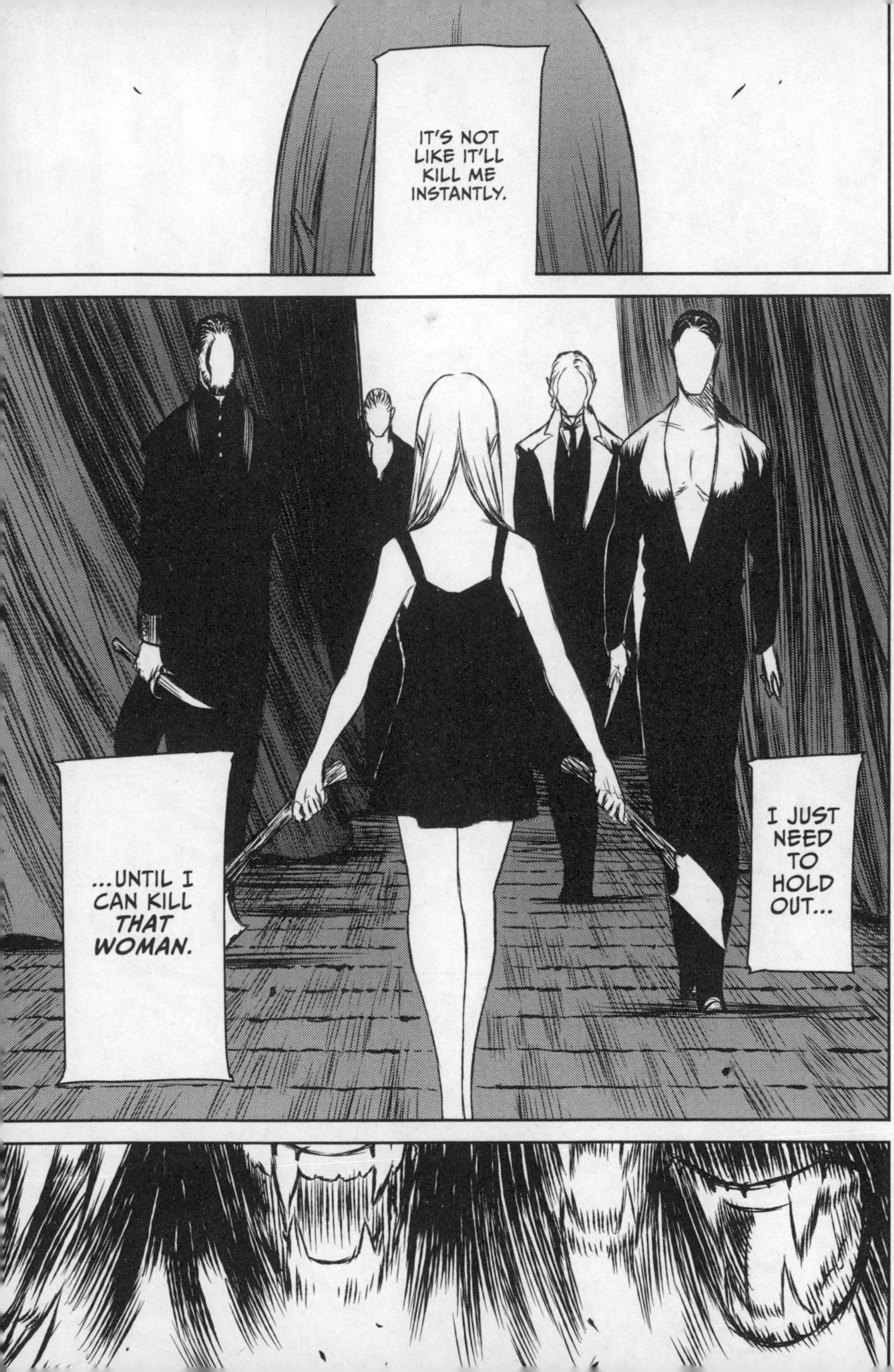
IT'S NOT LIKE IT'LL KILL ME INSTANTLY.
I JUST NEED TO HOLD OUT...
...UNTIL I CAN KILL *THAT WOMAN.*

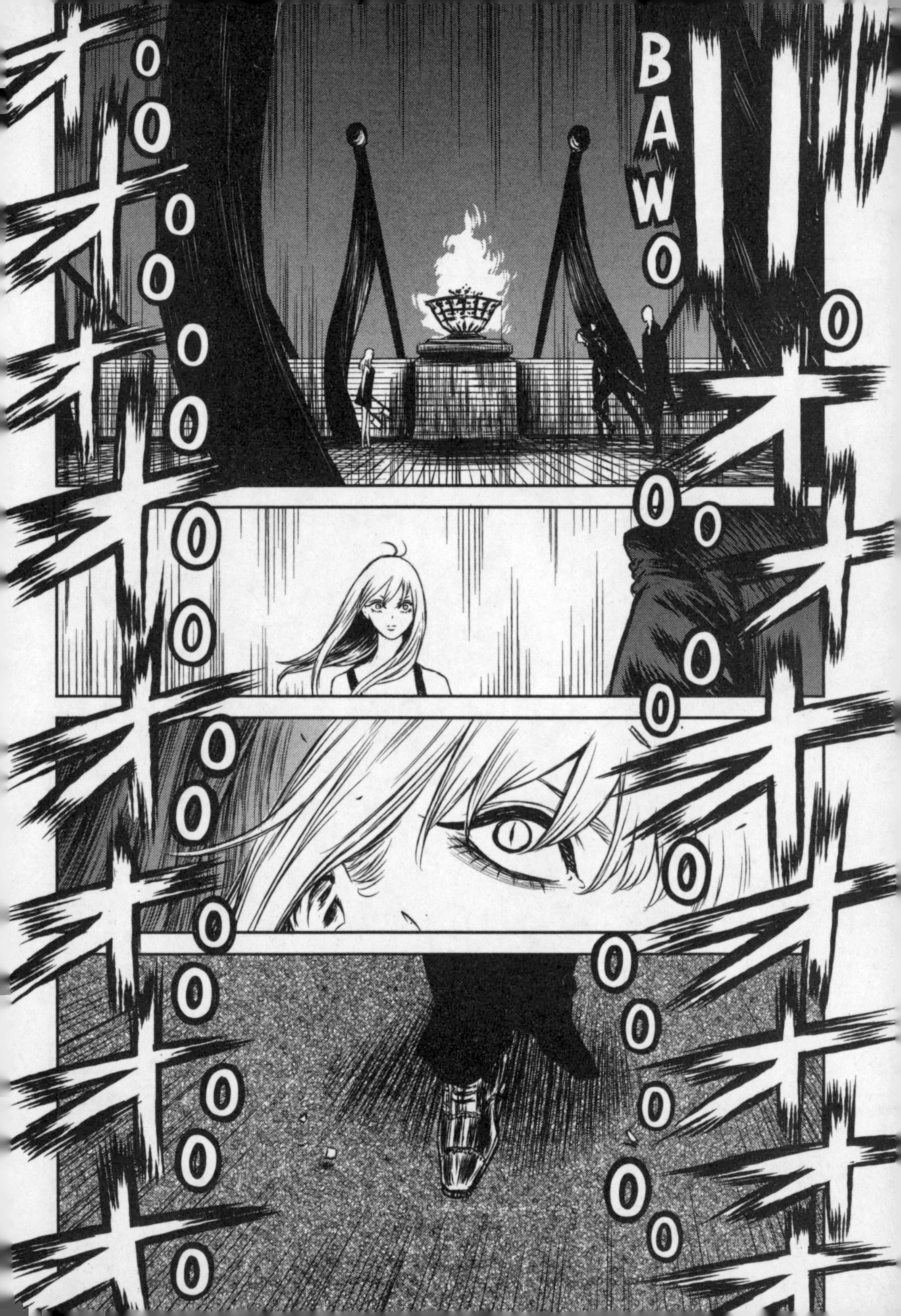

BAWOOOOOOOOOOOO
OOOOOOOOOOOOOOOOOO

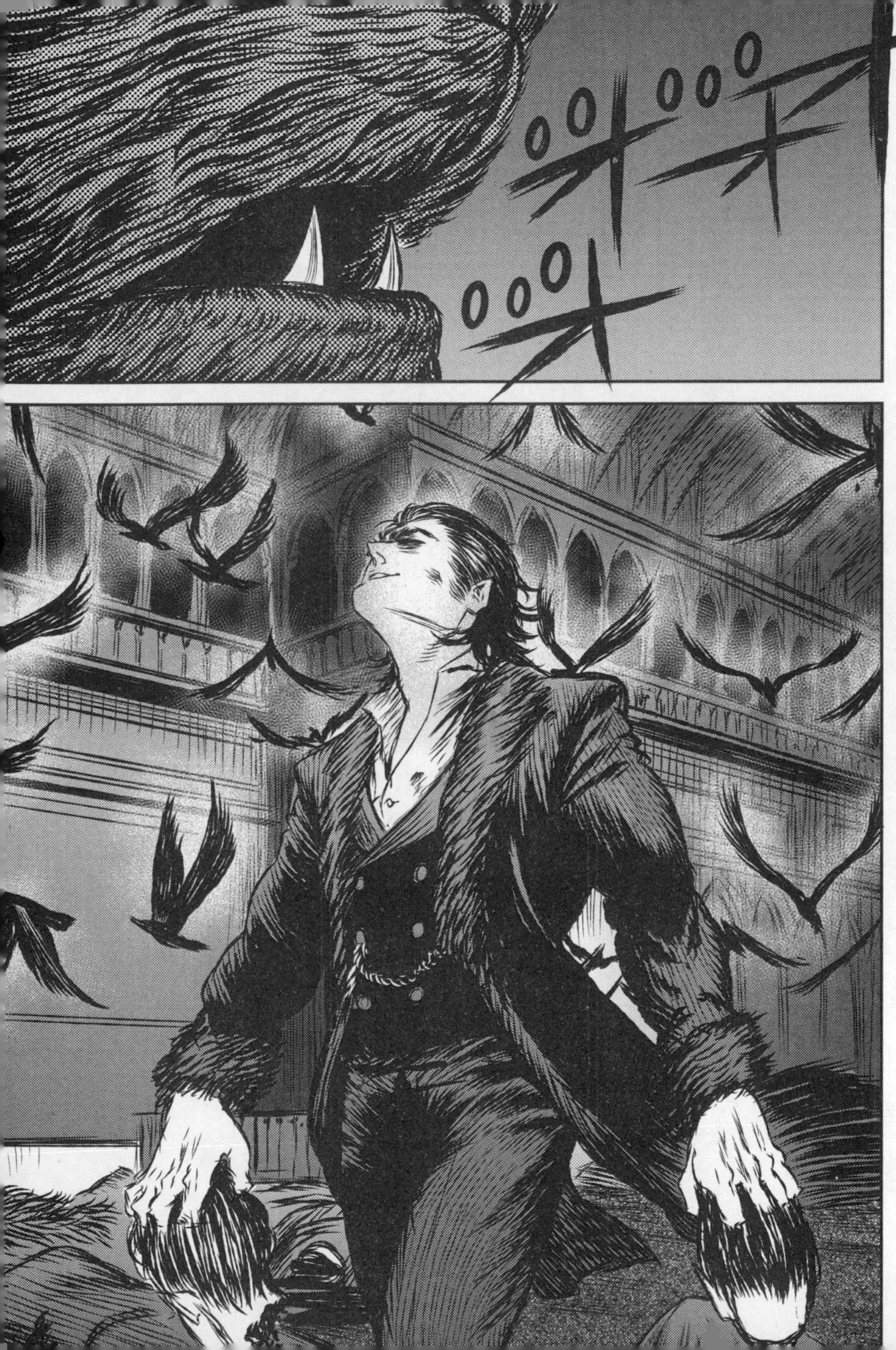

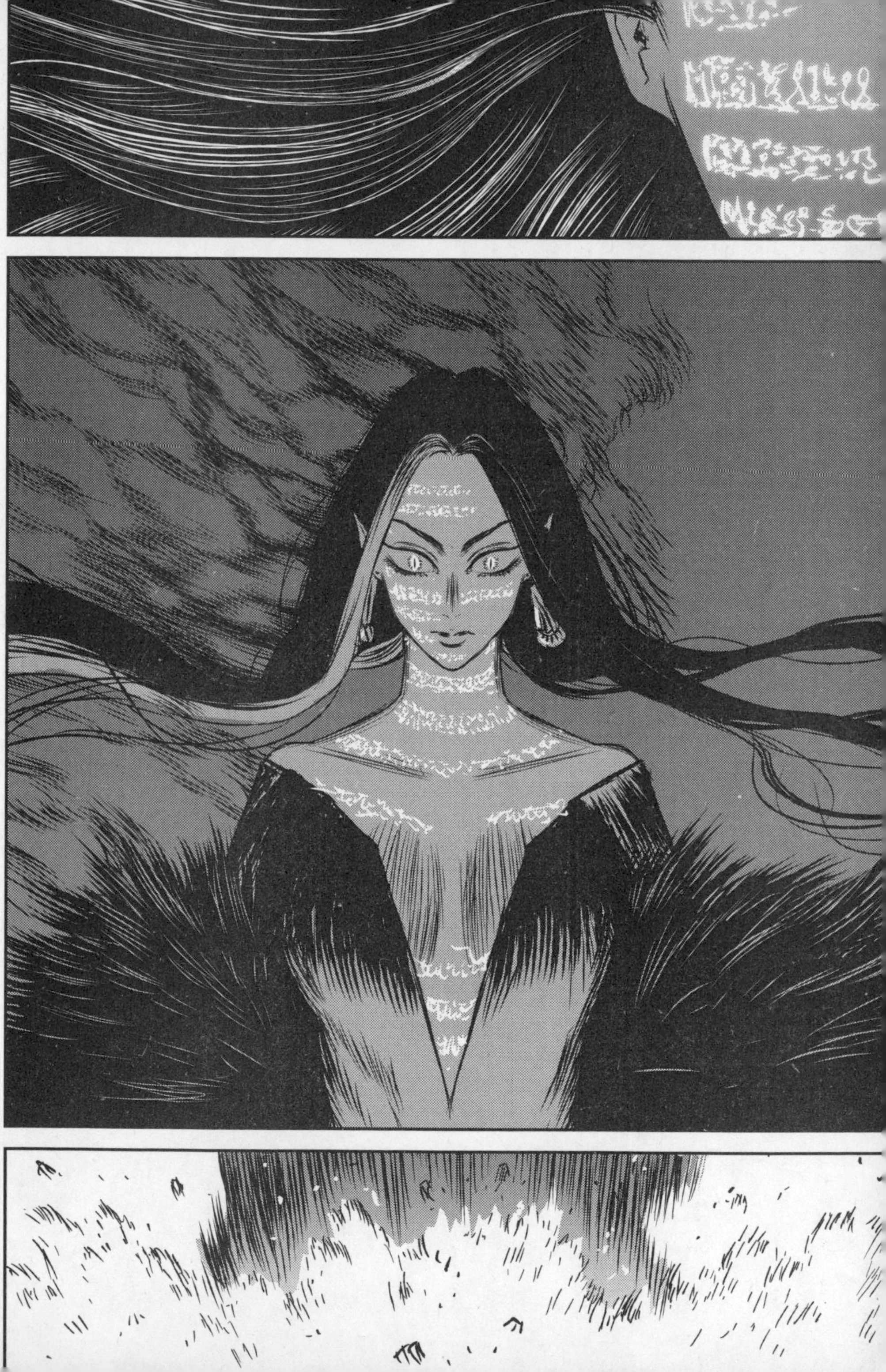

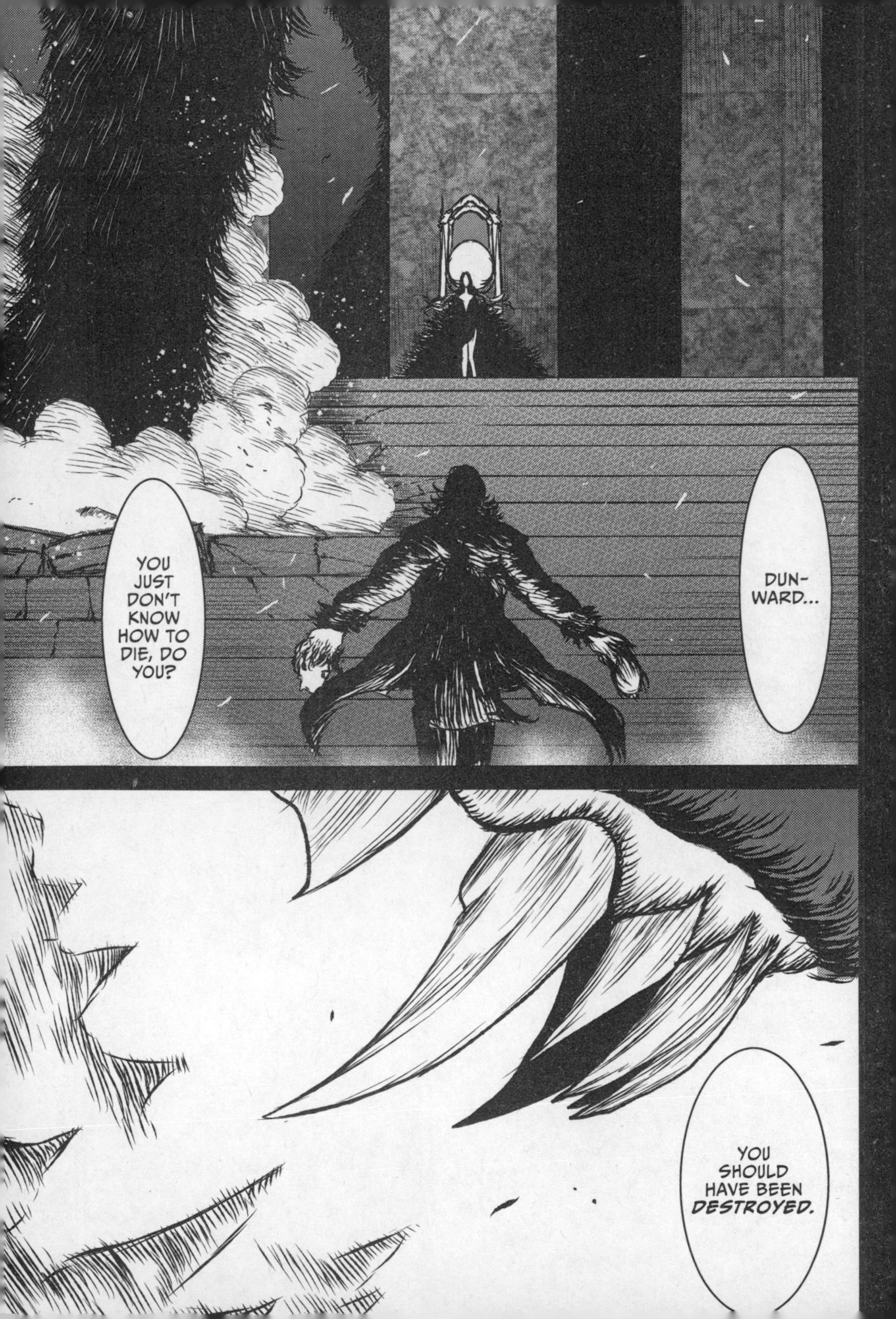
DUN-WARD...
YOU JUST DON'T KNOW HOW TO DIE, DO YOU?
YOU SHOULD HAVE BEEN *DESTROYED.*

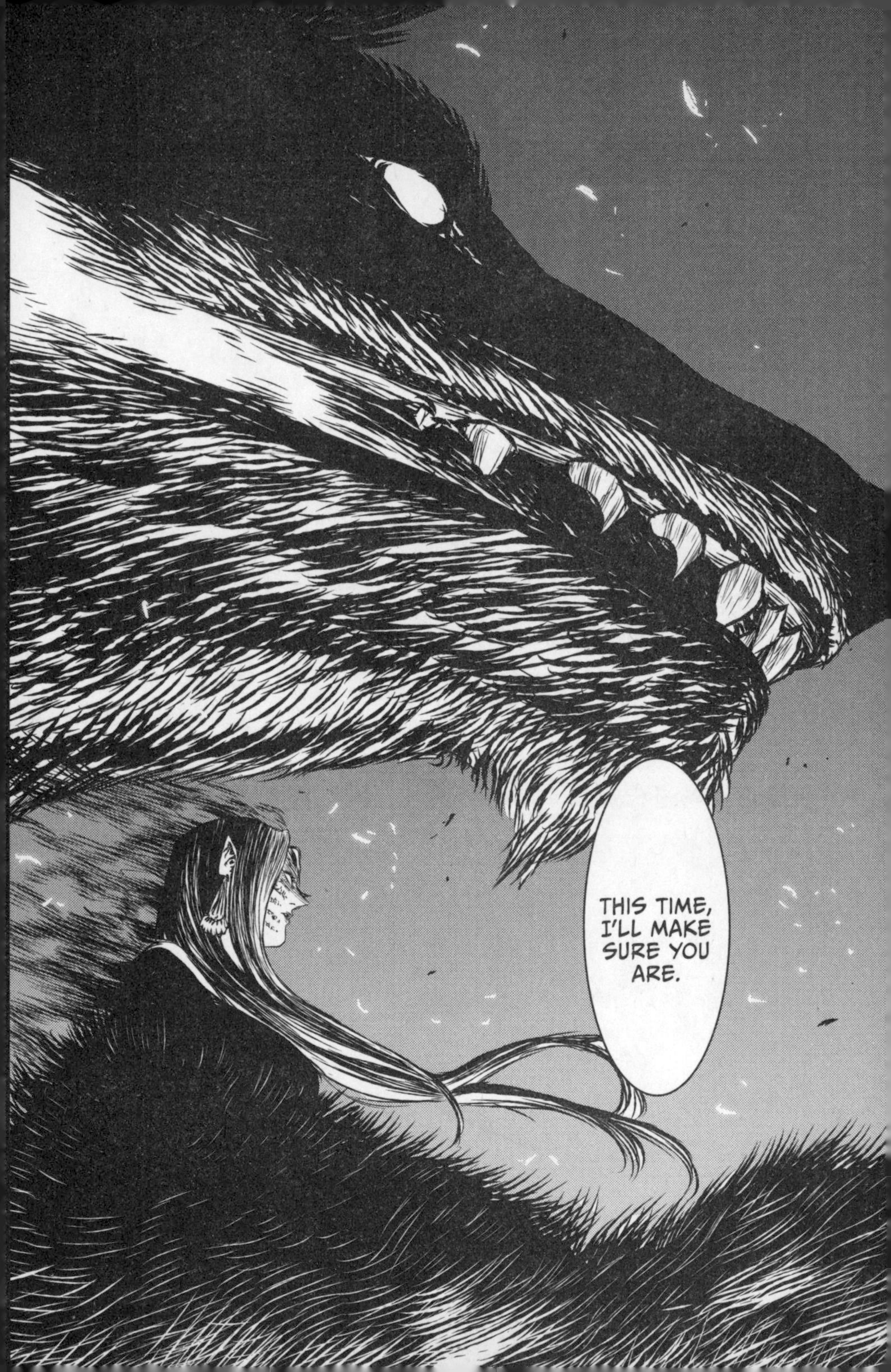
THIS TIME, I'LL MAKE SURE YOU ARE.

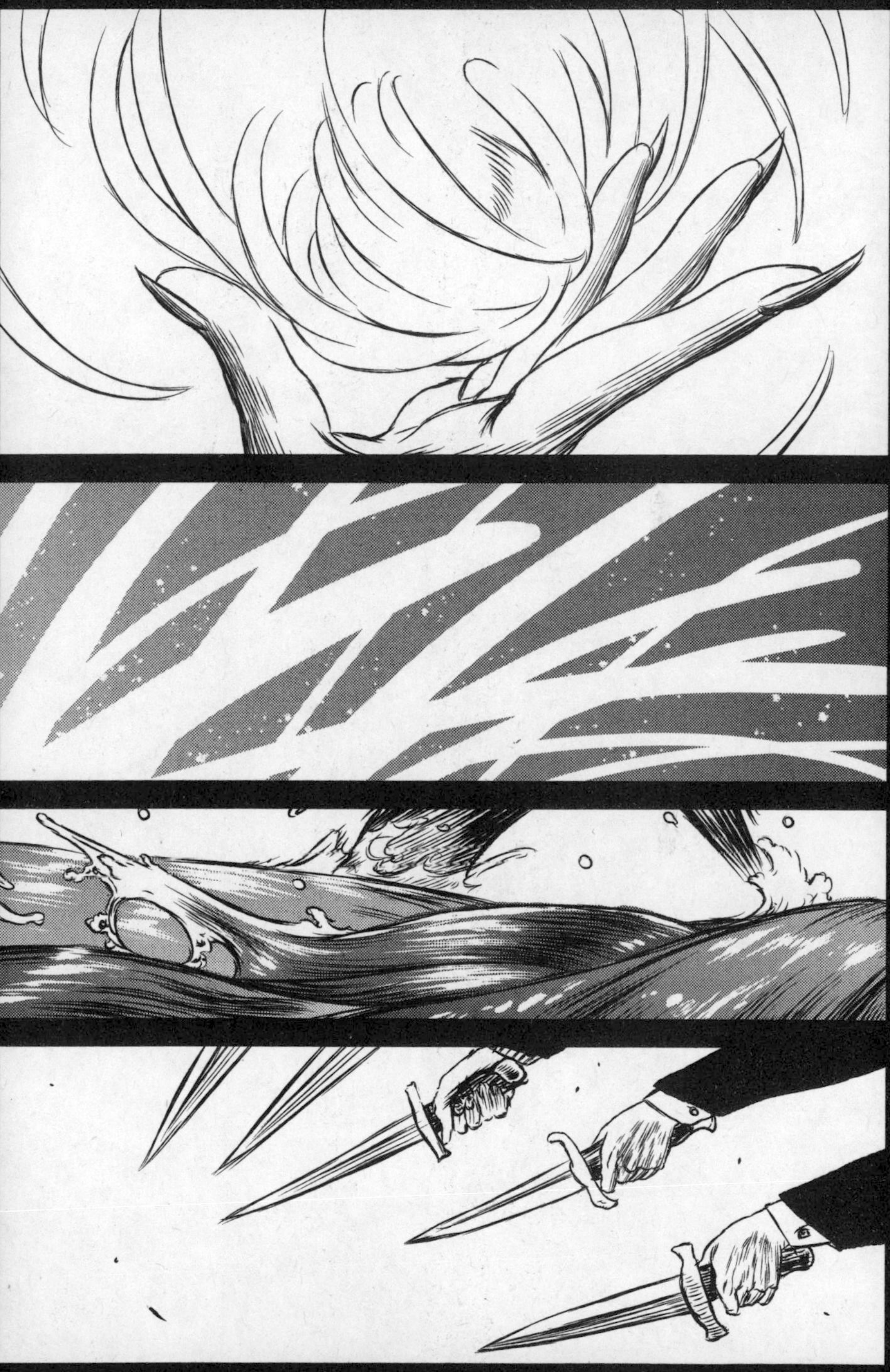

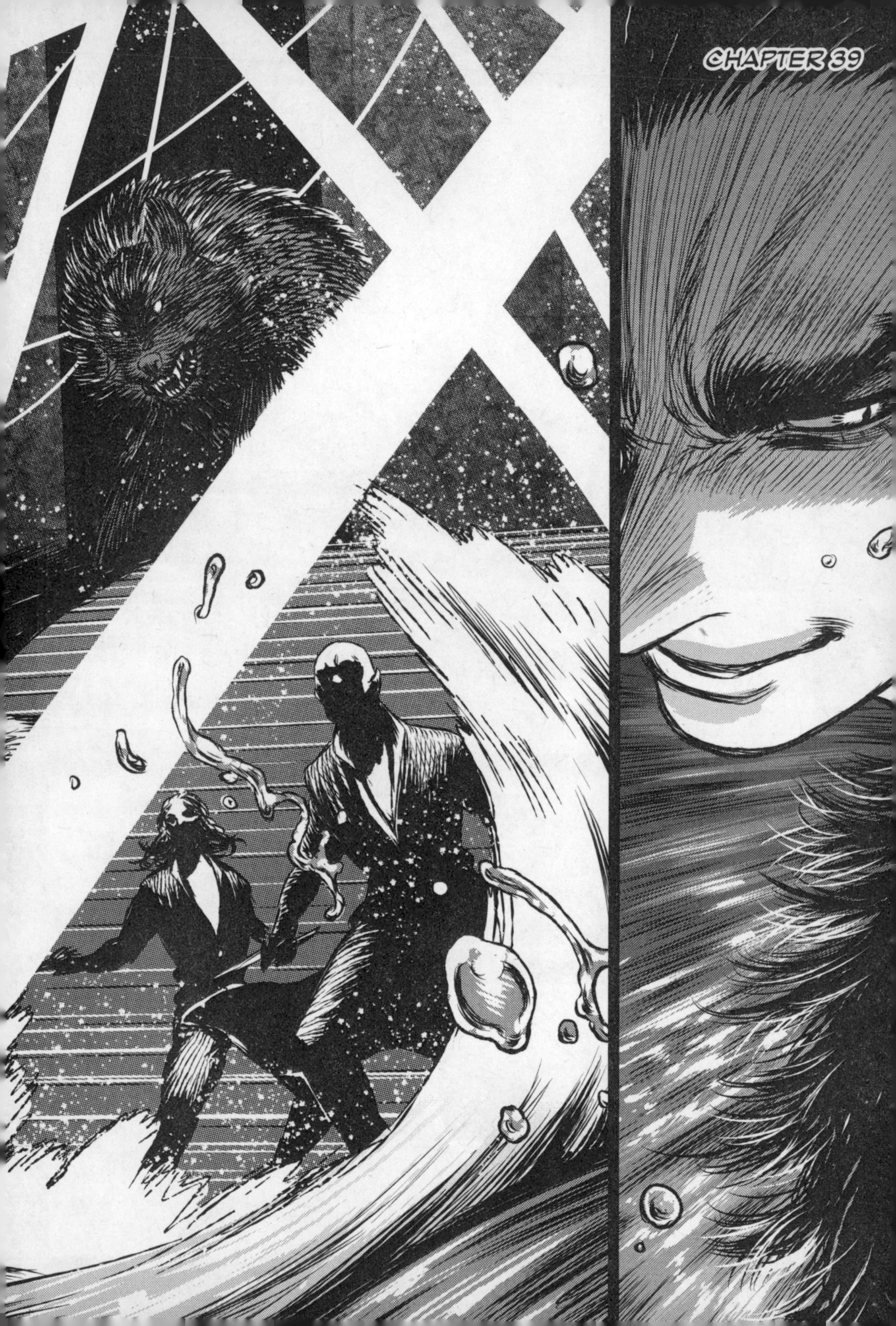
CHAPTER 39

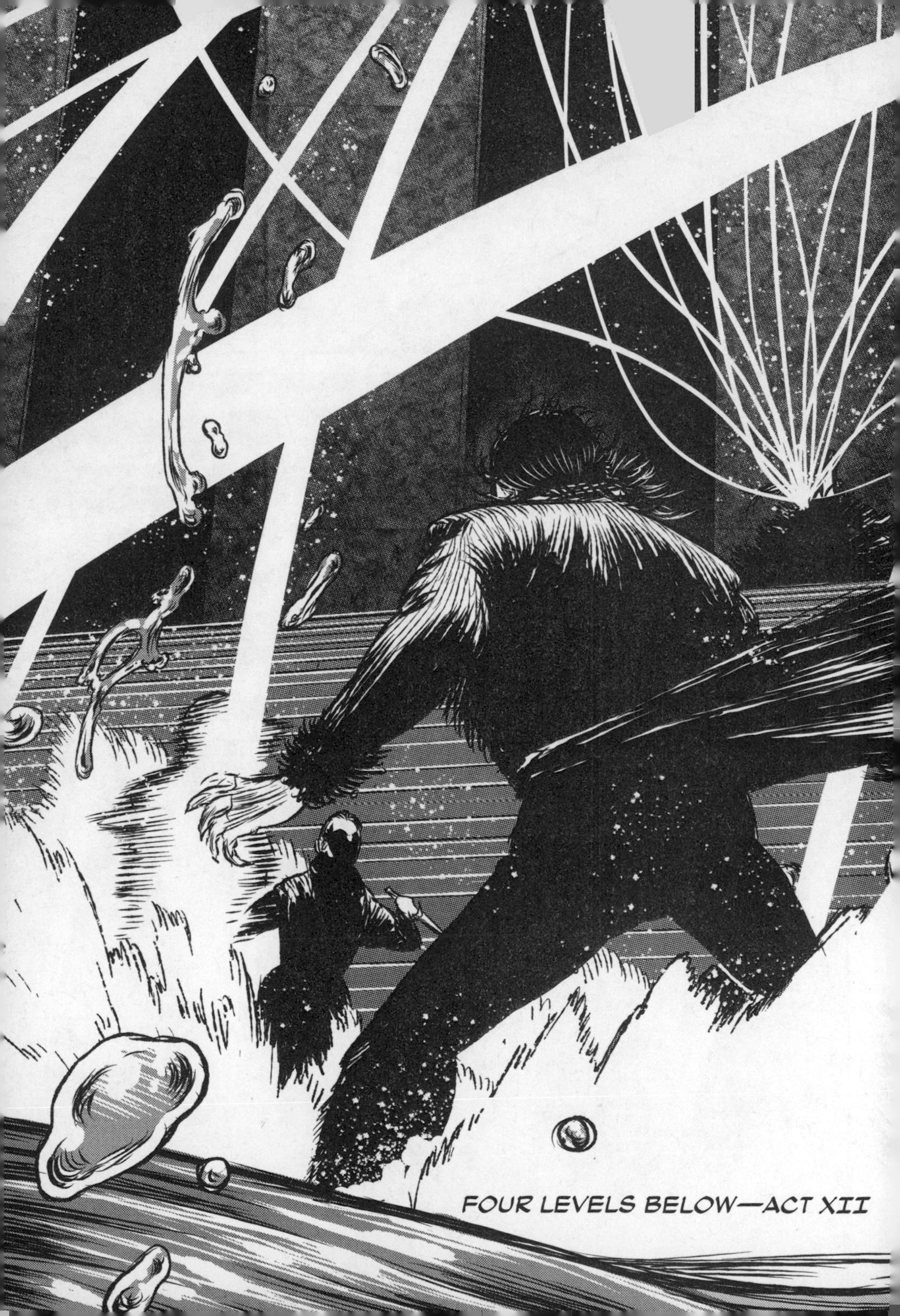
FOUR LEVELS BELOW—ACT XII

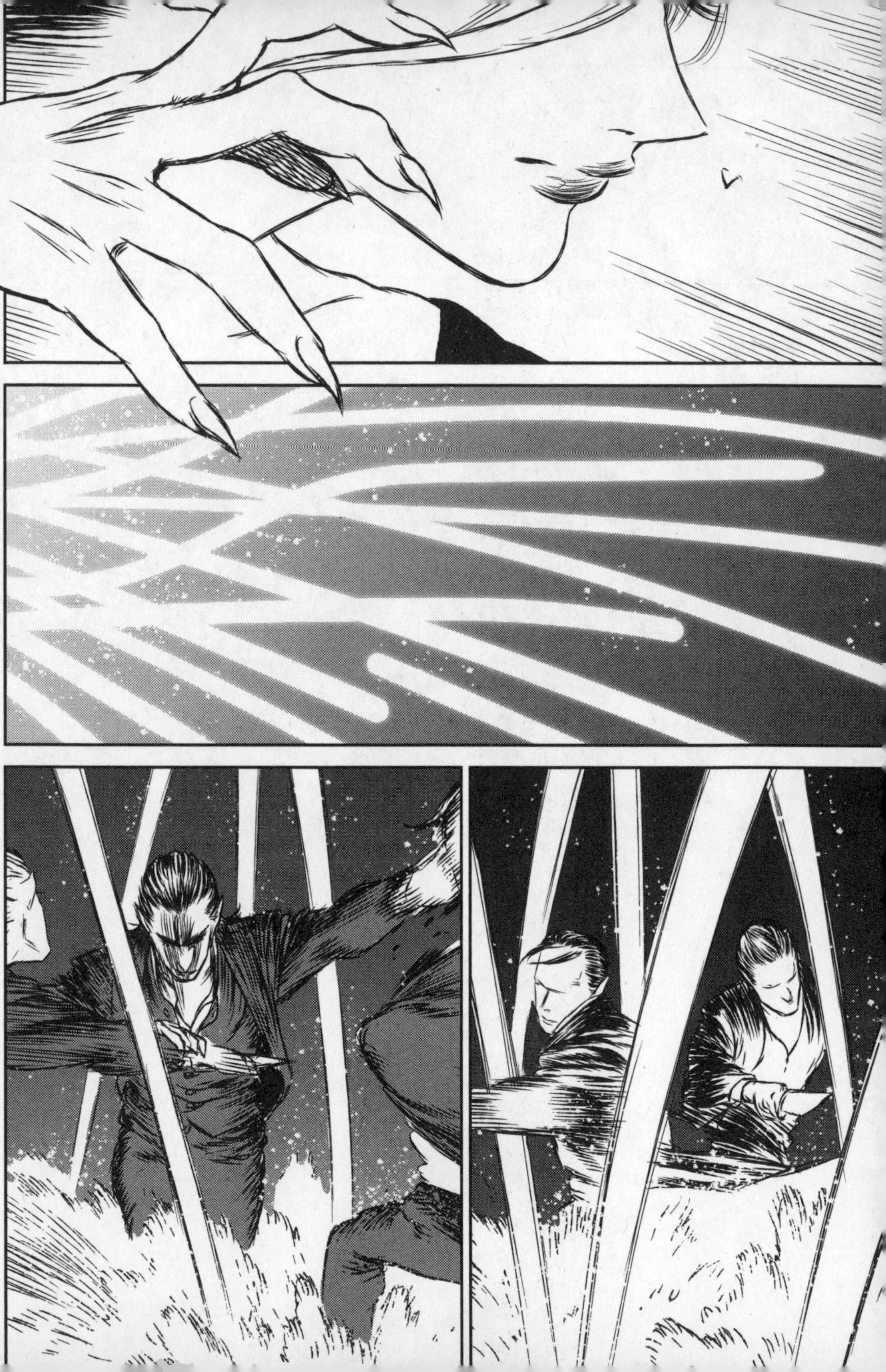

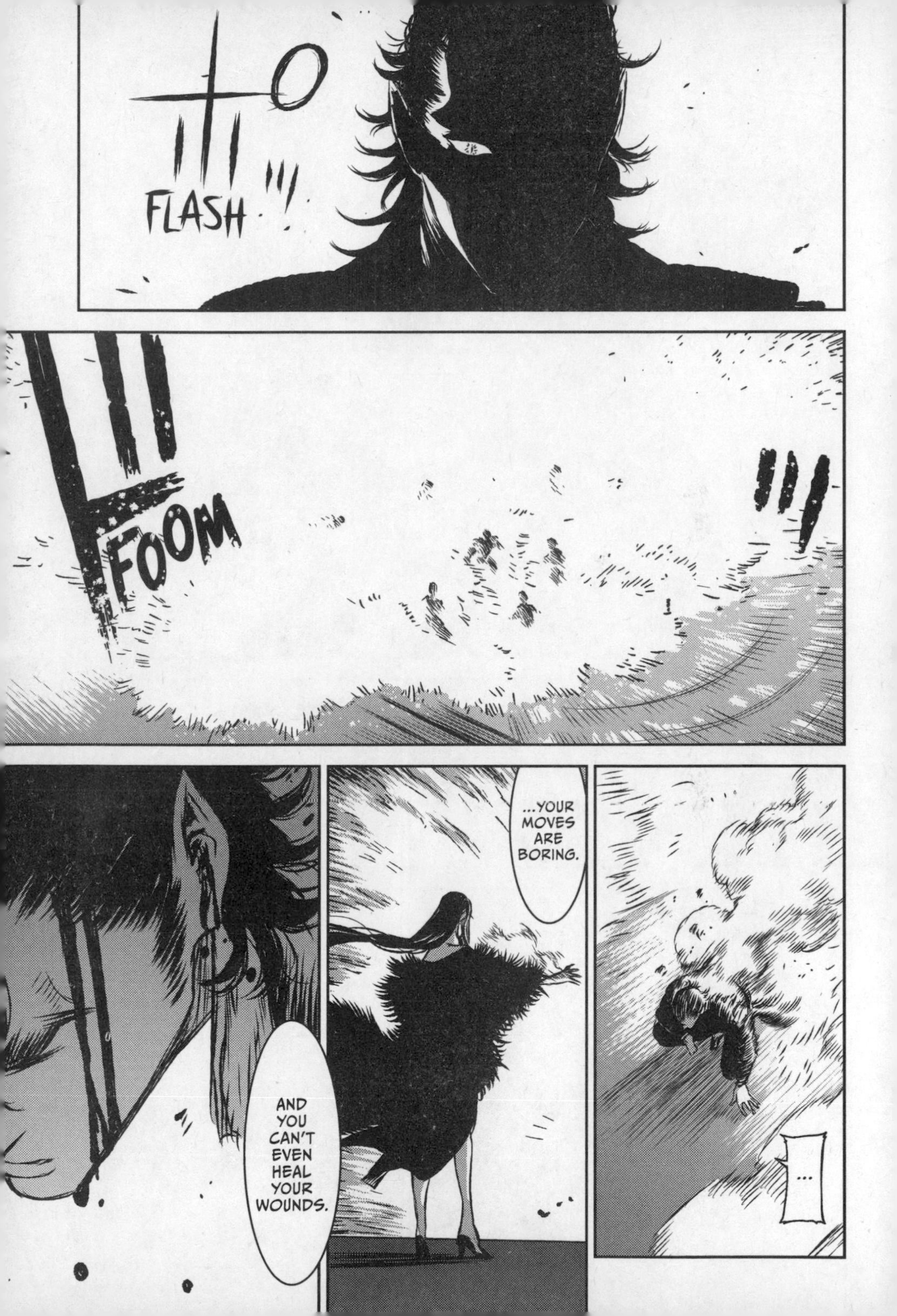
FLASH
FOOM
...
...YOUR MOVES ARE BORING.
AND YOU CAN'T EVEN HEAL YOUR WOUNDS.

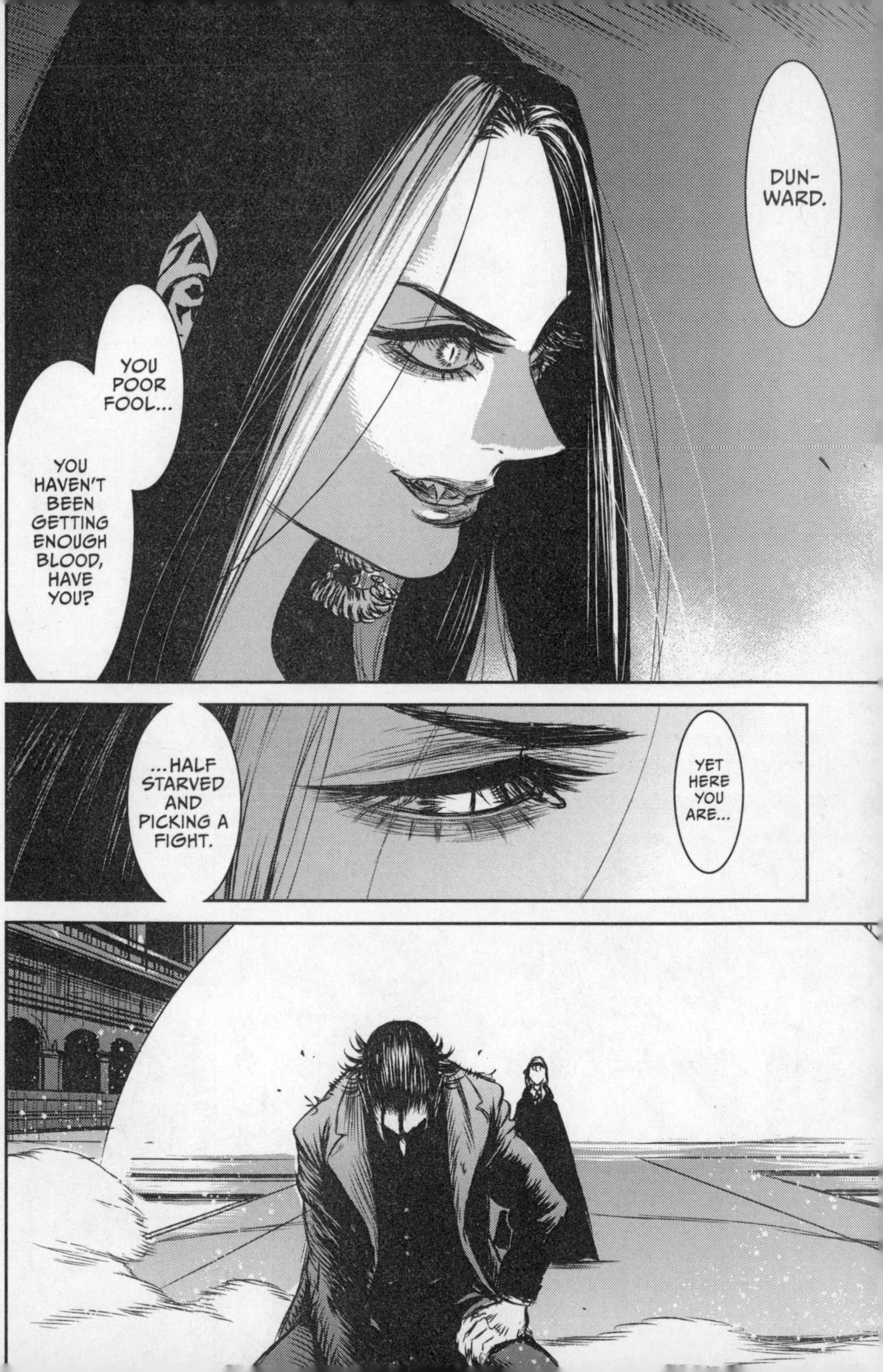
DUN-WARD.
YOU POOR FOOL...
YOU HAVEN'T BEEN GETTING ENOUGH BLOOD, HAVE YOU?
YET HERE YOU ARE...
...HALF STARVED AND PICKING A FIGHT.

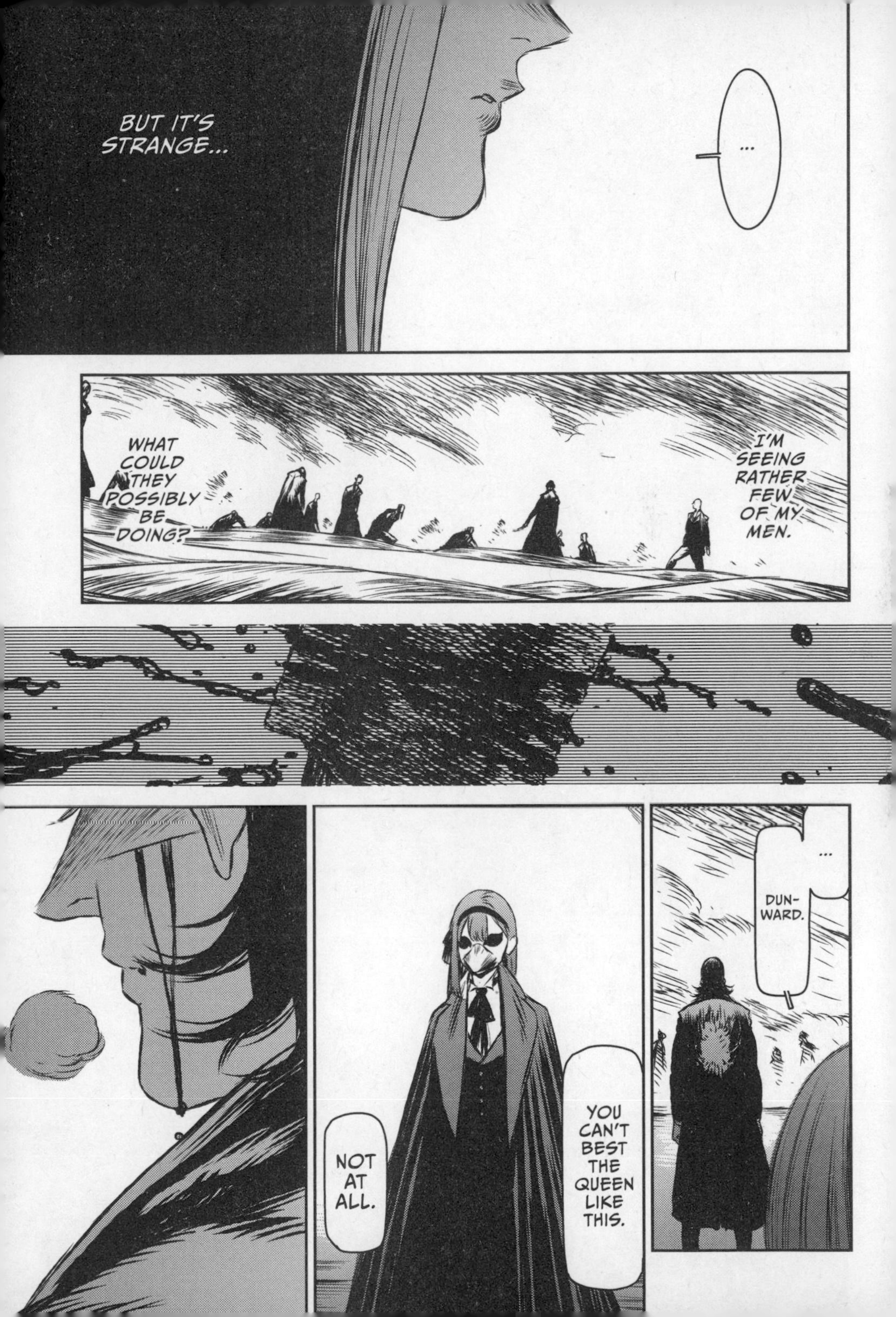
...
BUT IT'S STRANGE...
I'M SEEING RATHER FEW OF MY MEN.
WHAT COULD THEY POSSIBLY BE DOING?
...
DUN-WARD.
YOU CAN'T BEST THE QUEEN LIKE THIS.
NOT AT ALL.

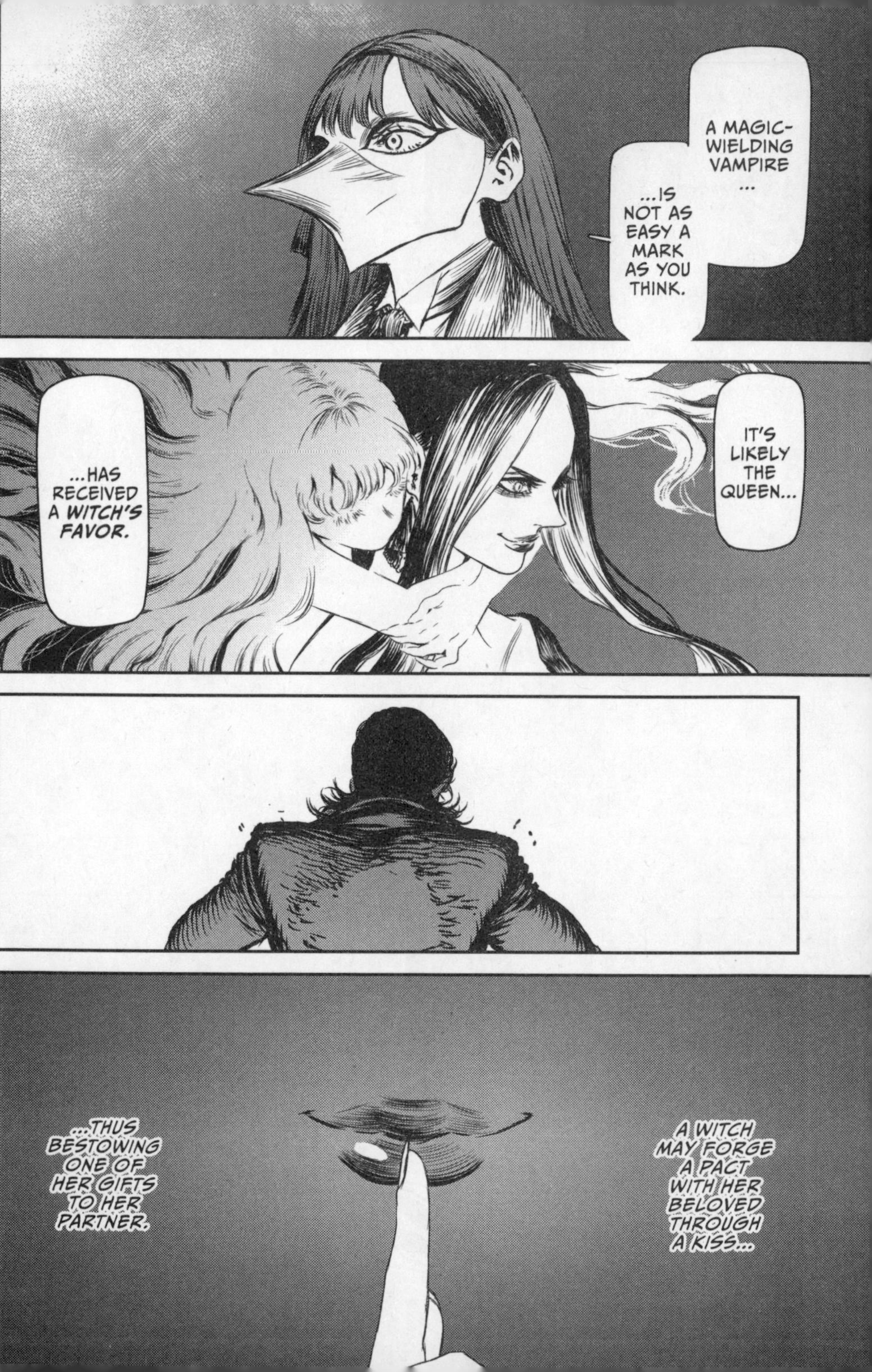
A MAGIC-WIELDING VAMPIRE...
...IS NOT AS EASY A MARK AS YOU THINK.
IT'S LIKELY THE QUEEN...
...HAS RECEIVED A *WITCH'S FAVOR*.
A WITCH MAY FORGE A PACT WITH HER BELOVED THROUGH A KISS...
...THUS BESTOWING ONE OF HER GIFTS TO HER PARTNER.

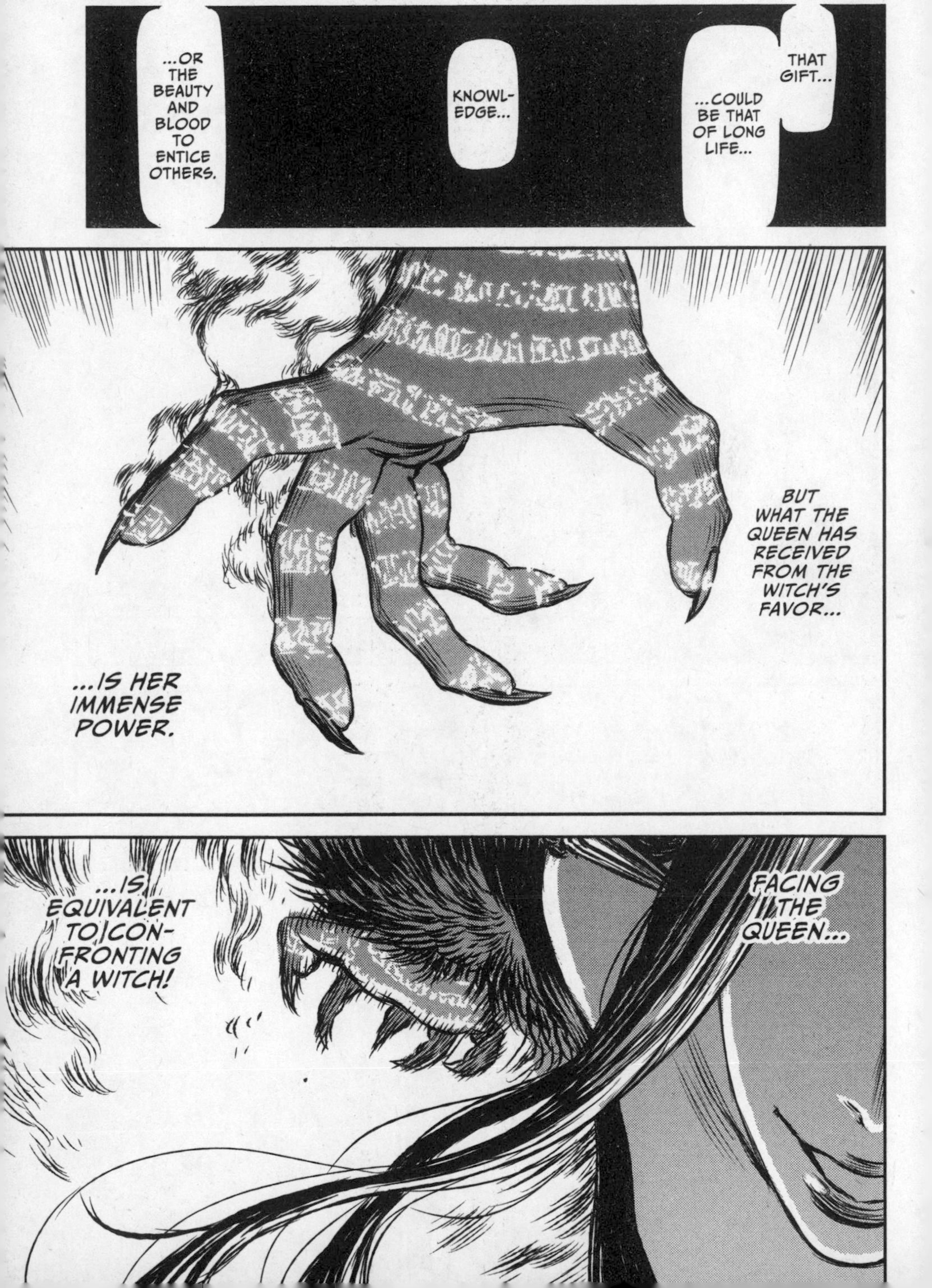
THAT GIFT...
...COULD BE THAT OF LONG LIFE...
KNOWL-EDGE...
...OR THE BEAUTY AND BLOOD TO ENTICE OTHERS.
BUT WHAT THE QUEEN HAS RECEIVED FROM THE WITCH'S FAVOR...
...IS HER IMMENSE POWER.
FACING THE QUEEN...
...IS EQUIVALENT TO CON-FRONTING A WITCH!

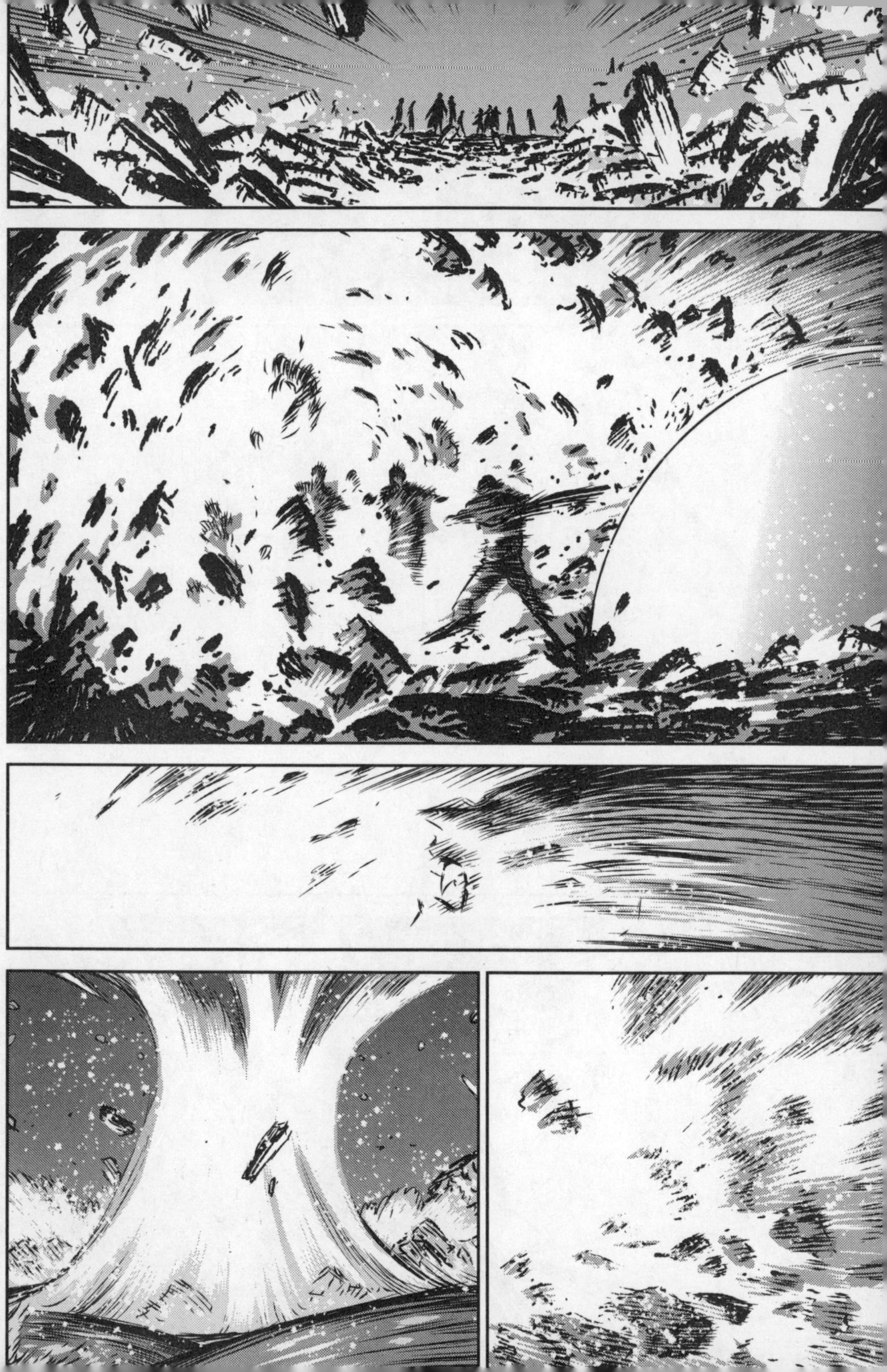

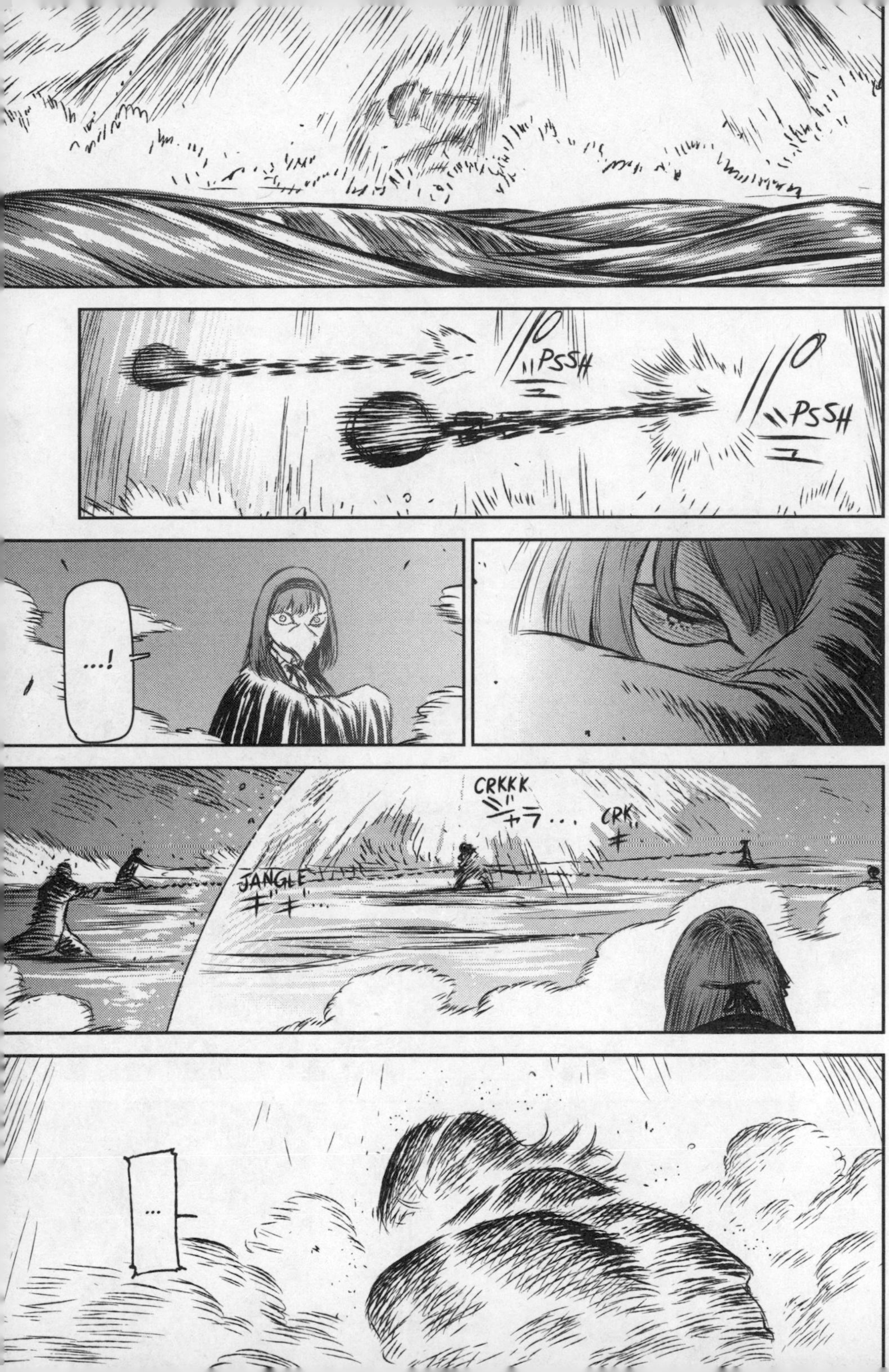
PSSH
PSSH
...!
CRK
CRKKK
JANGLE
...

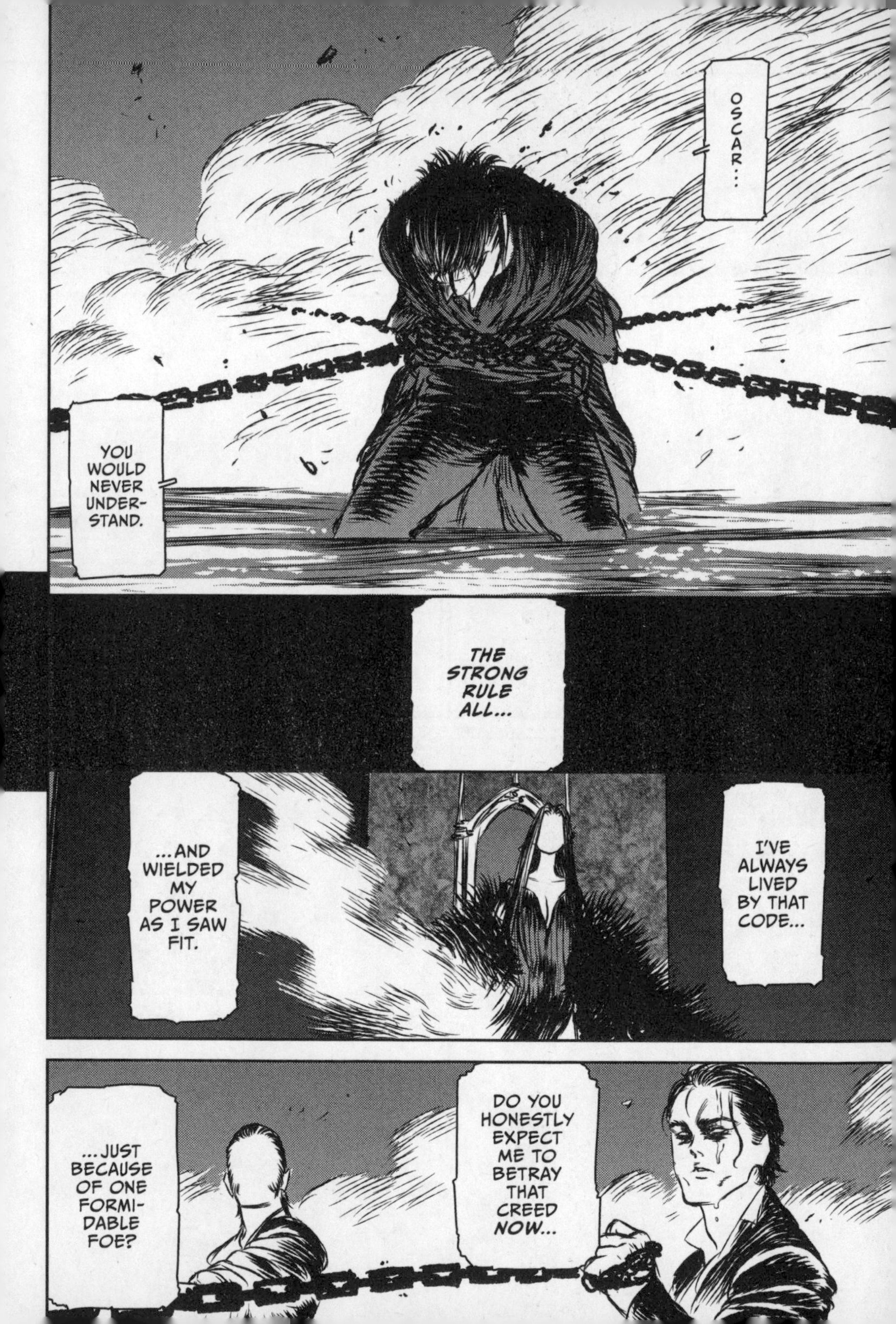
OSCAR...
YOU WOULD NEVER UNDER-STAND.
THE STRONG RULE ALL...
I'VE ALWAYS LIVED BY THAT CODE...
...AND WIELDED MY POWER AS I SAW FIT.
DO YOU HONESTLY EXPECT ME TO BETRAY THAT CREED NOW...
...JUST BECAUSE OF ONE FORMI-DABLE FOE?

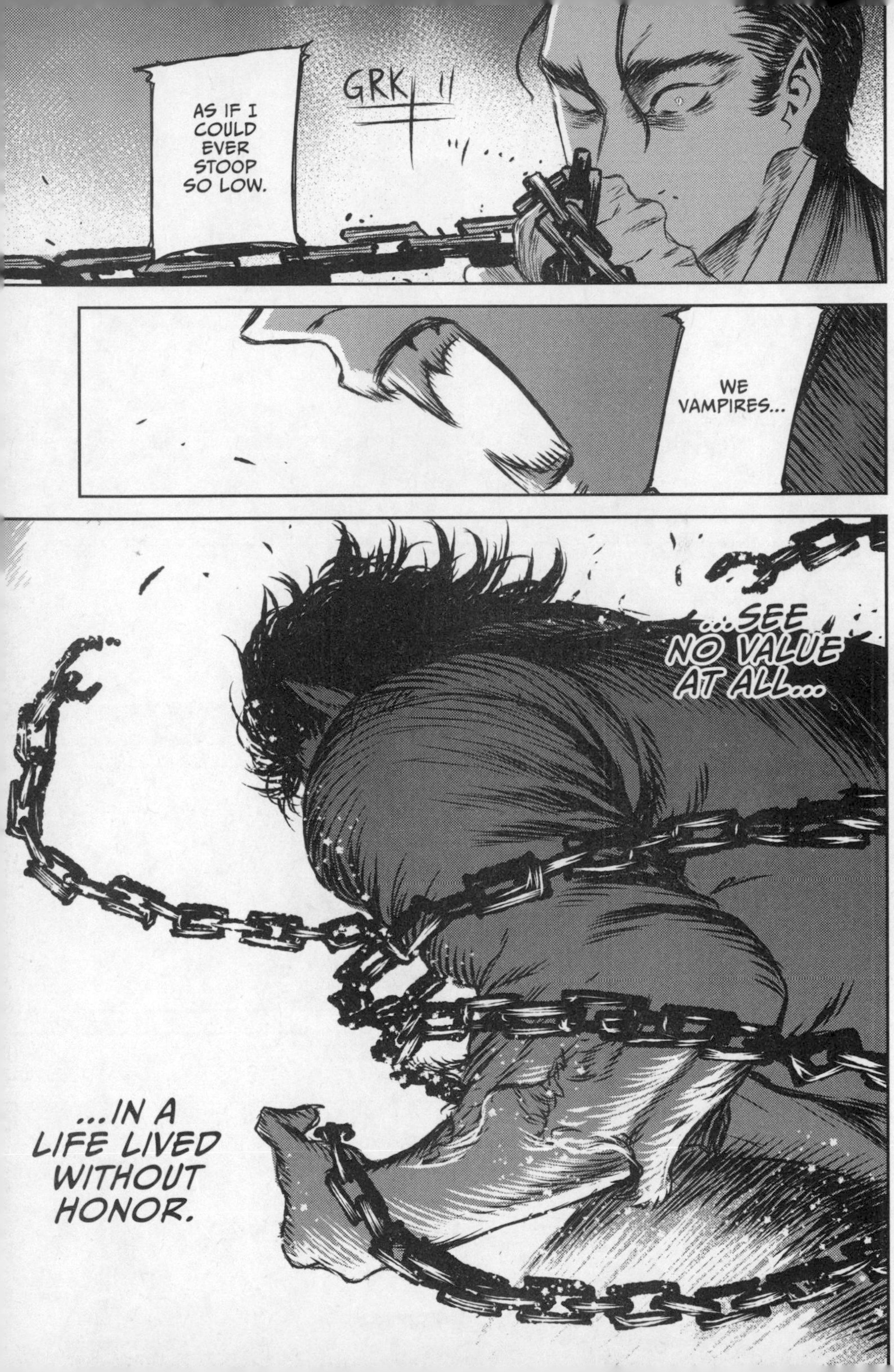
GRK
AS IF I COULD EVER STOOP SO LOW.
WE VAMPIRES...
...SEE NO VALUE AT ALL...
...IN A LIFE LIVED WITHOUT HONOR.

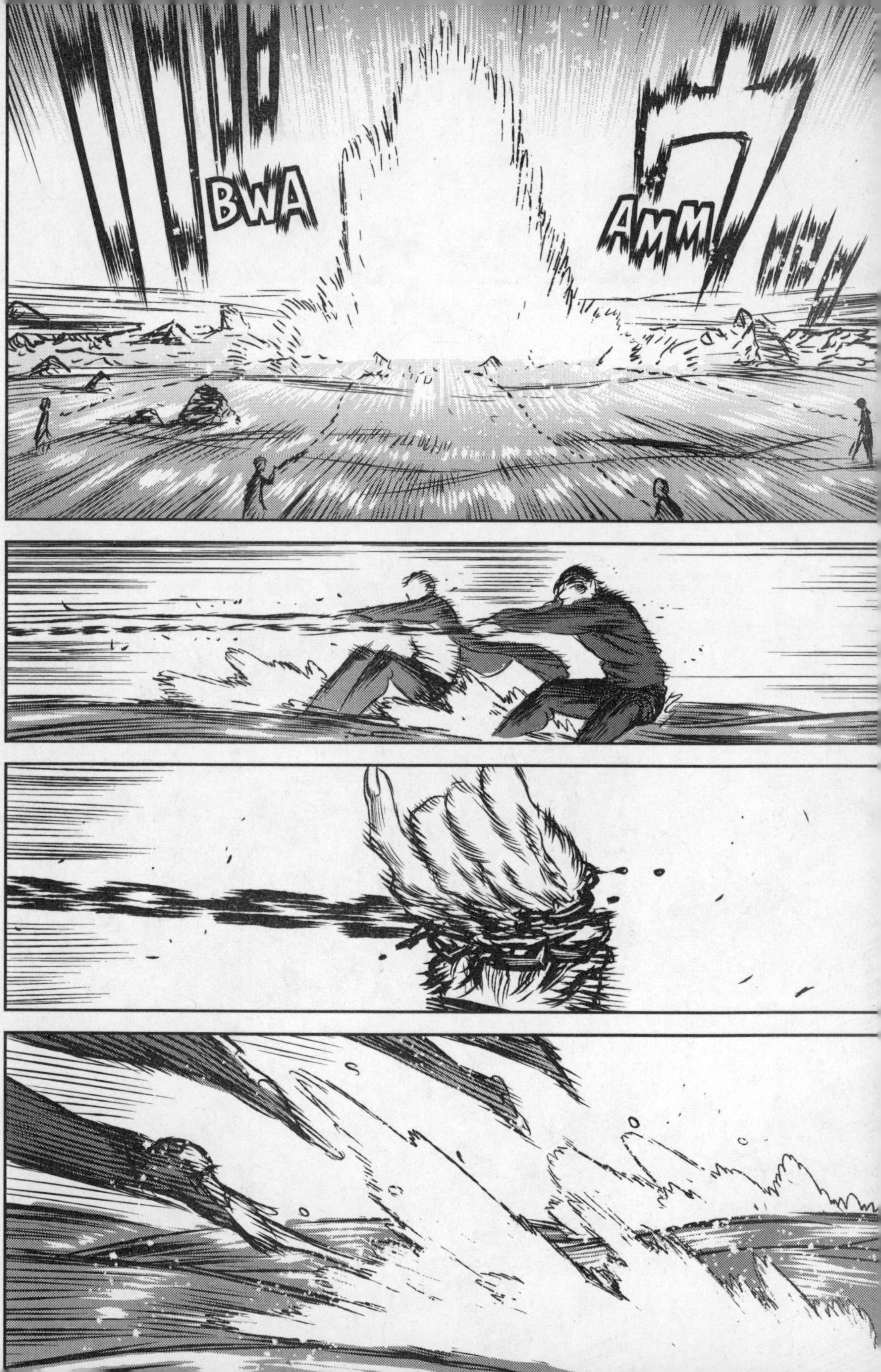
BWA
AMM

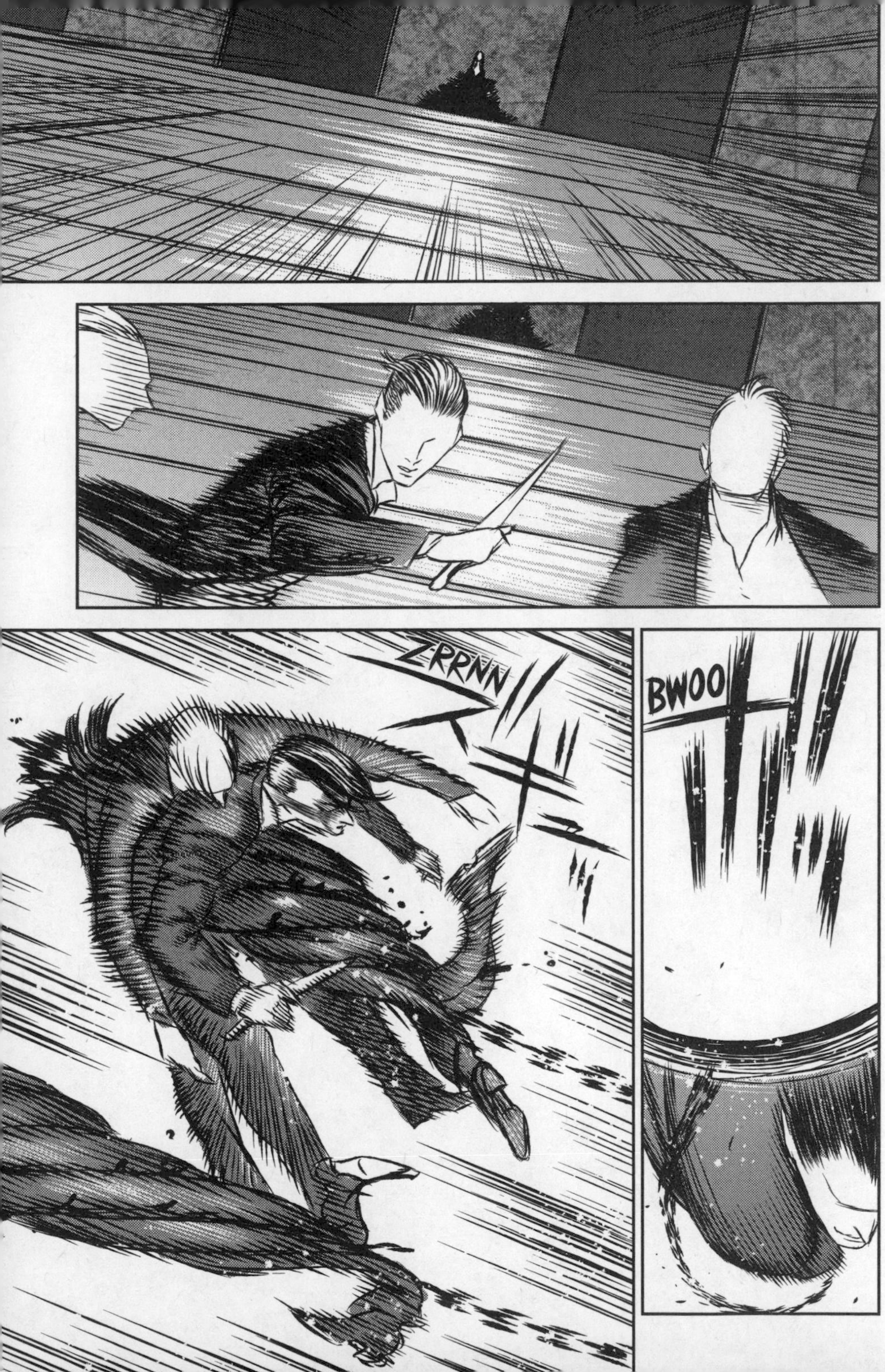
BWOO
ZRRNN

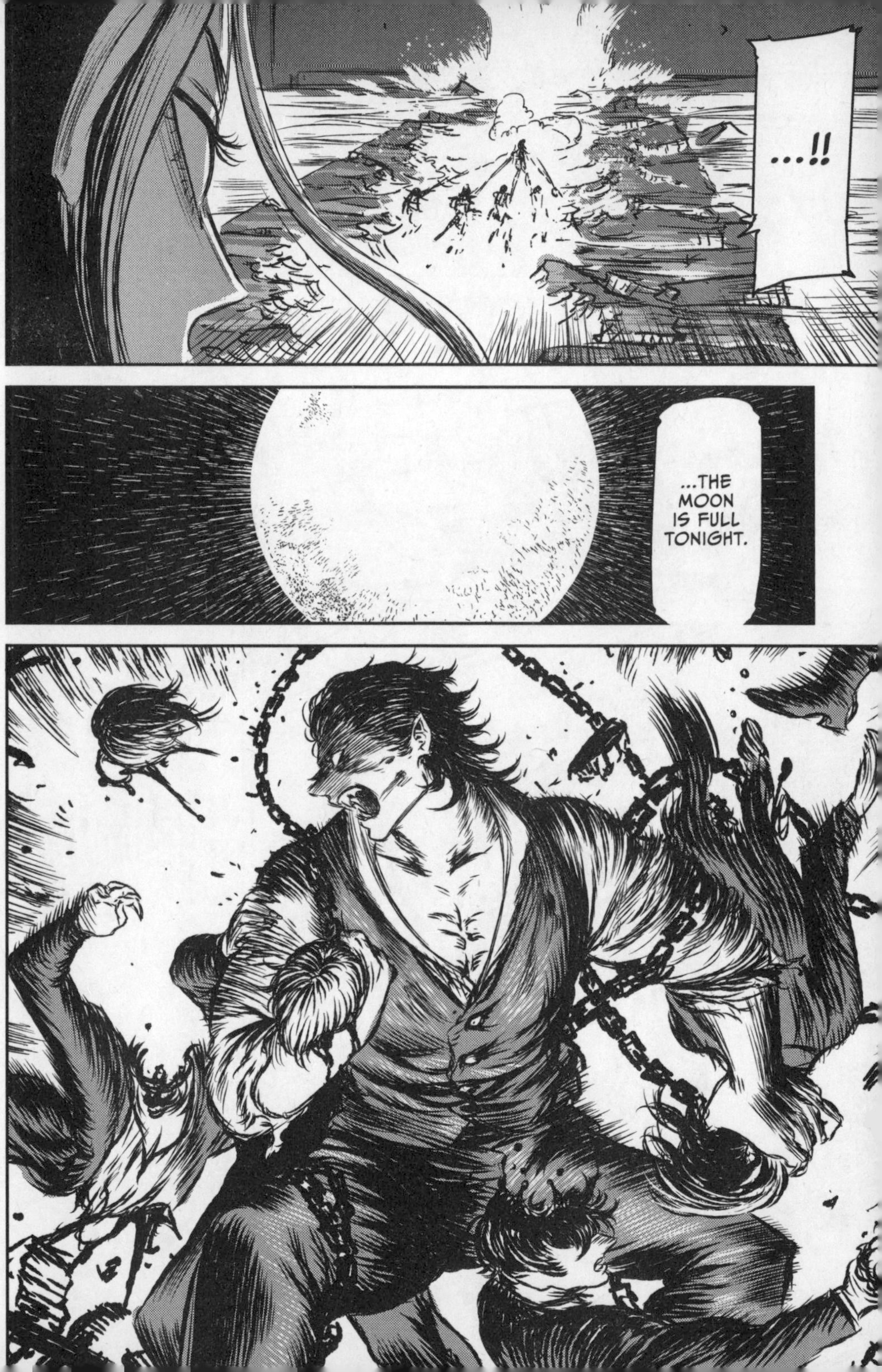
...!!
...THE MOON IS FULL TONIGHT.

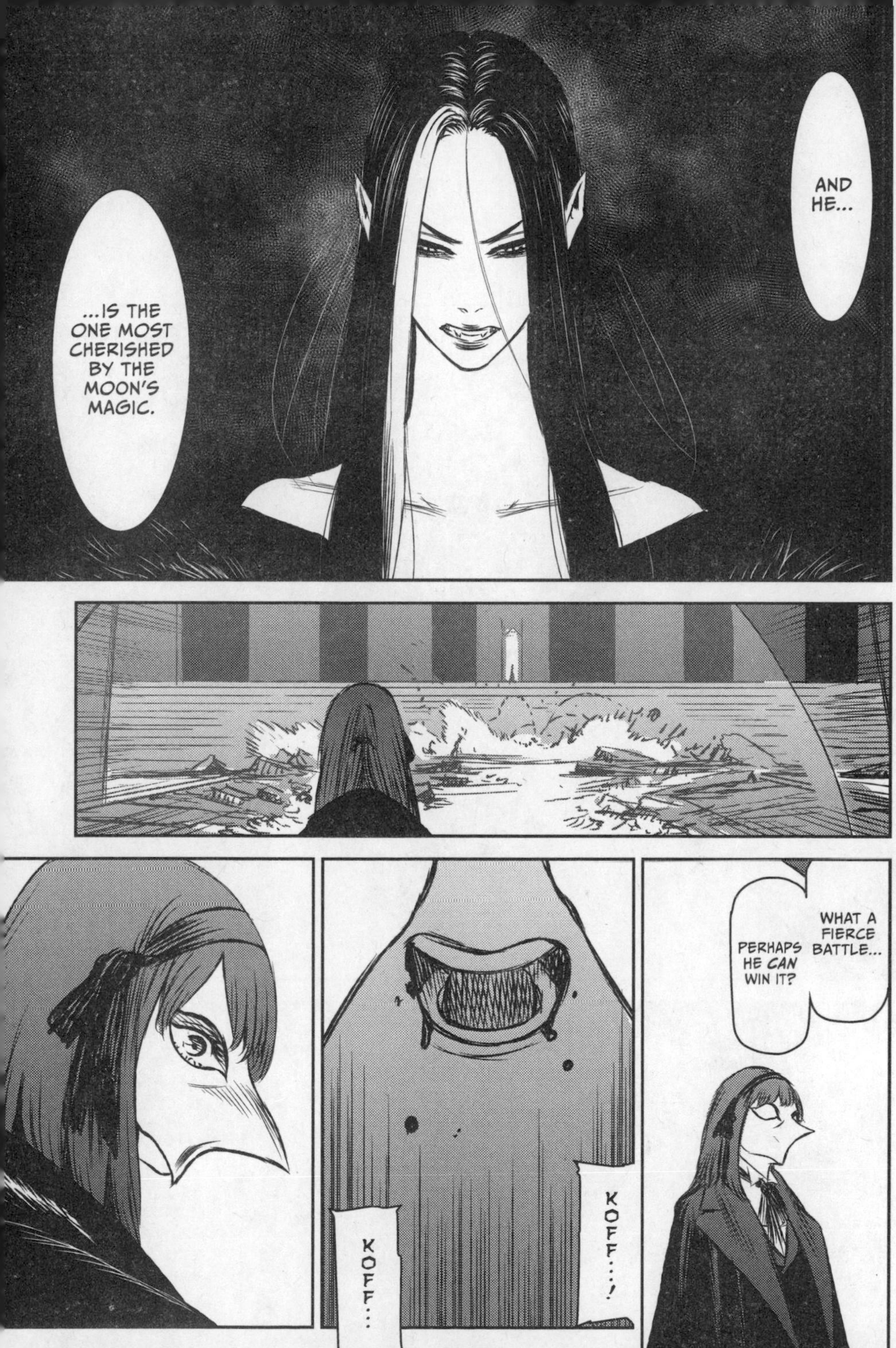
AND HE...
...IS THE ONE MOST CHERISHED BY THE MOON'S MAGIC.
WHAT A FIERCE BATTLE...
PERHAPS HE *CAN* WIN IT?
KOFF...!
KOFF...

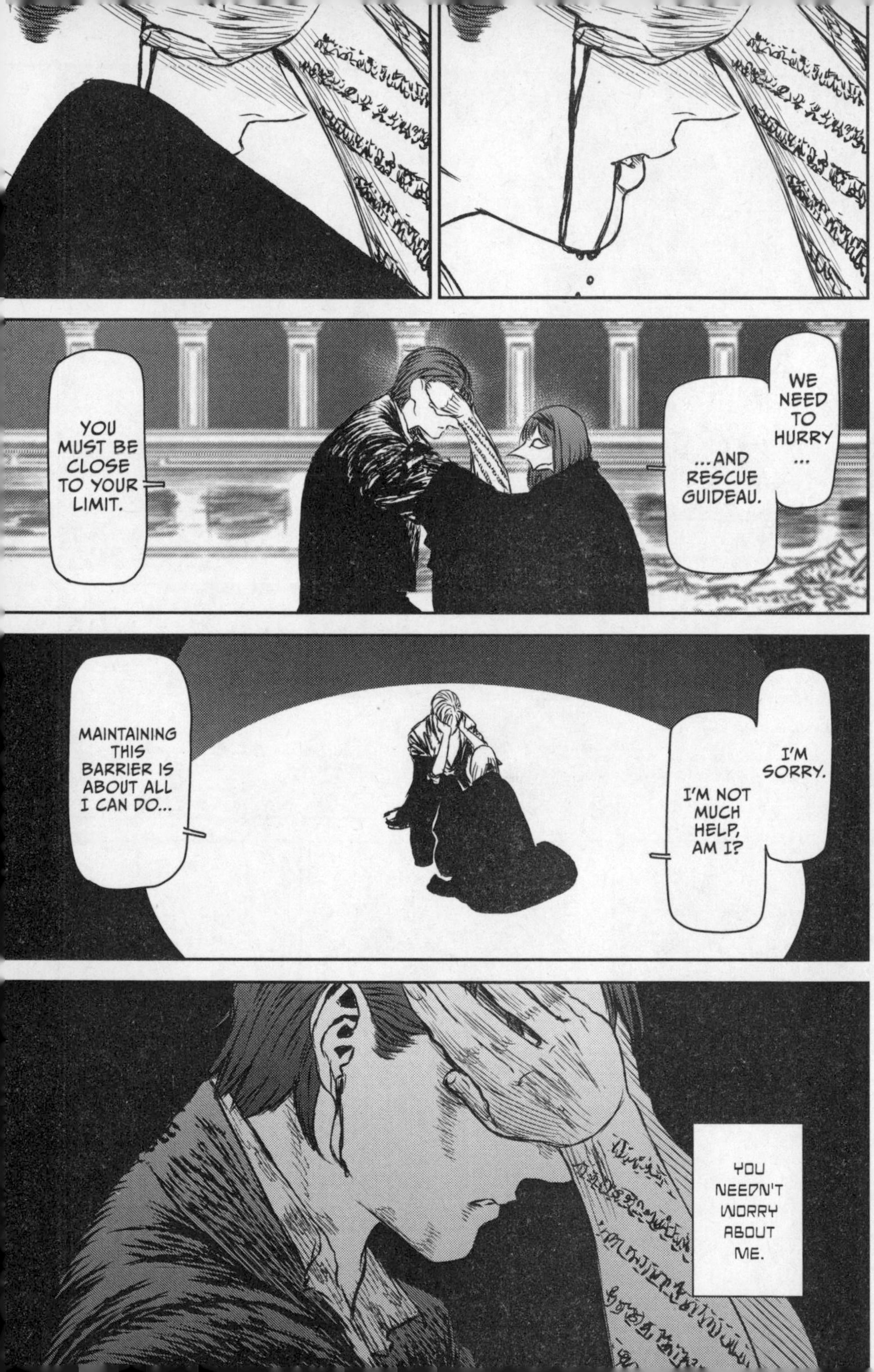
WE NEED TO HURRY ...
...AND RESCUE GUIDEAU.
YOU MUST BE CLOSE TO YOUR LIMIT.
I'M SORRY.
I'M NOT MUCH HELP, AM I?
MAINTAINING THIS BARRIER IS ABOUT ALL I CAN DO...
YOU NEEDN'T WORRY ABOUT ME.

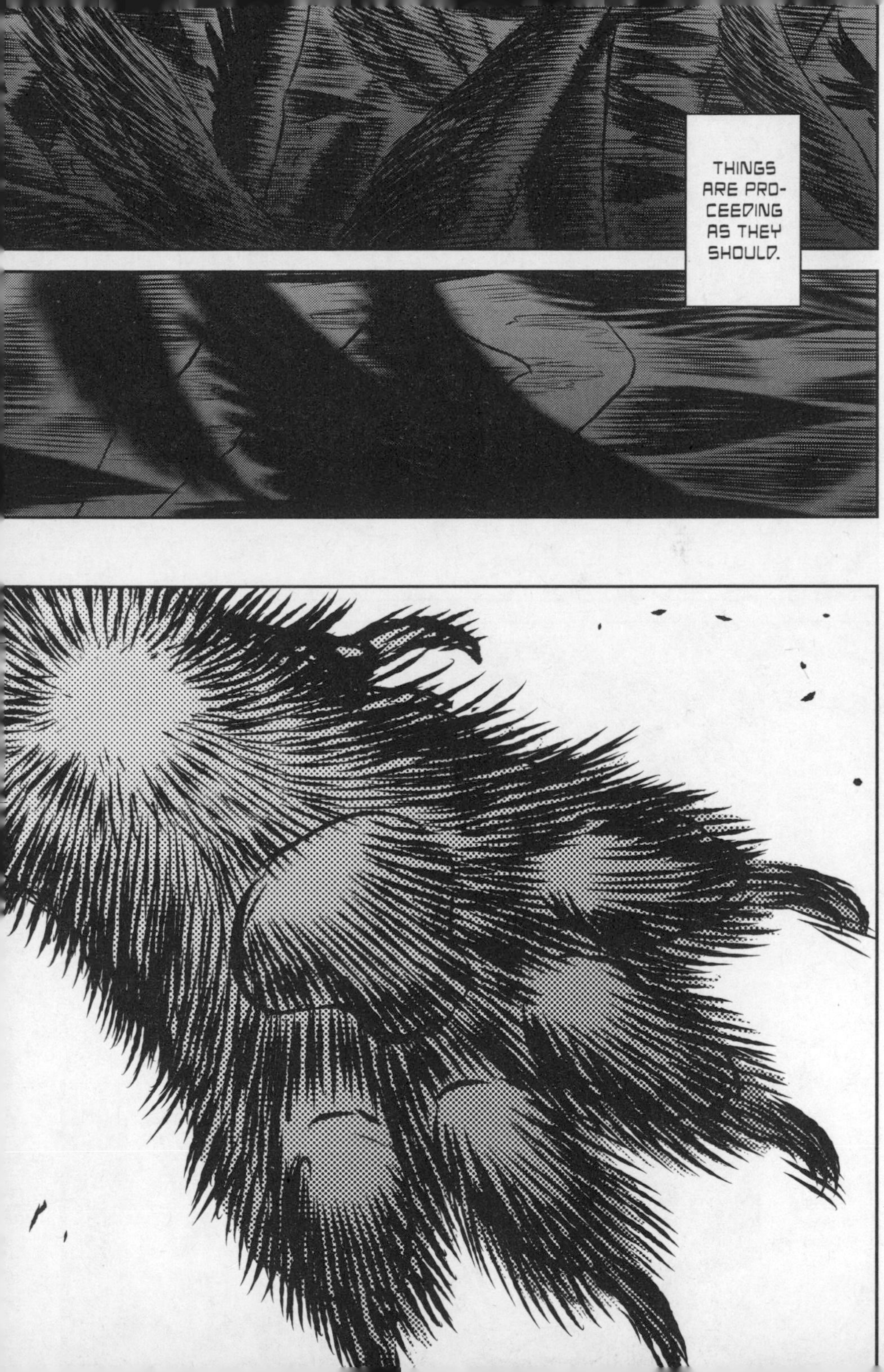
THINGS ARE PROCEEDING AS THEY SHOULD.

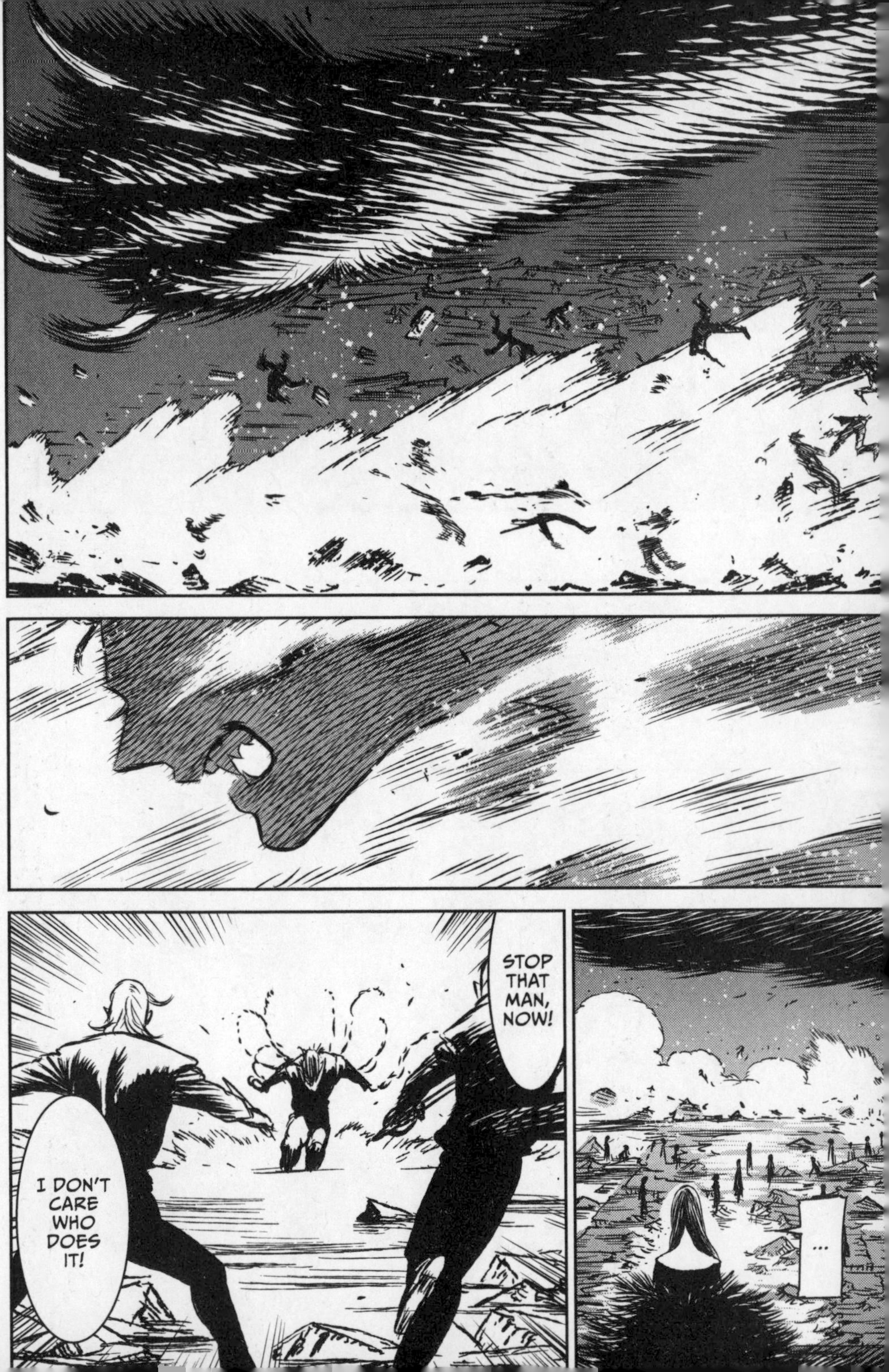
...
STOP THAT MAN, NOW!
I DON'T CARE WHO DOES IT!

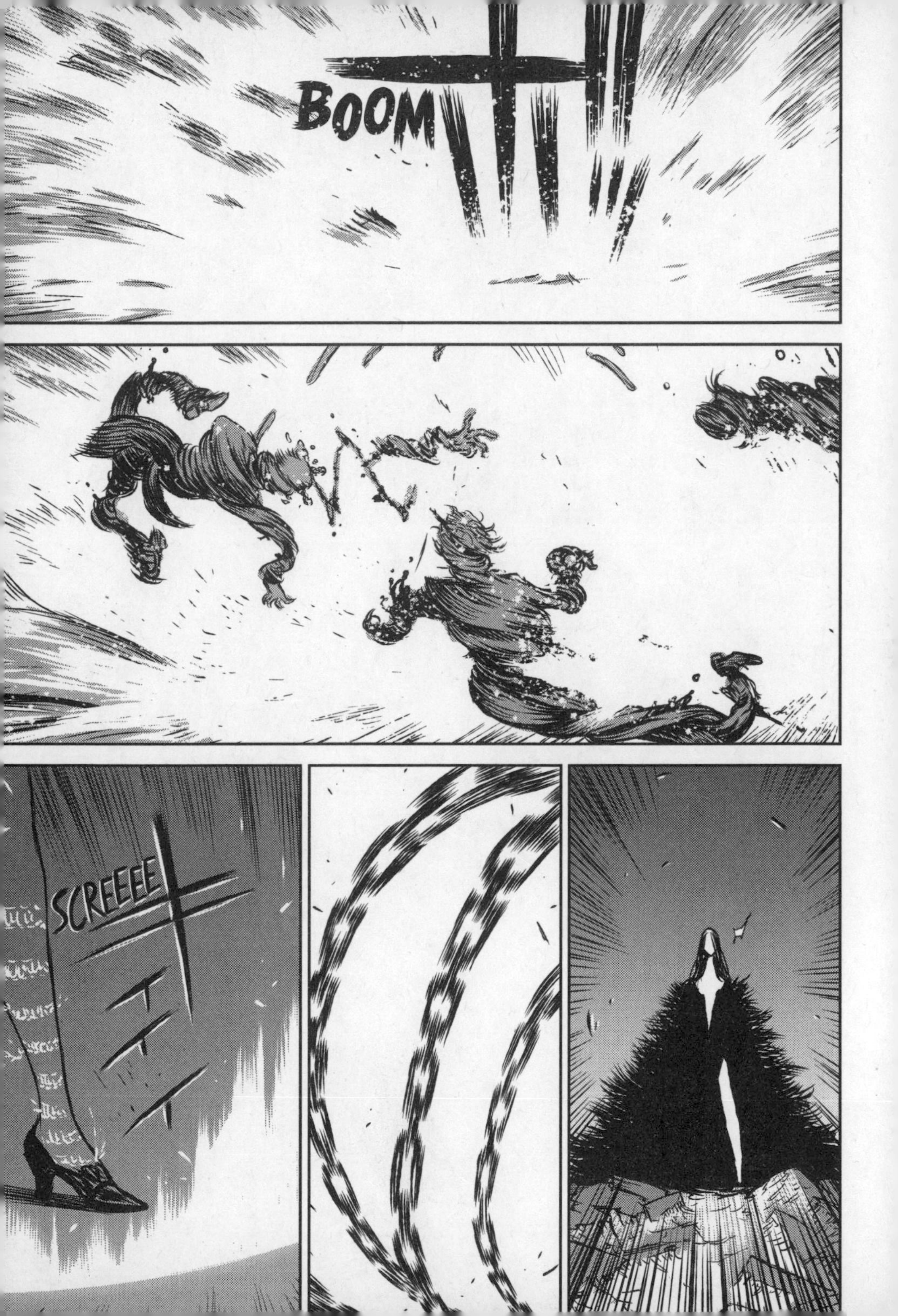
BOOM
SCREEEE

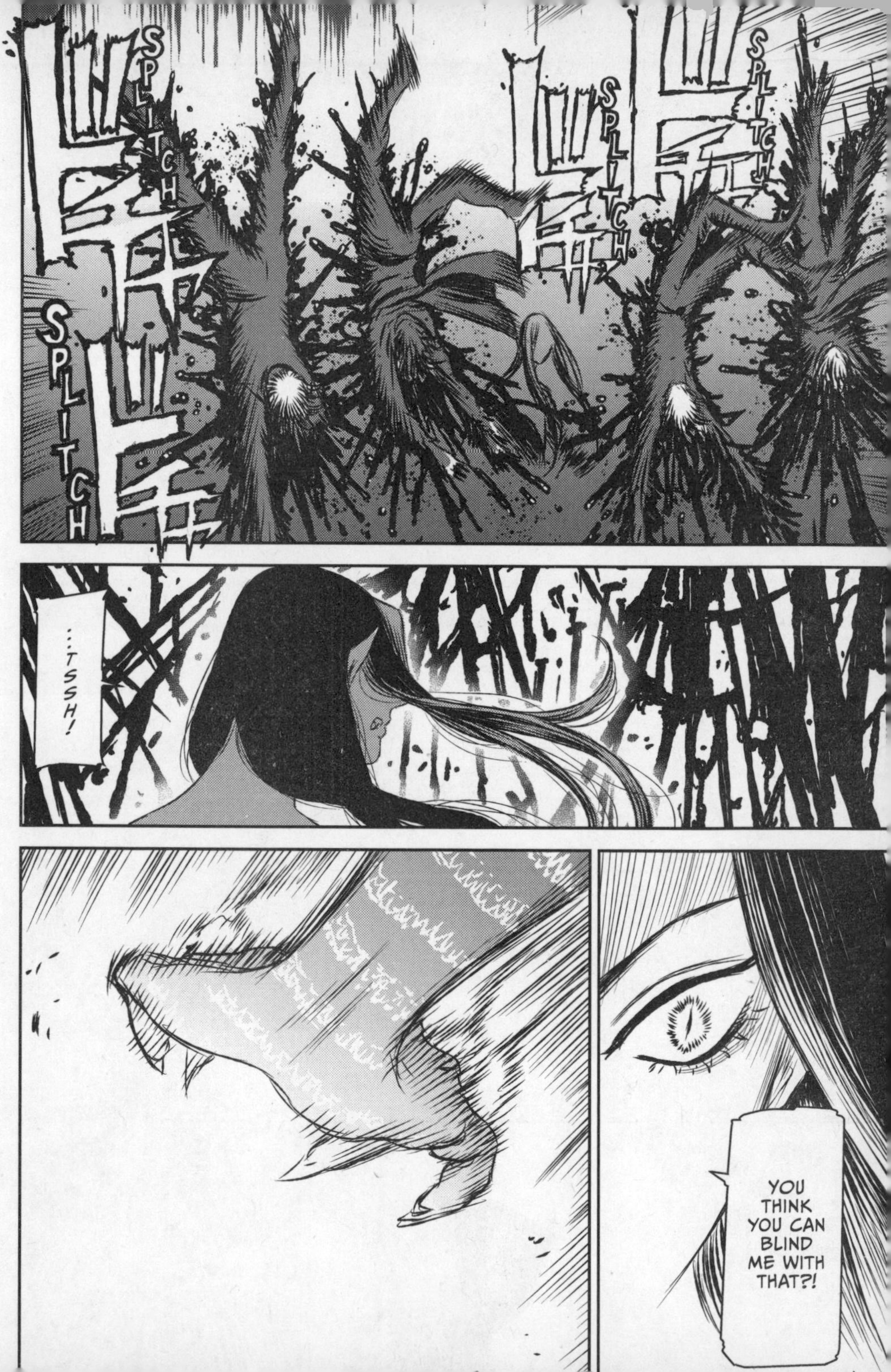
SPLITCH
SPLITCH
SPLITCH
SPLITCH
...TSSH!
YOU THINK YOU CAN BLIND ME WITH THAT?!

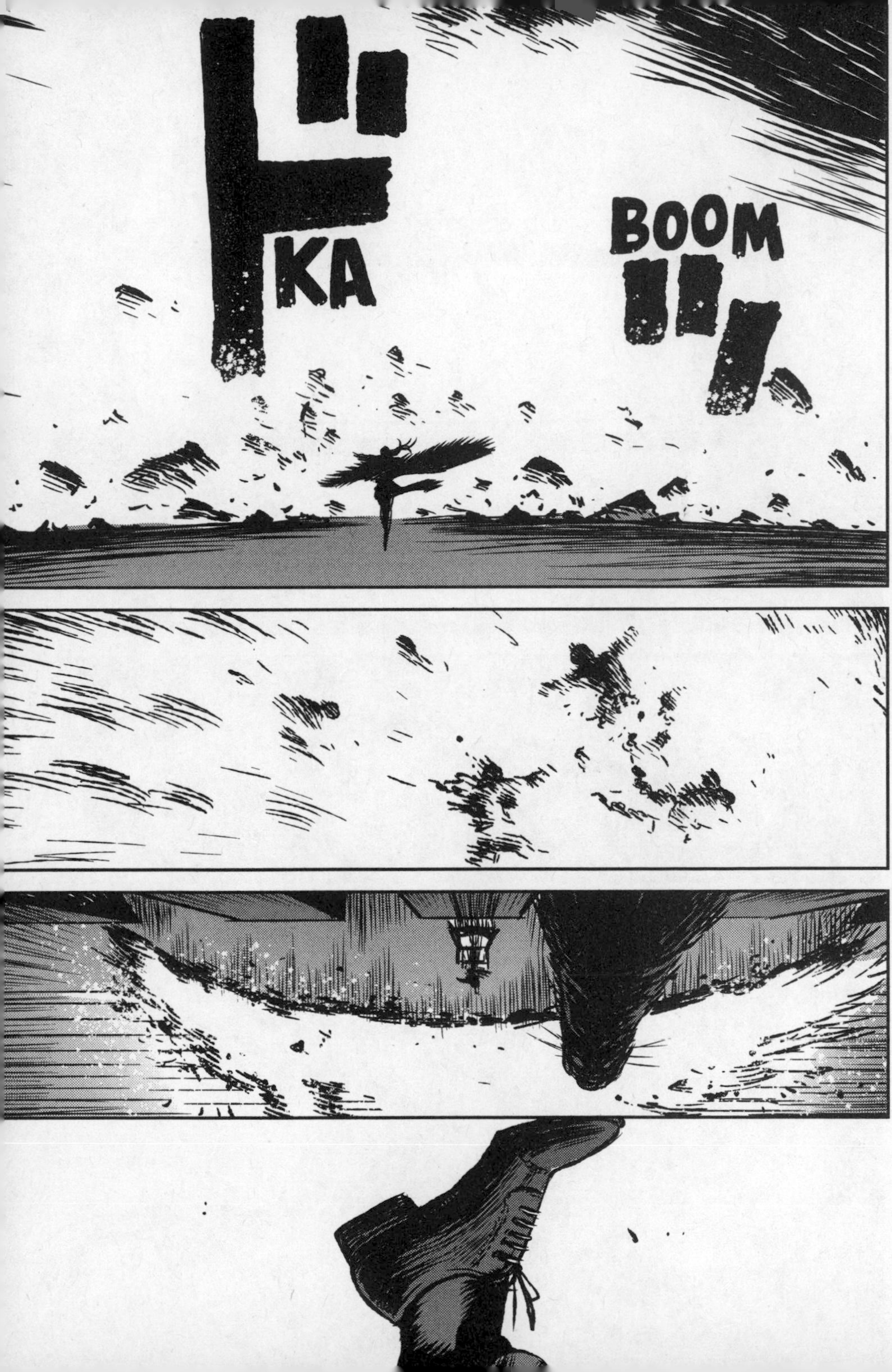
BOOM
ドKA

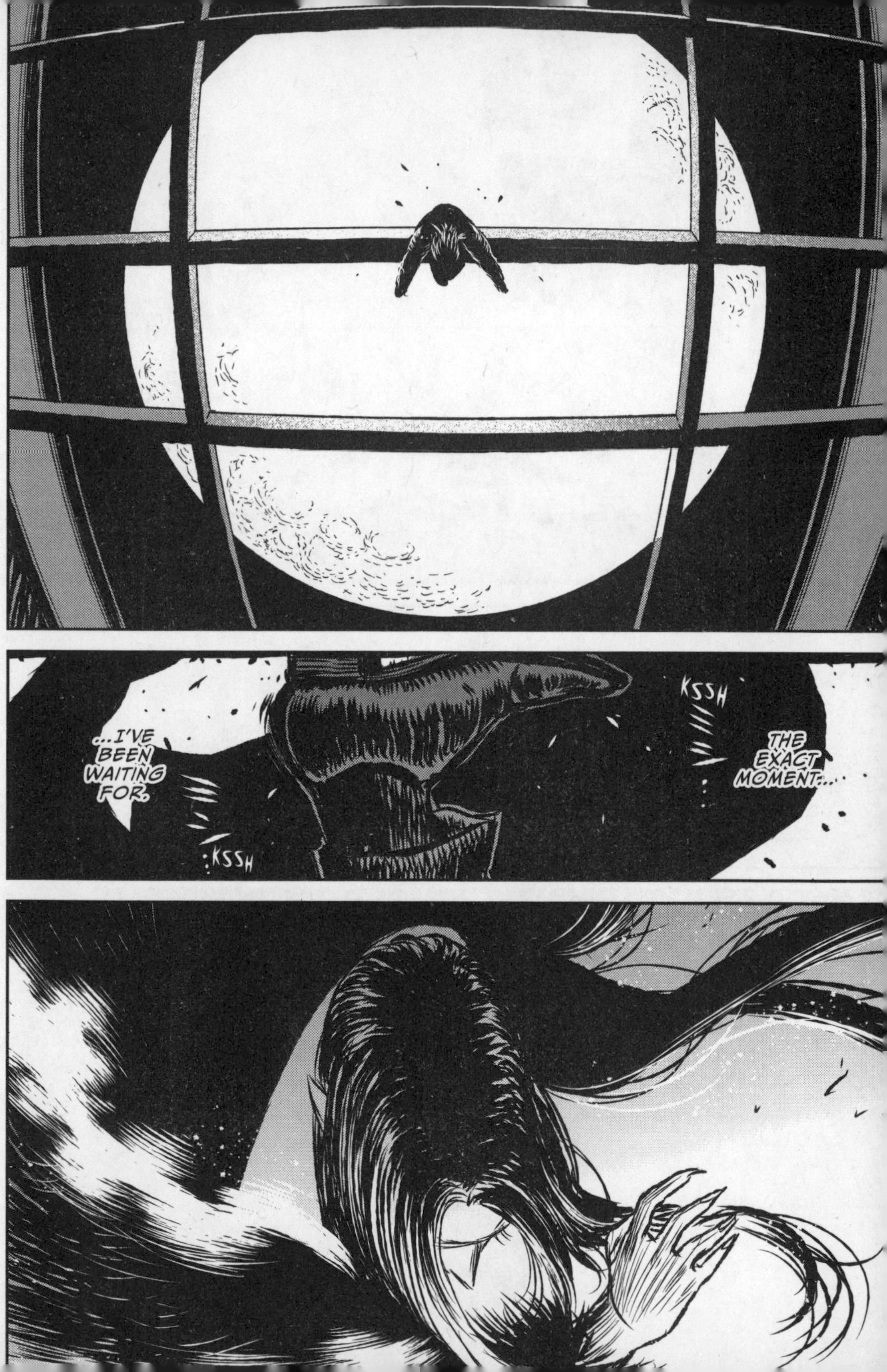
KSSH
THE EXACT MOMENT...
...I'VE BEEN WAITING FOR.
KSSH

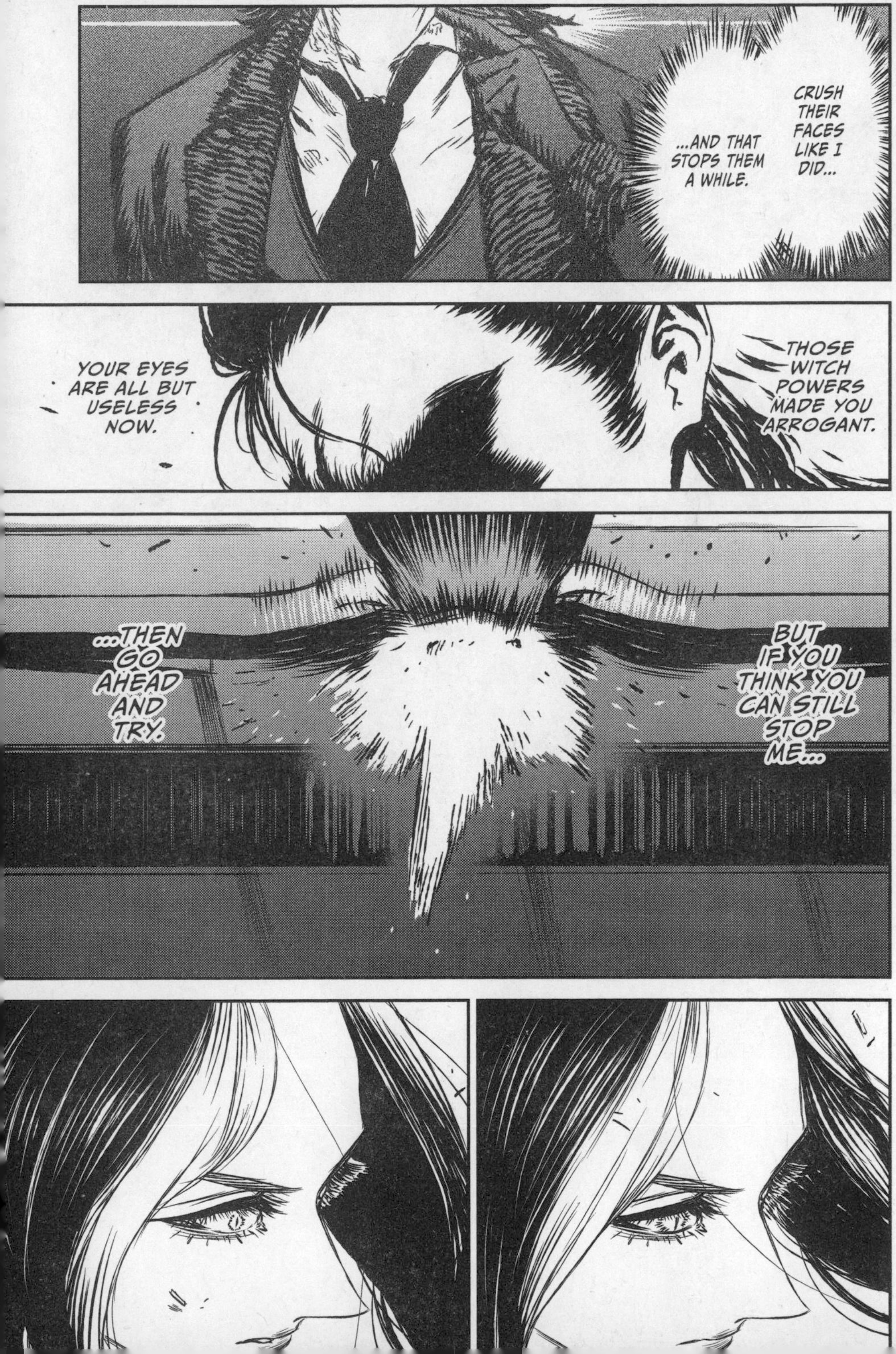
CRUSH THEIR FACES LIKE I DID...
...AND THAT STOPS THEM A WHILE.
THOSE WITCH POWERS MADE YOU ARROGANT.
YOUR EYES ARE ALL BUT USELESS NOW.
BUT IF YOU THINK YOU CAN STILL STOP ME...
...THEN GO AHEAD AND TRY.

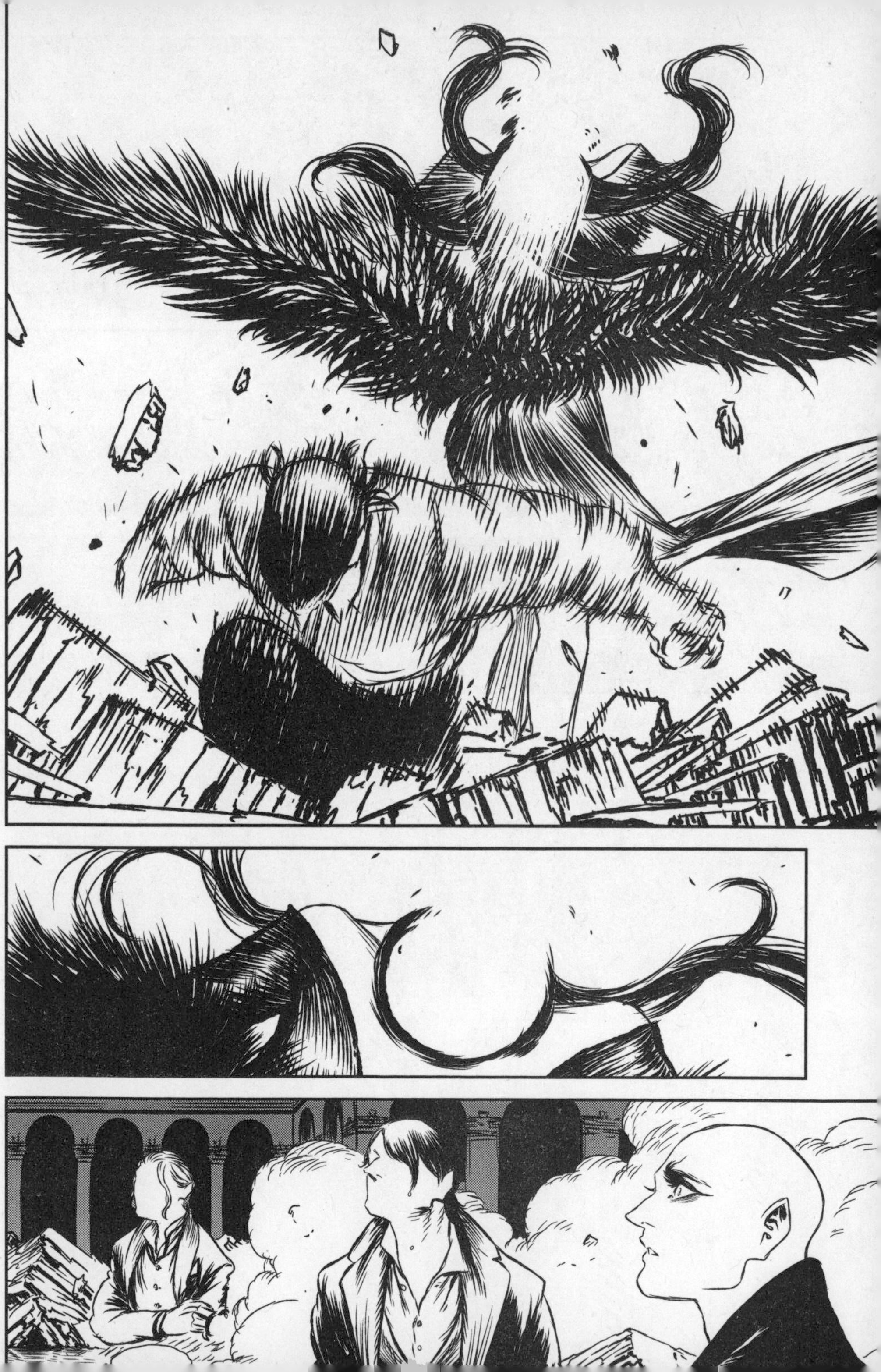

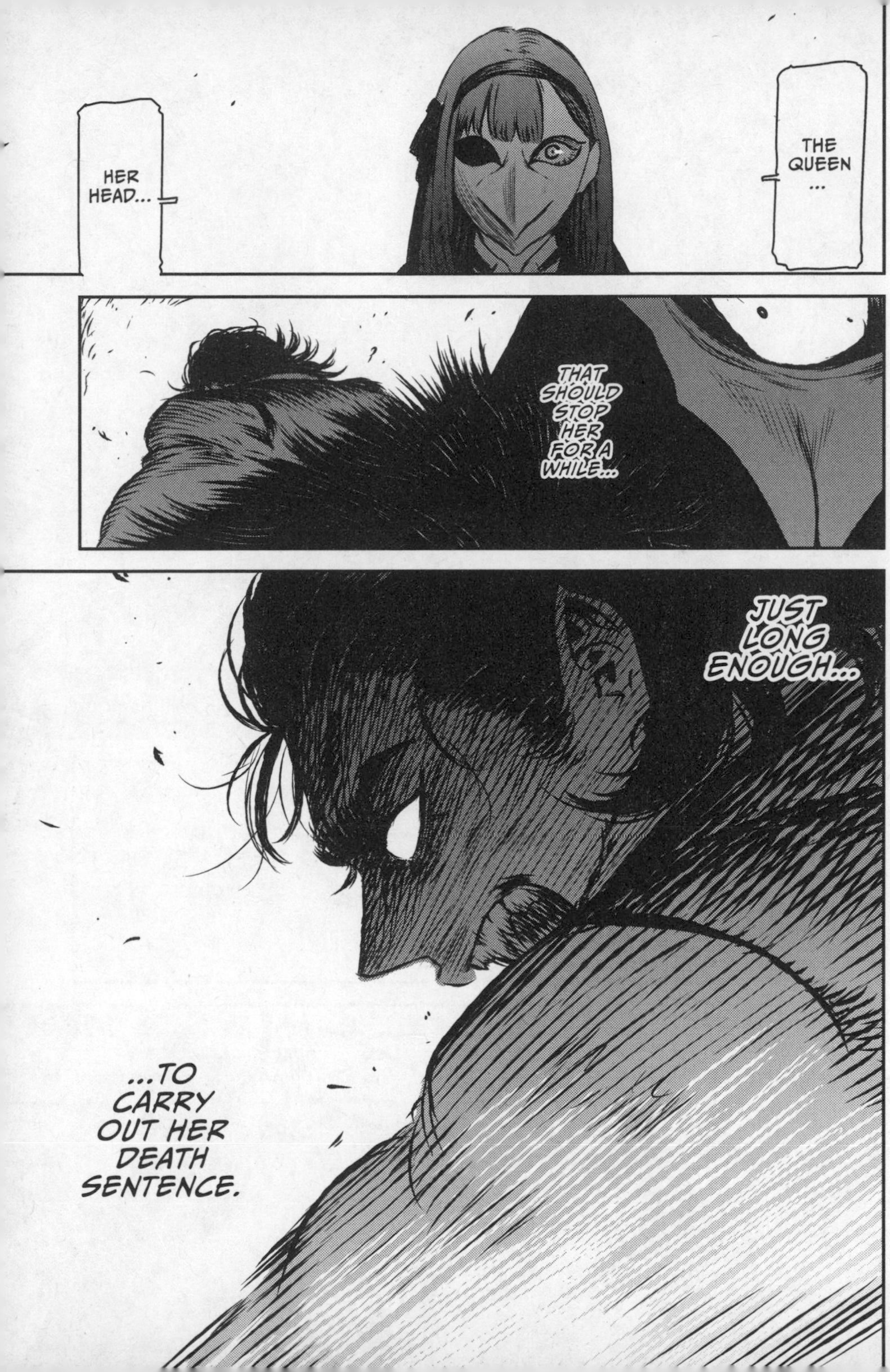
THE QUEEN ...
HER HEAD...
THAT SHOULD STOP HER FOR A WHILE...
JUST LONG ENOUGH...
...TO CARRY OUT HER DEATH SENTENCE.

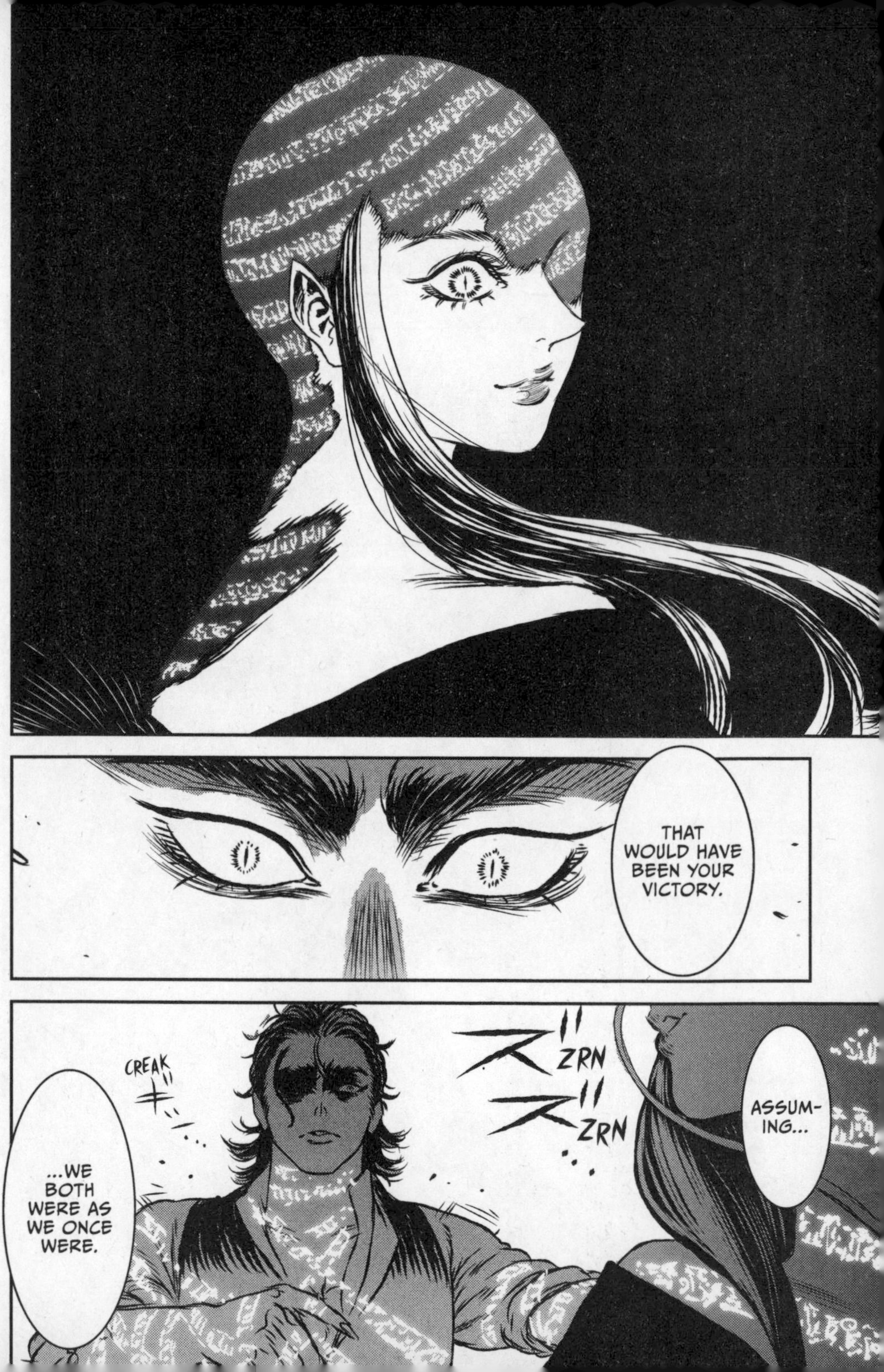
THAT WOULD HAVE BEEN YOUR VICTORY.
ASSUM-ING...
ZRN
ZRN
CREAK
...WE BOTH WERE AS WE ONCE WERE.

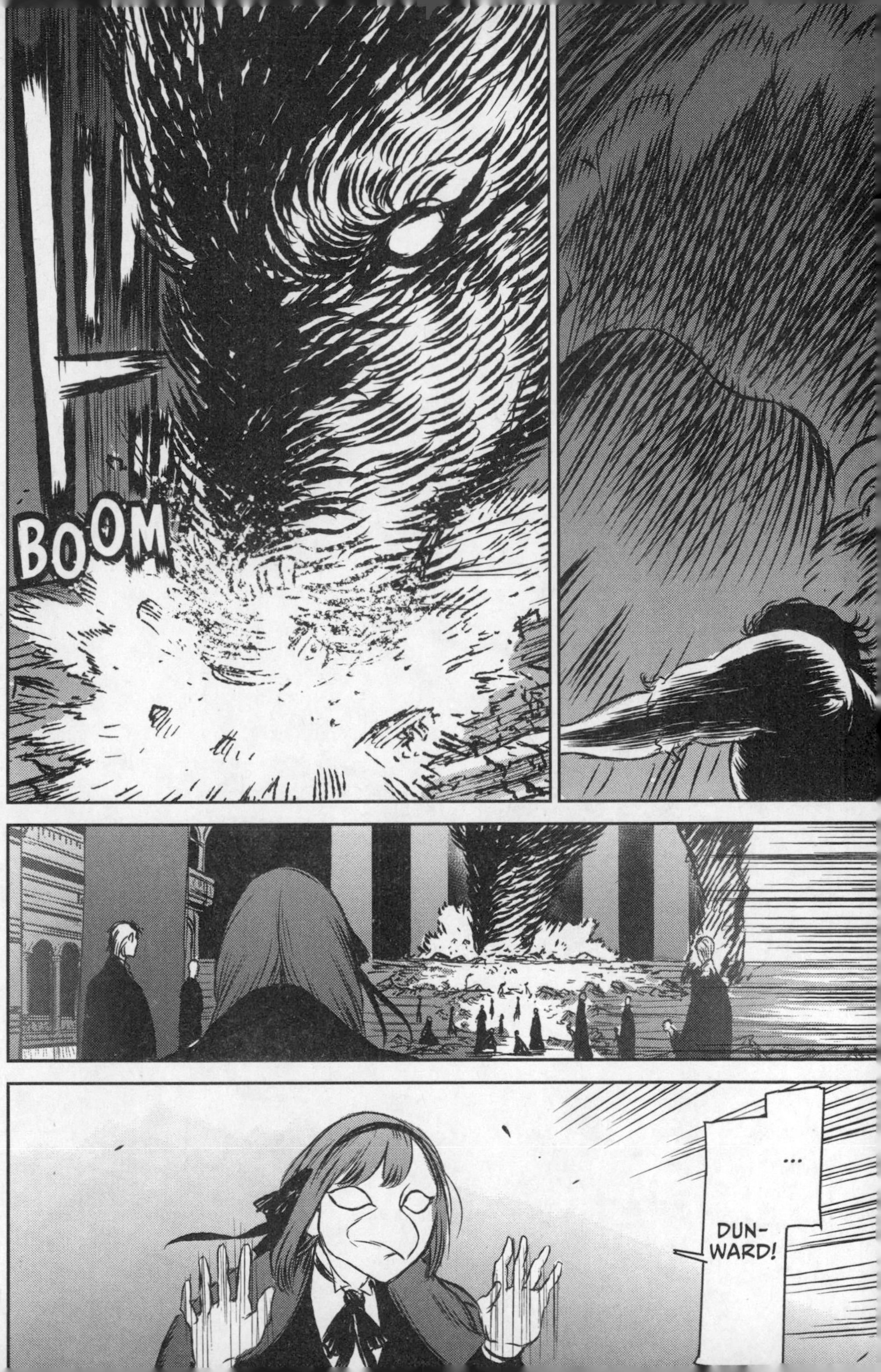
BOOM
...
DUN-
WARD!

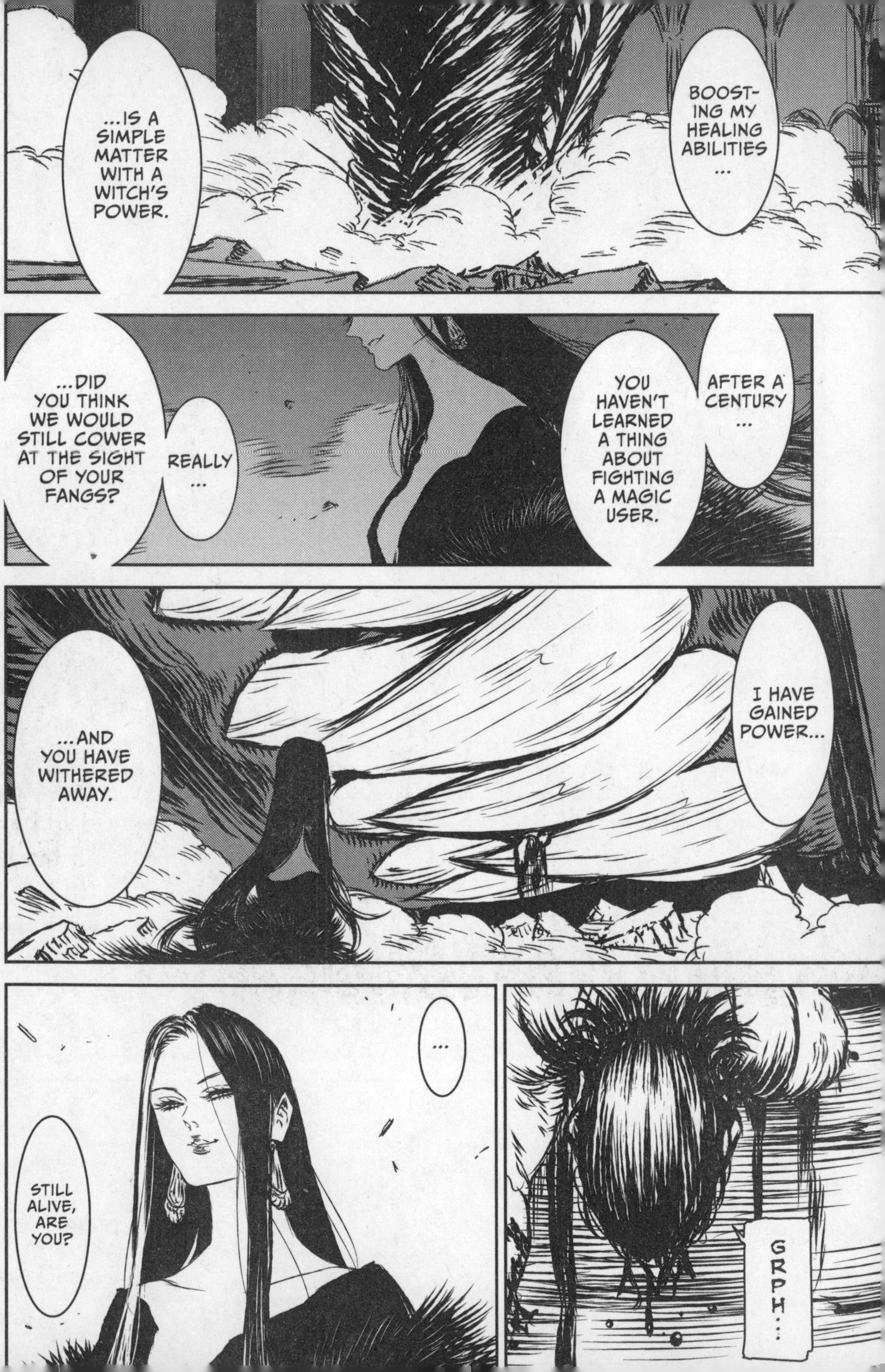
BOOST-ING MY HEALING ABILITIES ...
...IS A SIMPLE MATTER WITH A WITCH'S POWER.
AFTER A CENTURY ...
YOU HAVEN'T LEARNED A THING ABOUT FIGHTING A MAGIC USER.
REALLY ...
...DID YOU THINK WE WOULD STILL COWER AT THE SIGHT OF YOUR FANGS?
I HAVE GAINED POWER...
...AND YOU HAVE WITHERED AWAY.
GRPH...
...
STILL ALIVE, ARE YOU?

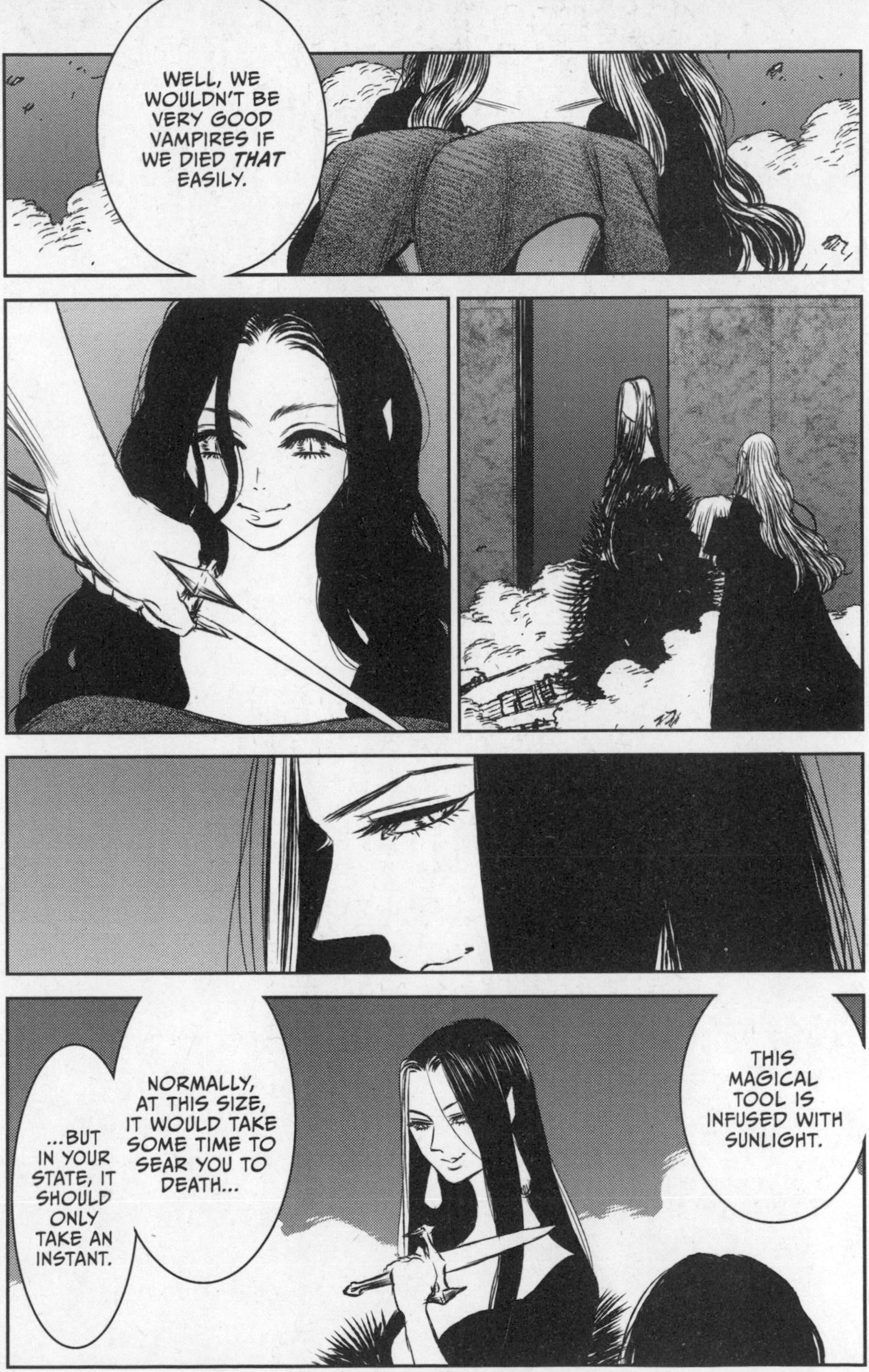
WELL, WE WOULDN'T BE VERY GOOD VAMPIRES IF WE DIED THAT EASILY.
THIS MAGICAL TOOL IS INFUSED WITH SUNLIGHT.
NORMALLY, AT THIS SIZE, IT WOULD TAKE SOME TIME TO SEAR YOU TO DEATH...
...BUT IN YOUR STATE, IT SHOULD ONLY TAKE AN INSTANT.

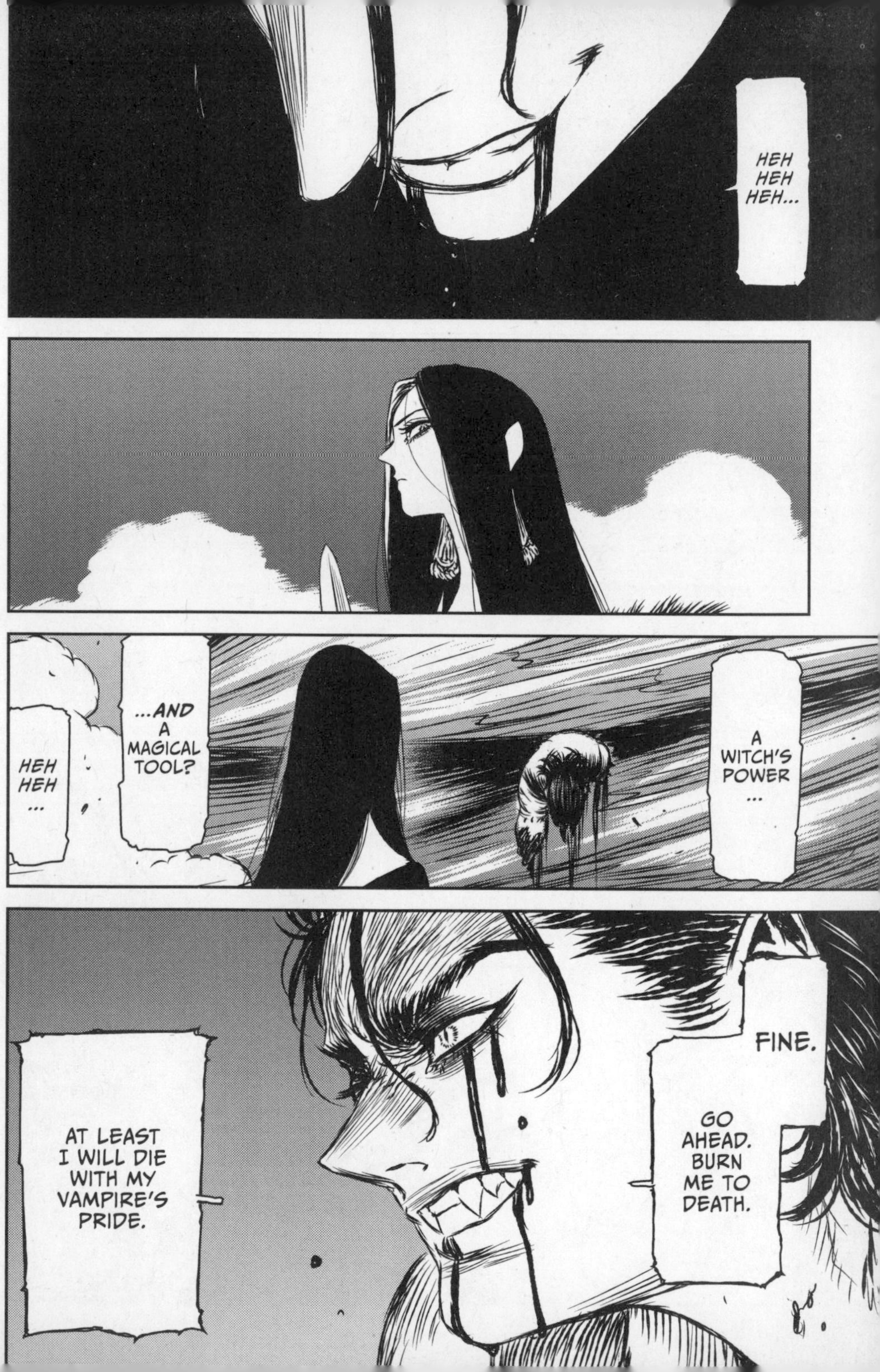
HEH HEH HEH...
A WITCH'S POWER ...
...AND A MAGICAL TOOL?
HEH HEH ...
FINE.
GO AHEAD. BURN ME TO DEATH.
AT LEAST I WILL DIE WITH MY VAMPIRE'S PRIDE.

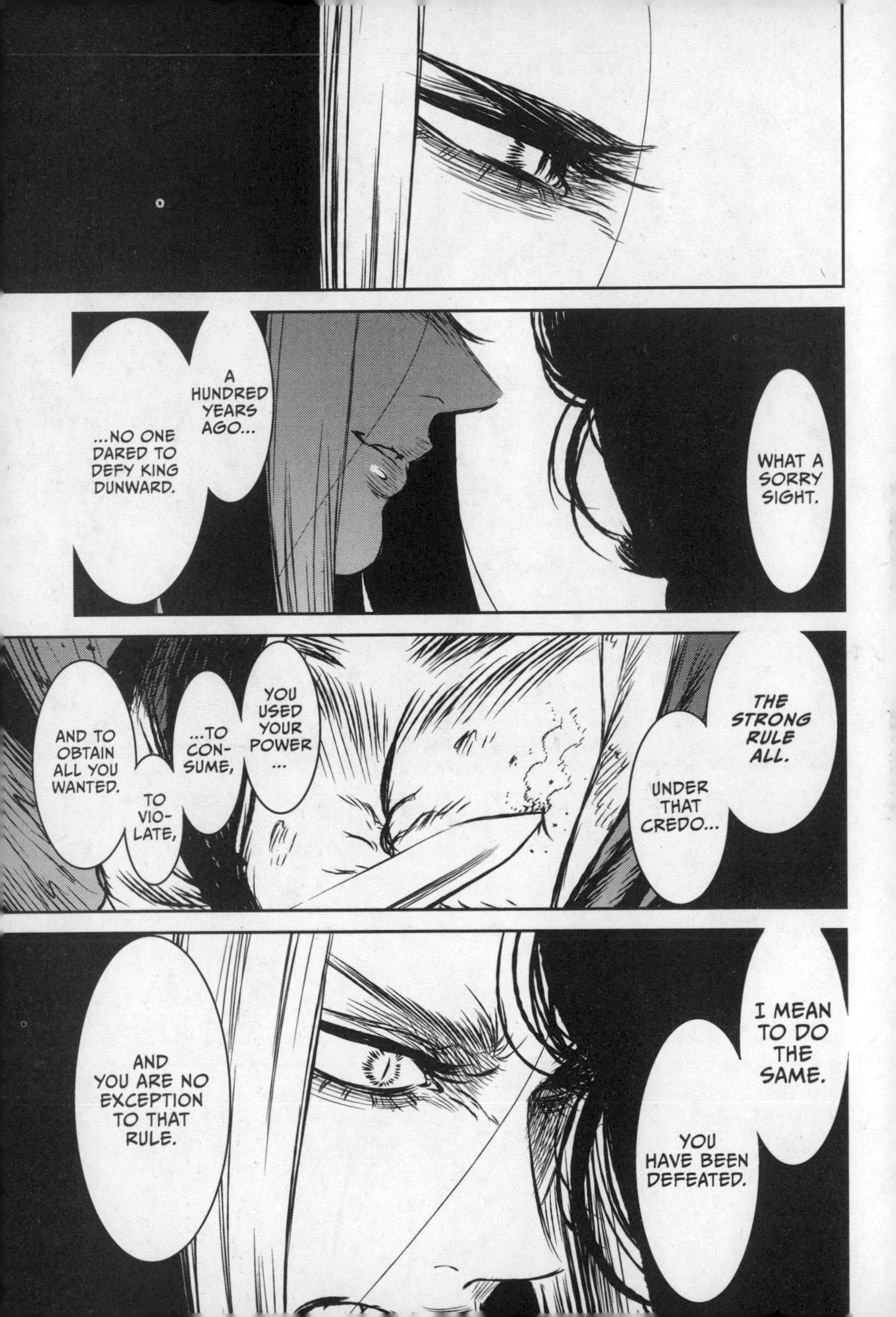
WHAT A SORRY SIGHT.
A HUNDRED YEARS AGO...
...NO ONE DARED TO DEFY KING DUNWARD.
THE STRONG RULE ALL.
UNDER THAT CREDO...
YOU USED YOUR POWER ...
...TO CON-SUME,
TO VIO-LATE,
AND TO OBTAIN ALL YOU WANTED.
I MEAN TO DO THE SAME.
YOU HAVE BEEN DEFEATED.
AND YOU ARE NO EXCEPTION TO THAT RULE.

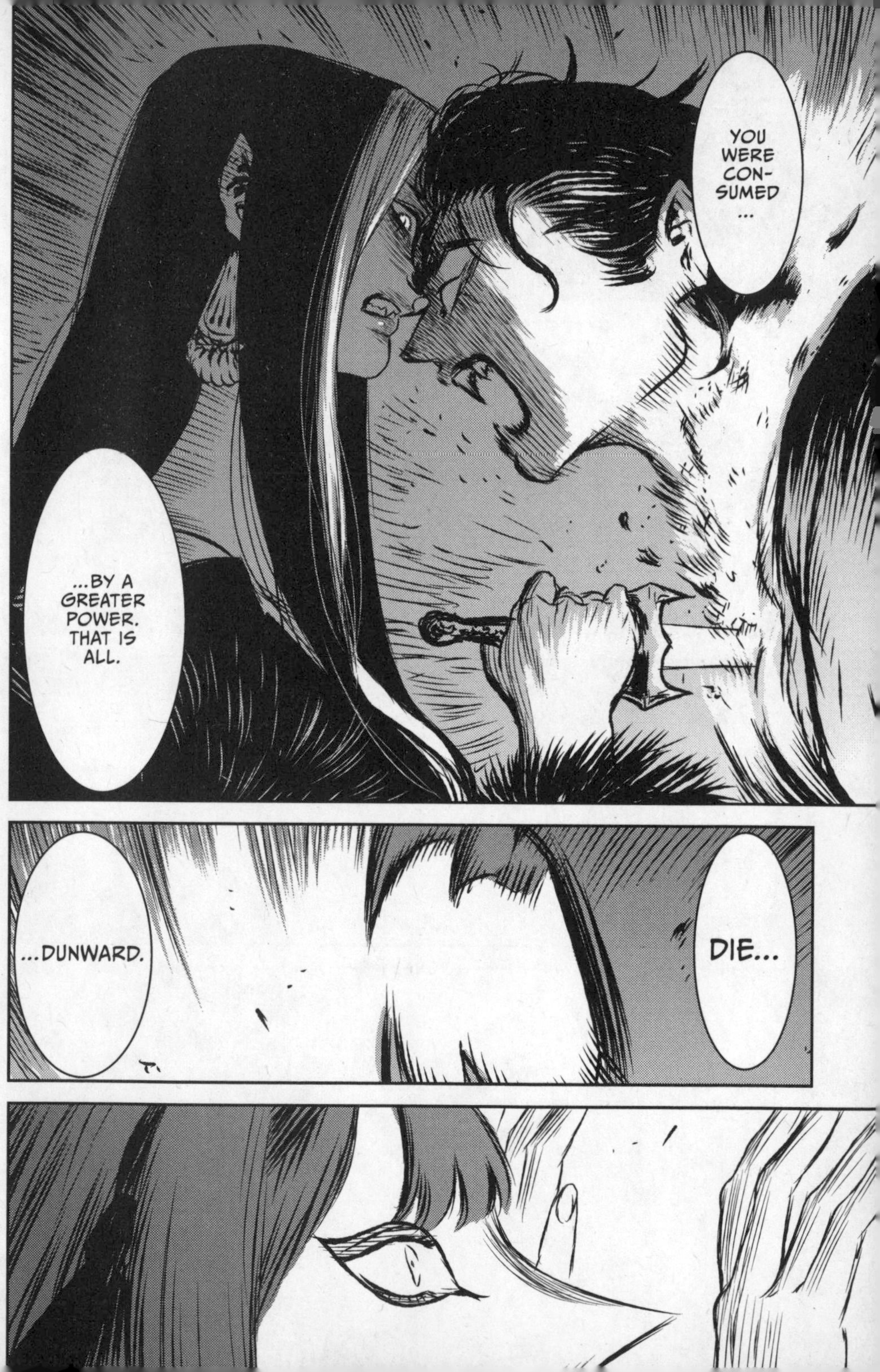
YOU WERE CON-SUMED ...
...BY A GREATER POWER. THAT IS ALL.
DIE...
...DUNWARD.

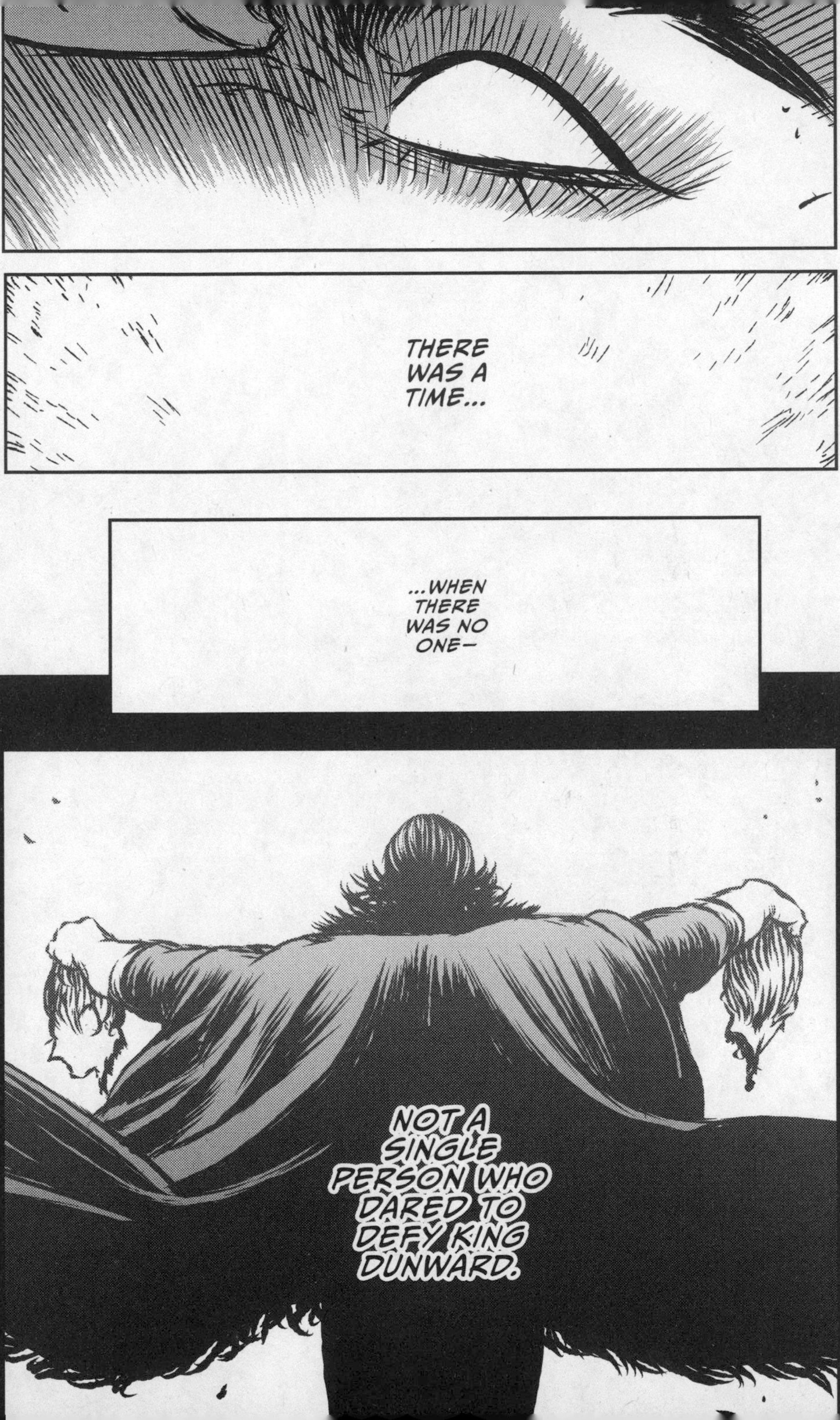
THERE WAS A TIME...
...WHEN THERE WAS NO ONE—
NOT A SINGLE PERSON WHO DARED TO DEFY KING DUNWARD.

THE WITCH AND THE BEAST

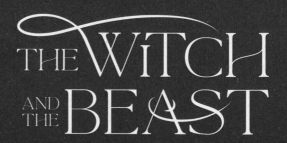

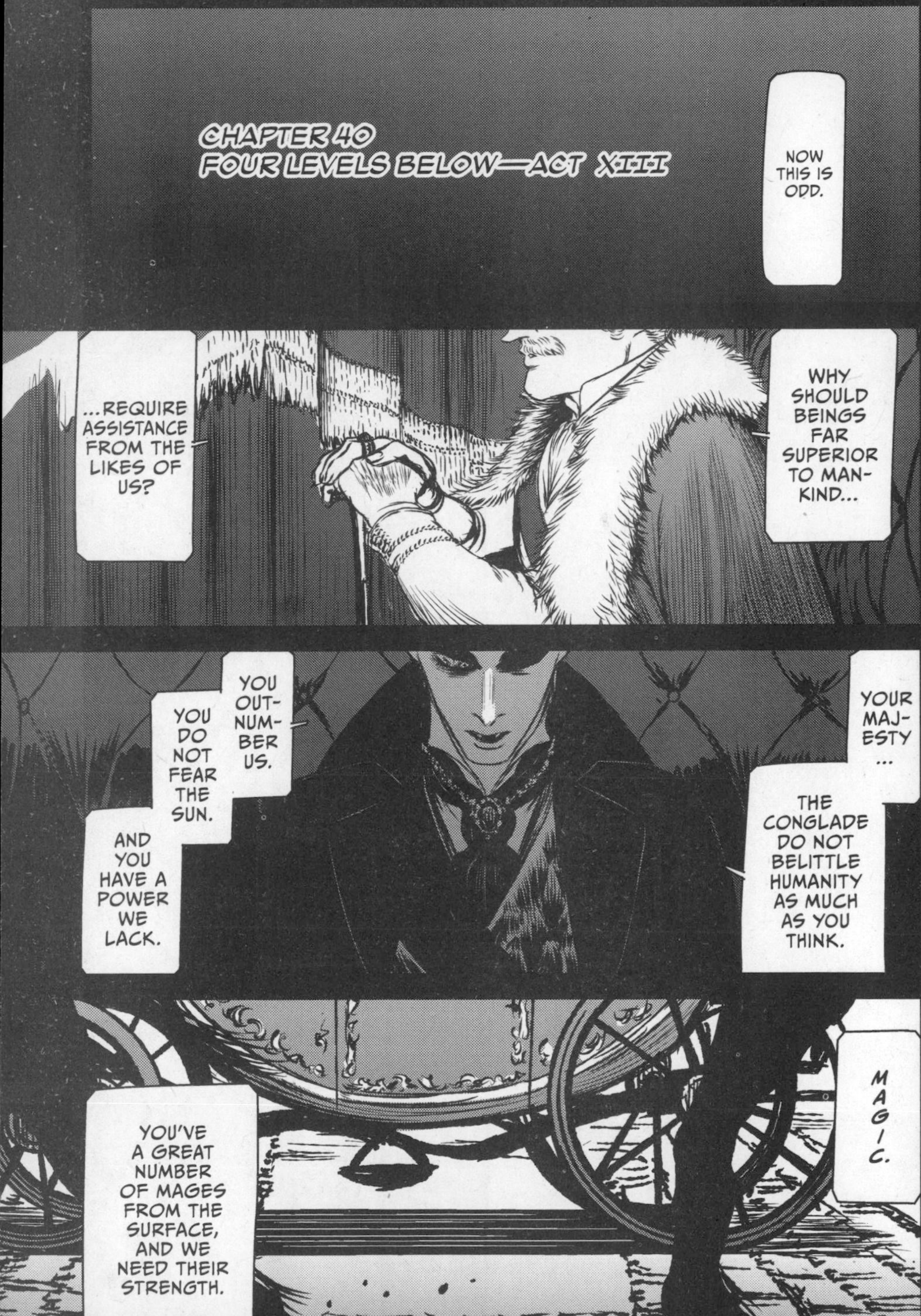
CHAPTER 40
FOUR LEVELS BELOW—ACT XIII
NOW THIS IS ODD.
WHY SHOULD BEINGS FAR SUPERIOR TO MAN-KIND...
...REQUIRE ASSISTANCE FROM THE LIKES OF US?
YOUR MAJ-ESTY...
THE CONGLADE DO NOT BELITTLE HUMANITY AS MUCH AS YOU THINK.
YOU OUT-NUM-BER US.
YOU DO NOT FEAR THE SUN.
AND YOU HAVE A POWER WE LACK.
MAGIC.
YOU'VE A GREAT NUMBER OF MAGES FROM THE SURFACE, AND WE NEED THEIR STRENGTH.

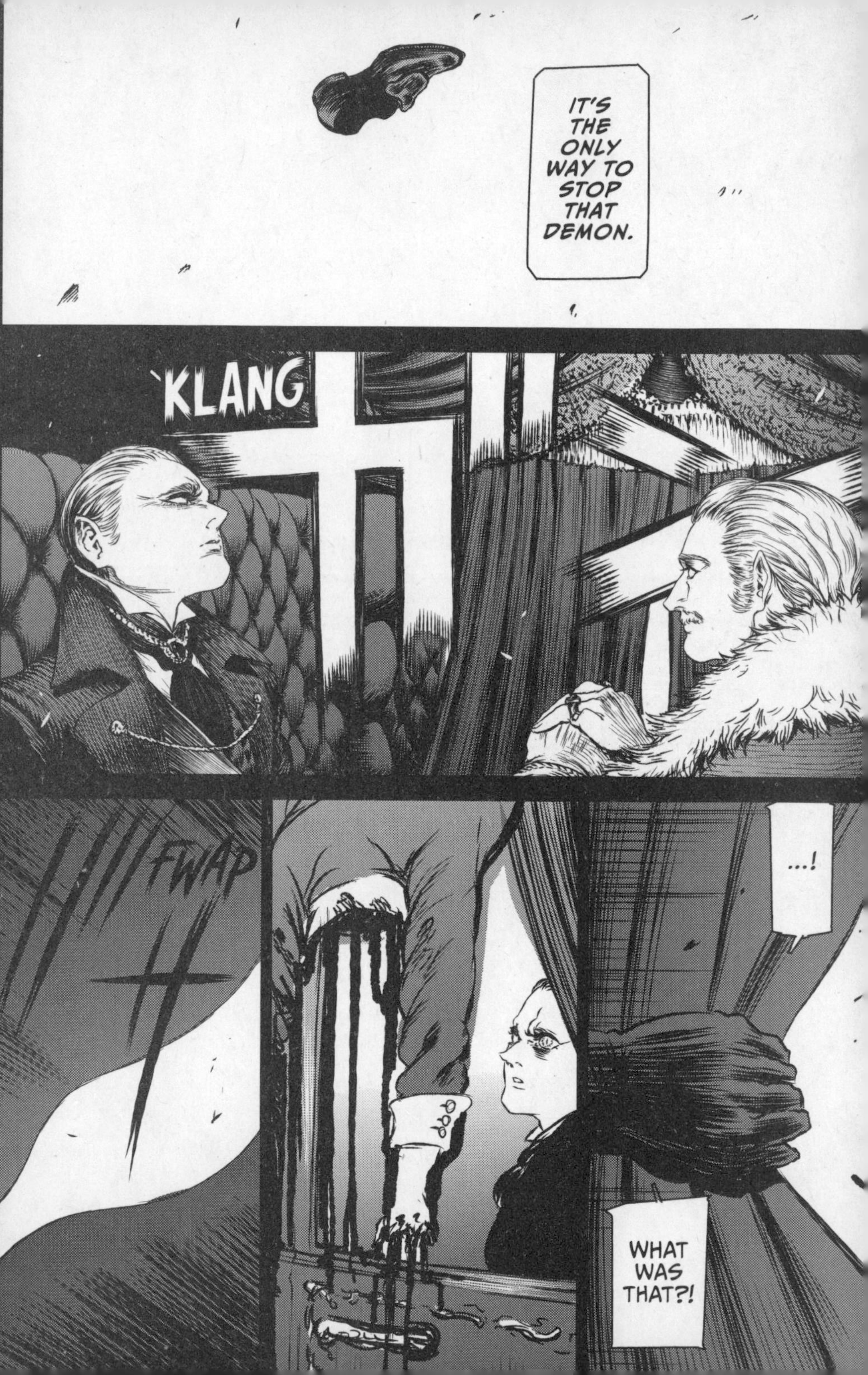
IT'S THE ONLY WAY TO STOP THAT DEMON.
KLANG
...!
WHAT WAS THAT?!
FWAP

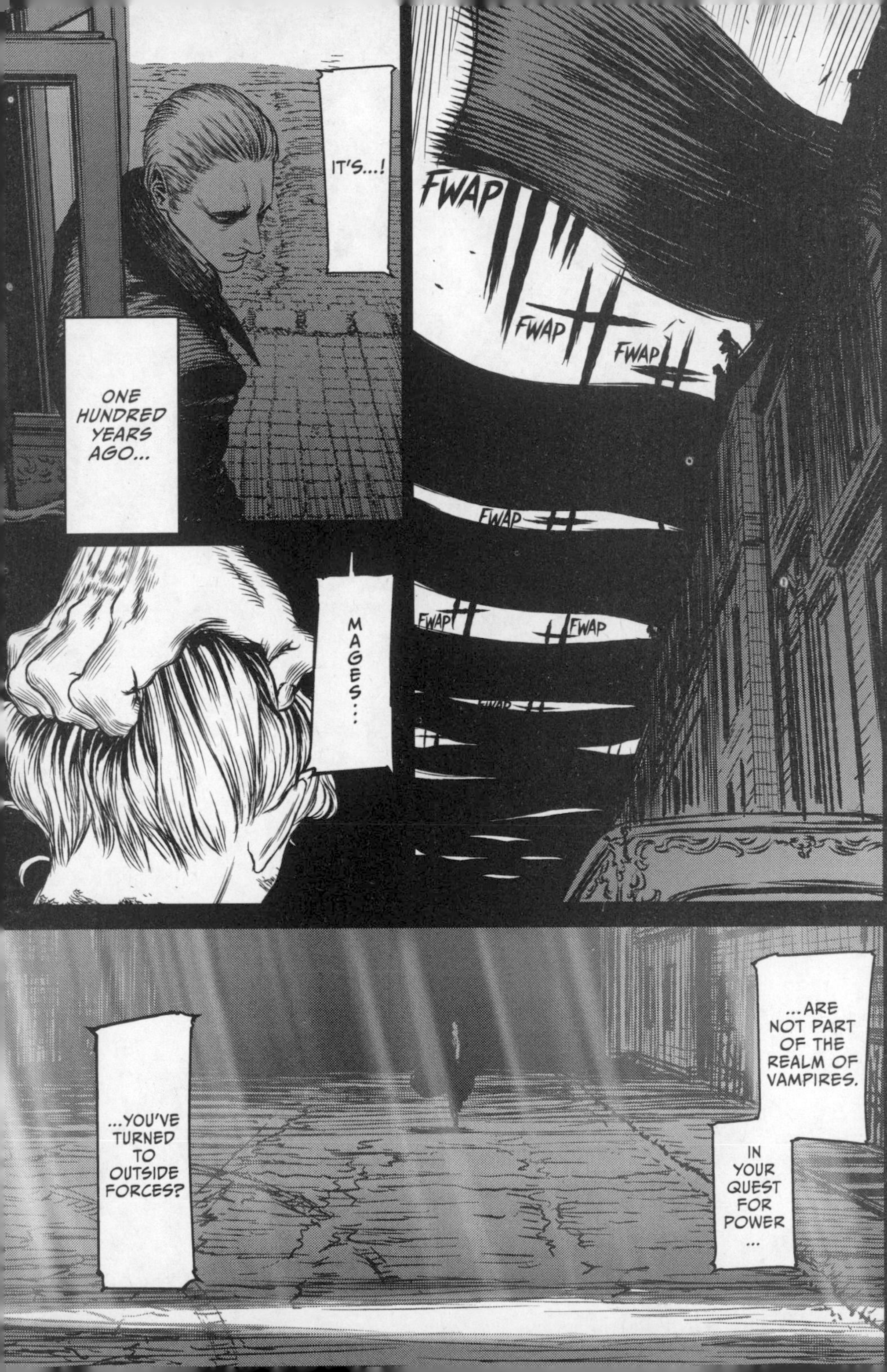
FWAP
FWAP
FWAP
FWAP
FWAP
FWAP
IT'S...!
ONE HUNDRED YEARS AGO...
MAGES...
...ARE NOT PART OF THE REALM OF VAMPIRES.
IN YOUR QUEST FOR POWER...
...YOU'VE TURNED TO OUTSIDE FORCES?

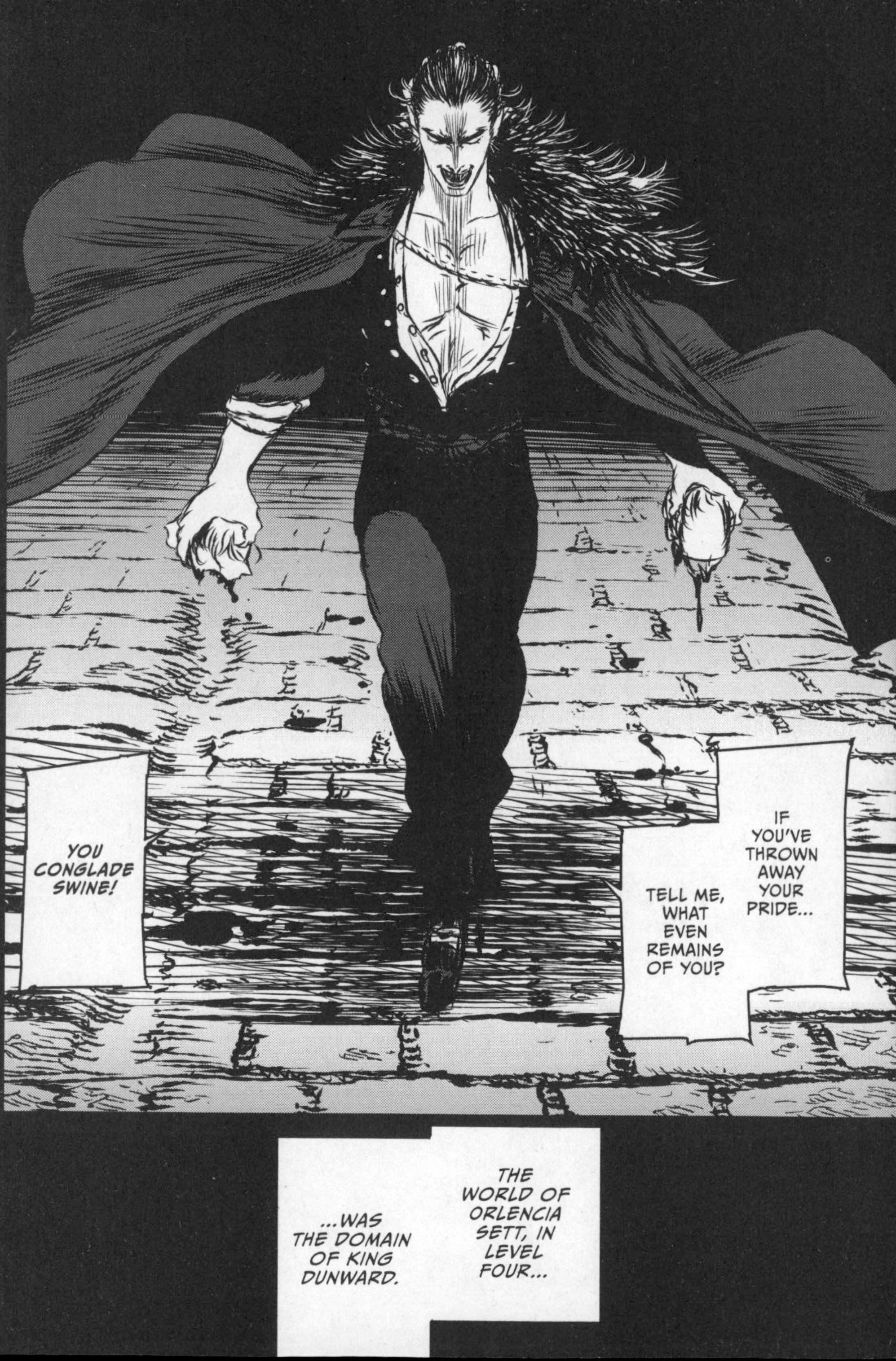
IF YOU'VE THROWN AWAY YOUR PRIDE...
TELL ME, WHAT EVEN REMAINS OF YOU?
YOU CONGLADE SWINE!
THE WORLD OF ORLENCIA SETT, IN LEVEL FOUR...
...WAS THE DOMAIN OF KING DUNWARD.

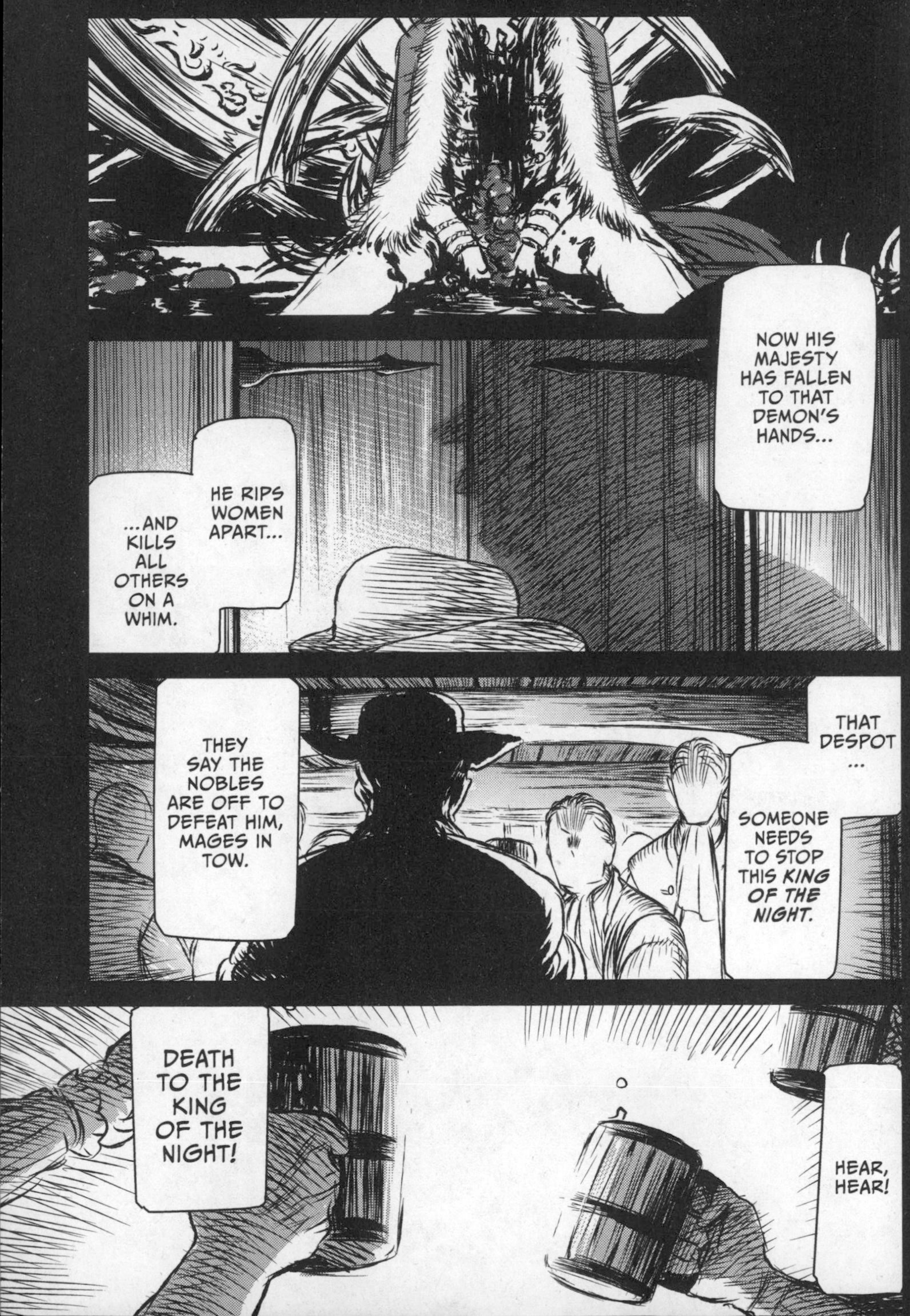
NOW HIS MAJESTY HAS FALLEN TO THAT DEMON'S HANDS...
HE RIPS WOMEN APART...
...AND KILLS ALL OTHERS ON A WHIM.
THAT DESPOT ...
SOMEONE NEEDS TO STOP THIS *KING OF THE NIGHT*.
THEY SAY THE NOBLES ARE OFF TO DEFEAT HIM, MAGES IN TOW.
DEATH TO THE KING OF THE NIGHT!
HEAR, HEAR!

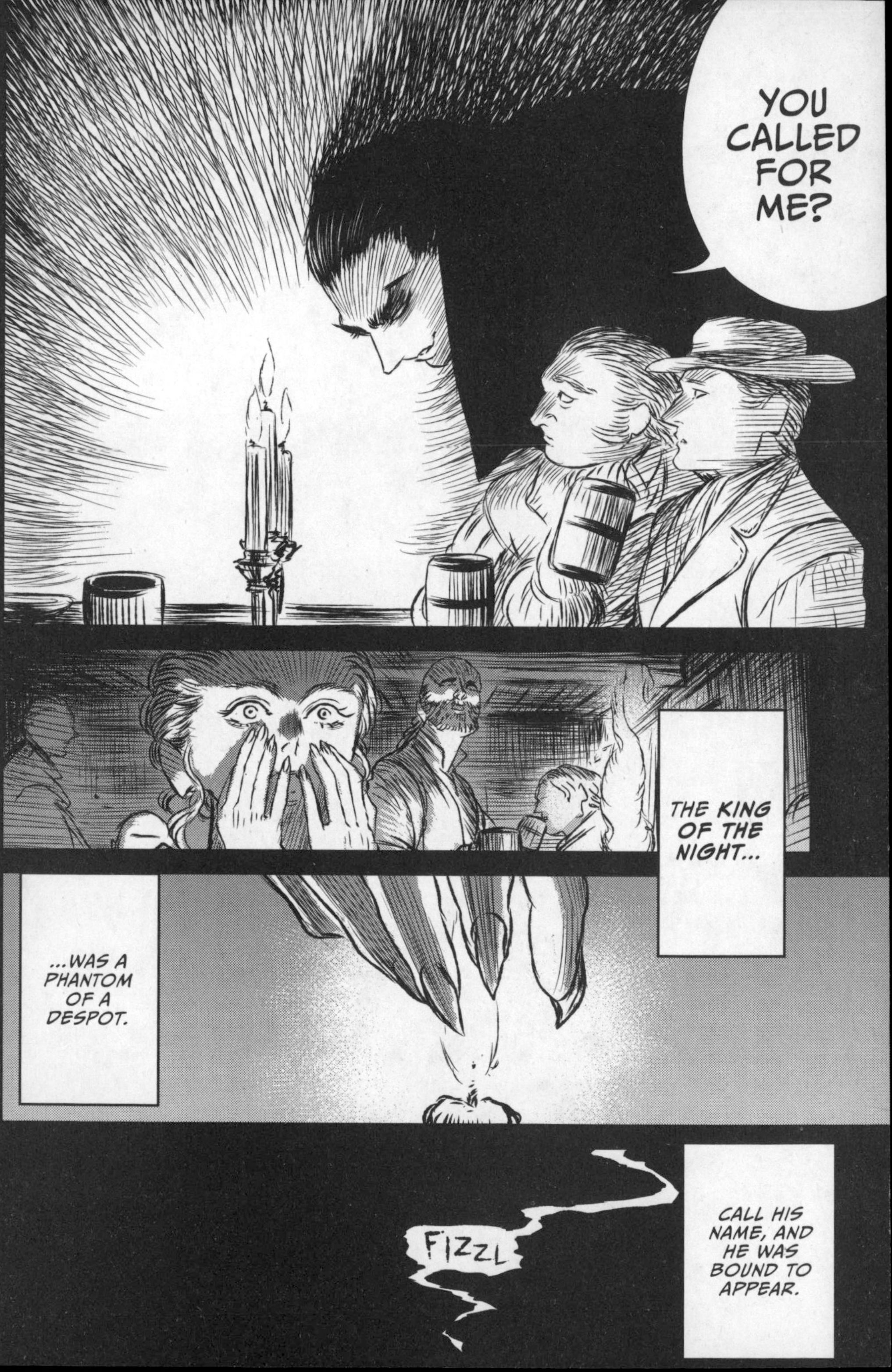
YOU CALLED FOR ME?
THE KING OF THE NIGHT...
...WAS A PHANTOM OF A DESPOT.
CALL HIS NAME, AND HE WAS BOUND TO APPEAR.
FIZZL

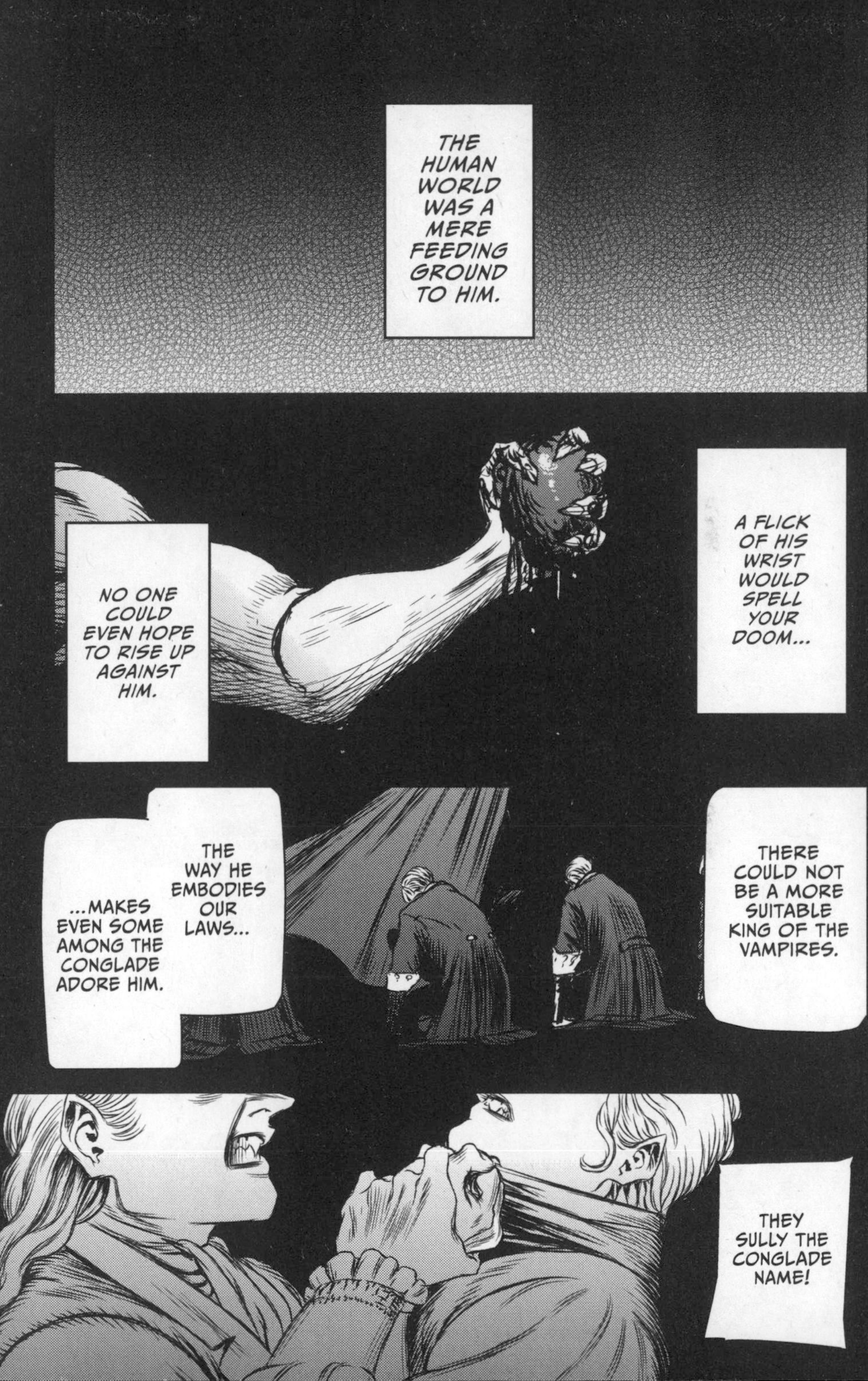
THE HUMAN WORLD WAS A MERE FEEDING GROUND TO HIM.
A FLICK OF HIS WRIST WOULD SPELL YOUR DOOM...
NO ONE COULD EVEN HOPE TO RISE UP AGAINST HIM.
THERE COULD NOT BE A MORE SUITABLE KING OF THE VAMPIRES.
THE WAY HE EMBODIES OUR LAWS...
...MAKES EVEN SOME AMONG THE CONGLADE ADORE HIM.
THEY SULLY THE CONGLADE NAME!

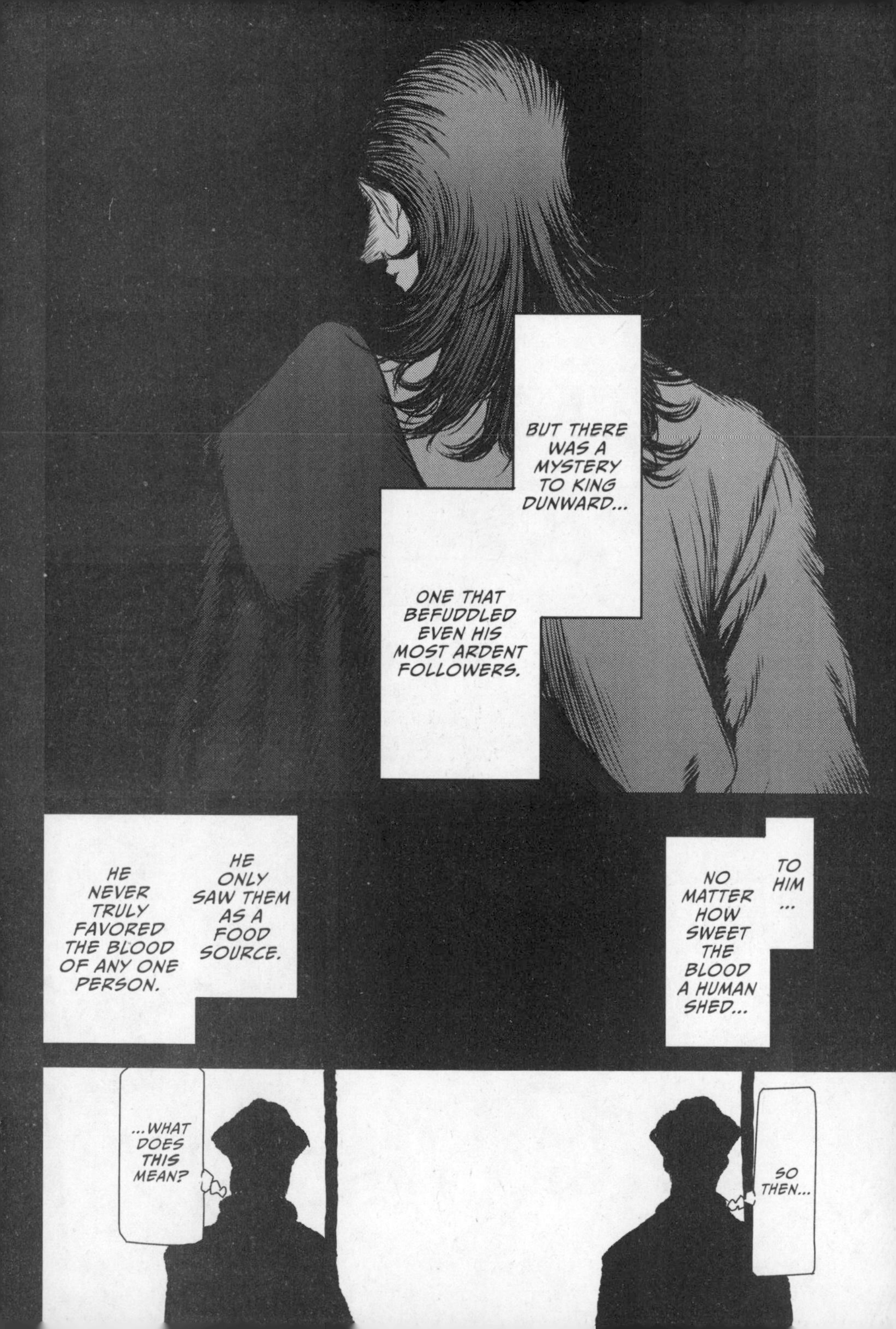
BUT THERE WAS A MYSTERY TO KING DUNWARD...
ONE THAT BEFUDDLED EVEN HIS MOST ARDENT FOLLOWERS.
TO HIM...
NO MATTER HOW SWEET THE BLOOD A HUMAN SHED...
HE ONLY SAW THEM AS A FOOD SOURCE.
HE NEVER TRULY FAVORED THE BLOOD OF ANY ONE PERSON.
SO THEN...
...WHAT DOES THIS MEAN?

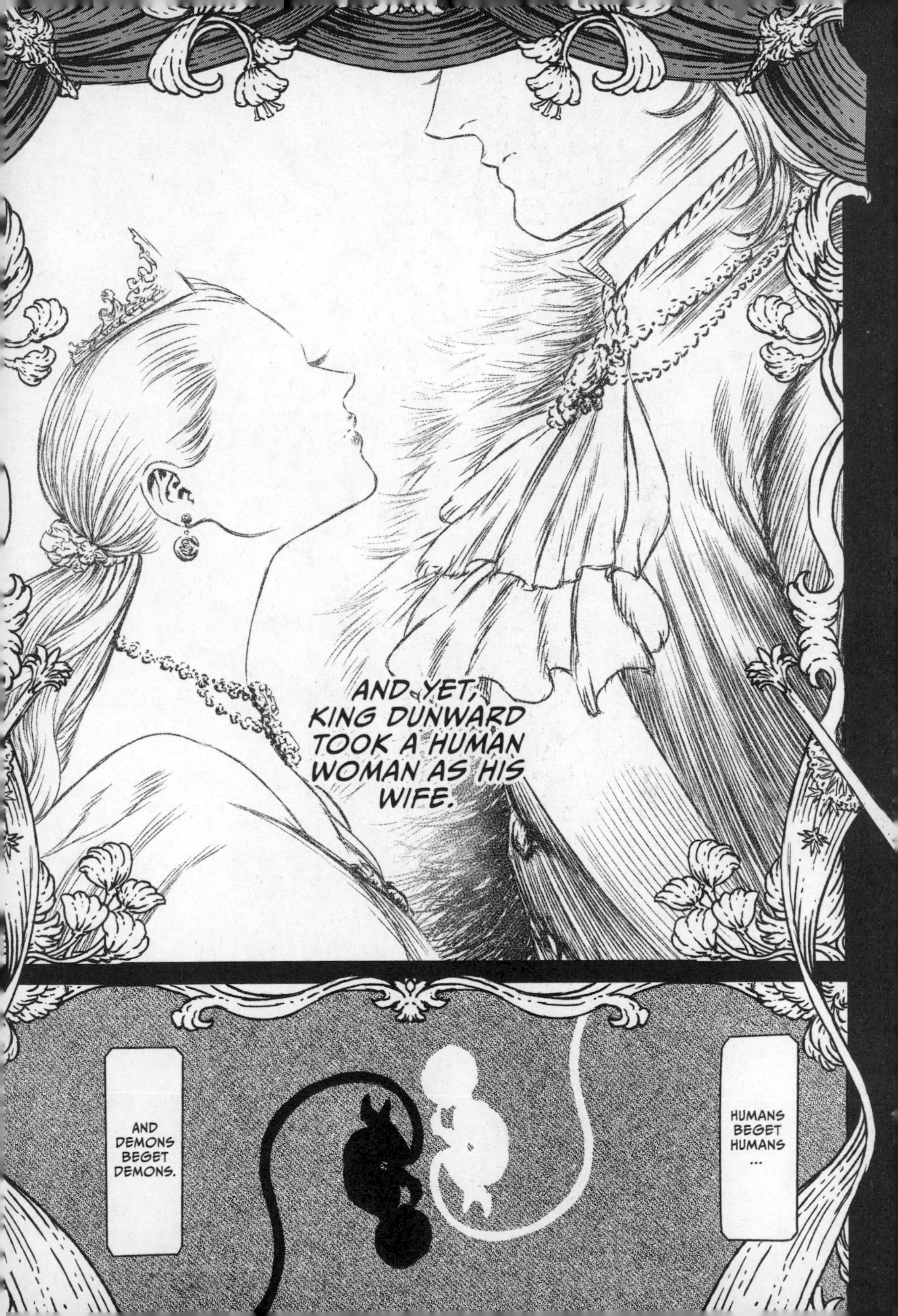
AND YET, KING DUNWARD TOOK A HUMAN WOMAN AS HIS WIFE.
HUMANS BEGET HUMANS ...
AND DEMONS BEGET DEMONS.

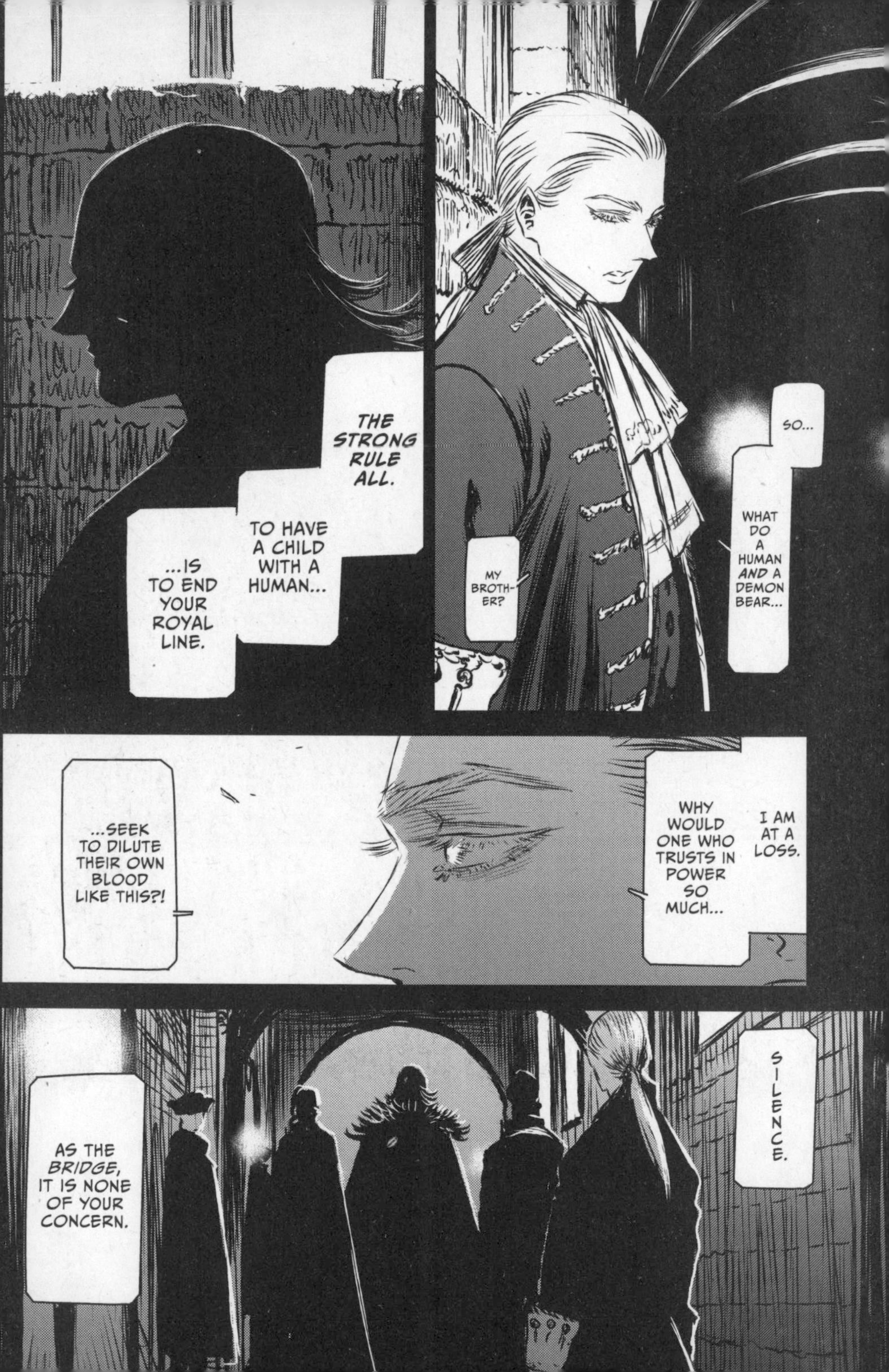
SO...
WHAT DO A HUMAN *AND* A DEMON BEAR...
MY BROTHER?
THE STRONG RULE ALL.
TO HAVE A CHILD WITH A HUMAN...
...IS TO END YOUR ROYAL LINE.
I AM AT A LOSS.
WHY WOULD ONE WHO TRUSTS IN POWER SO MUCH...
...SEEK TO DILUTE THEIR OWN BLOOD LIKE THIS?!
SILENCE.
AS THE *BRIDGE*, IT IS NONE OF YOUR CONCERN.

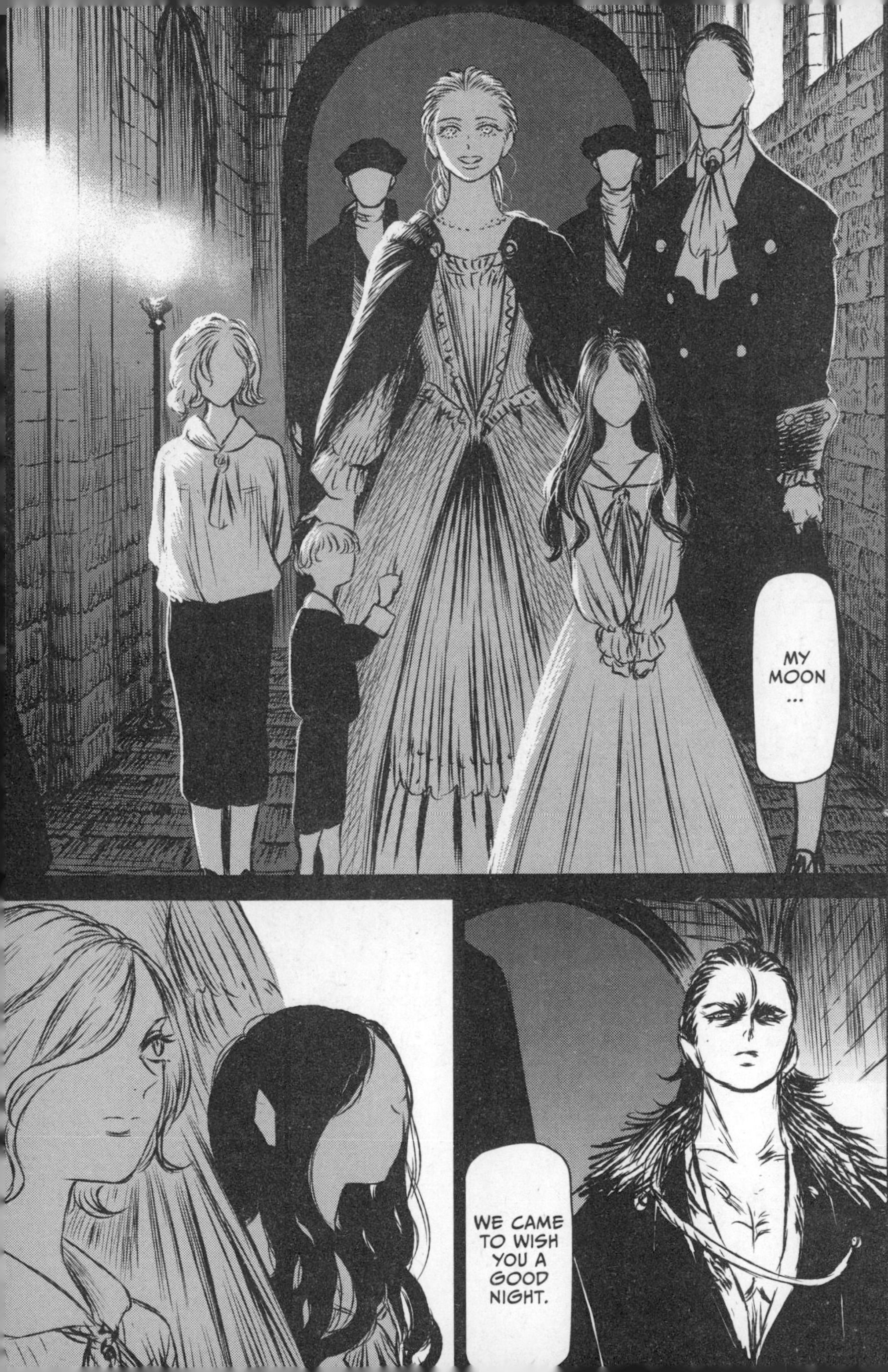
MY MOON ...
WE CAME TO WISH YOU A GOOD NIGHT.

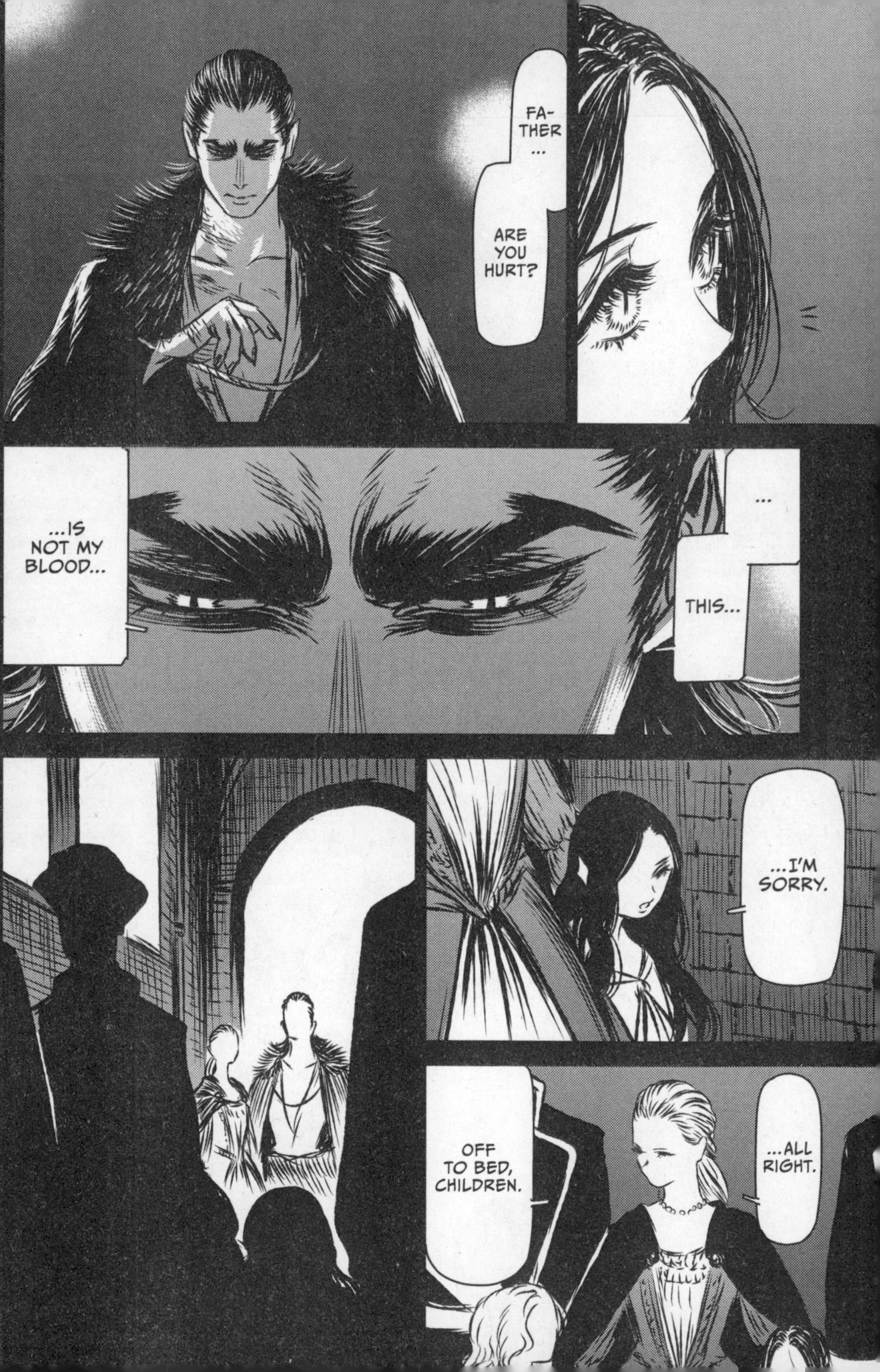
FA-THER...
ARE YOU HURT?
...
THIS...
...IS NOT MY BLOOD...
...I'M SORRY.
...ALL RIGHT.
OFF TO BED, CHILDREN.

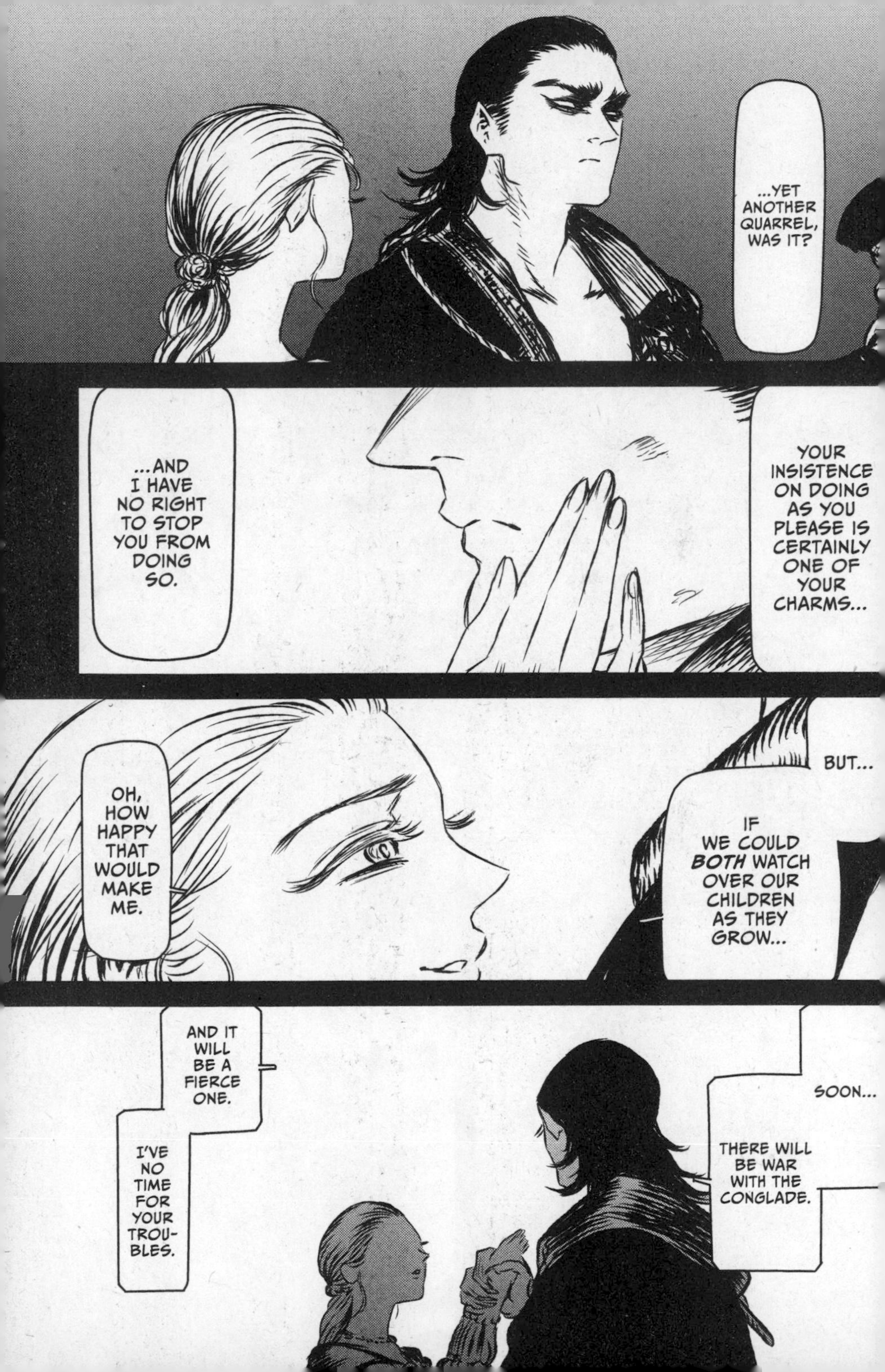
...YET ANOTHER QUARREL, WAS IT?
YOUR INSISTENCE ON DOING AS YOU PLEASE IS CERTAINLY ONE OF YOUR CHARMS...
...AND I HAVE NO RIGHT TO STOP YOU FROM DOING SO.
BUT...
IF WE COULD *BOTH* WATCH OVER OUR CHILDREN AS THEY GROW...
OH, HOW HAPPY THAT WOULD MAKE ME.
SOON...
THERE WILL BE WAR WITH THE CONGLADE.
AND IT WILL BE A FIERCE ONE.
I'VE NO TIME FOR YOUR TROUBLES.

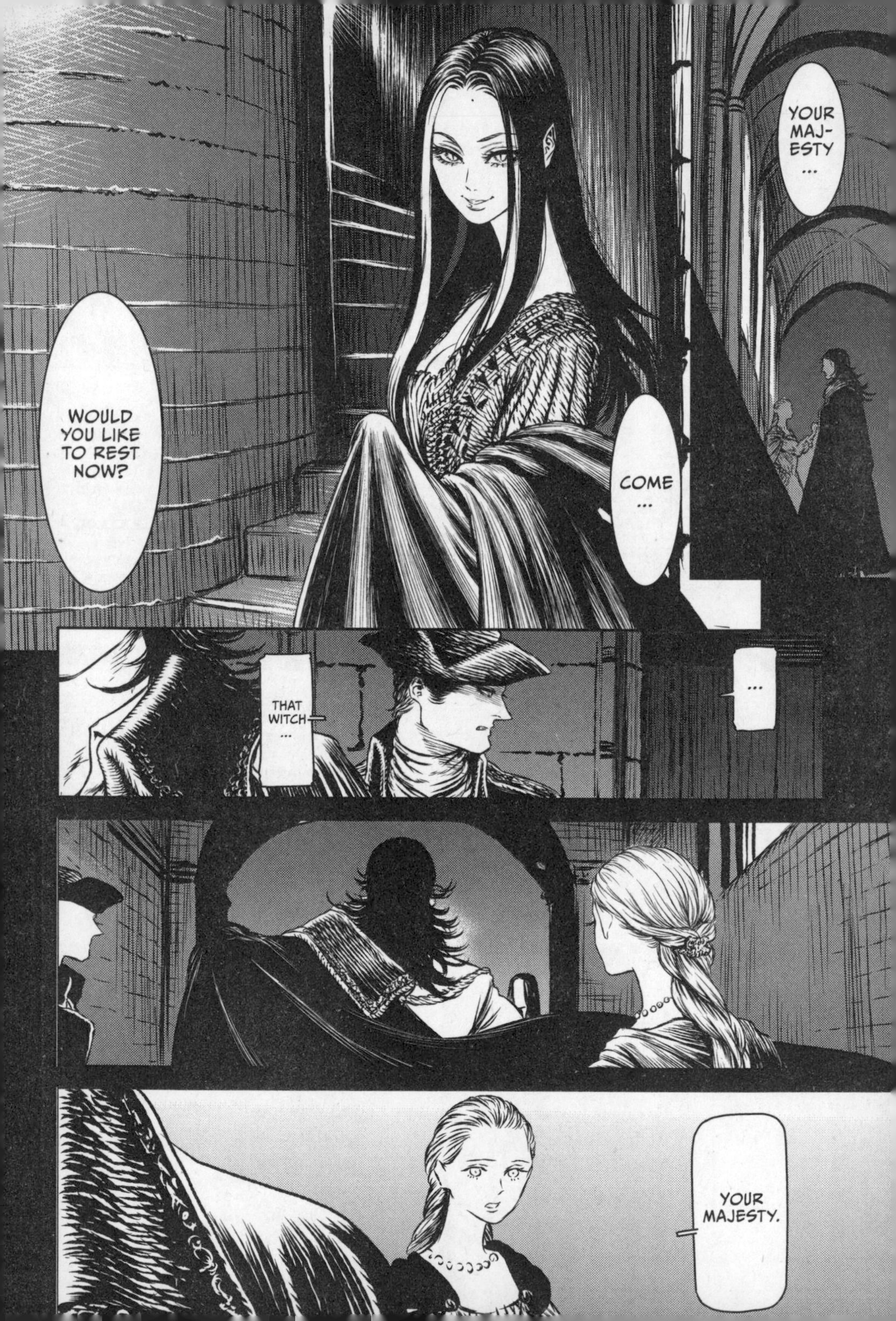
YOUR MAJ-ESTY ...
COME ...
WOULD YOU LIKE TO REST NOW?
...
THAT WITCH ...
YOUR MAJESTY.

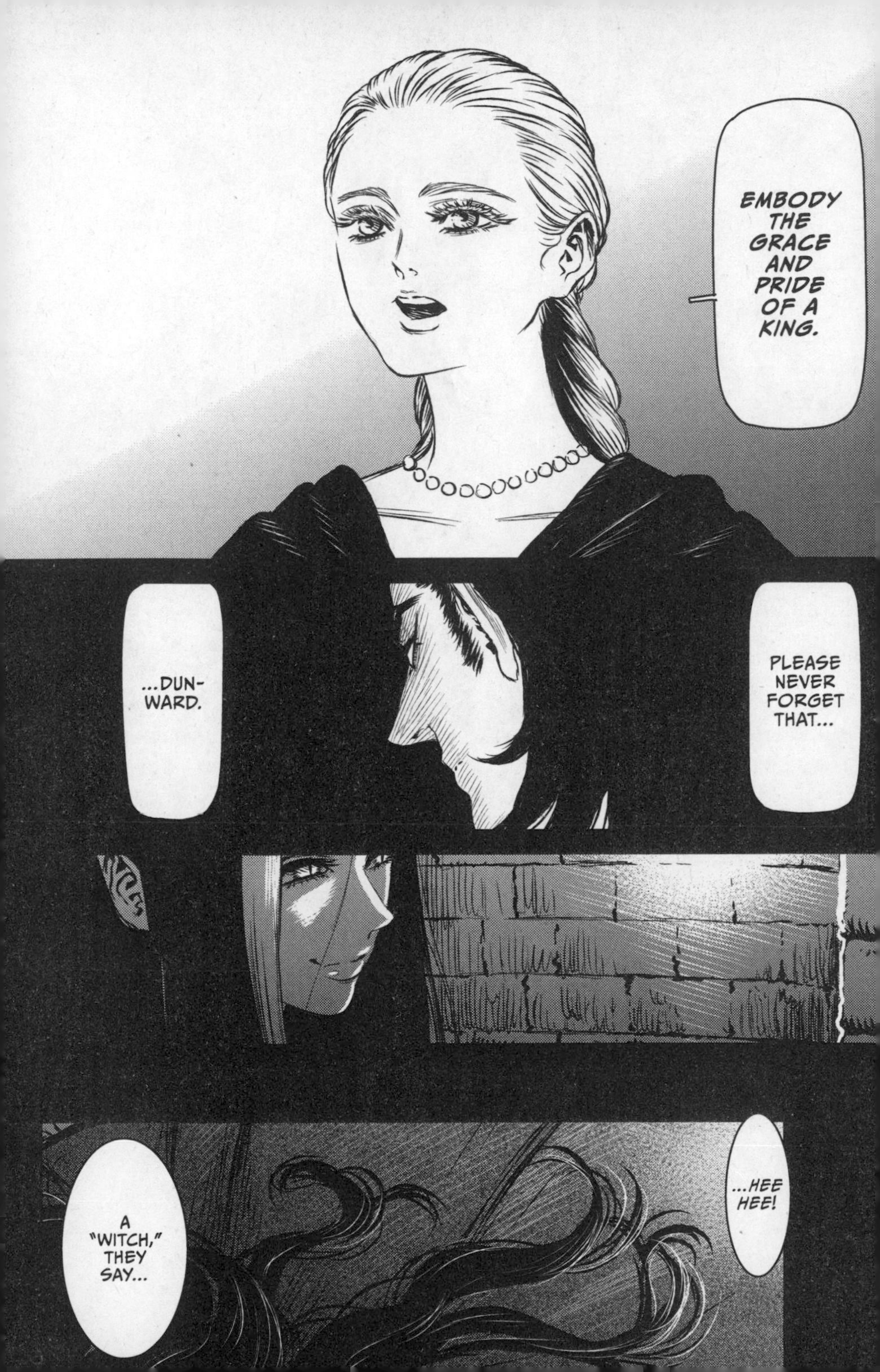
EMBODY THE GRACE AND PRIDE OF A KING.
PLEASE NEVER FORGET THAT...
...DUN-WARD.
...HEE HEE!
A "WITCH," THEY SAY...

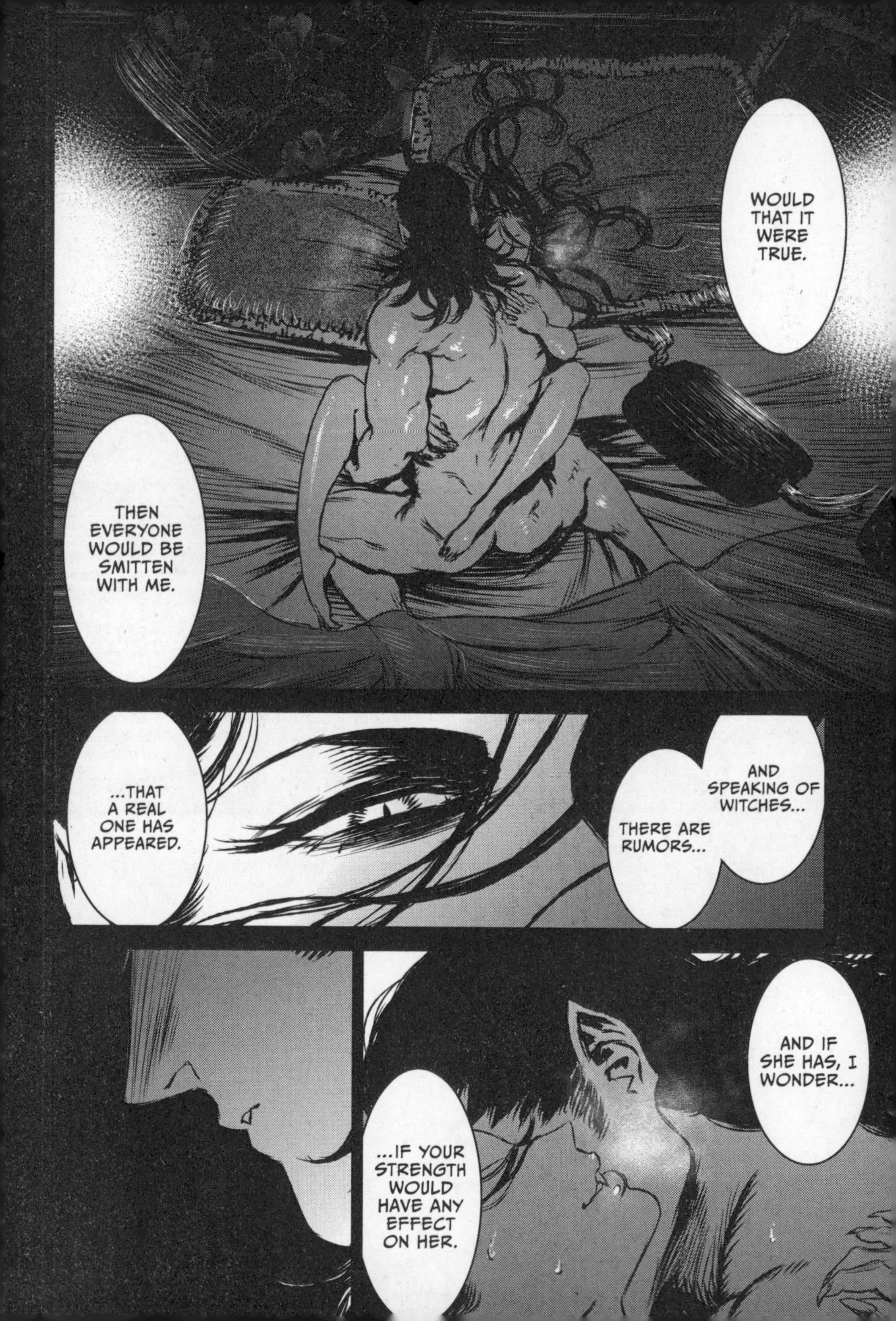
WOULD THAT IT WERE TRUE.
THEN EVERYONE WOULD BE SMITTEN WITH ME.
AND SPEAKING OF WITCHES...
THERE ARE RUMORS...
...THAT A REAL ONE HAS APPEARED.
AND IF SHE HAS, I WONDER...
...IF YOUR STRENGTH WOULD HAVE ANY EFFECT ON HER.

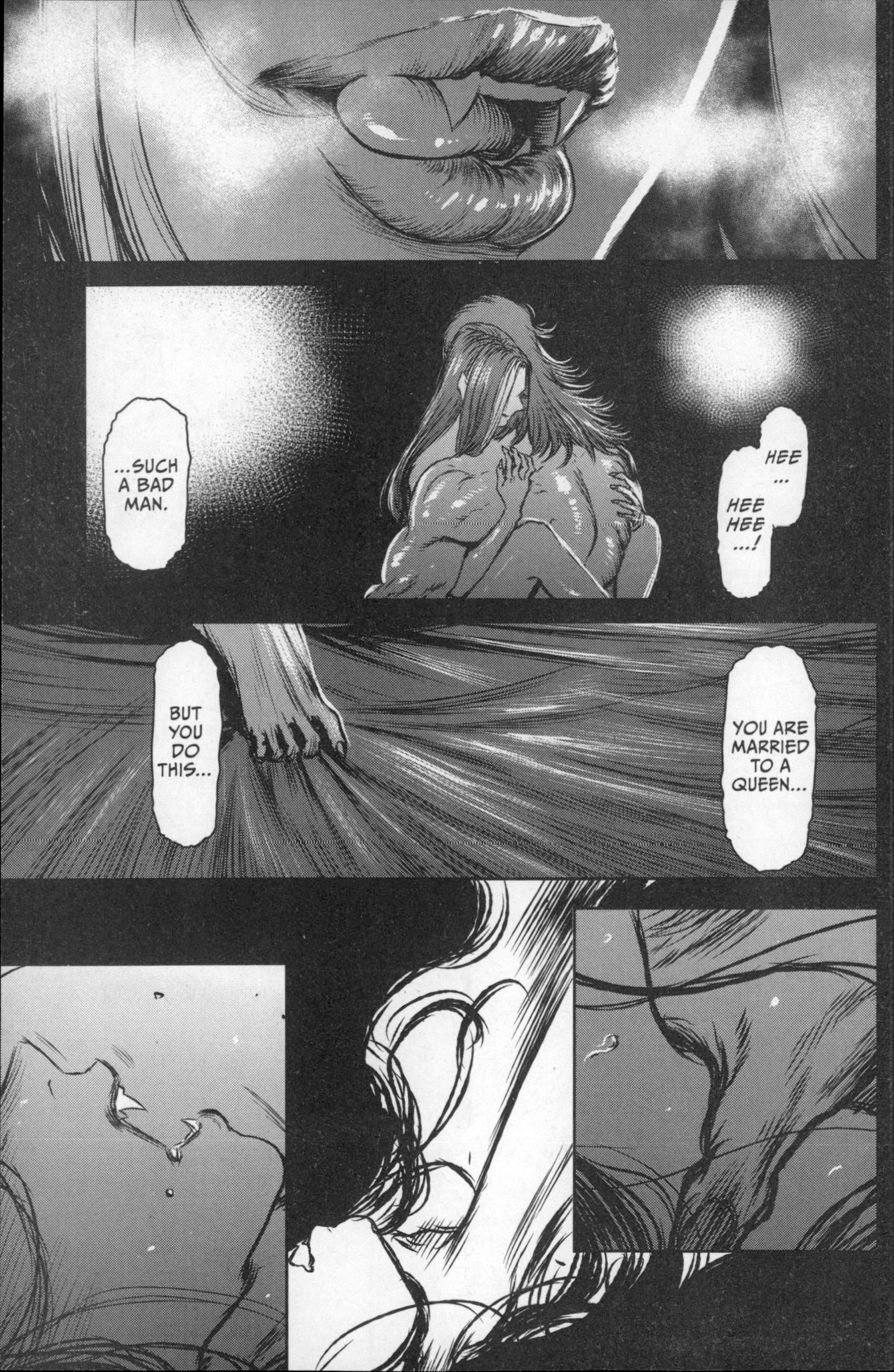
HEE ... HEE HEE ...!
...SUCH A BAD MAN.
YOU ARE MARRIED TO A QUEEN...
BUT YOU DO THIS...

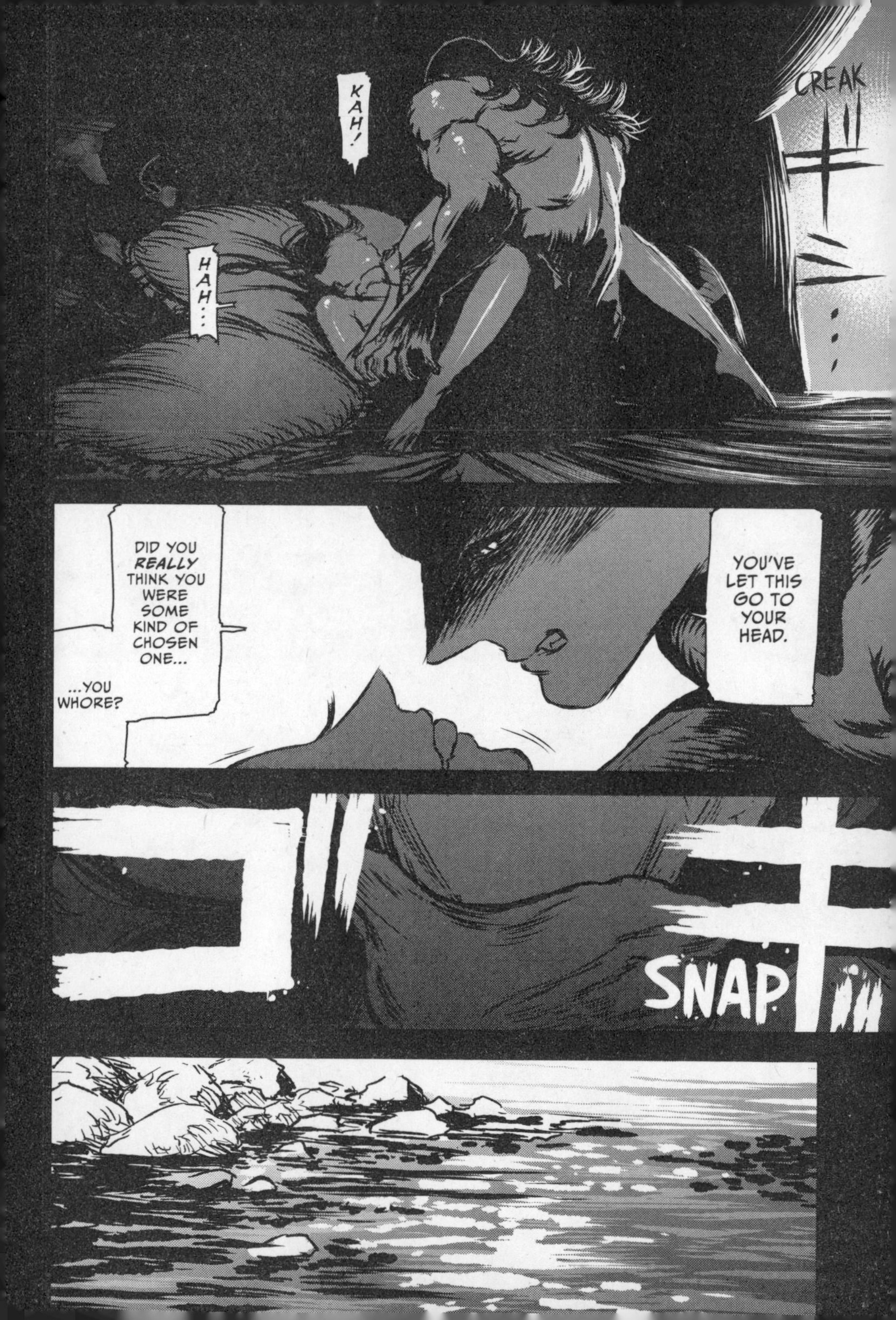
CREAK
KAH!
HAH...
YOU'VE LET THIS GO TO YOUR HEAD.
DID YOU *REALLY* THINK YOU WERE SOME KIND OF CHOSEN ONE...
...YOU WHORE?
SNAP

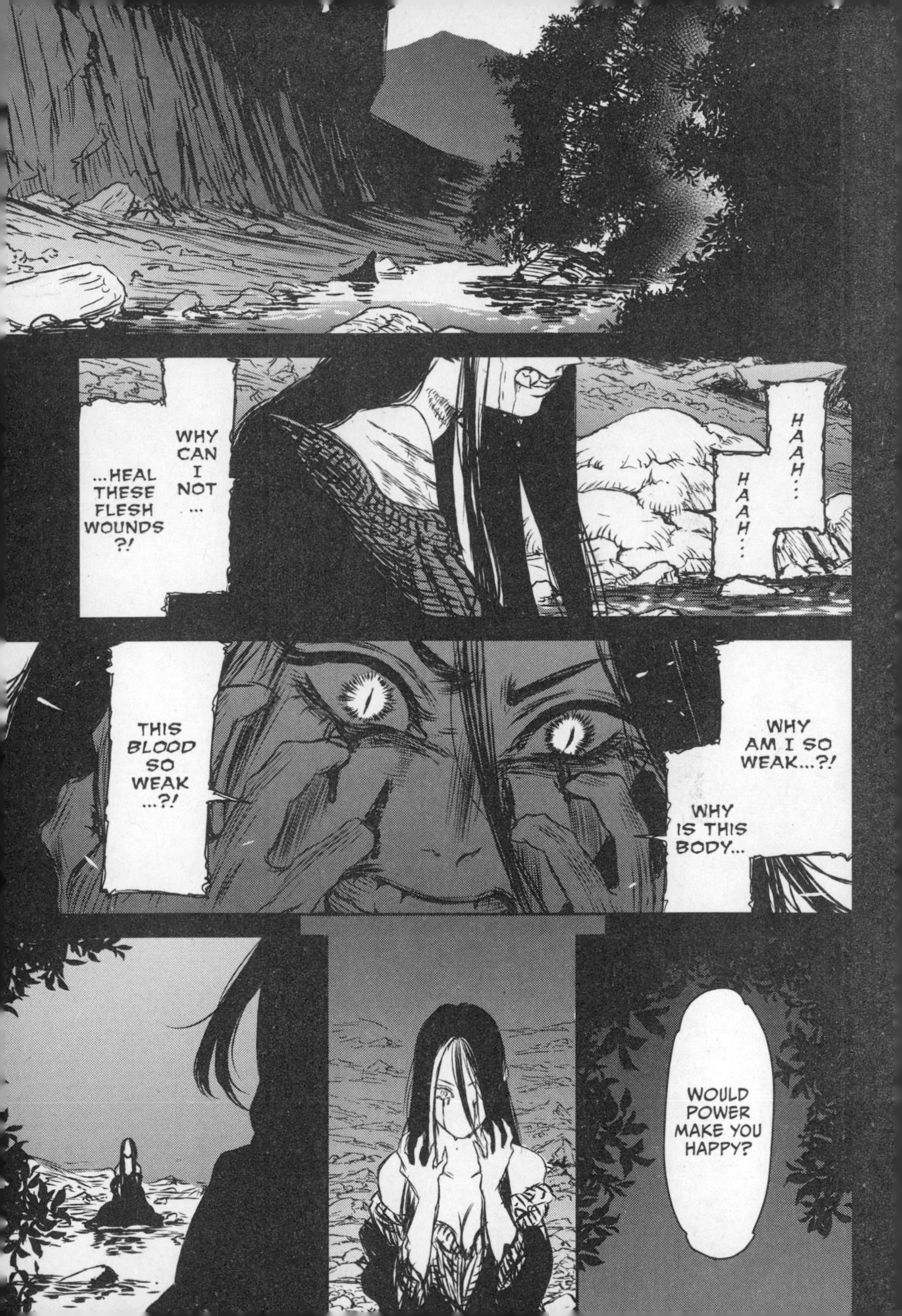
HAAH...
HAAH...
WHY CAN I NOT ...
...HEAL THESE FLESH WOUNDS ?!
WHY AM I SO WEAK...?!
WHY IS THIS BODY...
THIS BLOOD SO WEAK ...?!
WOULD POWER MAKE YOU HAPPY?

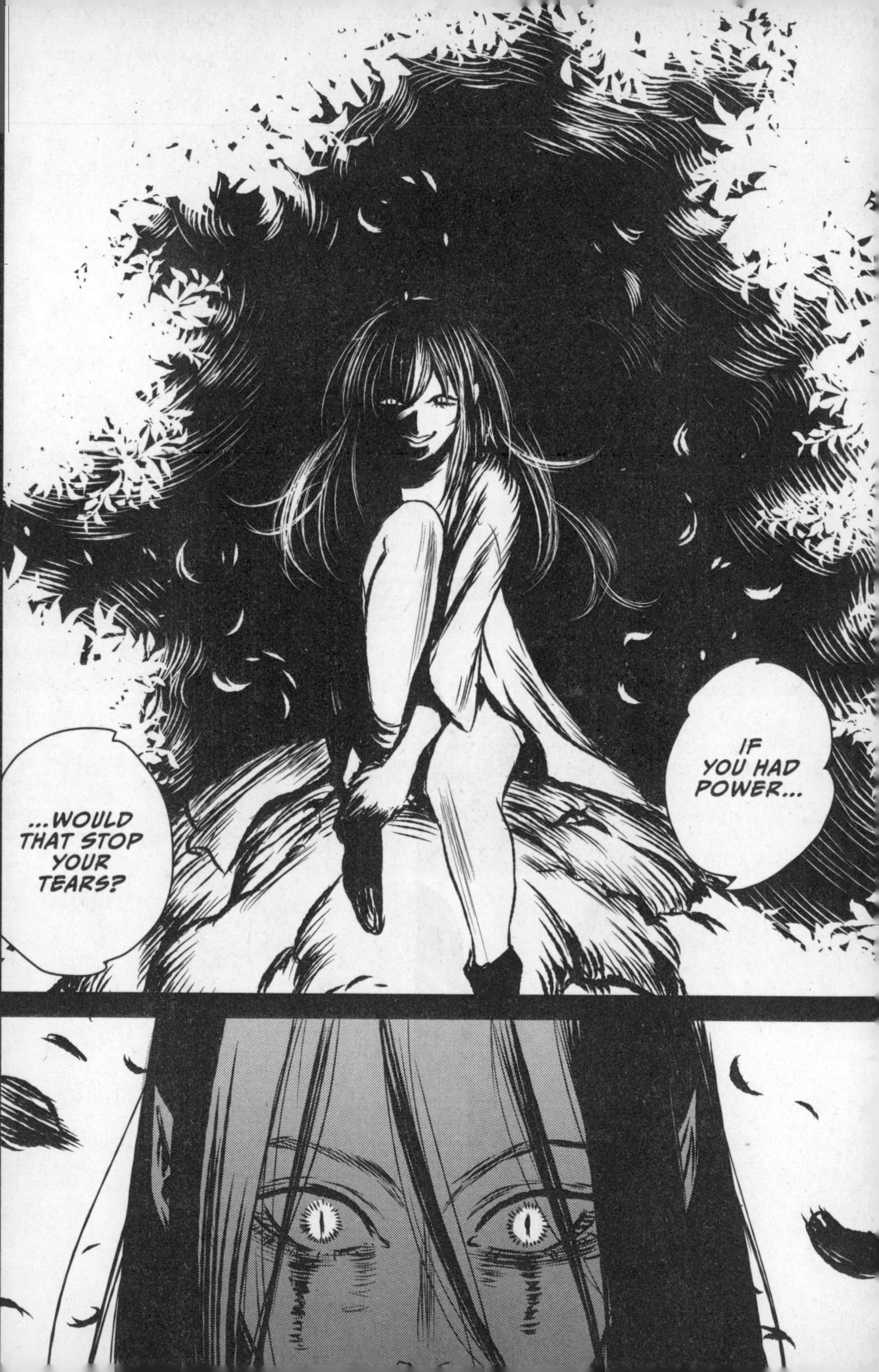
IF YOU HAD POWER...
...WOULD THAT STOP YOUR TEARS?

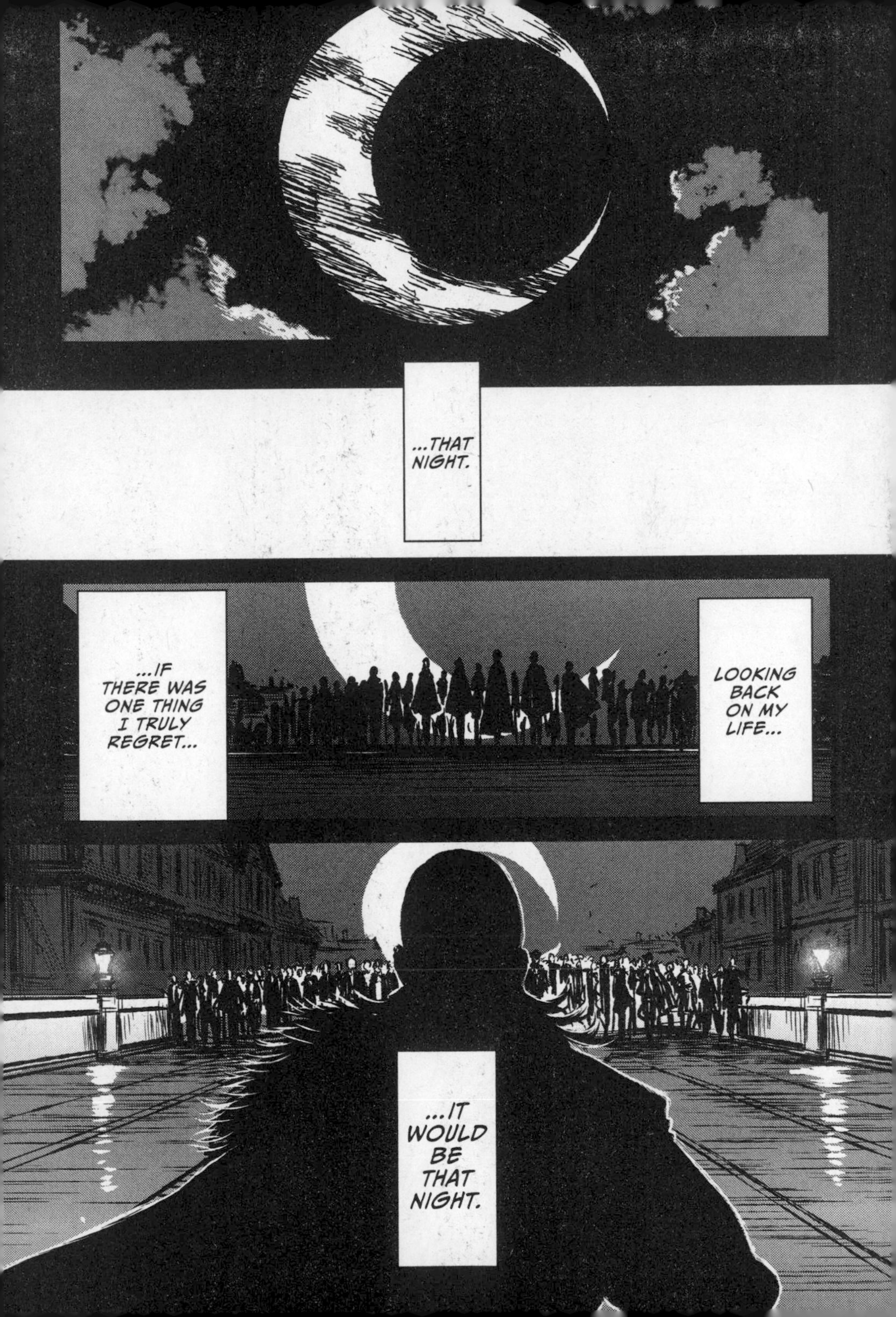
...THAT NIGHT.
LOOKING BACK ON MY LIFE...
...IF THERE WAS ONE THING I TRULY REGRET...
...IT WOULD BE THAT NIGHT.

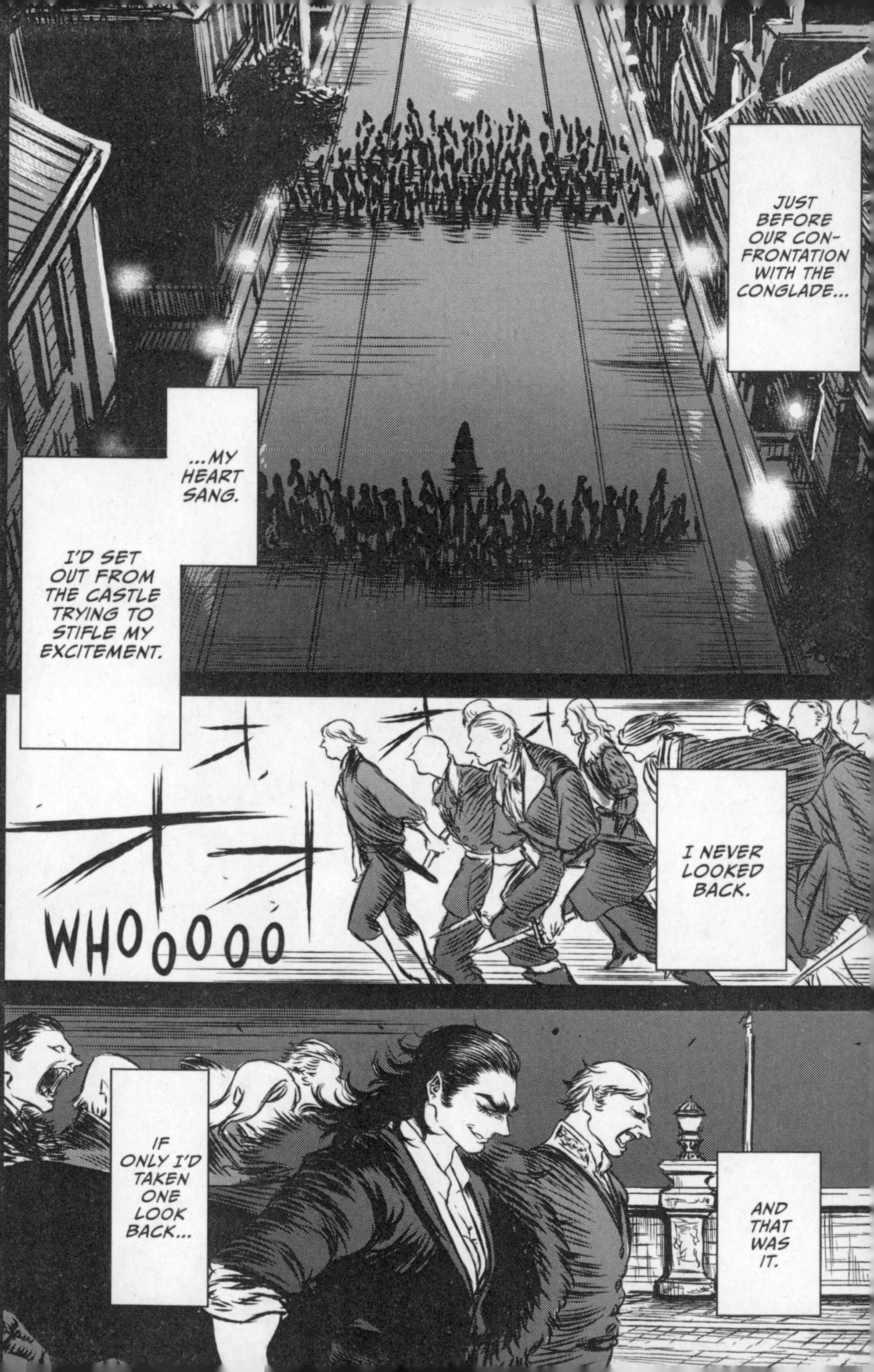
JUST BEFORE OUR CON-FRONTATION WITH THE CONGLADE...
...MY HEART SANG.
I'D SET OUT FROM THE CASTLE TRYING TO STIFLE MY EXCITEMENT.
I NEVER LOOKED BACK.
WHOOOOOO
AND THAT WAS IT.
IF ONLY I'D TAKEN ONE LOOK BACK...

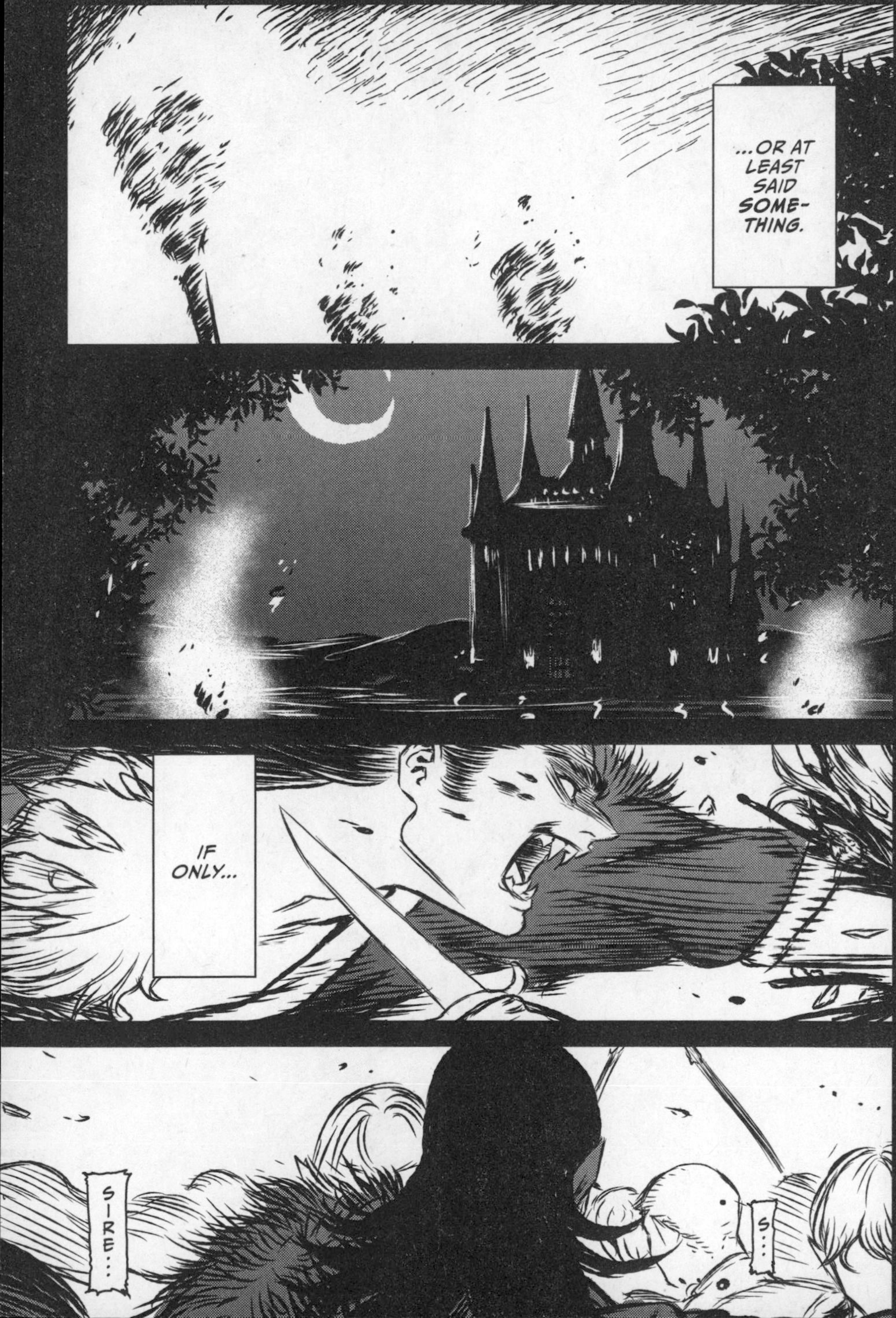
...OR AT LEAST SAID SOME-THING.
IF ONLY...
S...
SIRE...

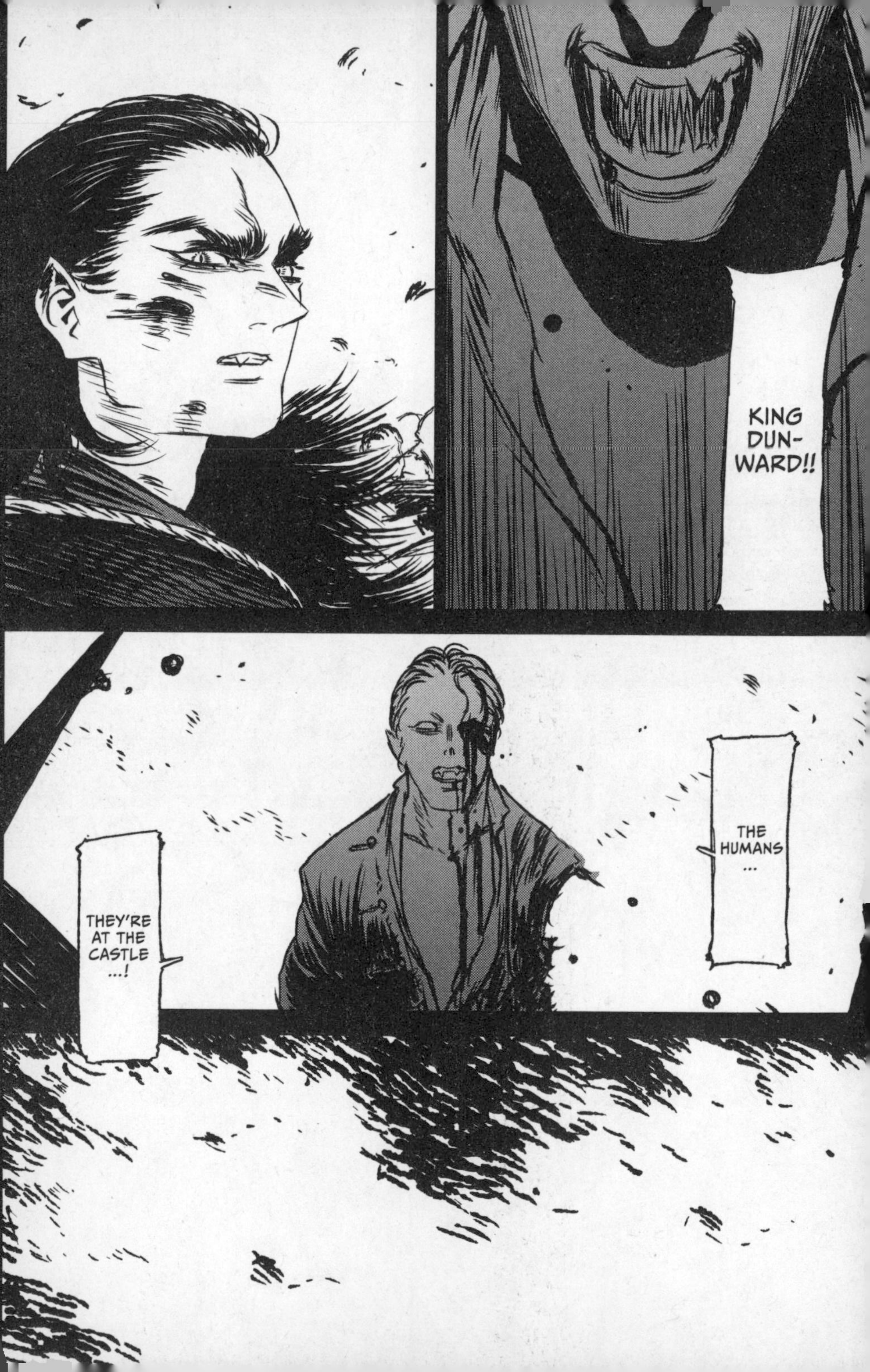
KING DUN-WARD!!
THE HUMANS ...
THEY'RE AT THE CASTLE ...!

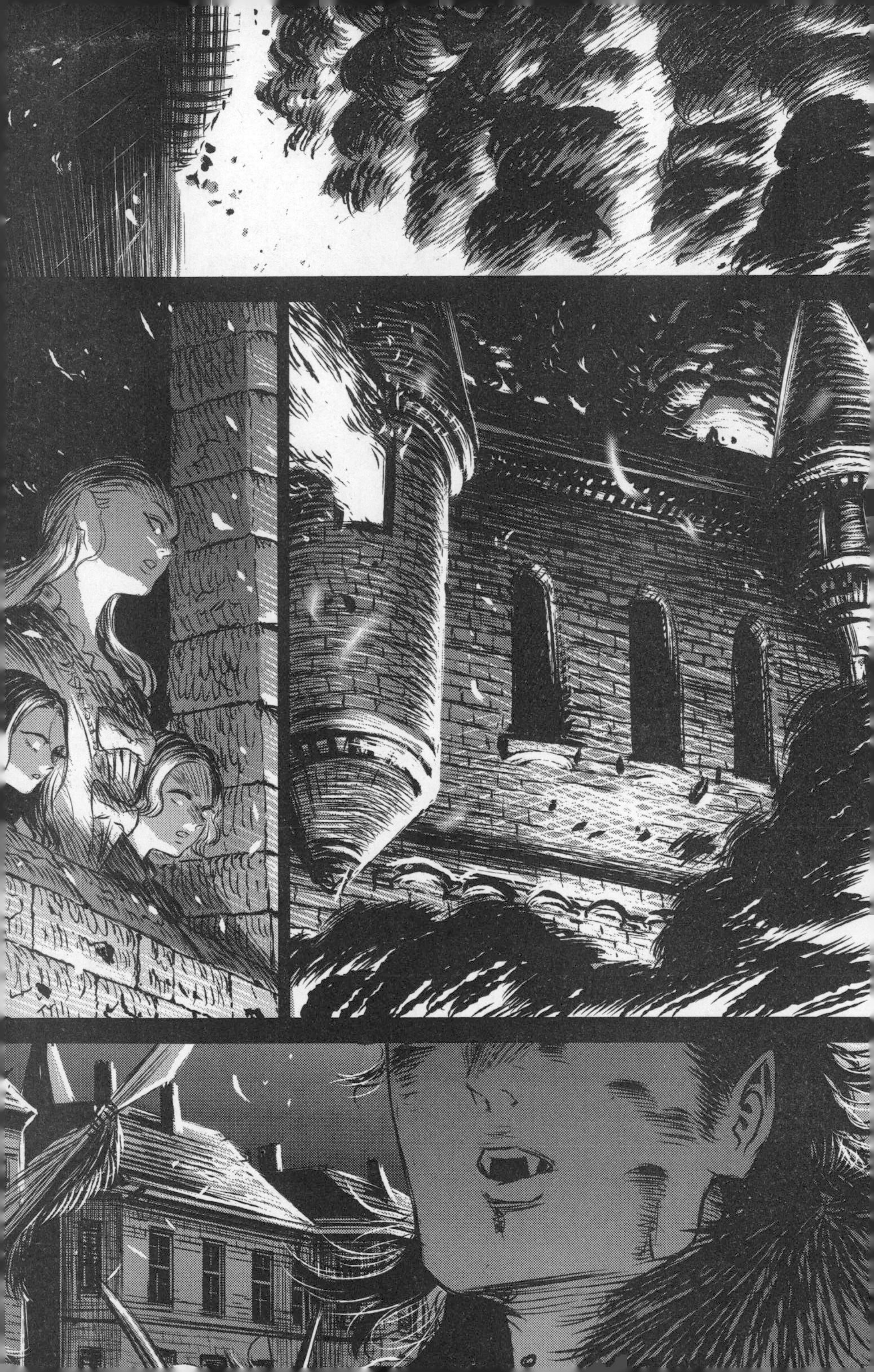

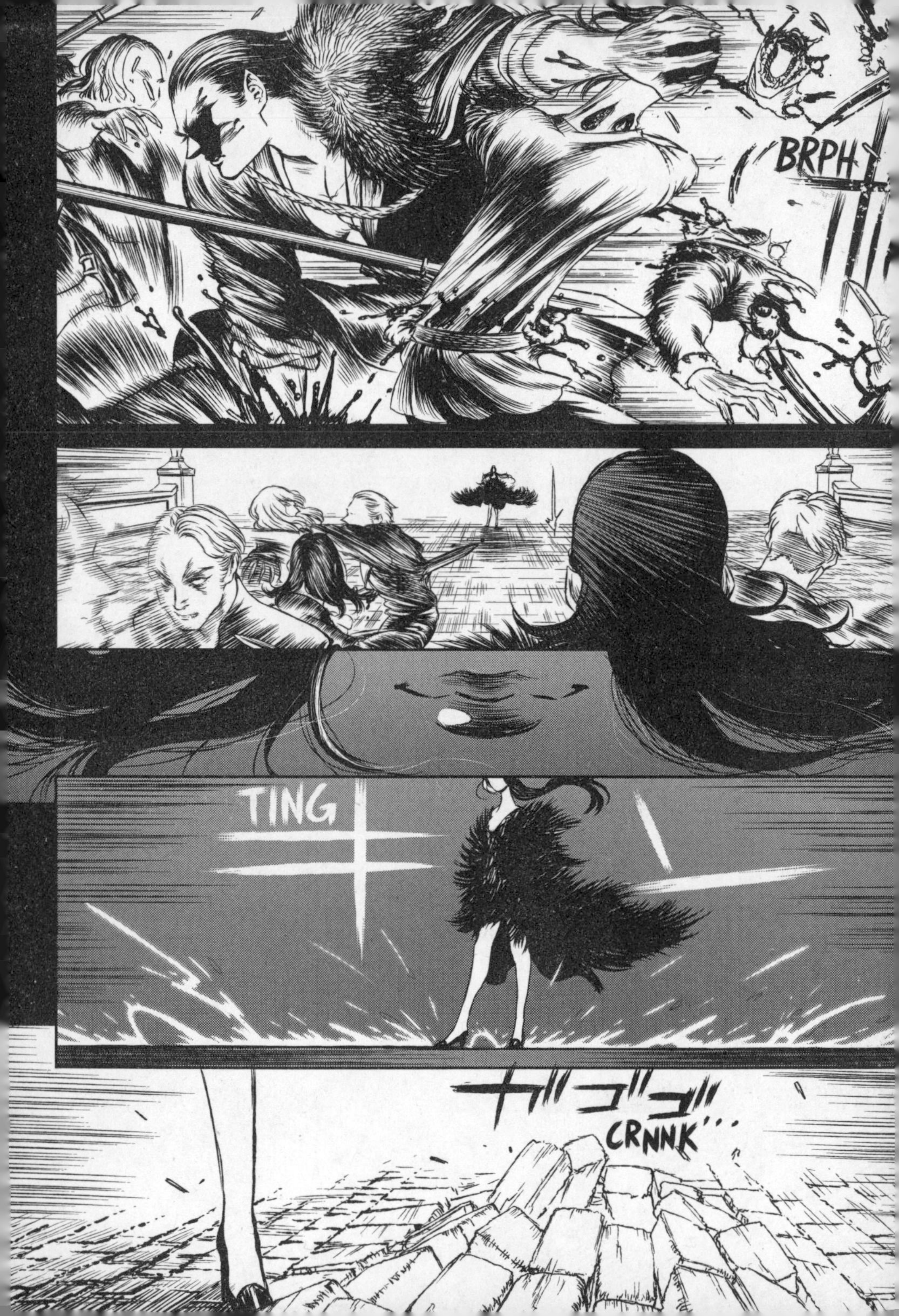
BRPH
TING
ガゴゴ
CRNNK...

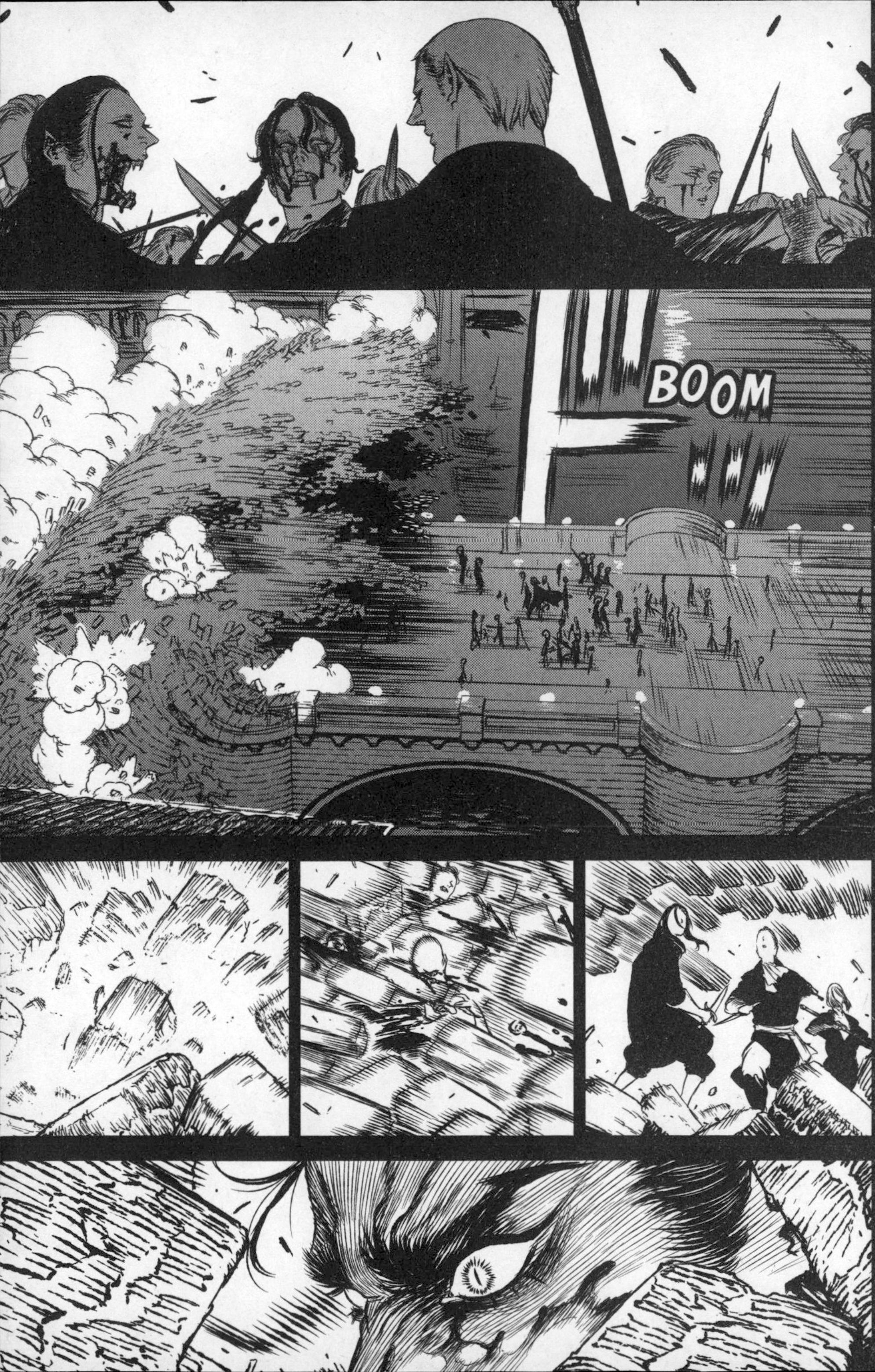
BOOM

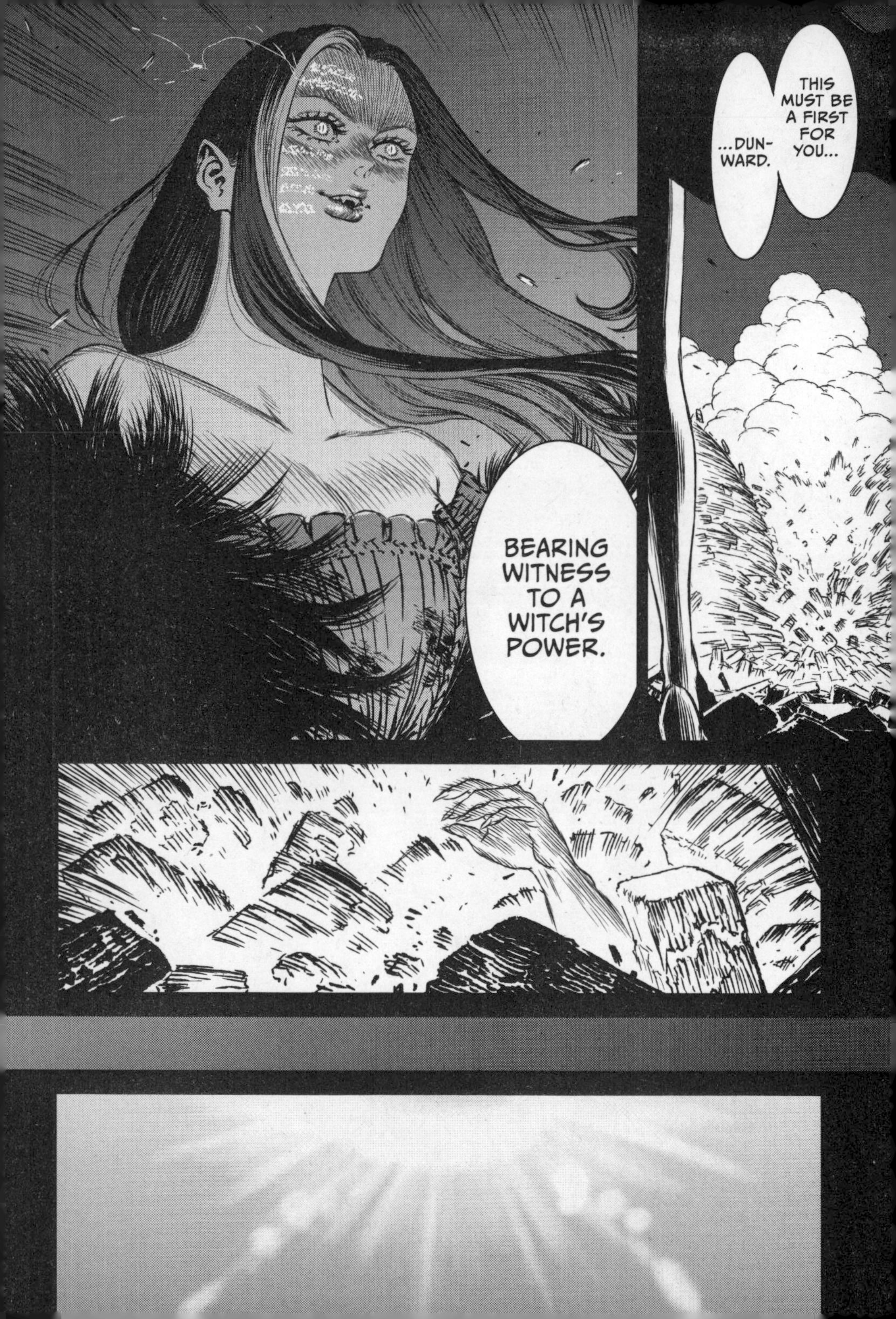
THIS MUST BE A FIRST FOR YOU...
...DUNWARD.
BEARING WITNESS TO A WITCH'S POWER.

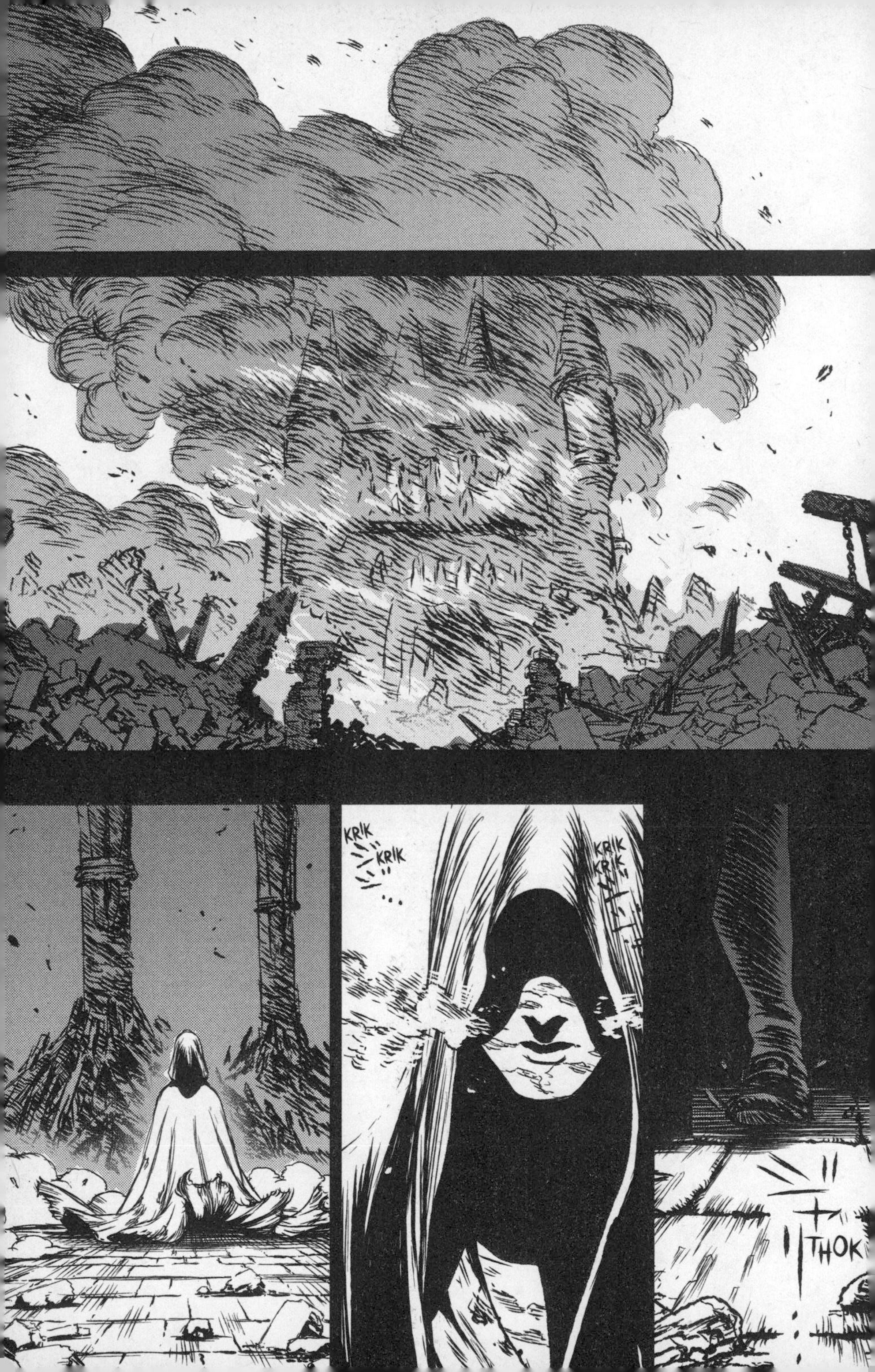
THOK
KRIK
KRIK
KRIK
KRIK

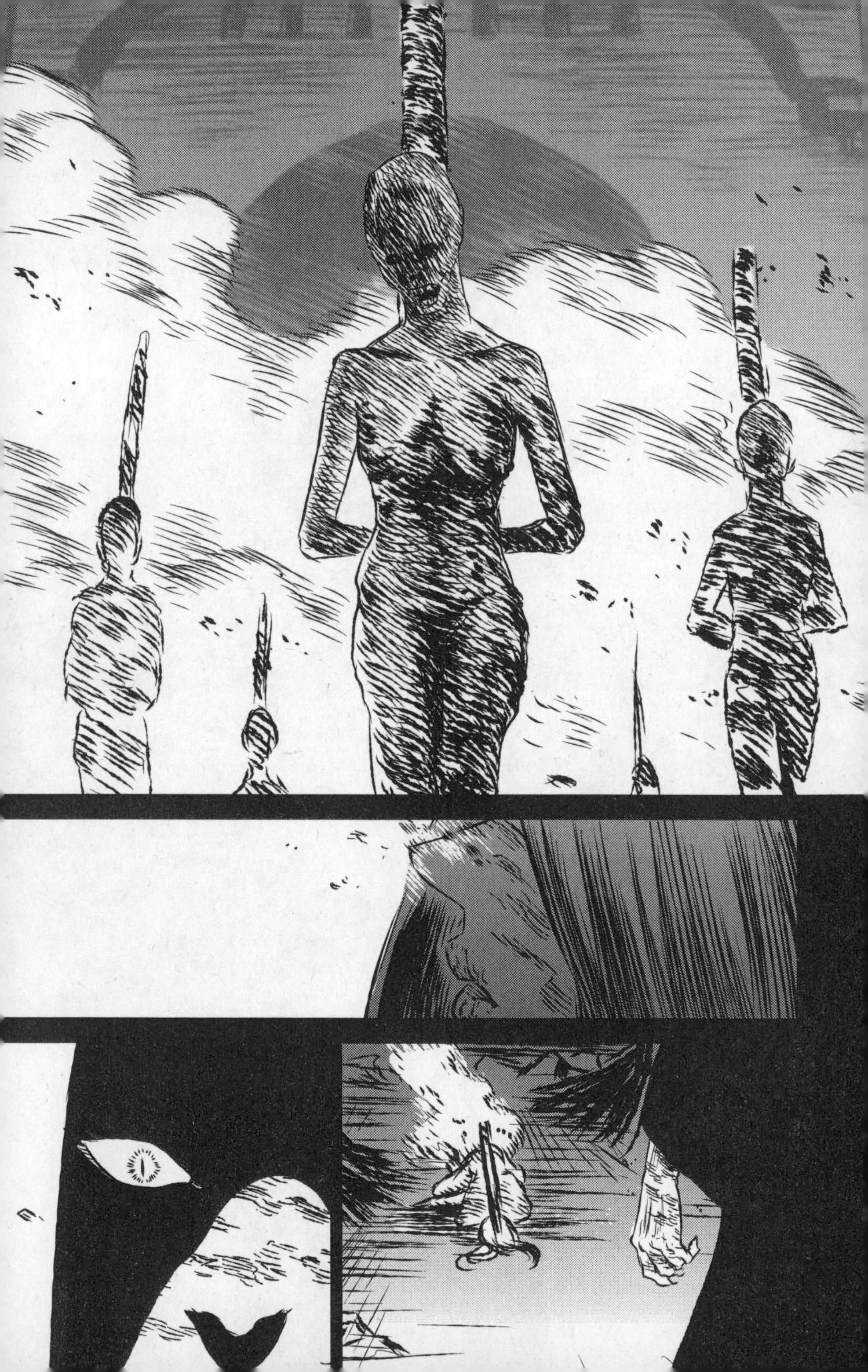

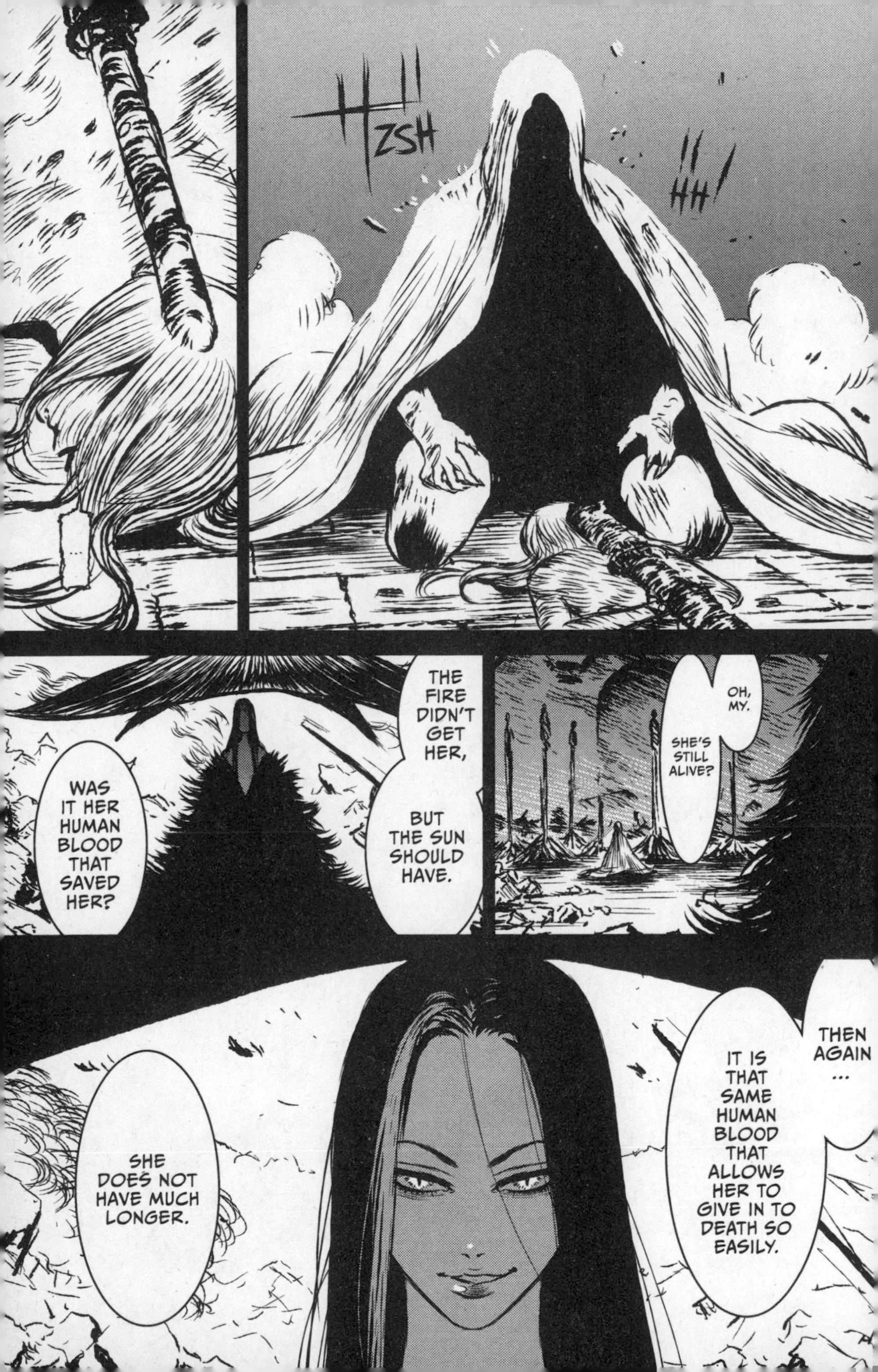
ZSH
!! HH!
...
OH, MY.
SHE'S STILL ALIVE?
THE FIRE DIDN'T GET HER,
BUT THE SUN SHOULD HAVE.
WAS IT HER HUMAN BLOOD THAT SAVED HER?
THEN AGAIN ...
IT IS THAT SAME HUMAN BLOOD THAT ALLOWS HER TO GIVE IN TO DEATH SO EASILY.
SHE DOES NOT HAVE MUCH LONGER.

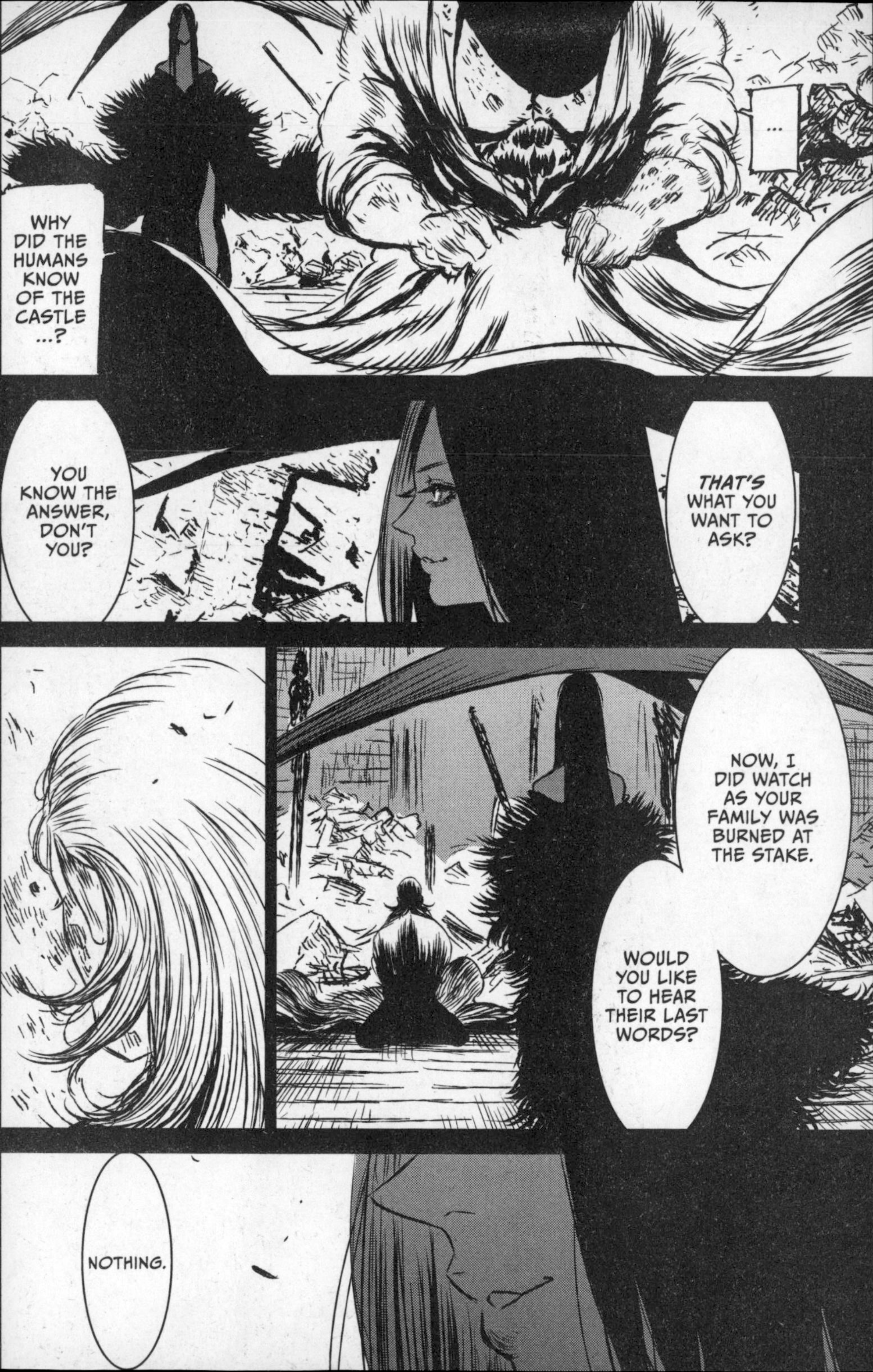
...
WHY DID THE HUMANS KNOW OF THE CASTLE ...?
THAT'S WHAT YOU WANT TO ASK?
YOU KNOW THE ANSWER, DON'T YOU?
NOW, I DID WATCH AS YOUR FAMILY WAS BURNED AT THE STAKE.
WOULD YOU LIKE TO HEAR THEIR LAST WORDS?
NOTHING.

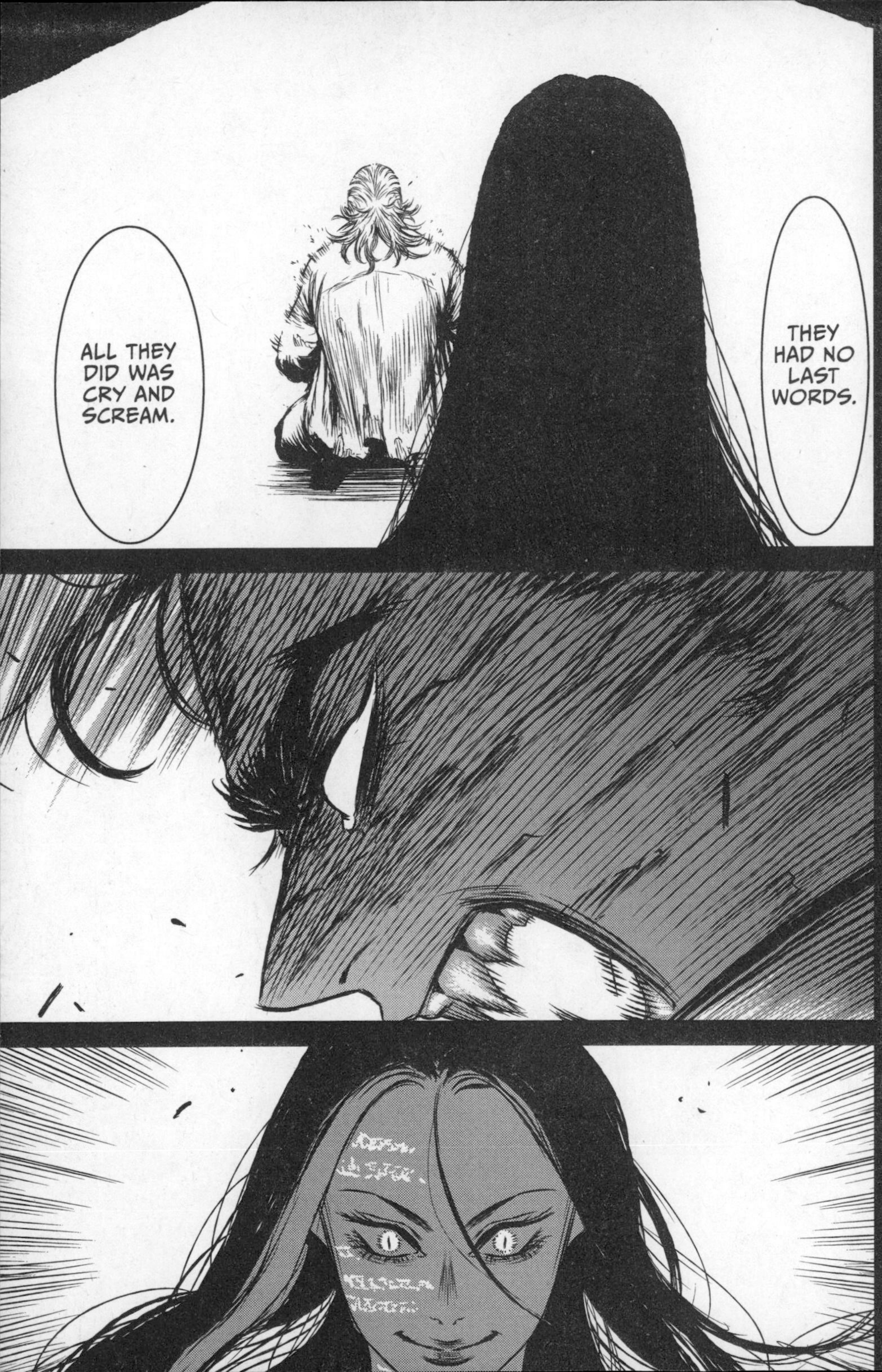
THEY HAD NO LAST WORDS.
ALL THEY DID WAS CRY AND SCREAM.

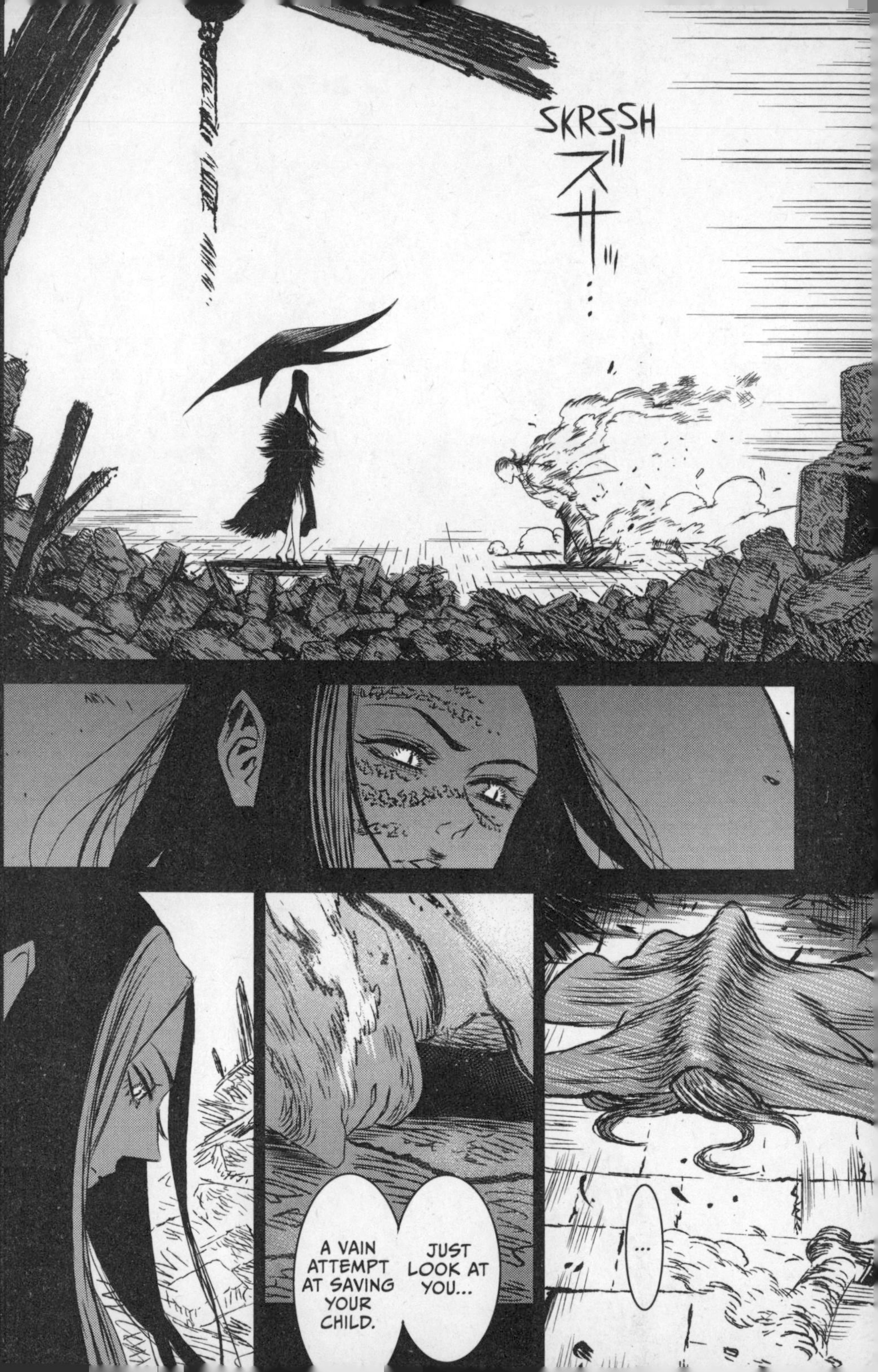
SKRSSH
ズザッ…
…
JUST LOOK AT YOU…
A VAIN ATTEMPT AT SAVING YOUR CHILD.

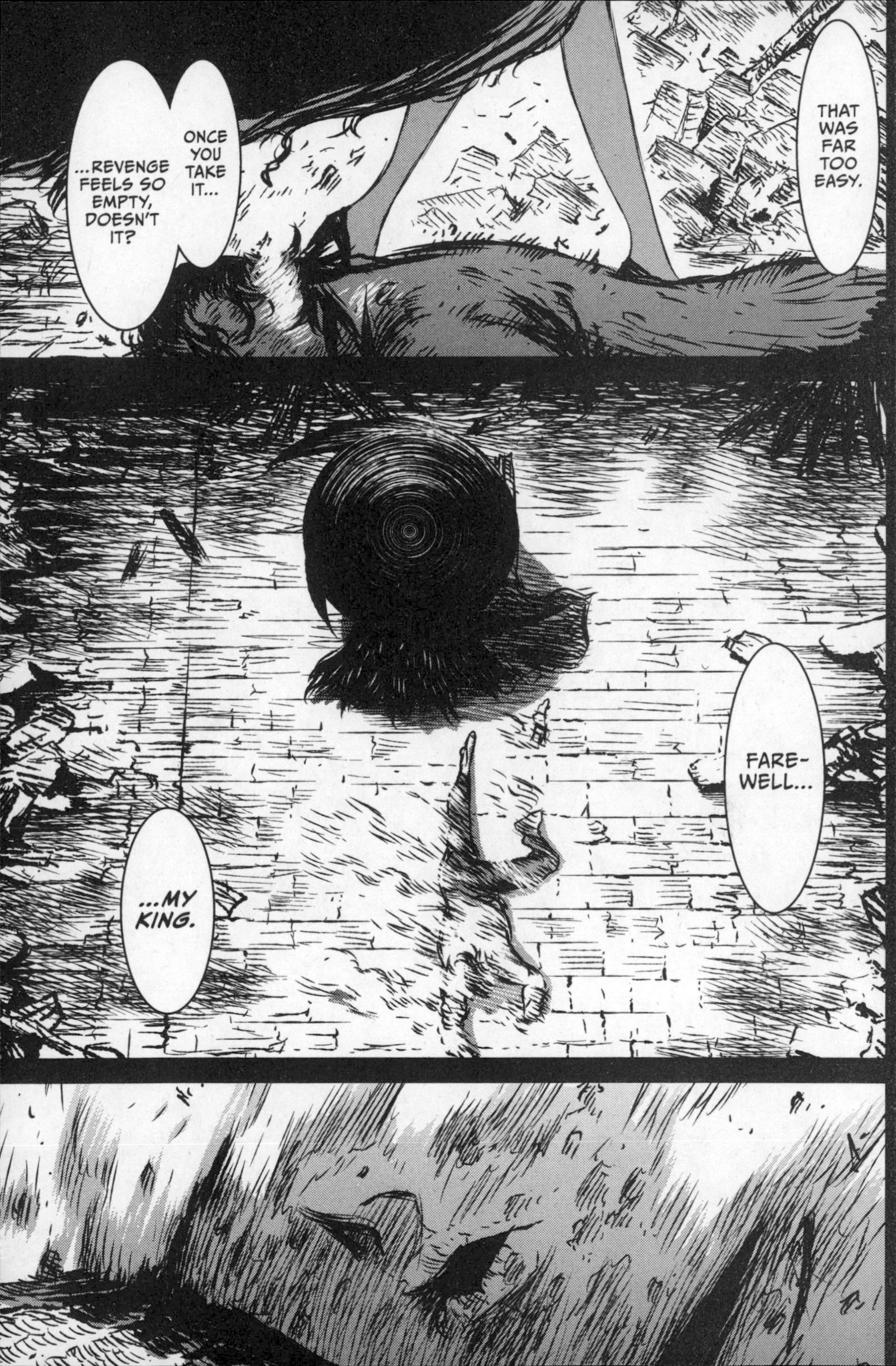
THAT WAS FAR TOO EASY.
ONCE YOU TAKE IT...
...REVENGE FEELS SO EMPTY, DOESN'T IT?
FARE-WELL...
...MY KING.

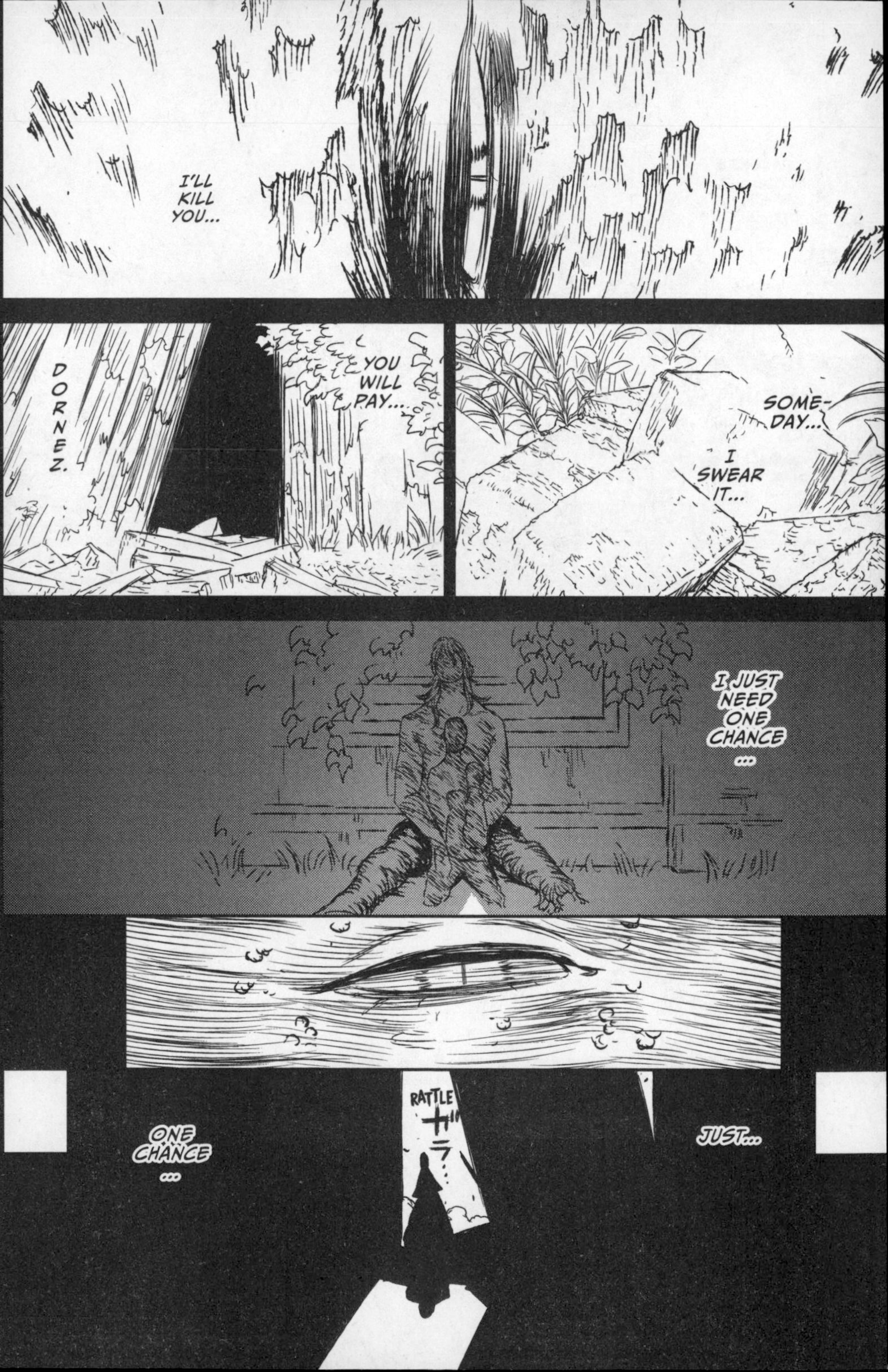
I'LL KILL YOU...
SOME-DAY...
I SWEAR IT...
YOU WILL PAY...
DORNEZ.
I JUST NEED ONE CHANCE ...
JUST...
RATTLE
ONE CHANCE ...

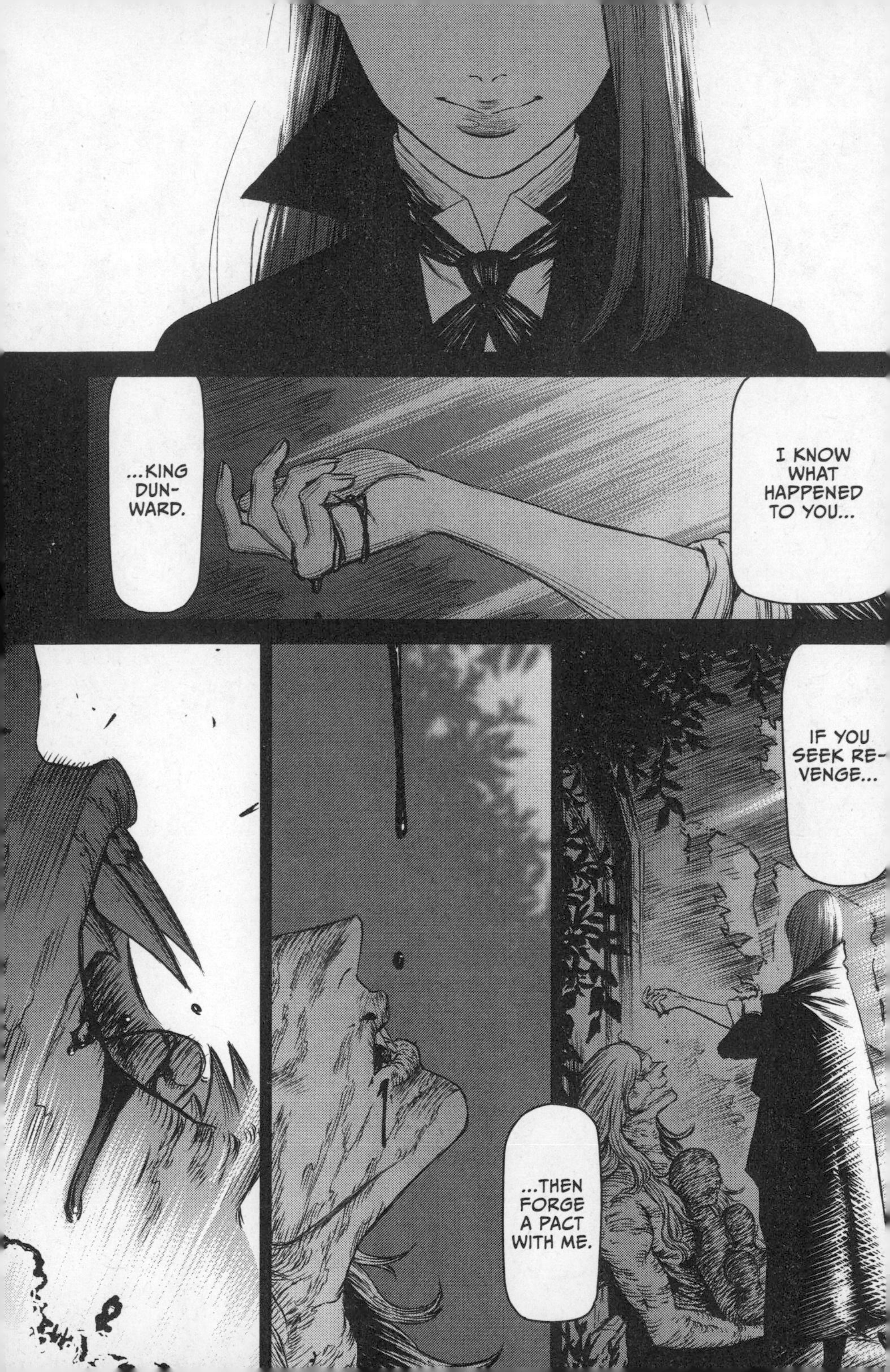
I KNOW WHAT HAPPENED TO YOU...
...KING DUN-WARD.
IF YOU SEEK RE-VENGE...
...THEN FORGE A PACT WITH ME.

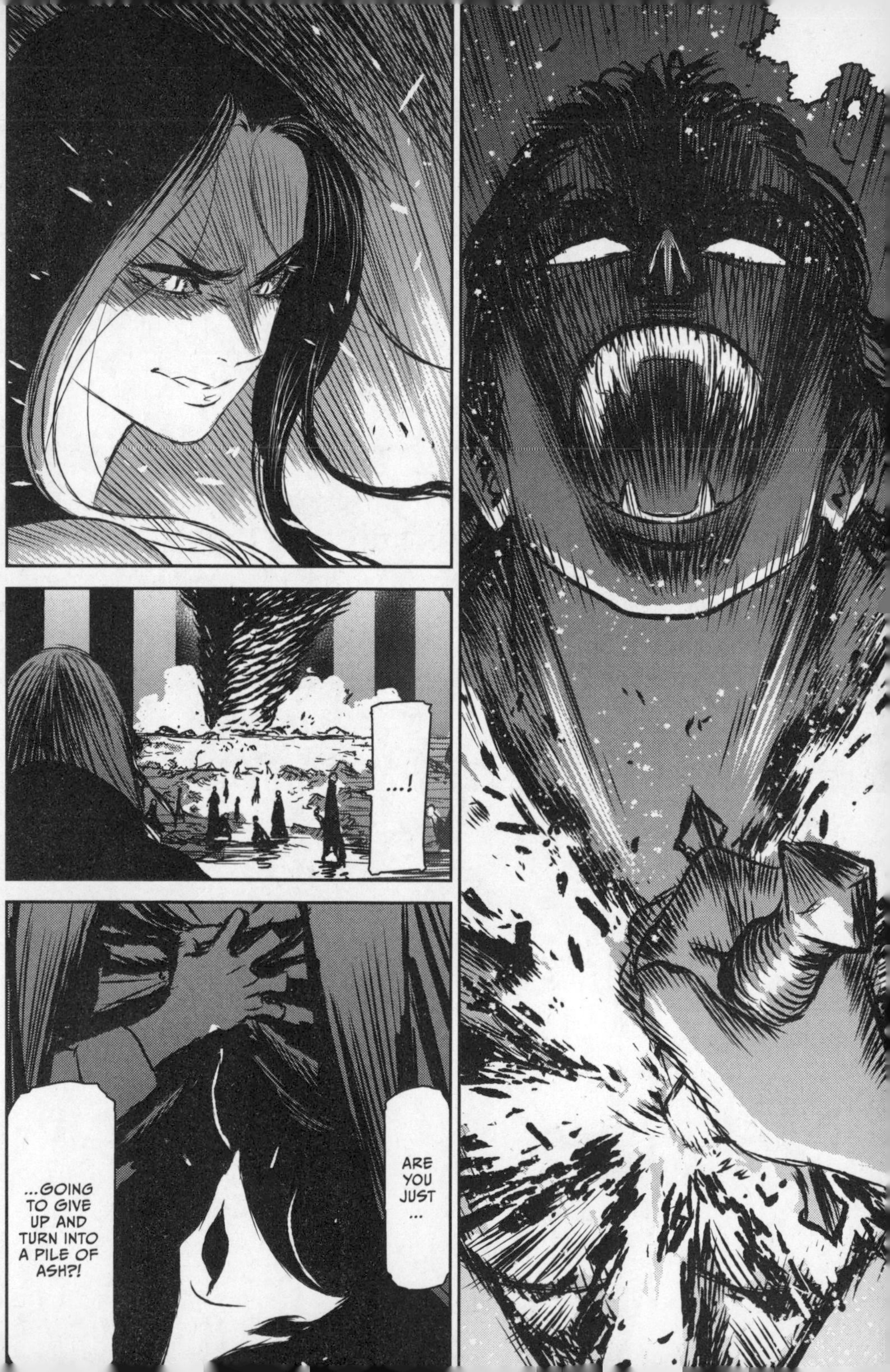
...!
ARE YOU JUST ...
...GOING TO GIVE UP AND TURN INTO A PILE OF ASH?!

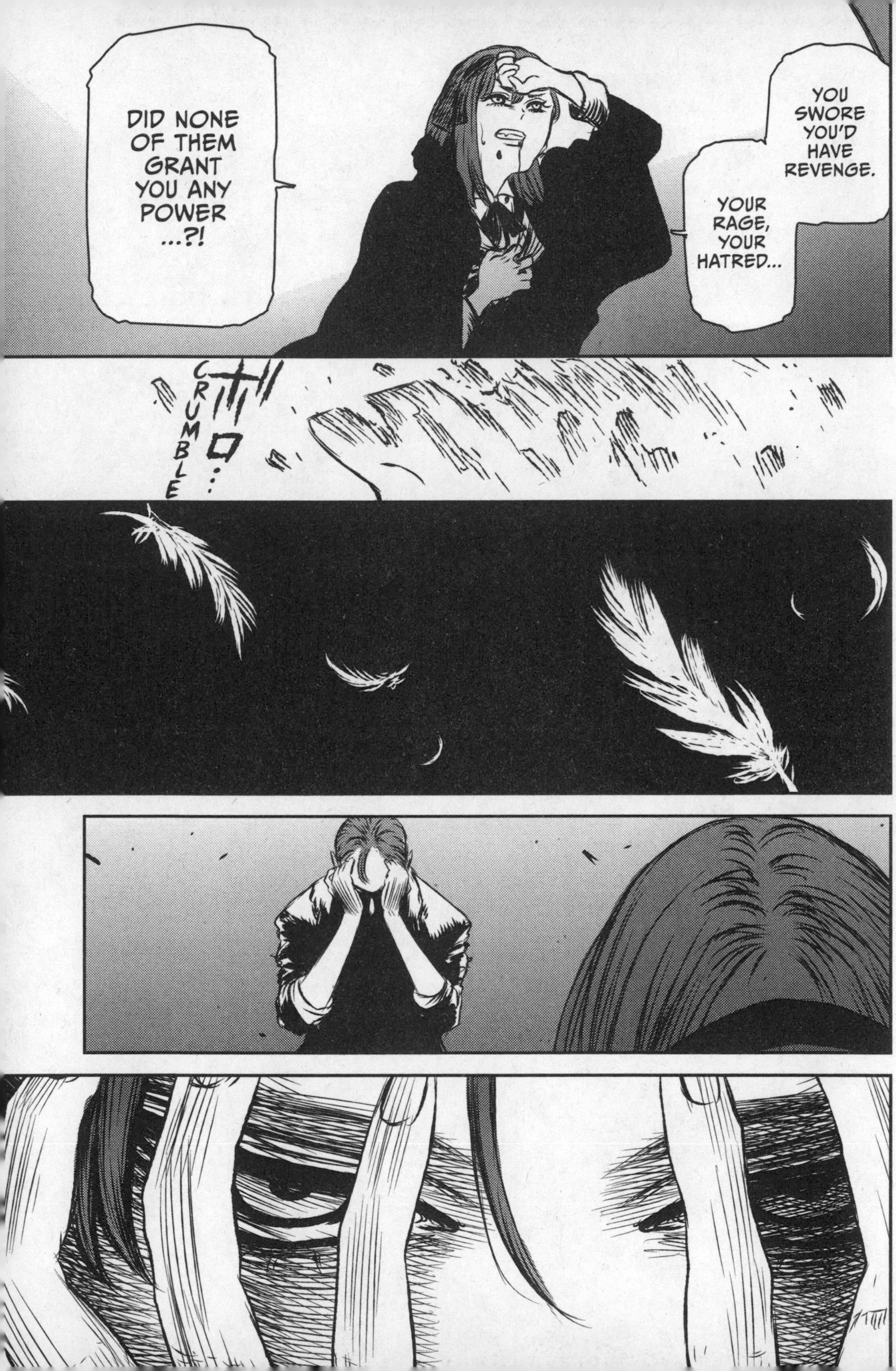
YOU SWORE YOU'D HAVE REVENGE.
YOUR RAGE, YOUR HATRED...
DID NONE OF THEM GRANT YOU ANY POWER ...?!
CRUMBLE

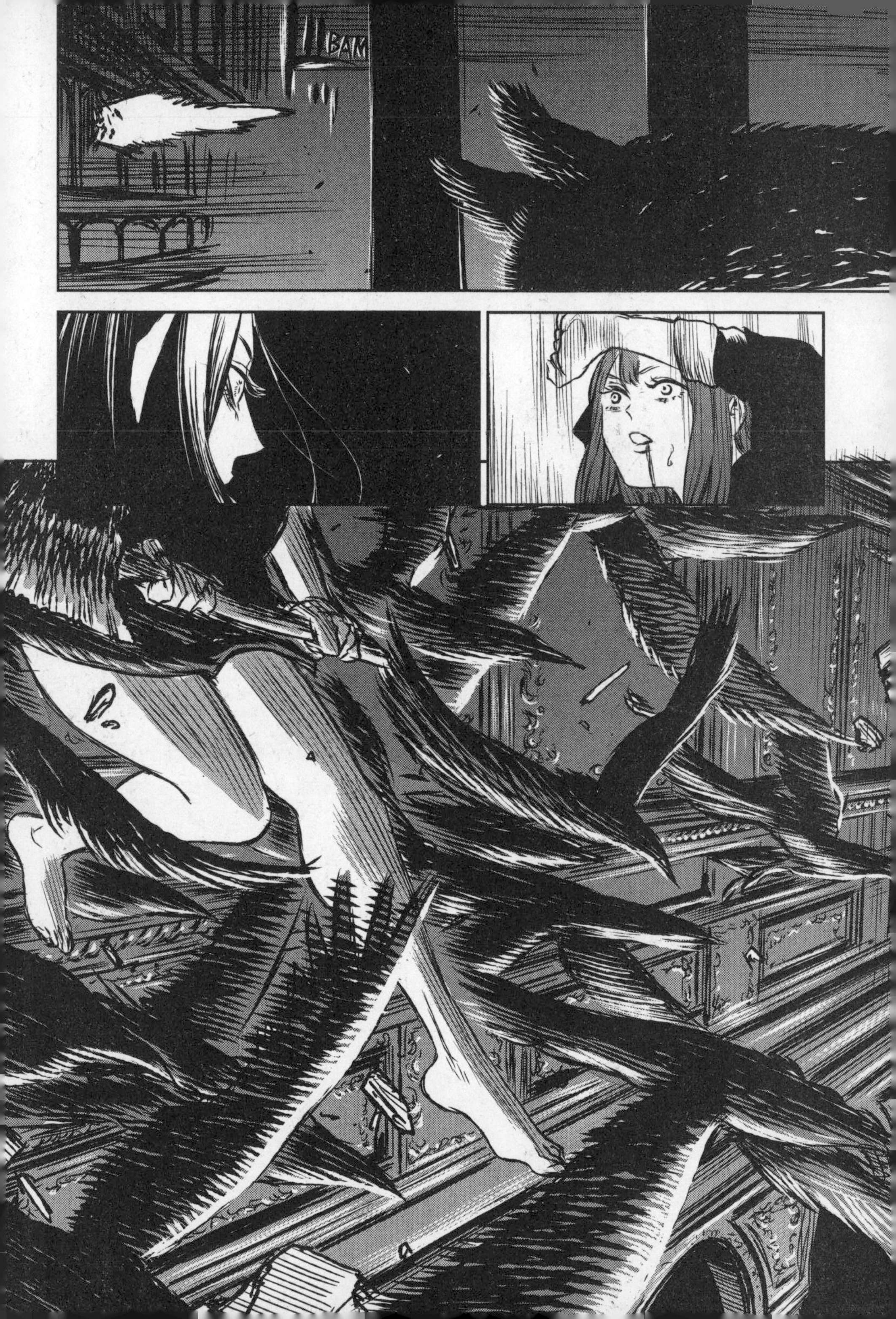
BAM

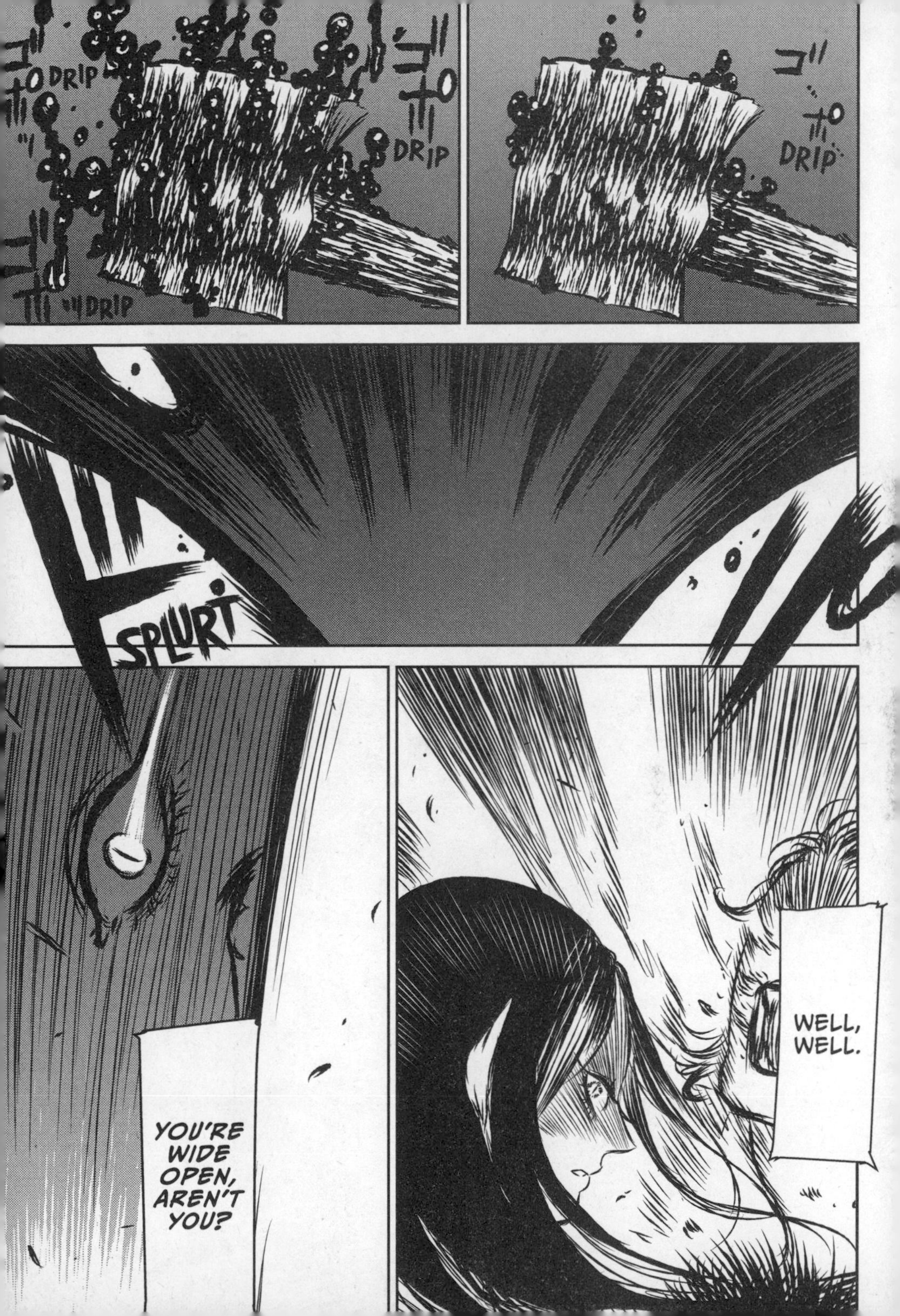
DRIP
DRIP
DRIP
DRIP
SPLURT
WELL, WELL.
YOU'RE WIDE OPEN, AREN'T YOU?

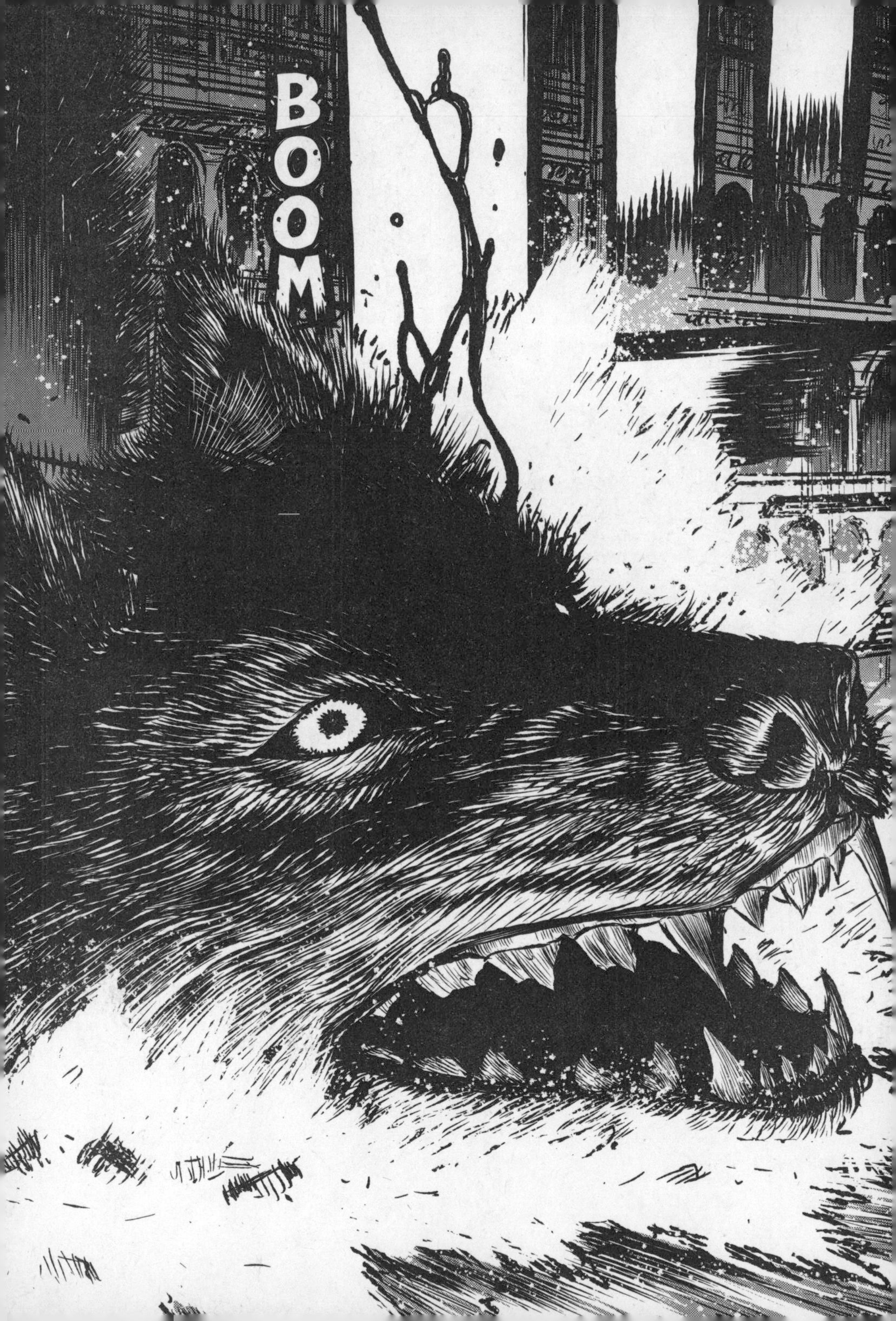
BOOM

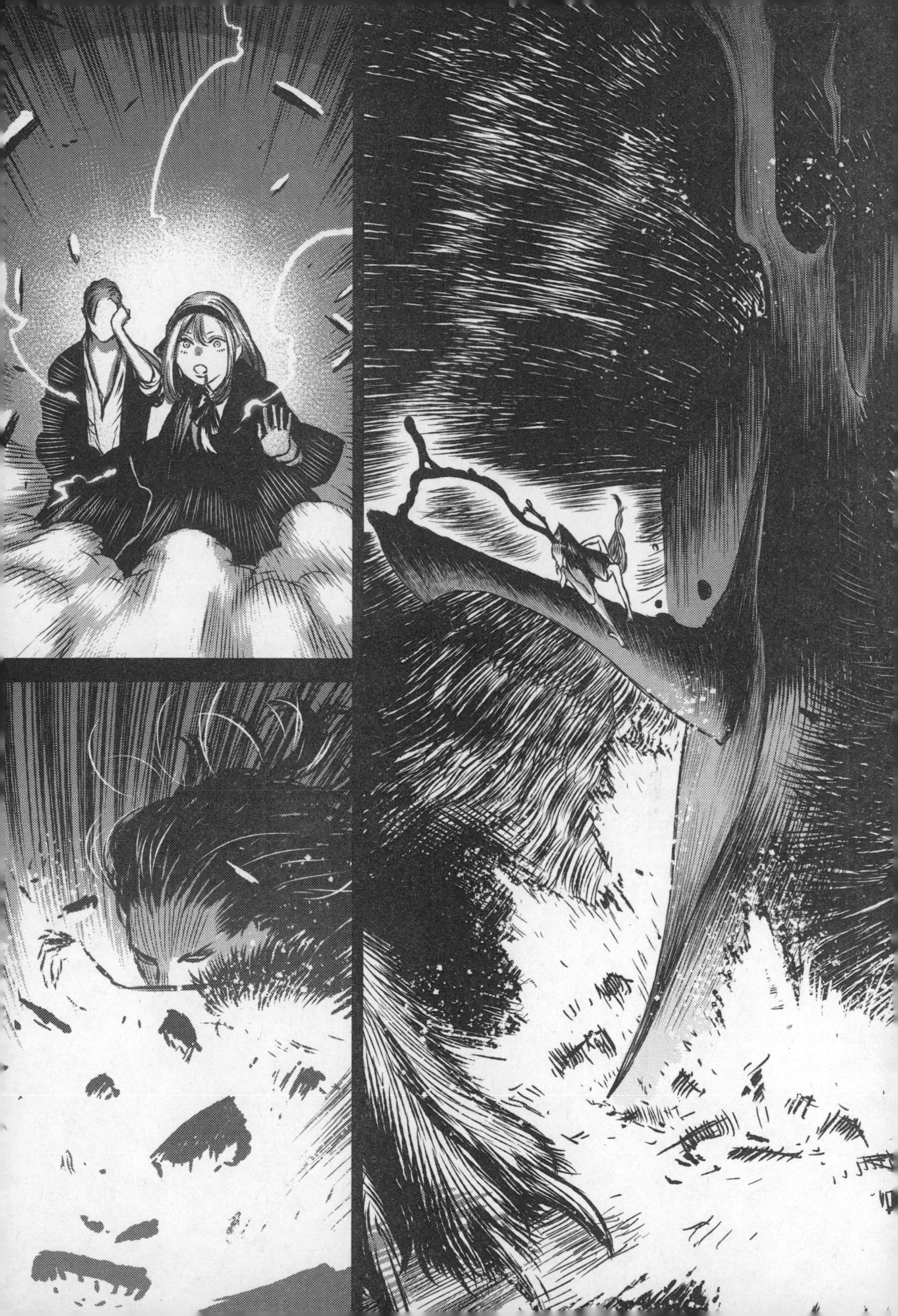

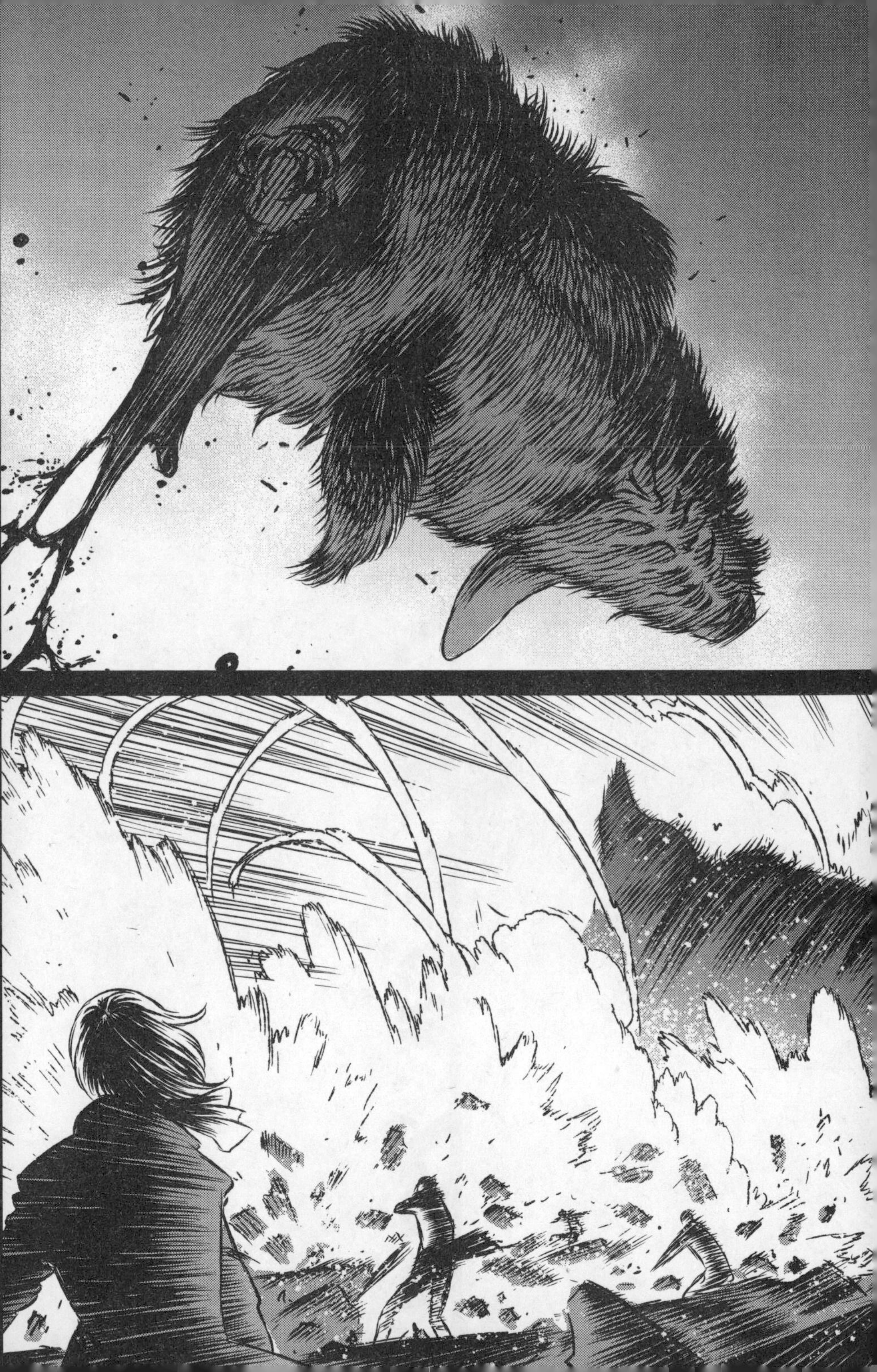

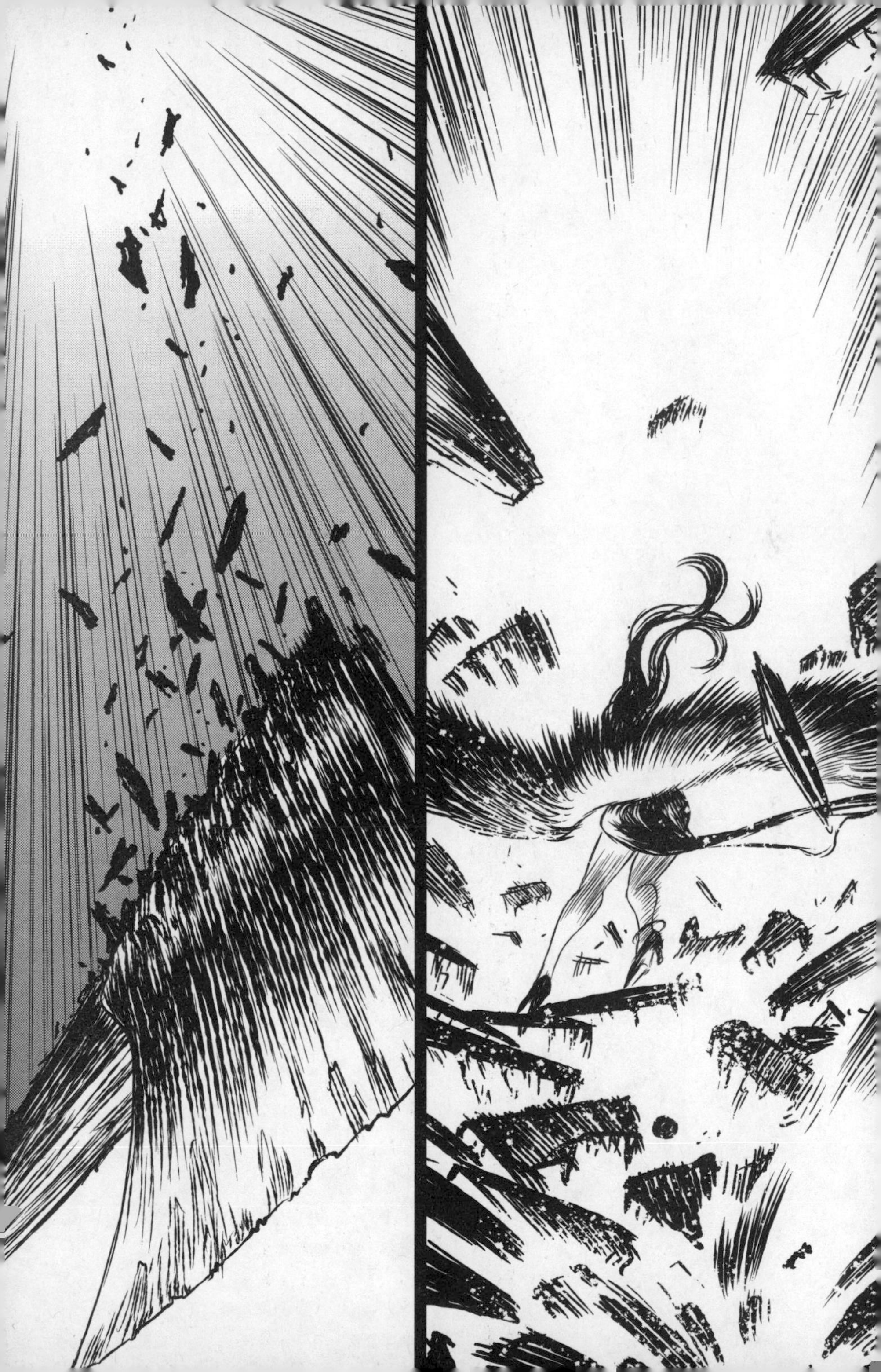

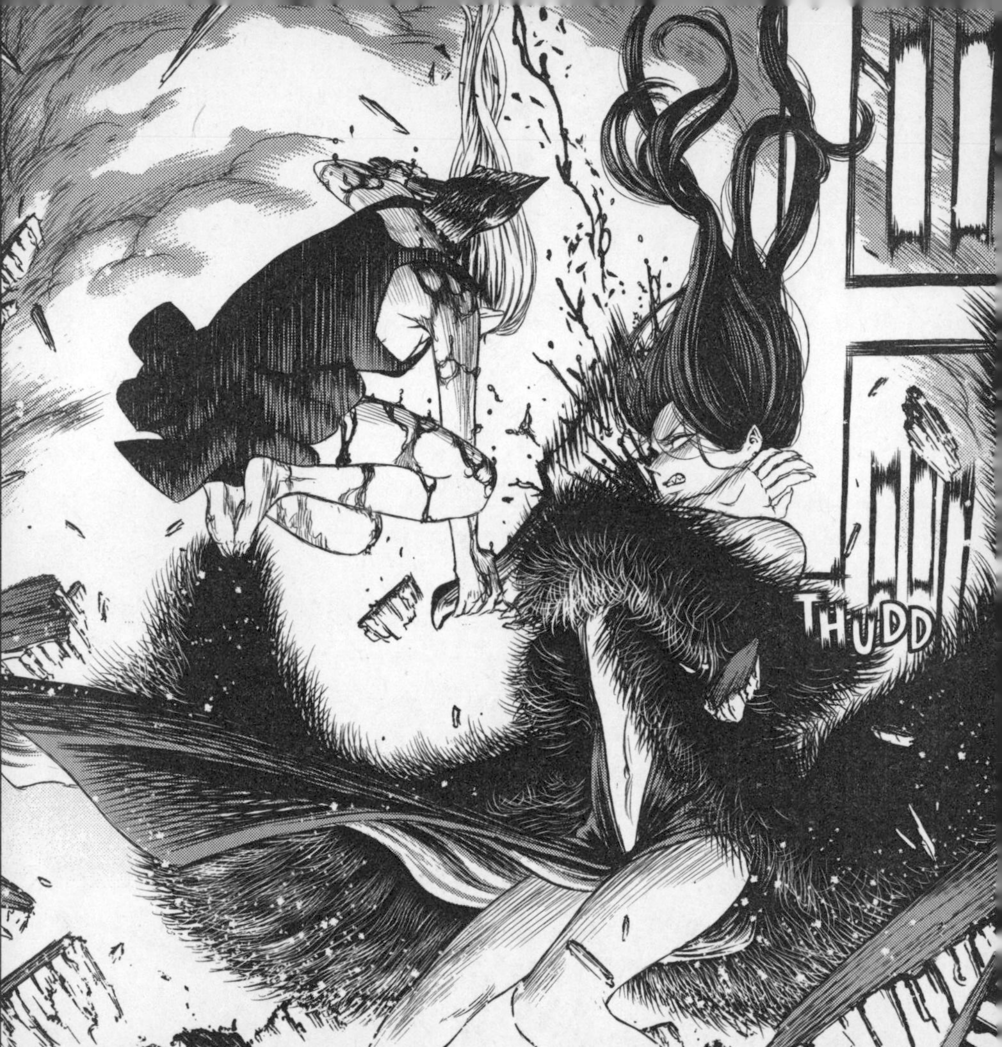
THUDD
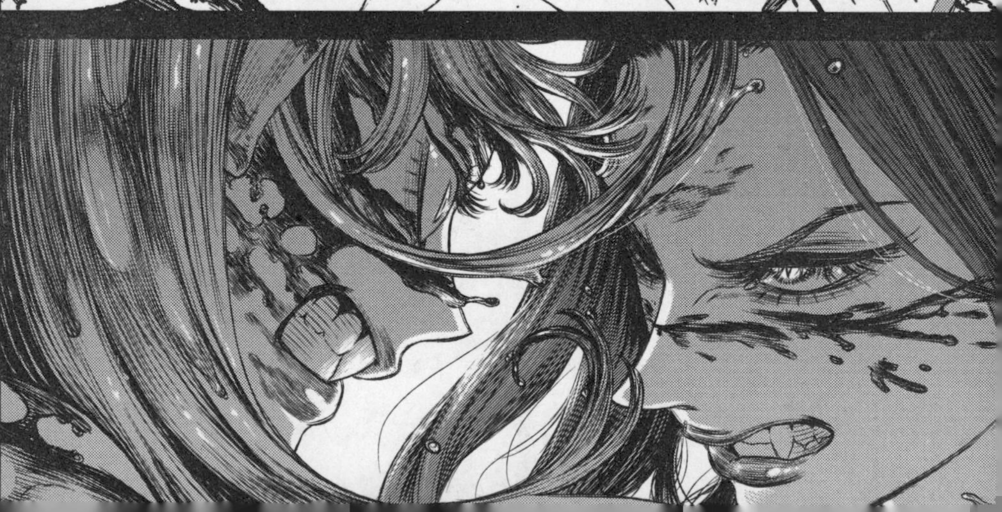

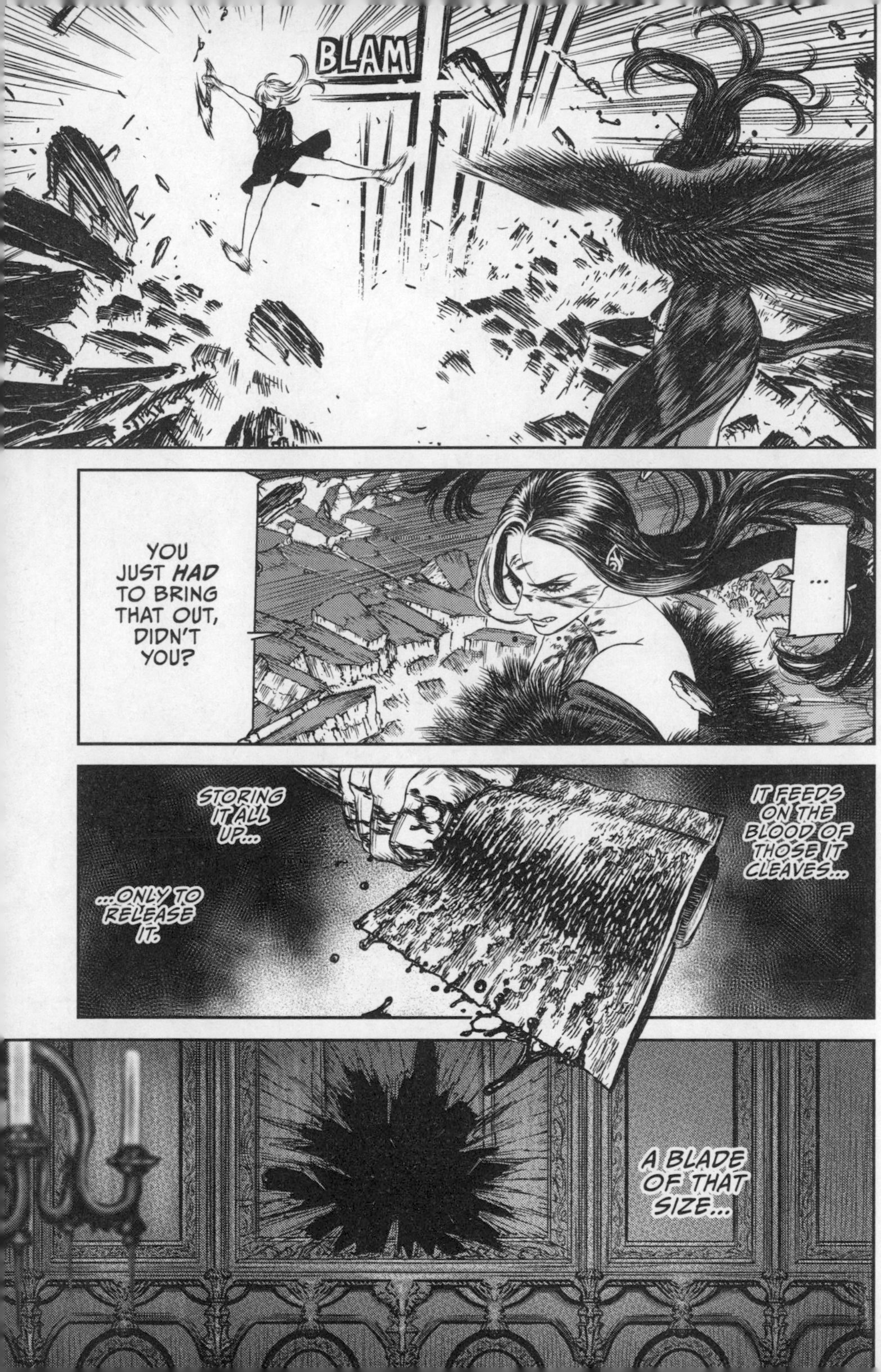
BLAM
...
YOU JUST *HAD* TO BRING THAT OUT, DIDN'T YOU?
IT FEEDS ON THE BLOOD OF THOSE IT CLEAVES...
STORING IT ALL UP...
...ONLY TO RELEASE IT.
A BLADE OF THAT SIZE...

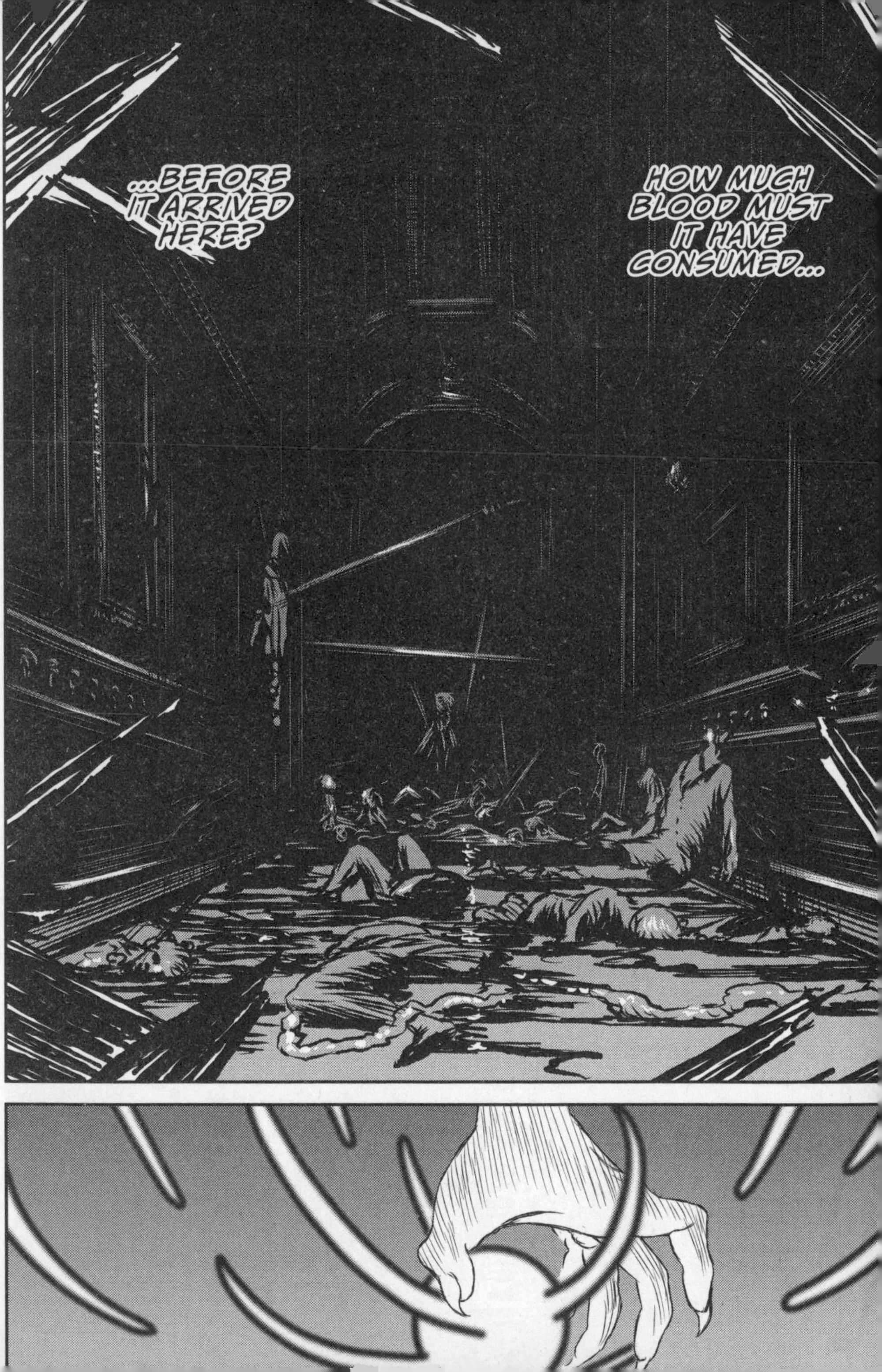
HOW MUCH BLOOD MUST IT HAVE CONSUMED...
...BEFORE IT ARRIVED HERE?

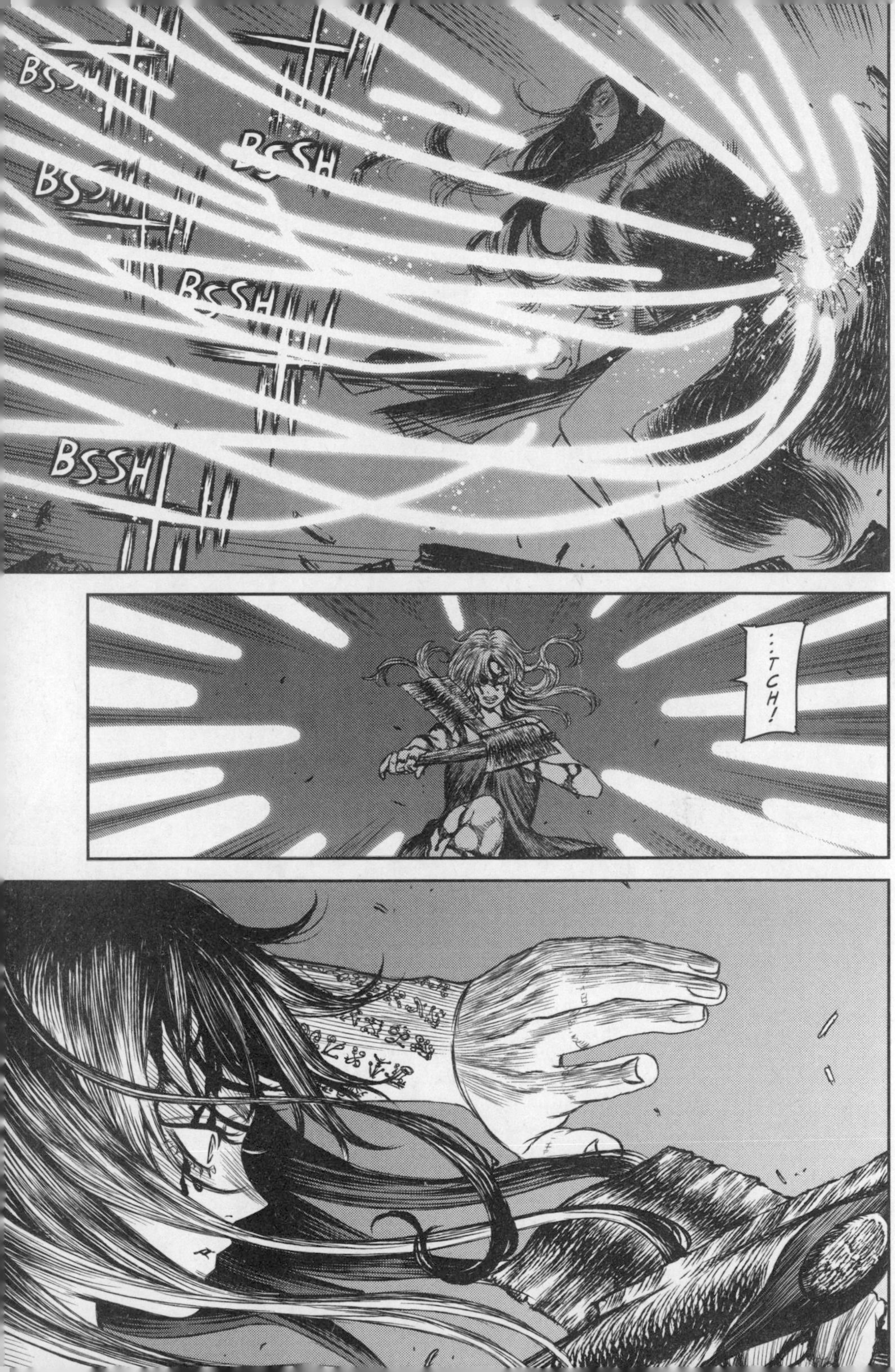
BSSH
BSSH
BSSH
BSSH
BSSH
...TCH!

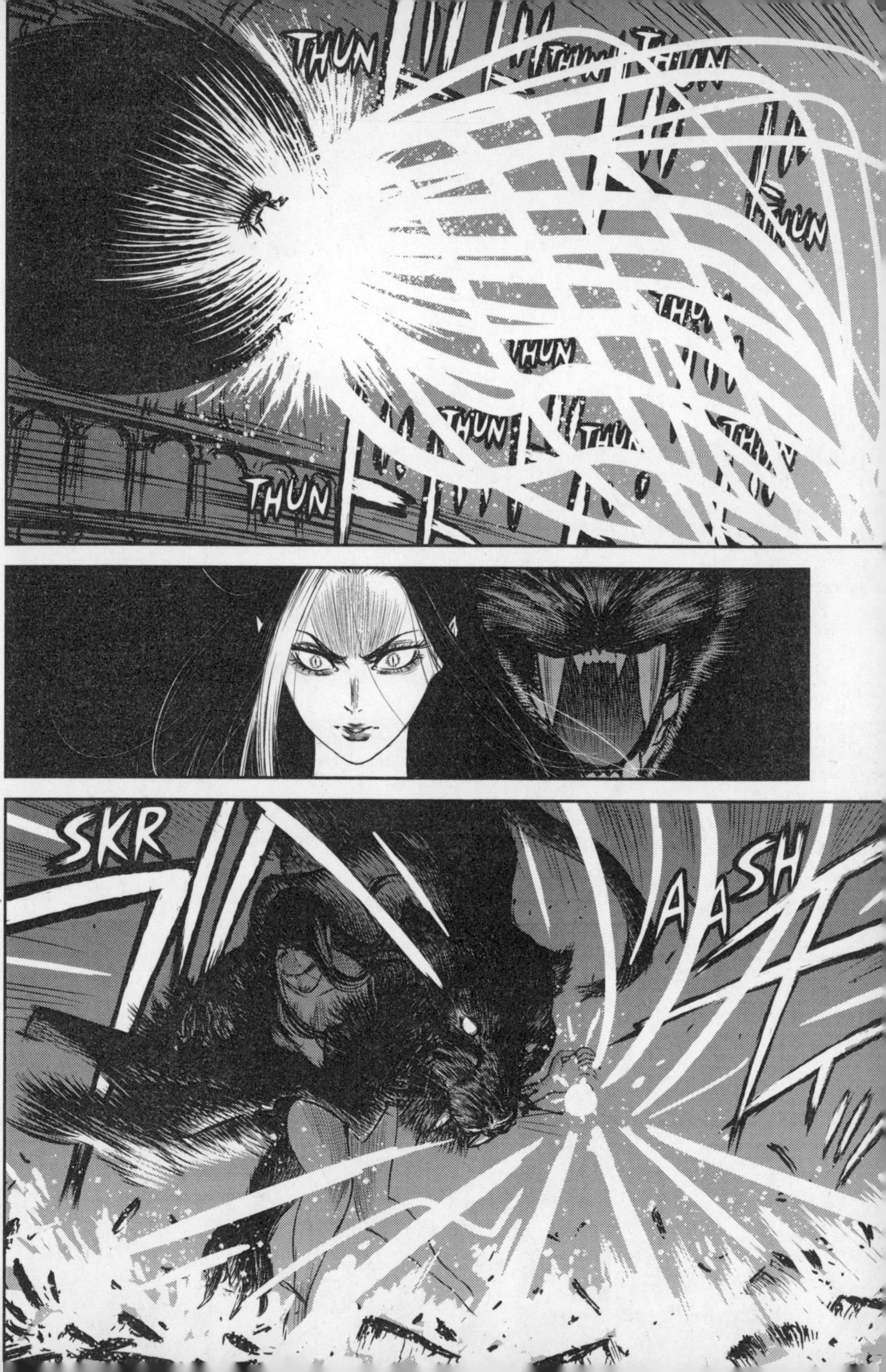
THUN
THUN
THUN
THUN
THUN
THUN
THUN
THUN
THUN
THUN
SKR
AASH

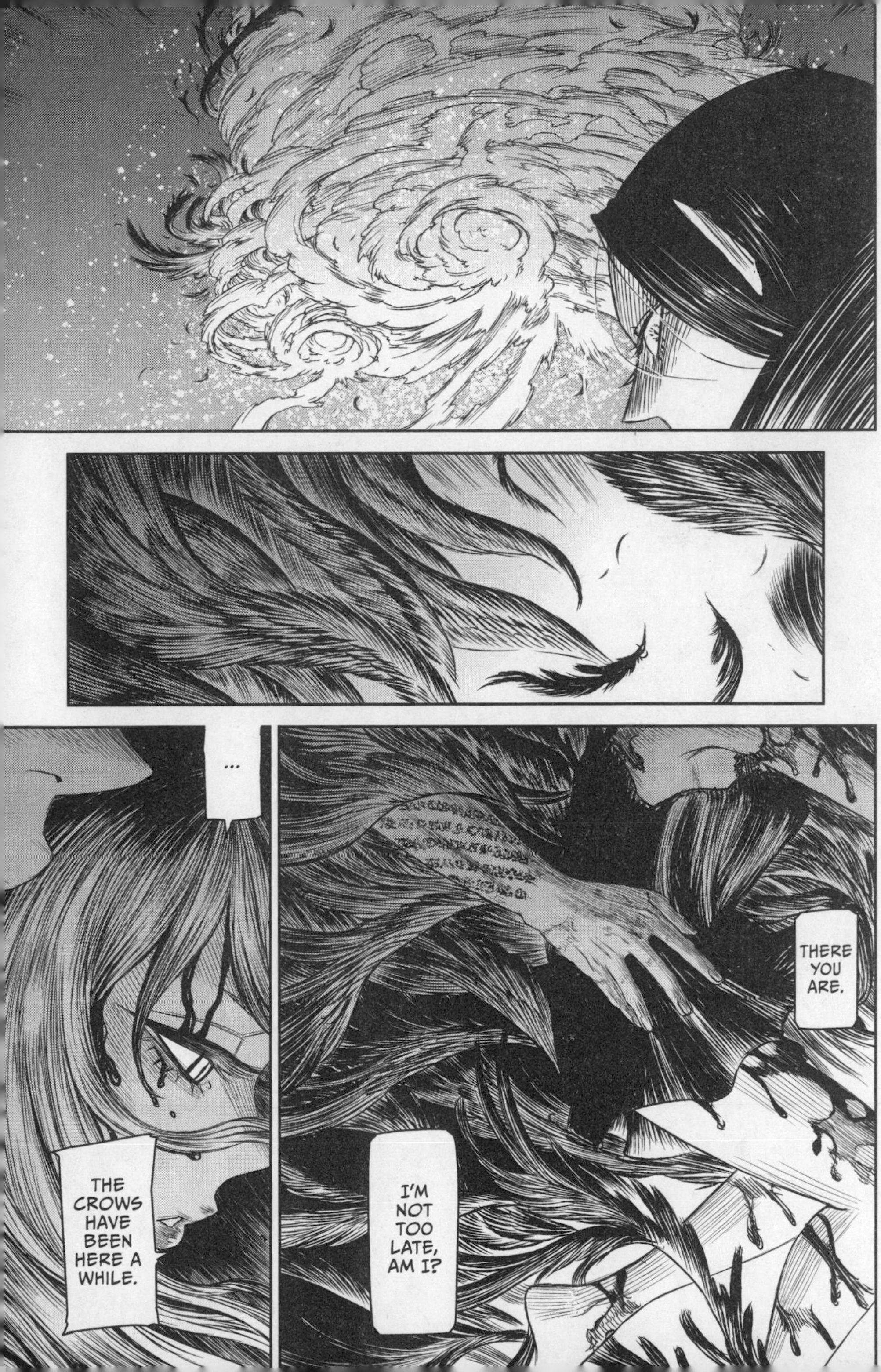
THERE YOU ARE.
I'M NOT TOO LATE, AM I?
...
THE CROWS HAVE BEEN HERE A WHILE.

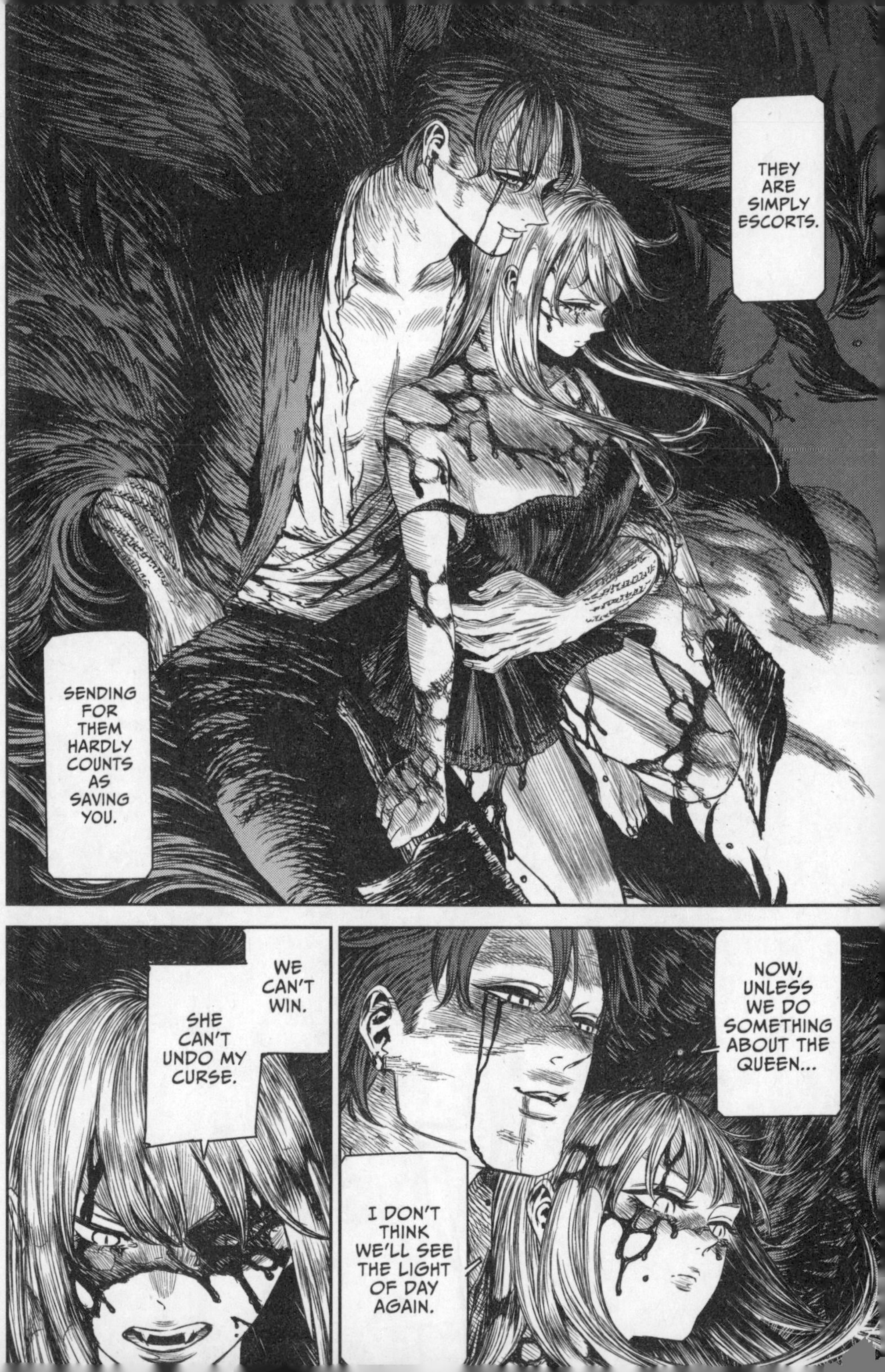
THEY ARE SIMPLY ESCORTS.
SENDING FOR THEM HARDLY COUNTS AS SAVING YOU.
NOW, UNLESS WE DO SOMETHING ABOUT THE QUEEN...
I DON'T THINK WE'LL SEE THE LIGHT OF DAY AGAIN.
WE CAN'T WIN.
SHE CAN'T UNDO MY CURSE.

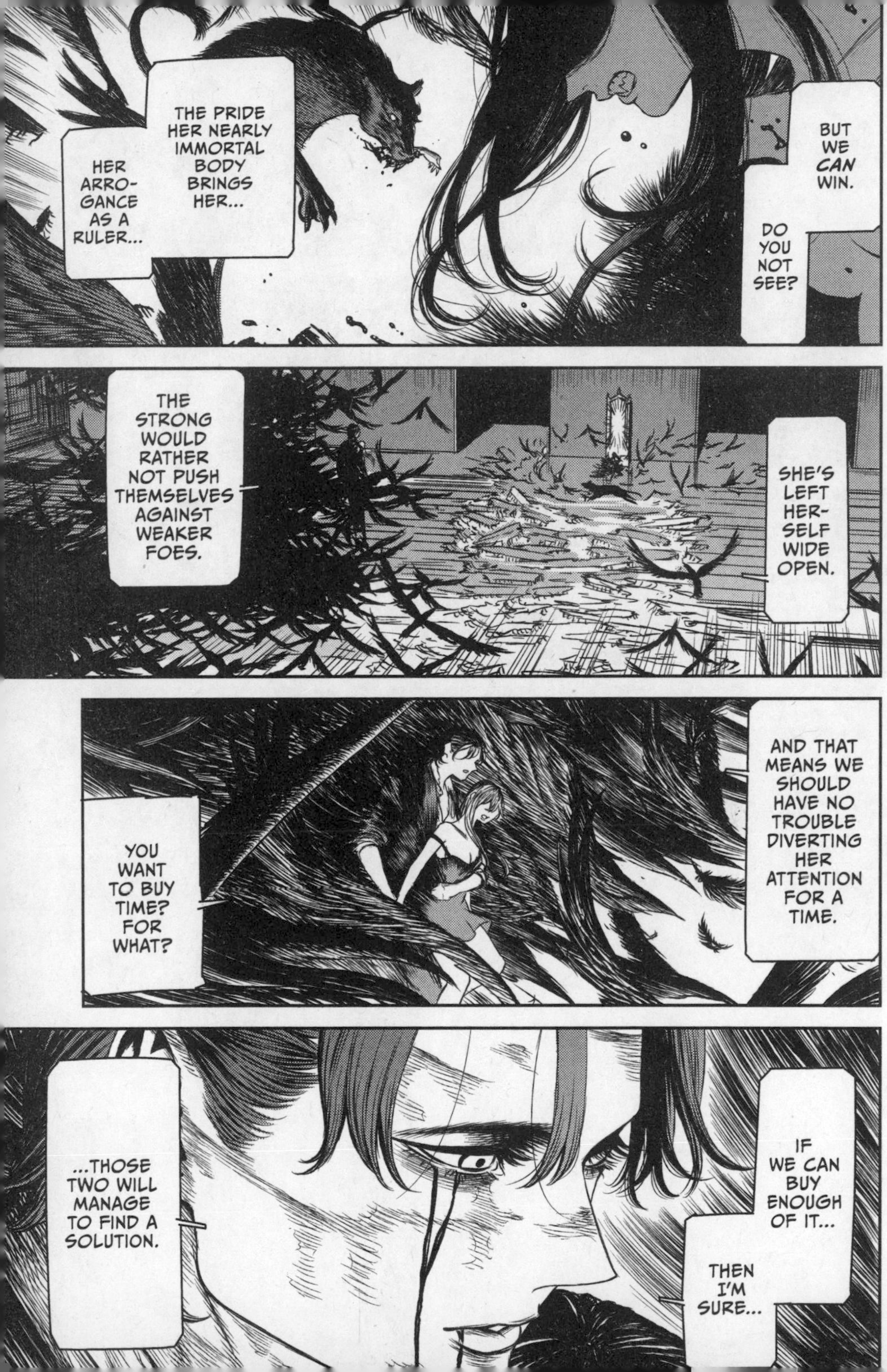
BUT WE *CAN* WIN.
DO YOU NOT SEE?
THE PRIDE HER NEARLY IMMORTAL BODY BRINGS HER...
HER ARROGANCE AS A RULER...
SHE'S LEFT HERSELF WIDE OPEN.
THE STRONG WOULD RATHER NOT PUSH THEMSELVES AGAINST WEAKER FOES.
AND THAT MEANS WE SHOULD HAVE NO TROUBLE DIVERTING HER ATTENTION FOR A TIME.
YOU WANT TO BUY TIME? FOR WHAT?
IF WE CAN BUY ENOUGH OF IT...
THEN I'M SURE...
...THOSE TWO WILL MANAGE TO FIND A SOLUTION.

BR-SSSH

...AND YOU'RE **SURE** ABOUT THAT?

HMM...

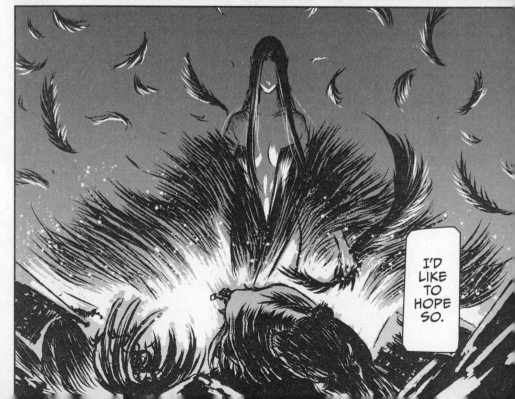

I'D LIKE TO HOPE SO.

...
THAT AXE... I KNOW OF IT.
IT'S A MAGICAL TOOL...
BUT ITS STRENGTH DEPENDS ON ITS WIELDER.
SIMPLY POSSESSING IT...
...WOULD NOT BE ENOUGH TO DICE UP ALL OF THOSE MEN.
THAT POWER...
WHERE DOES IT COME FROM?
AND IT'S NOT JUST PHYSICAL POWER, OR SPEED.
I'M SURE THAT GUIDEAU...
...HAS HER OWN UNIQUE STRENGTHS AND EXPERIENCES.

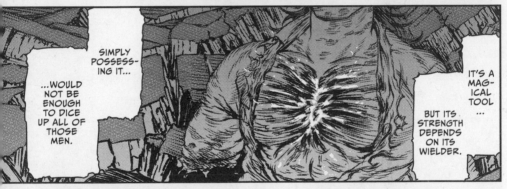

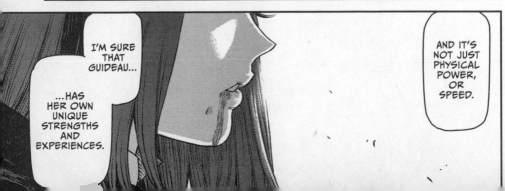

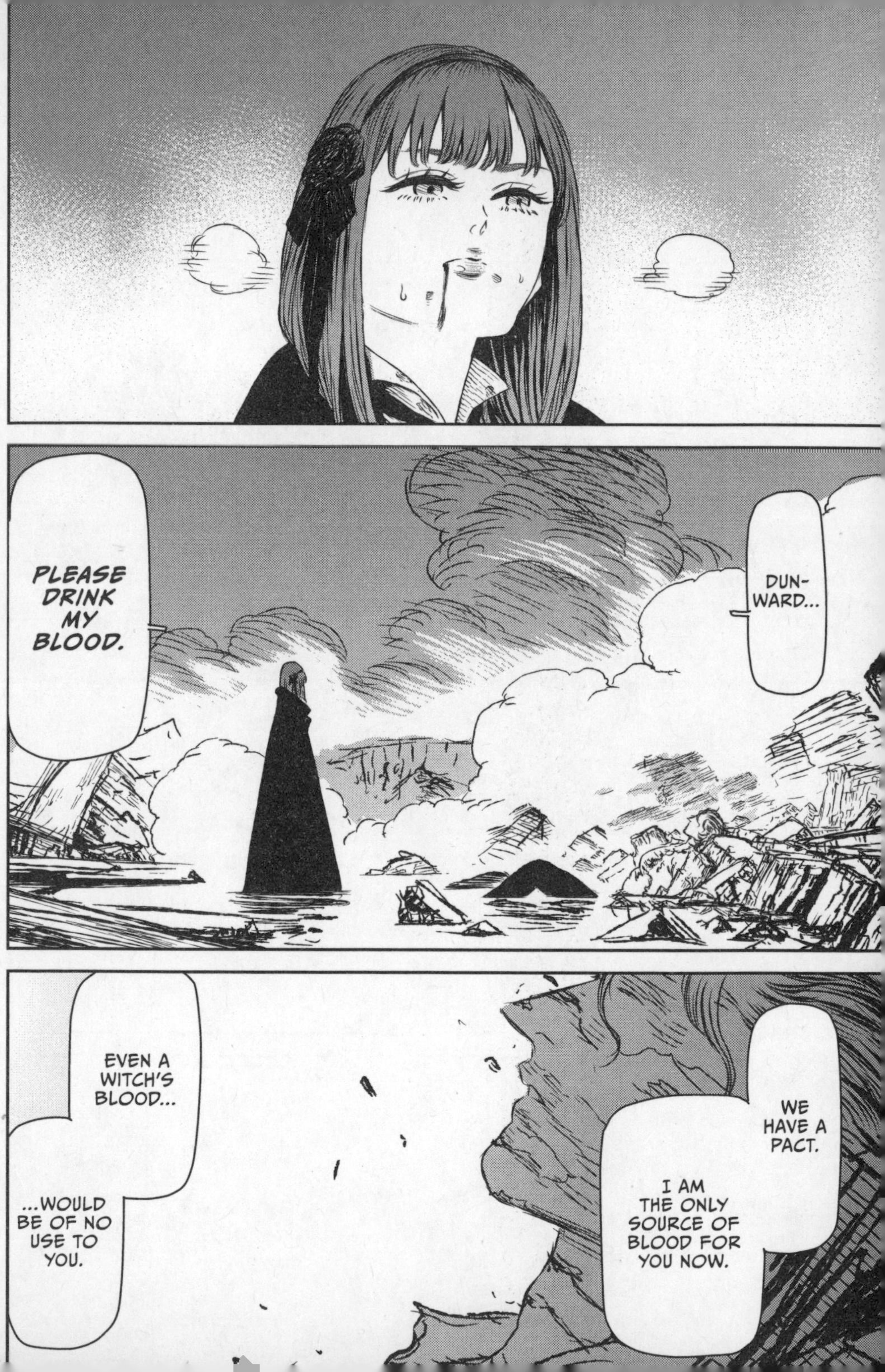
DUN-WARD...
PLEASE DRINK MY BLOOD.
WE HAVE A PACT.
I AM THE ONLY SOURCE OF BLOOD FOR YOU NOW.
EVEN A WITCH'S BLOOD...
...WOULD BE OF NO USE TO YOU.

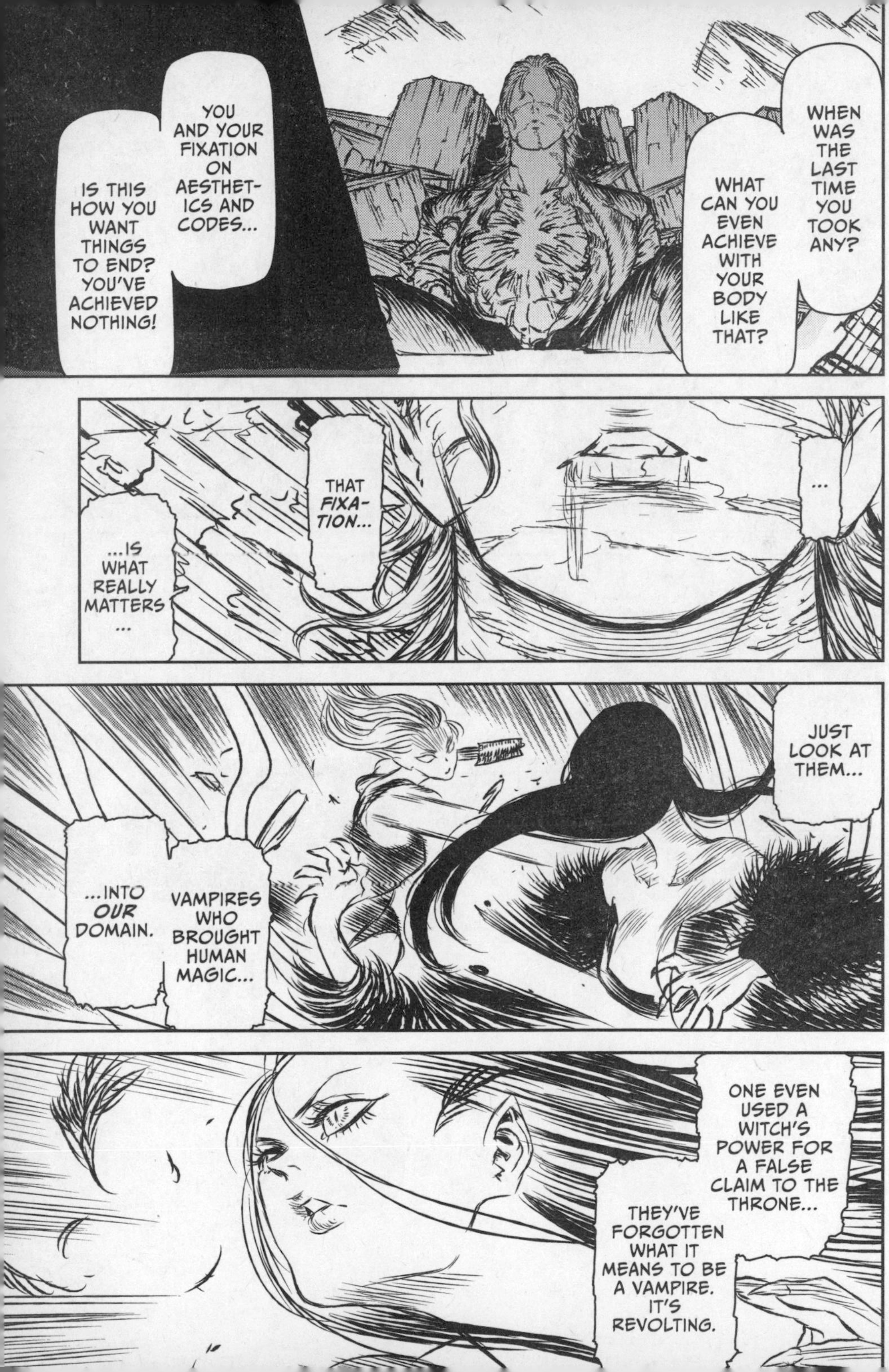
WHEN WAS THE LAST TIME YOU TOOK ANY?
WHAT CAN YOU EVEN ACHIEVE WITH YOUR BODY LIKE THAT?
YOU AND YOUR FIXATION ON AESTHETICS AND CODES...
IS THIS HOW YOU WANT THINGS TO END? YOU'VE ACHIEVED NOTHING!
...
THAT *FIXATION*...
...IS WHAT REALLY MATTERS...
JUST LOOK AT THEM...
VAMPIRES WHO BROUGHT HUMAN MAGIC...
...INTO *OUR* DOMAIN.
ONE EVEN USED A WITCH'S POWER FOR A FALSE CLAIM TO THE THRONE...
THEY'VE FORGOTTEN WHAT IT MEANS TO BE A VAMPIRE. IT'S REVOLTING.

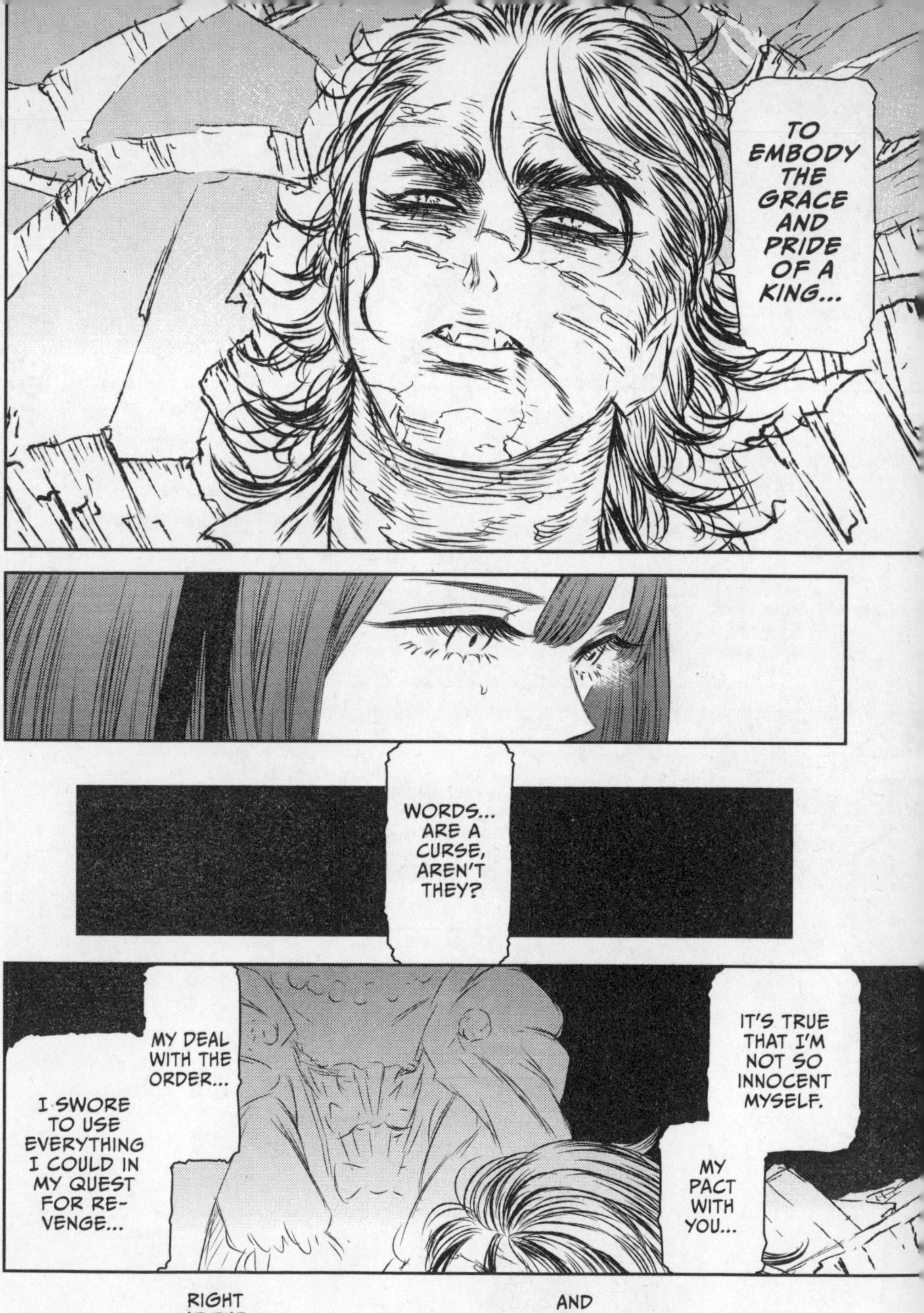
TO EMBODY THE GRACE AND PRIDE OF A KING...
WORDS... ARE A CURSE, AREN'T THEY?
IT'S TRUE THAT I'M NOT SO INNOCENT MYSELF.
MY PACT WITH YOU...
MY DEAL WITH THE ORDER...
I SWORE TO USE EVERYTHING I COULD IN MY QUEST FOR RE-VENGE...
AND YET...
RIGHT AT THE END...

THAT CURSE...

...COMES BACK TO HAUNT ME...

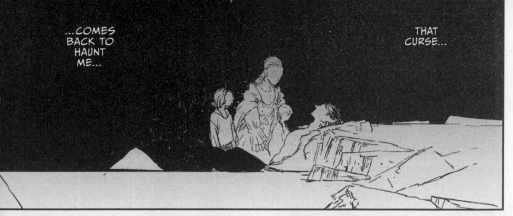

...WHAT A SURPRISE.

...WASN'T FOR JUST YOUR OWN SAKE AFTER ALL.

YOUR REVENGE...

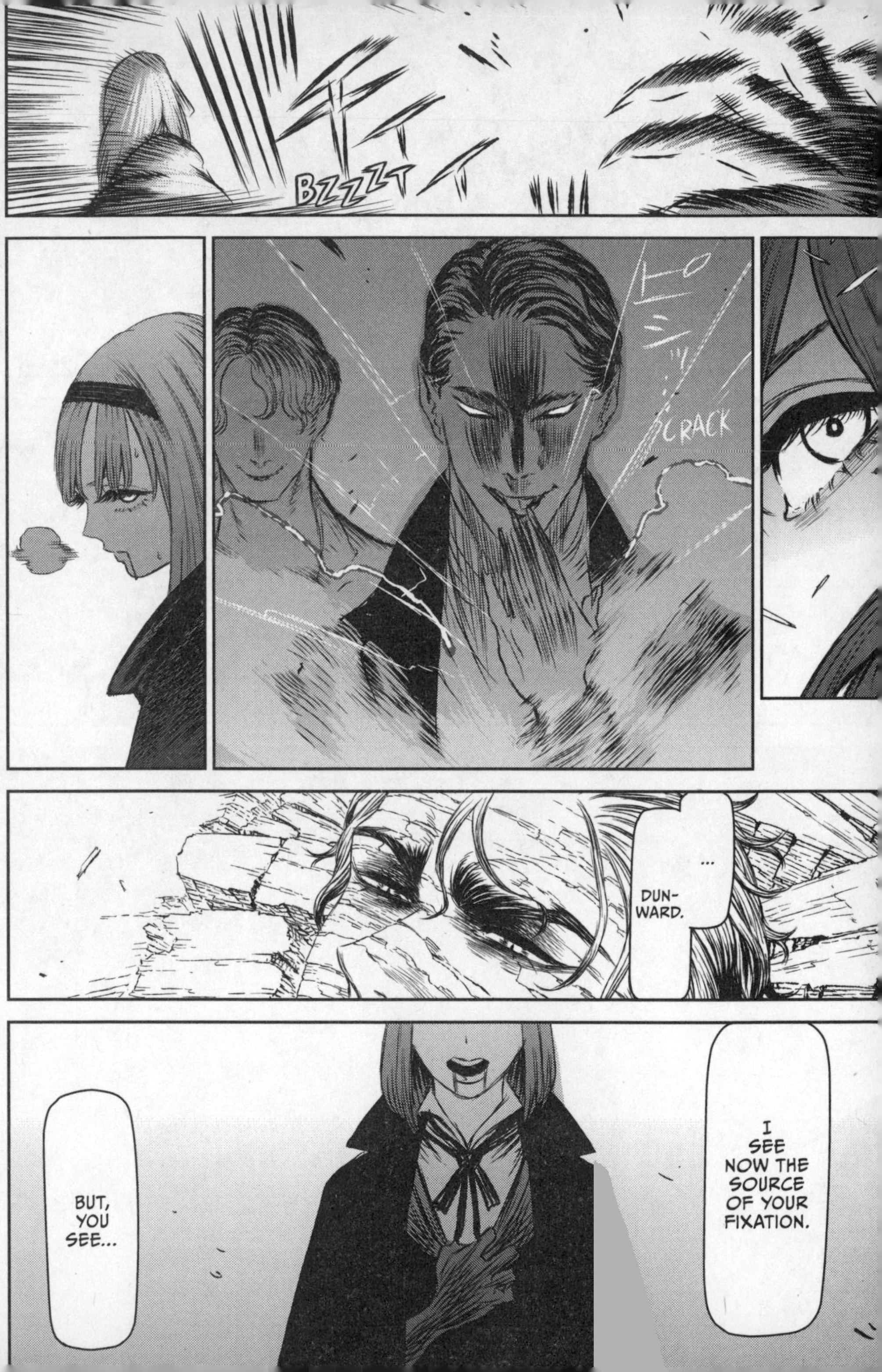
BZZZZT
CRACK
... DUN-WARD.
I SEE NOW THE SOURCE OF YOUR FIXATION.
BUT, YOU SEE...

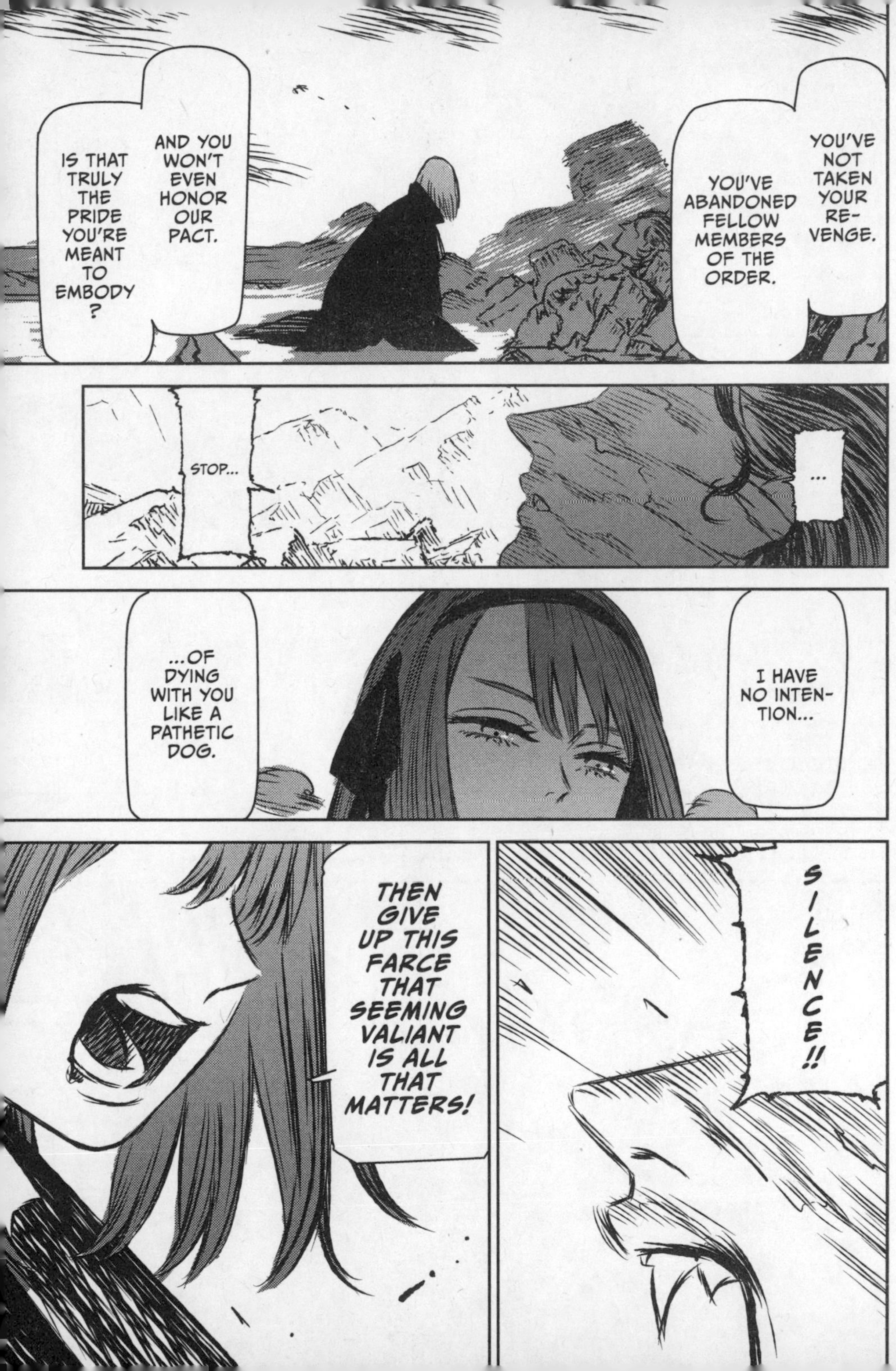
YOU'VE NOT TAKEN YOUR RE- VENGE.
YOU'VE ABANDONED FELLOW MEMBERS OF THE ORDER.
AND YOU WON'T EVEN HONOR OUR PACT.
IS THAT TRULY THE PRIDE YOU'RE MEANT TO EMBODY ?
...
STOP...
I HAVE NO INTEN- TION...
...OF DYING WITH YOU LIKE A PATHETIC DOG.
SILENCE!!
THEN GIVE UP THIS FARCE THAT SEEMING VALIANT IS ALL THAT MATTERS!

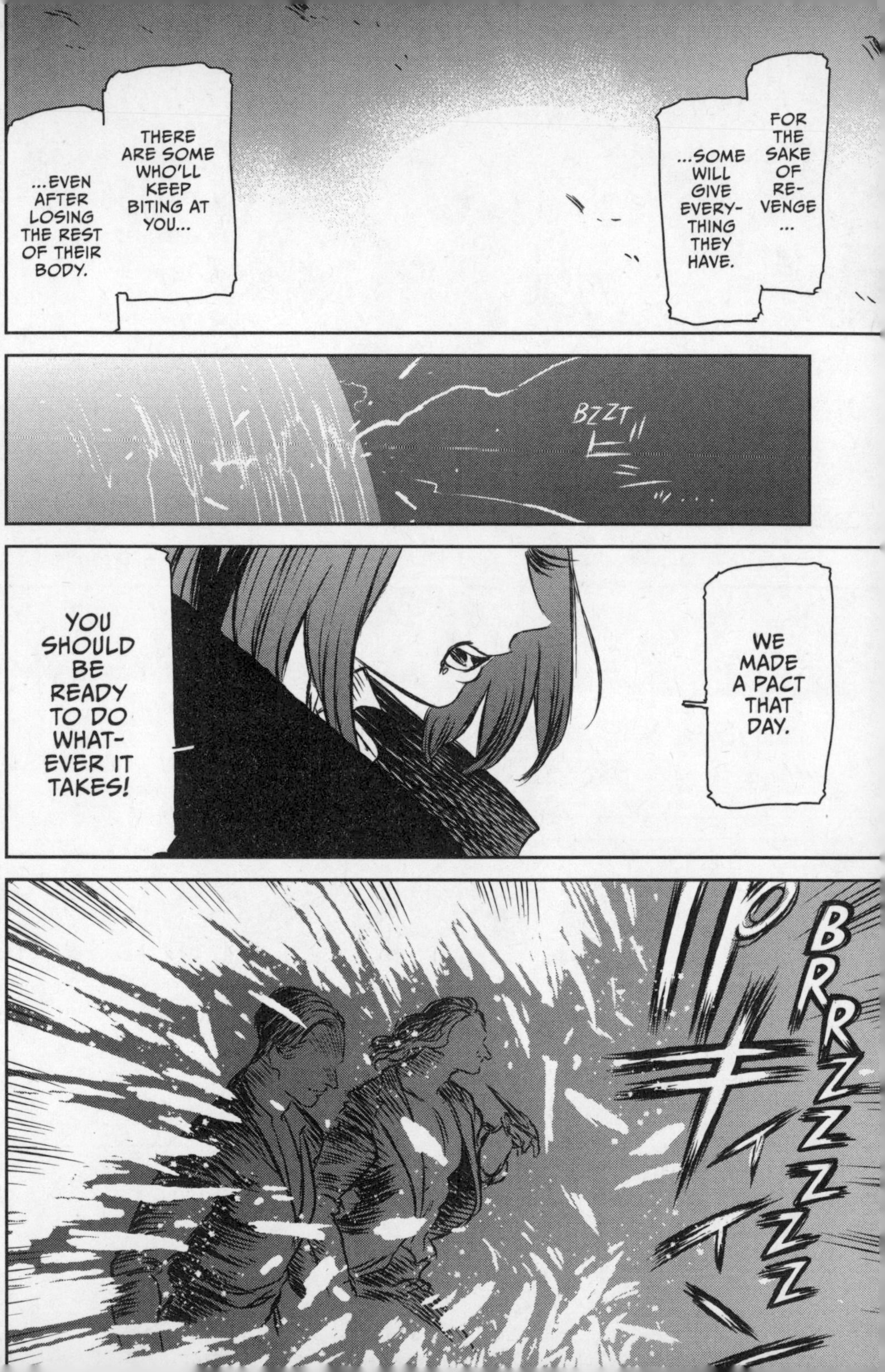
FOR THE SAKE OF RE-VENGE...
...SOME WILL GIVE EVERY-THING THEY HAVE.
THERE ARE SOME WHO'LL KEEP BITING AT YOU...
...EVEN AFTER LOSING THE REST OF THEIR BODY.
BZZT
WE MADE A PACT THAT DAY.
YOU SHOULD BE READY TO DO WHAT-EVER IT TAKES!
BRRZZZZZZZ

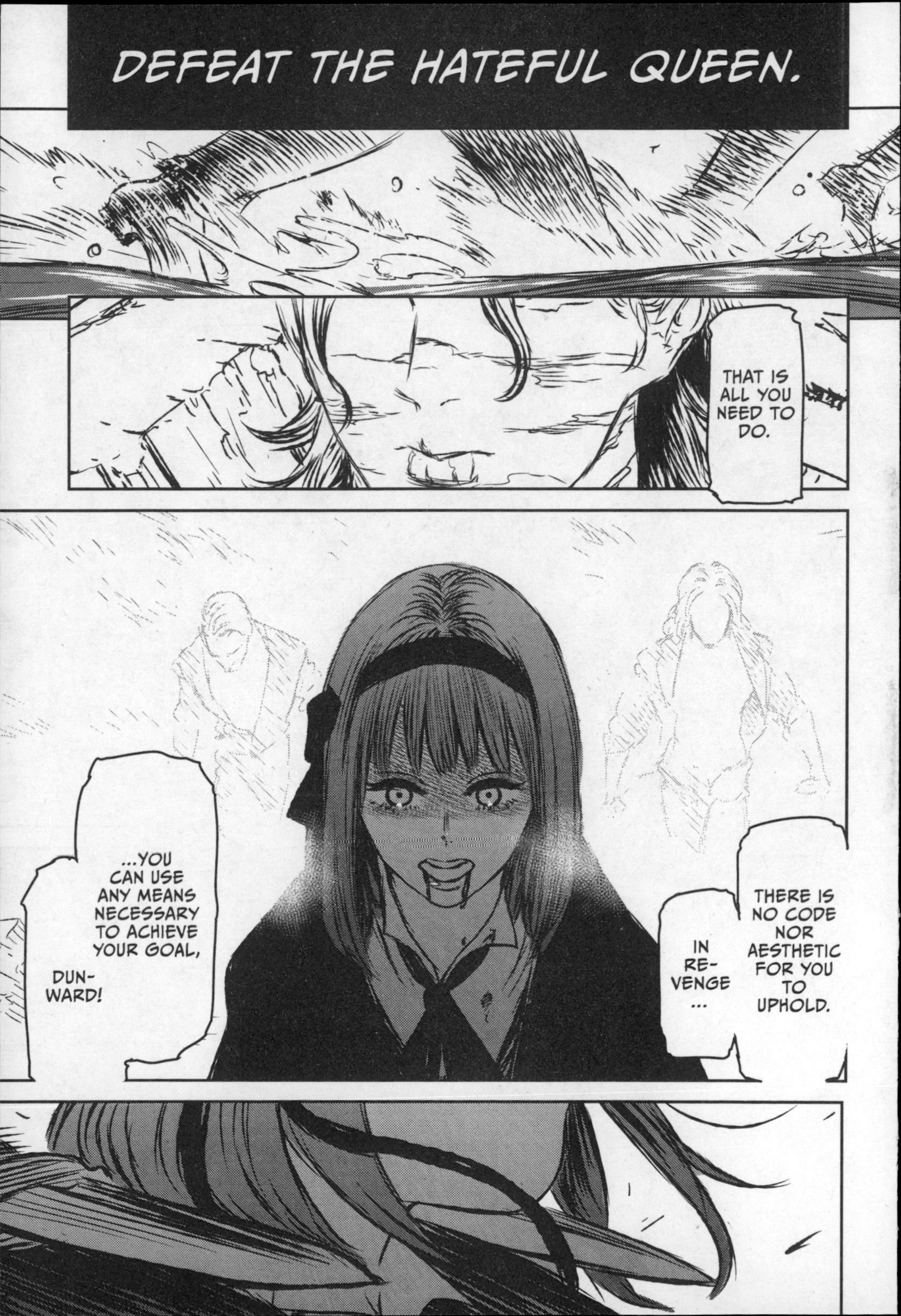
DEFEAT THE HATEFUL QUEEN.
THAT IS ALL YOU NEED TO DO.
THERE IS NO CODE NOR AESTHETIC FOR YOU TO UPHOLD.
IN RE-VENGE ...
...YOU CAN USE ANY MEANS NECESSARY TO ACHIEVE YOUR GOAL,
DUN-WARD!

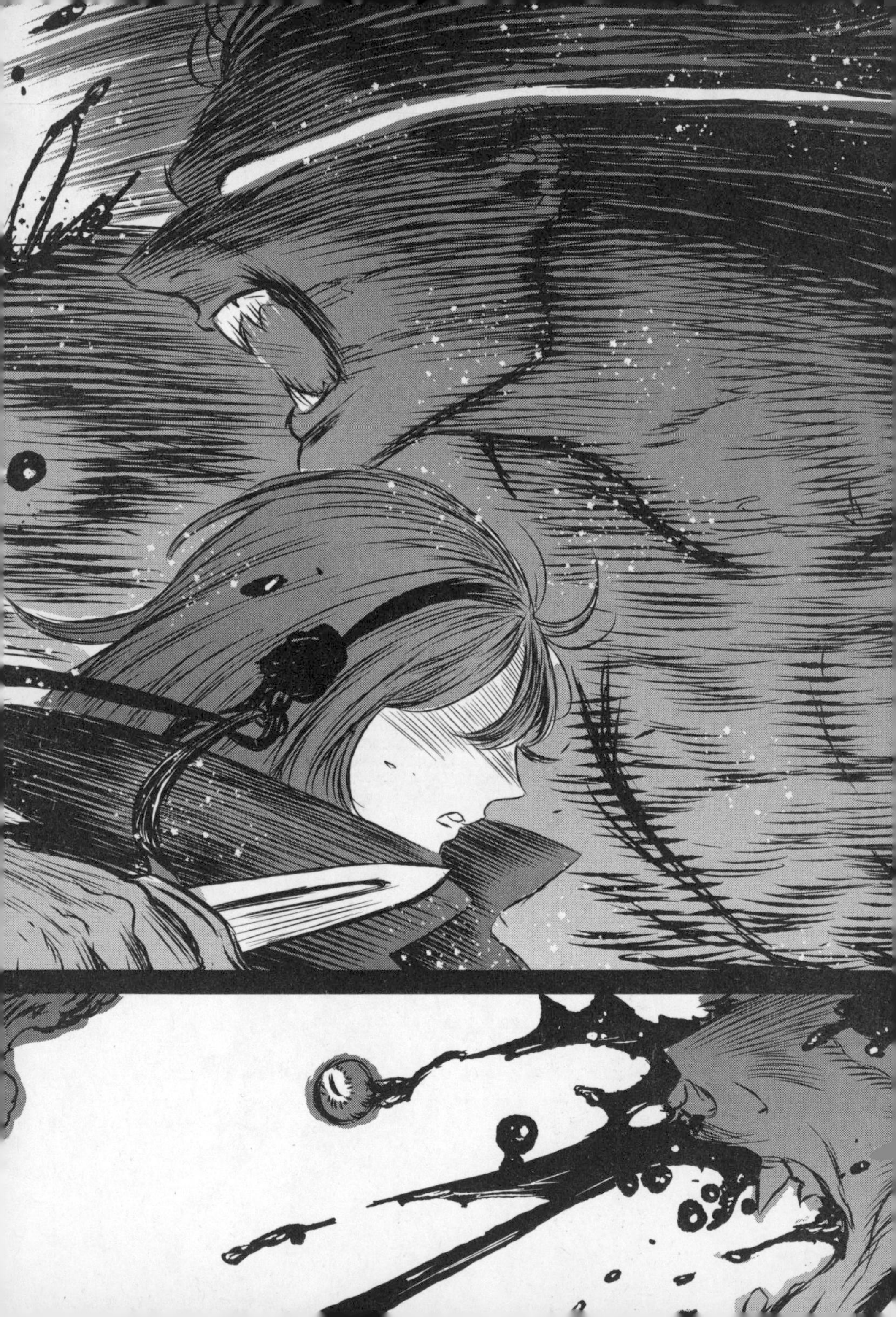

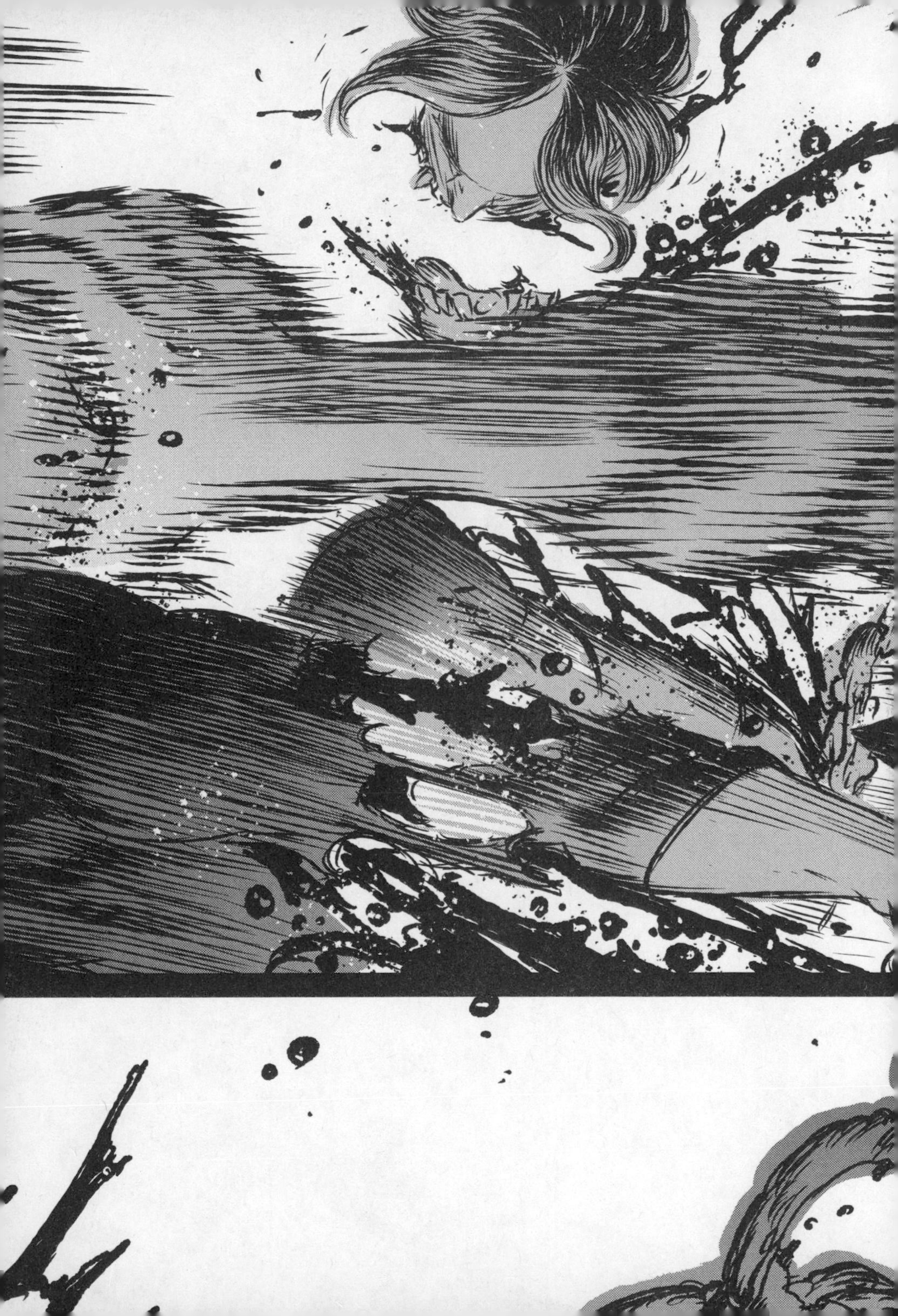

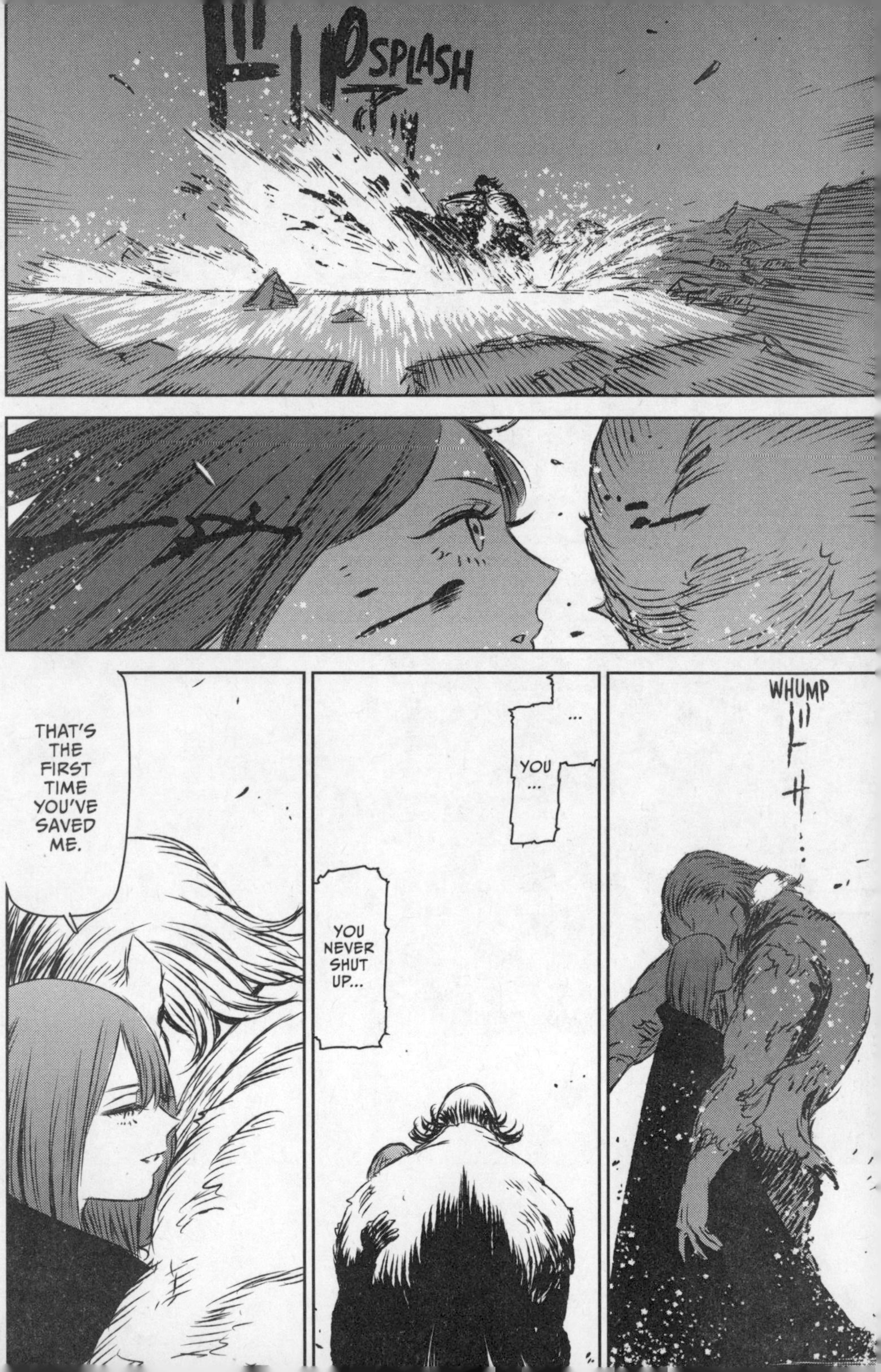
SPLASH
WHUMP
... YOU ...
YOU NEVER SHUT UP...
THAT'S THE FIRST TIME YOU'VE SAVED ME.

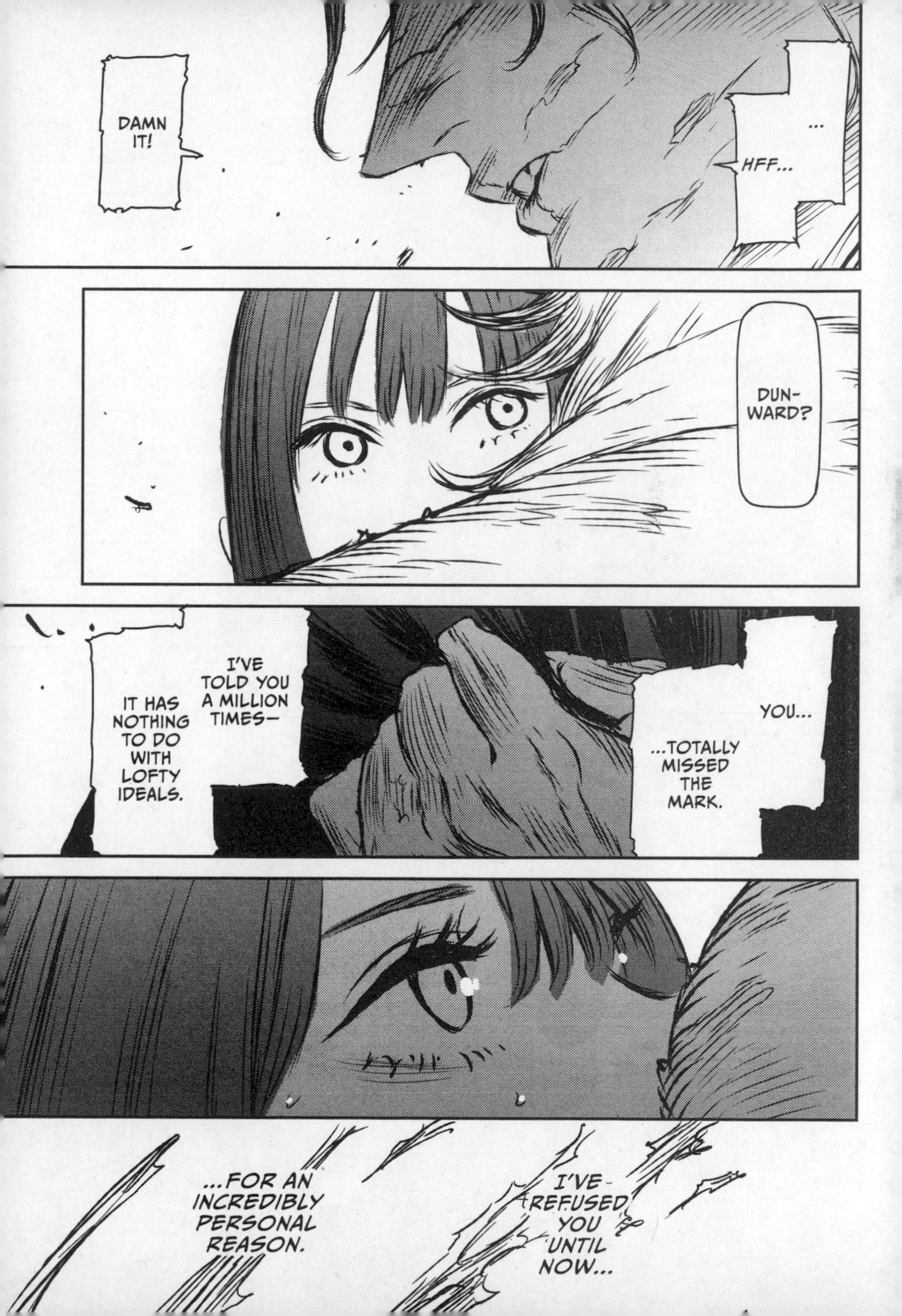
...
HFF...
DAMN IT!
DUN-WARD?
YOU...
...TOTALLY MISSED THE MARK.
I'VE TOLD YOU A MILLION TIMES—
IT HAS NOTHING TO DO WITH LOFTY IDEALS.
I'VE REFUSED YOU UNTIL NOW...
...FOR AN INCREDIBLY PERSONAL REASON.

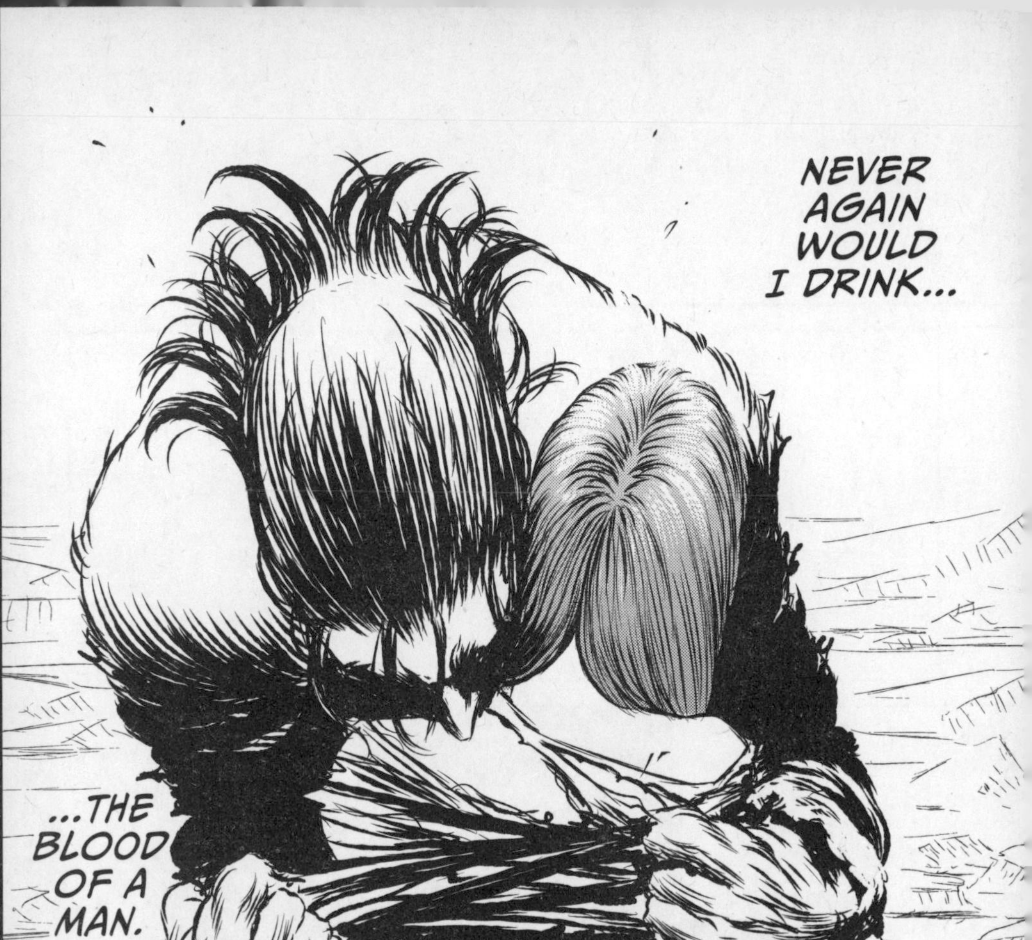
NEVER AGAIN WOULD I DRINK...
...THE BLOOD OF A MAN.

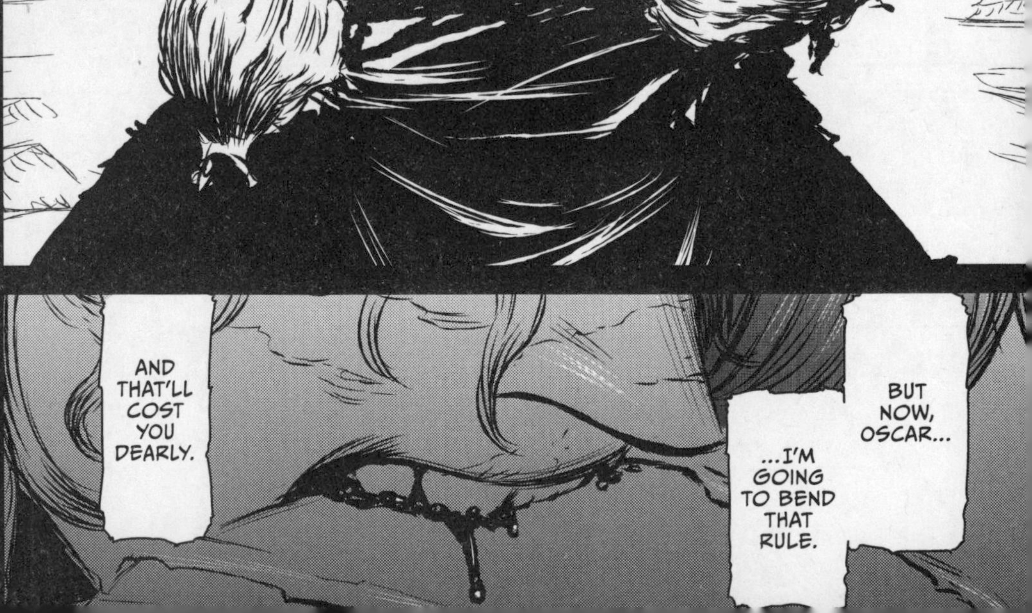
BUT NOW, OSCAR...
...I'M GOING TO BEND THAT RULE.
AND THAT'LL COST YOU DEARLY.

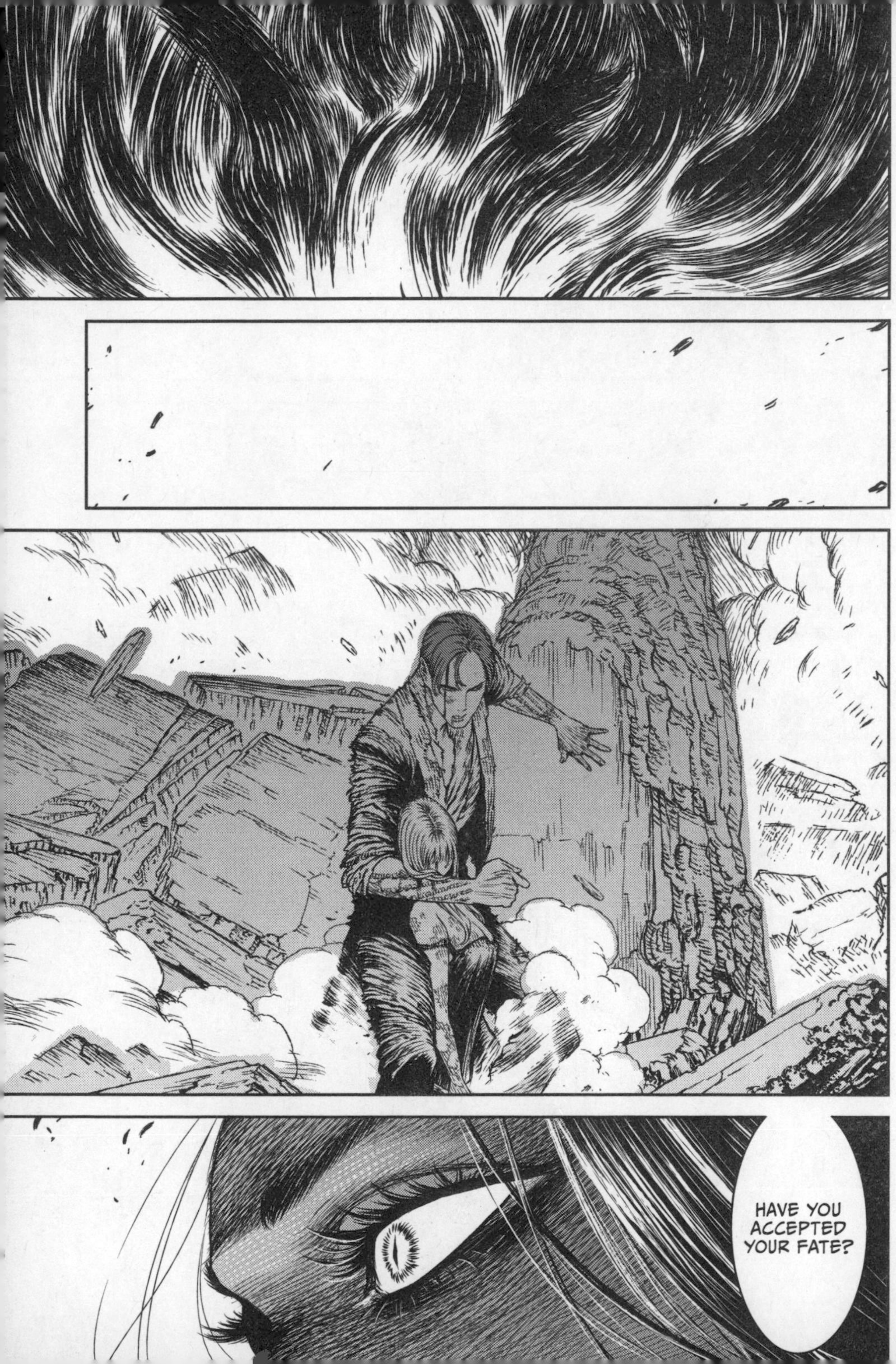
HAVE YOU ACCEPTED YOUR FATE?

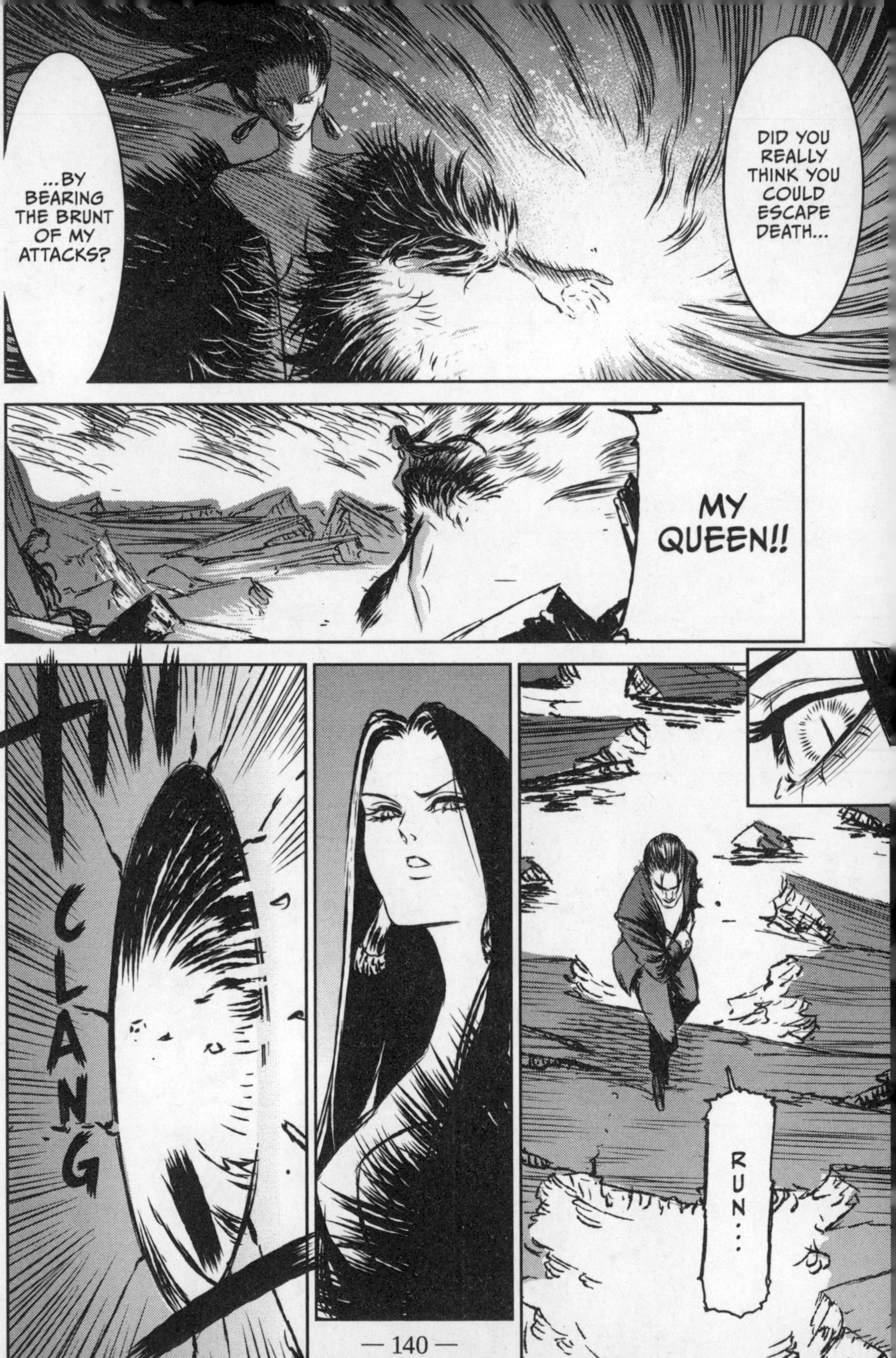
DID YOU REALLY THINK YOU COULD ESCAPE DEATH...
...BY BEARING THE BRUNT OF MY ATTACKS?
MY QUEEN!!
RUN...
CLANG

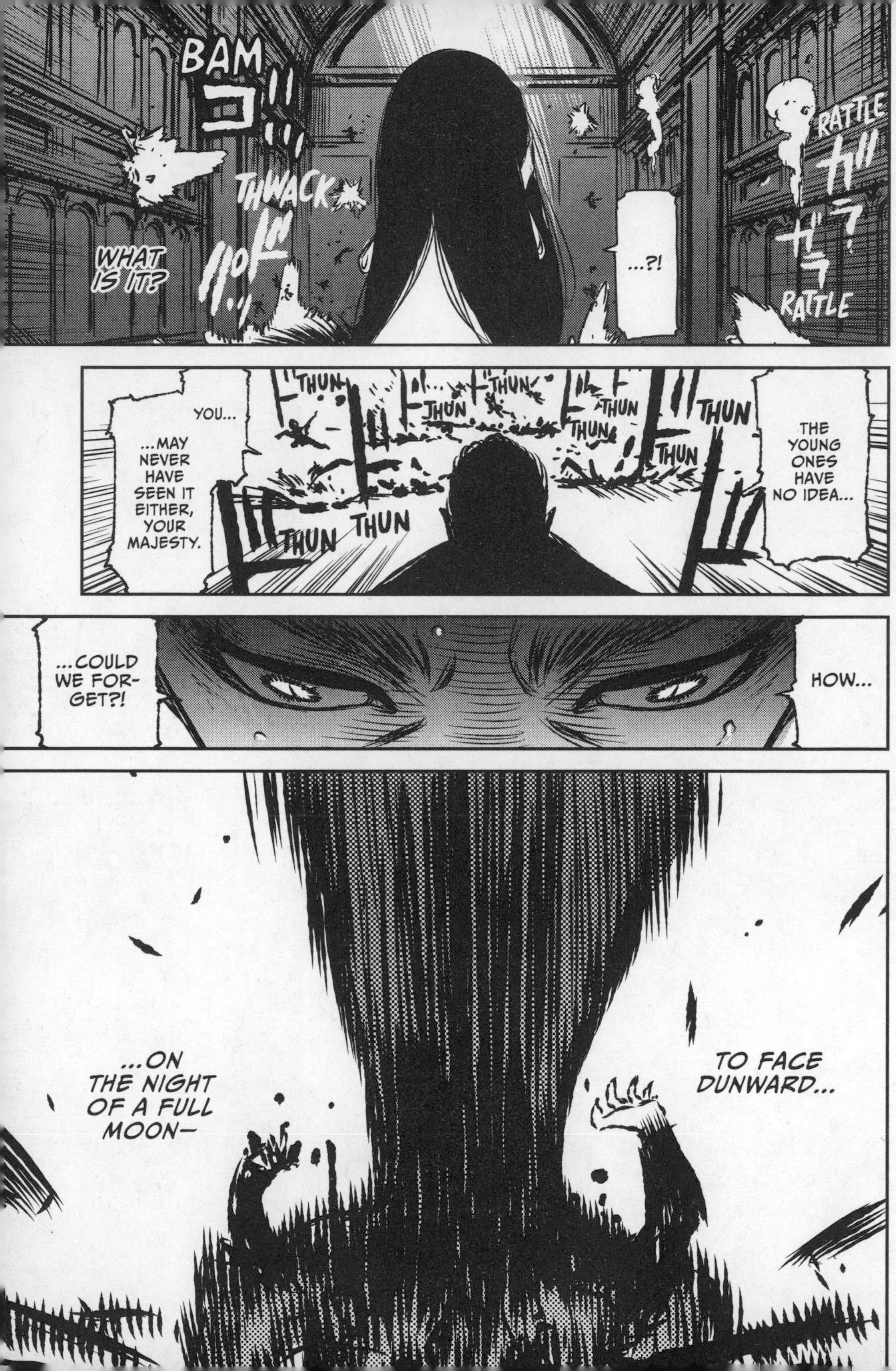
RATTLE
RATTLE
...?!
BAM
THWACK
WHAT IS IT?
THE YOUNG ONES HAVE NO IDEA...
THUN THUN THUN THUN THUN THUN THUN THUN
YOU...
...MAY NEVER HAVE SEEN IT EITHER, YOUR MAJESTY.
HOW...
...COULD WE FOR-GET?!
TO FACE DUNWARD...
...ON THE NIGHT OF A FULL MOON—

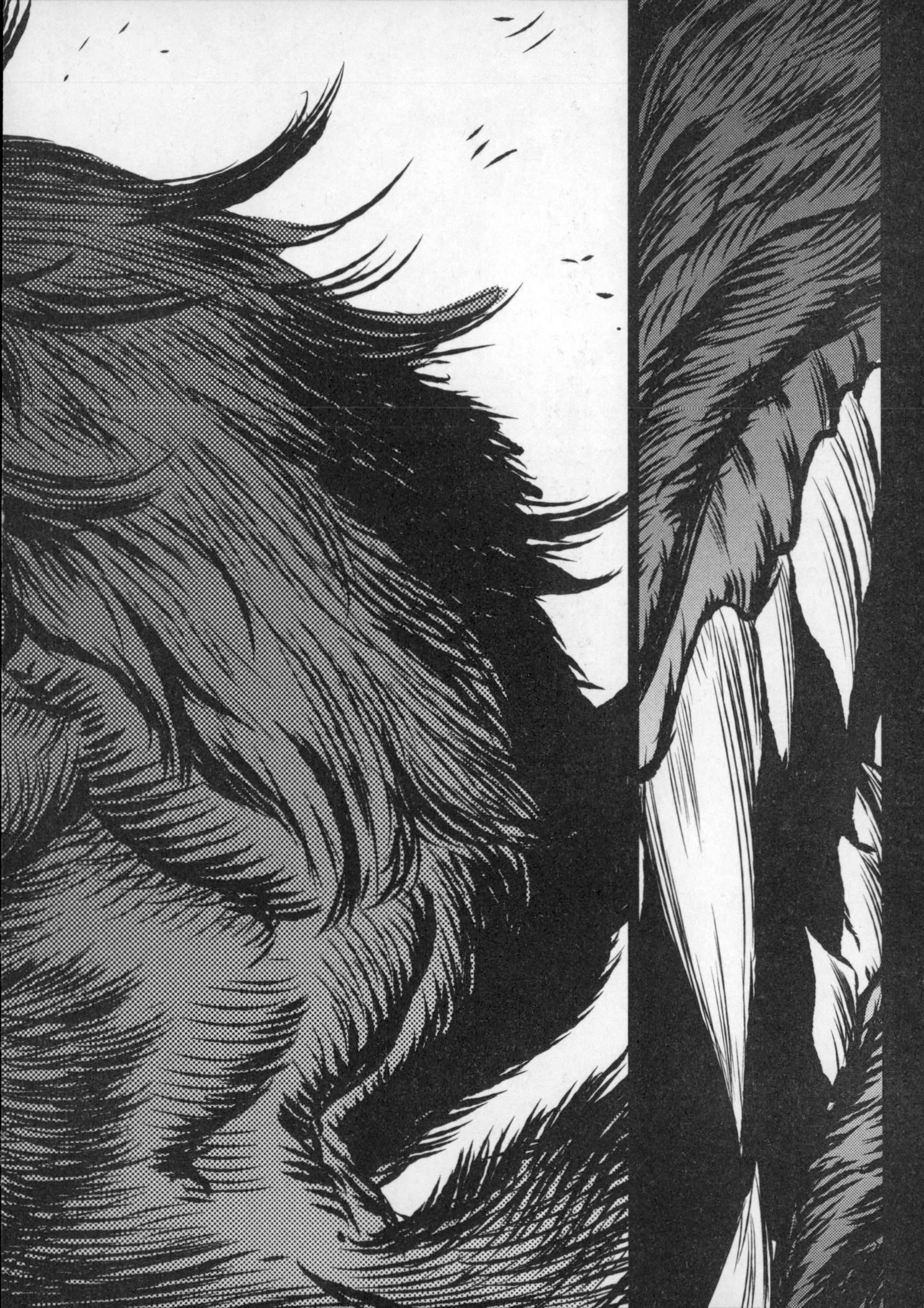

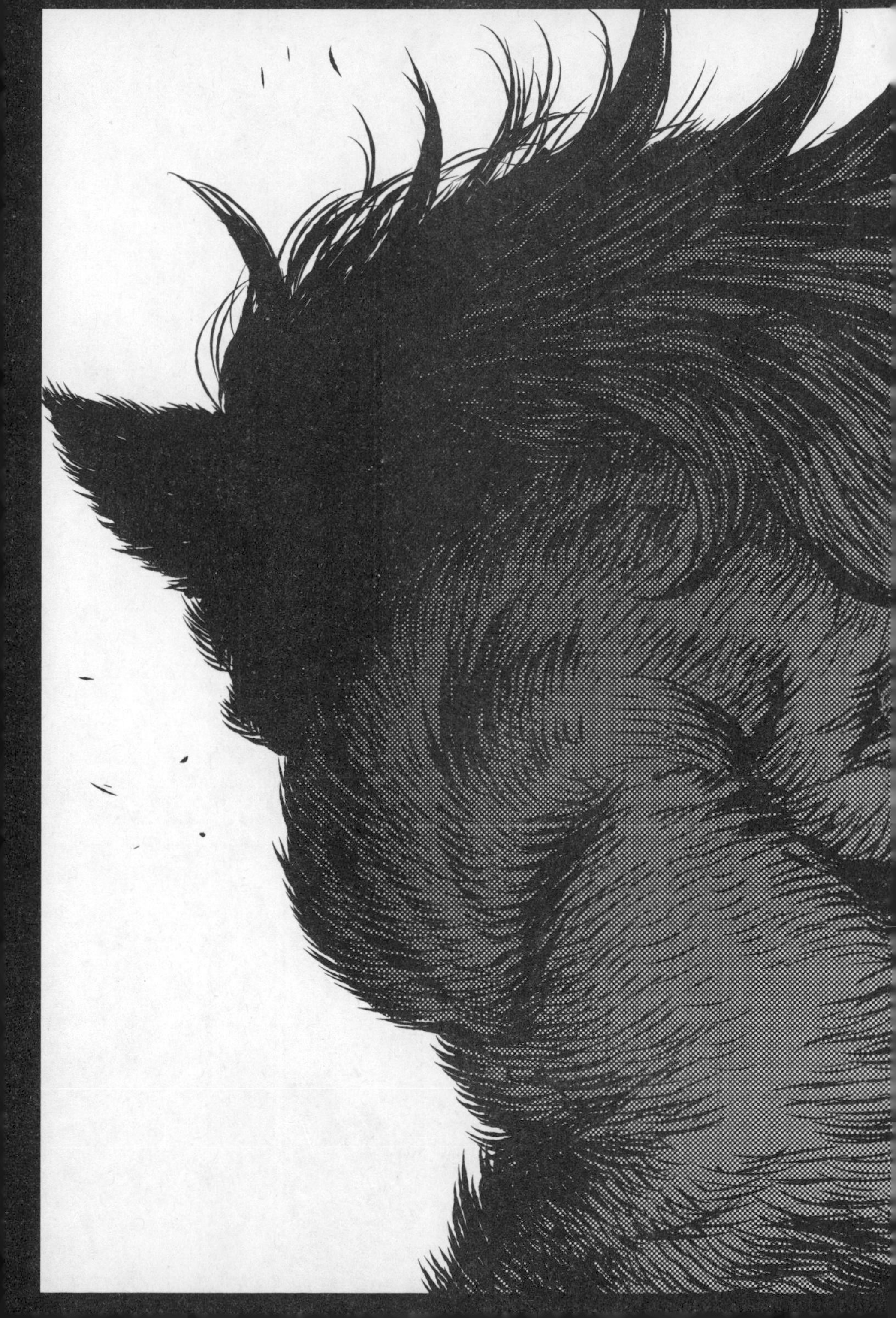

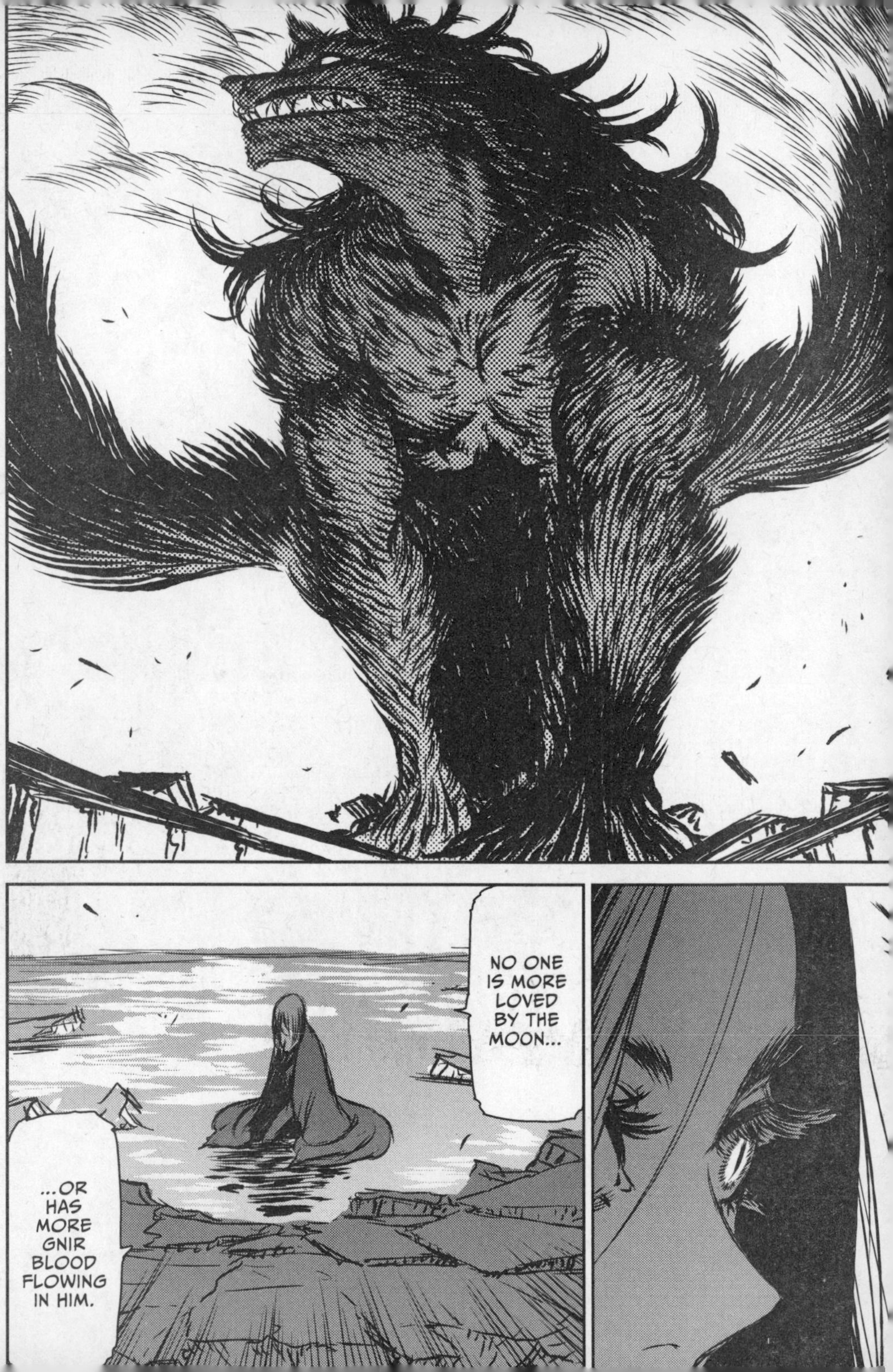
NO ONE IS MORE LOVED BY THE MOON...
...OR HAS MORE GNIR BLOOD FLOWING IN HIM.

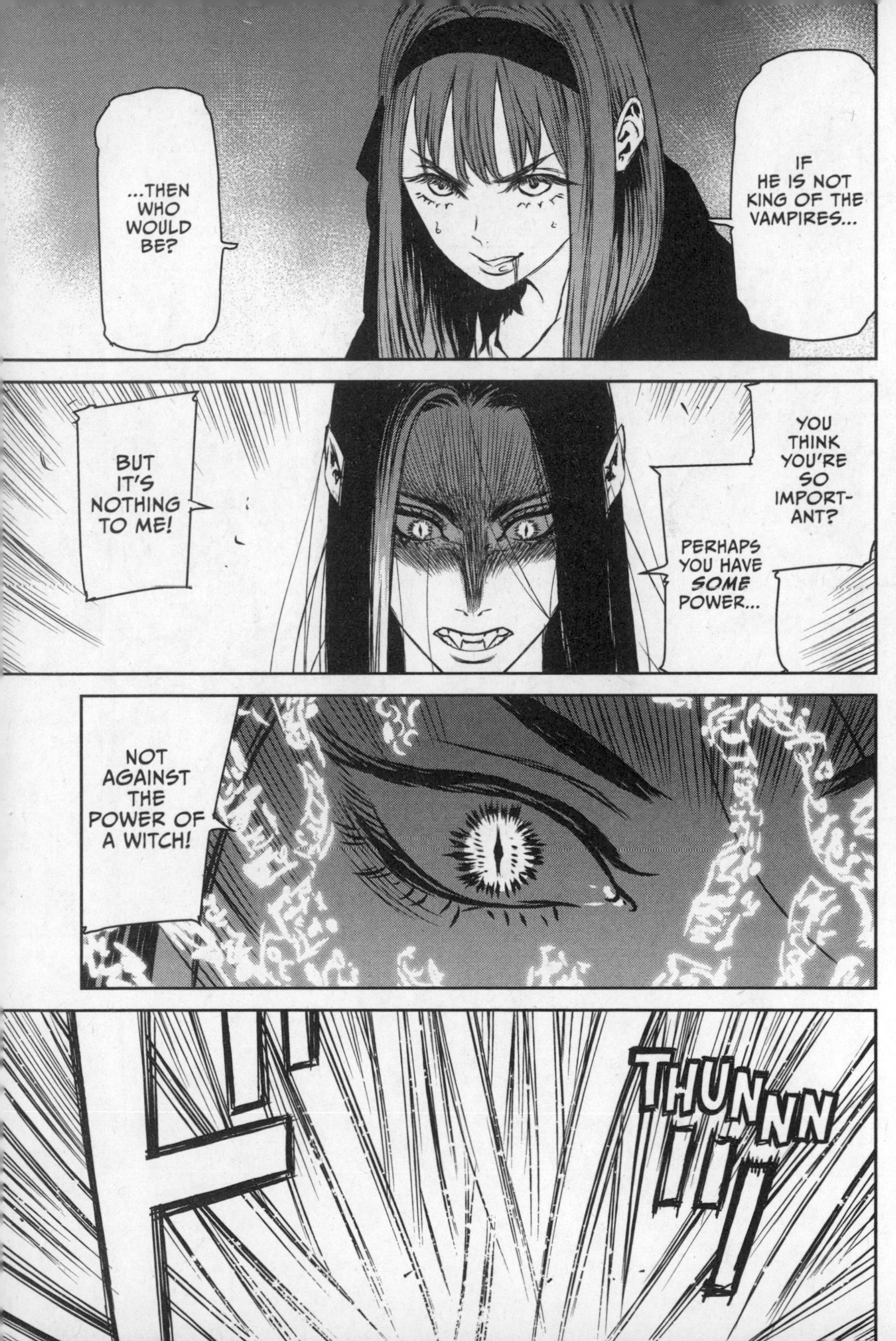
IF HE IS NOT KING OF THE VAMPIRES...
...THEN WHO WOULD BE?
YOU THINK YOU'RE SO IMPORTANT?
PERHAPS YOU HAVE *SOME* POWER...
BUT IT'S NOTHING TO ME!
NOT AGAINST THE POWER OF A WITCH!
THUNNNN

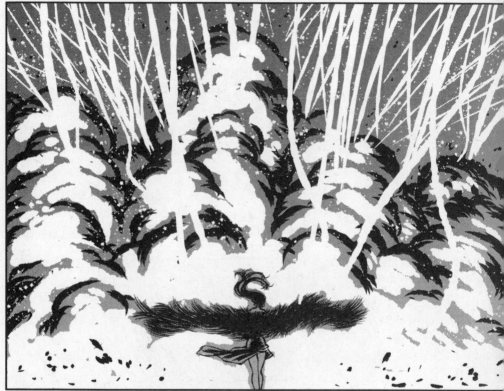

PERHAPS EVEN THIS FORM...

...WILL NOT BE ENOUGH TO DEFEAT A WITCH.

YES...

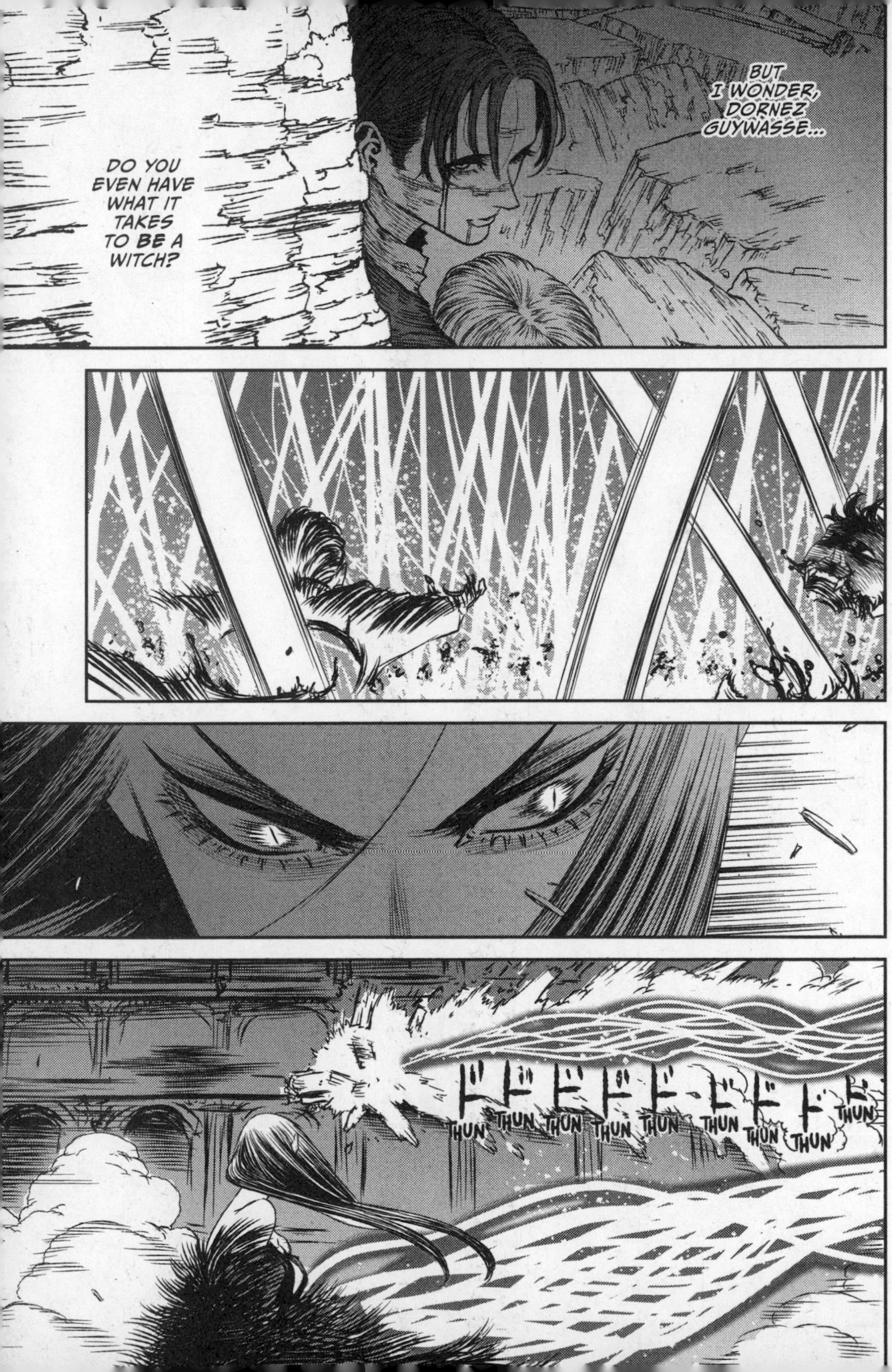
BUT I WONDER, DORNEZ GUYWASSE...
DO YOU EVEN HAVE WHAT IT TAKES TO BE A WITCH?
THUN THUN THUN THUN THUN THUN THUN THUN THUN

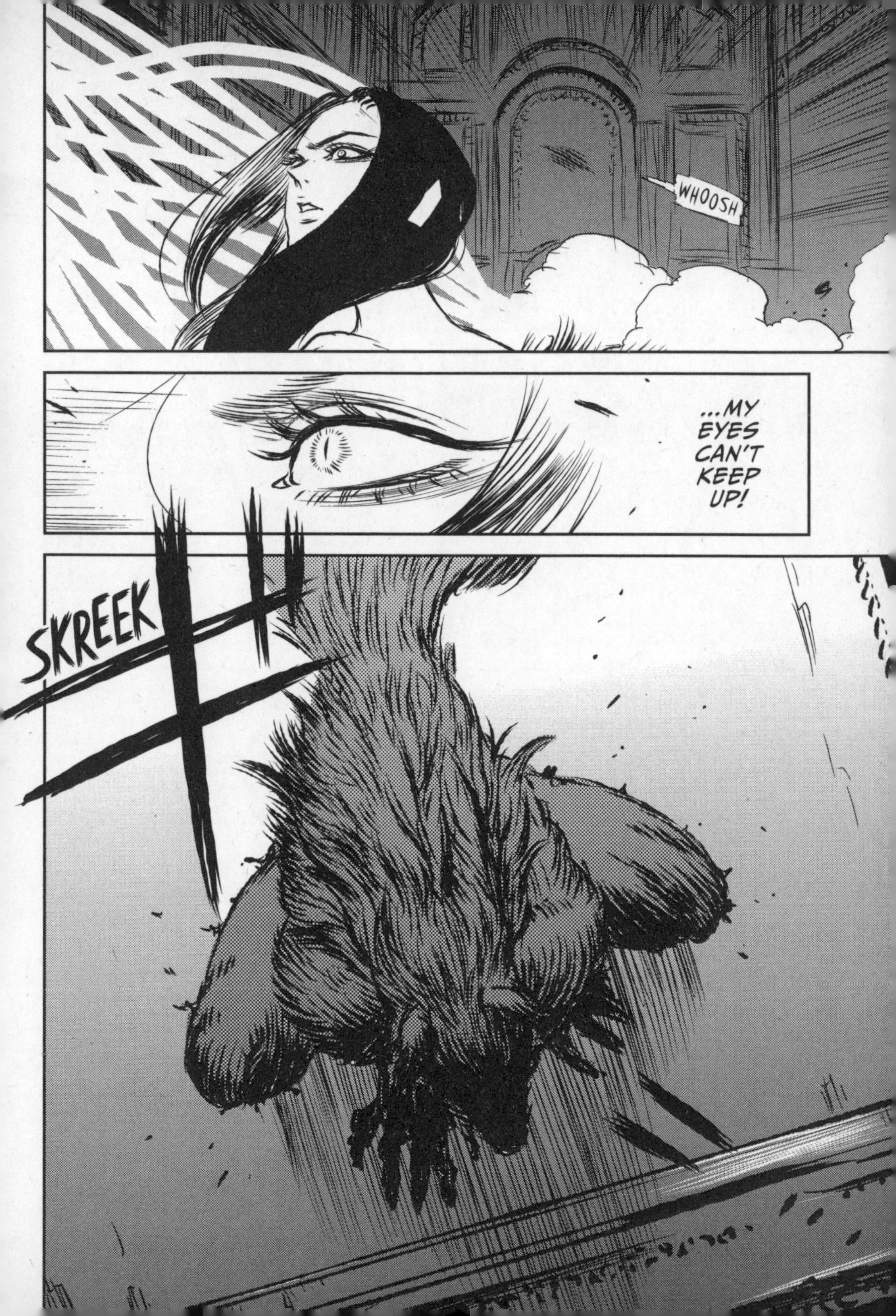
WHOOSH
...MY EYES CAN'T KEEP UP!
SKREEK

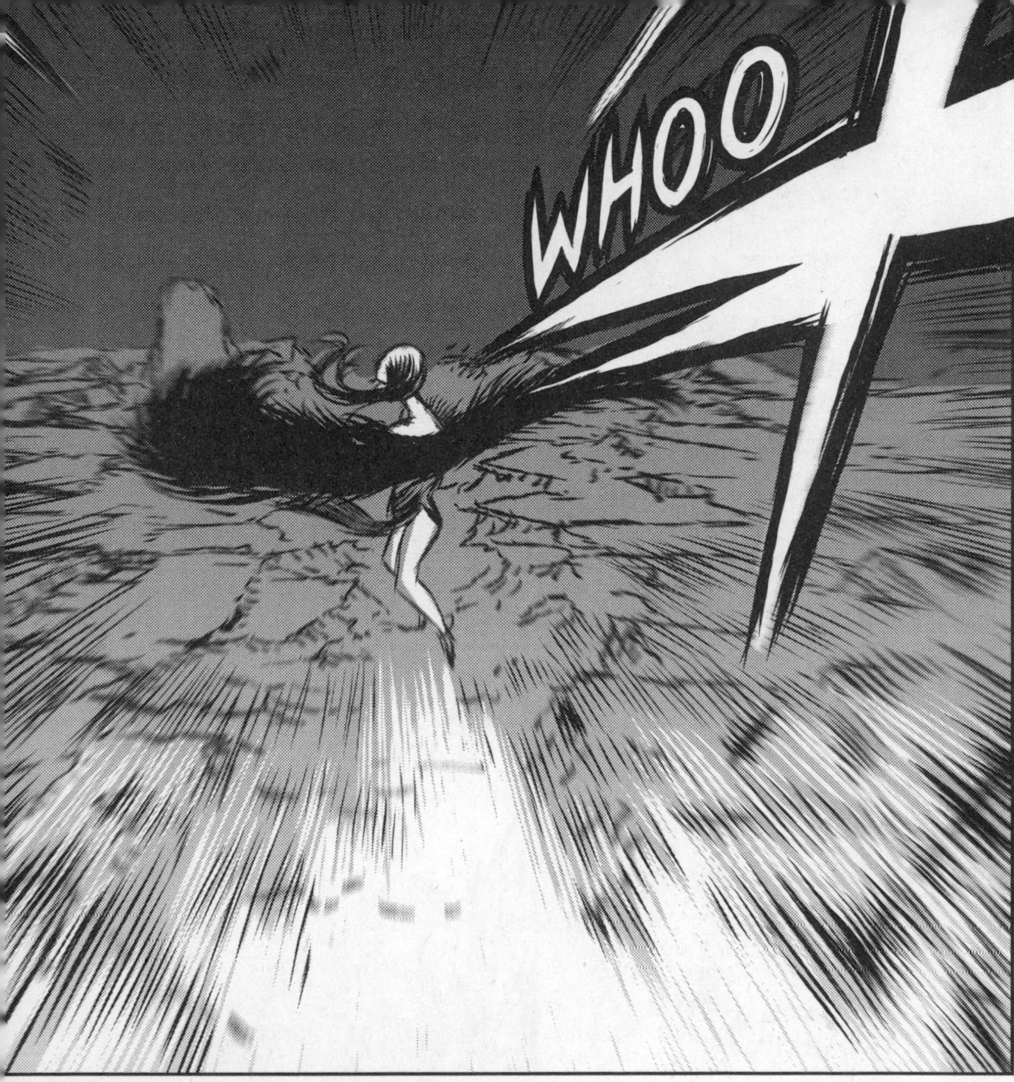
WHOO
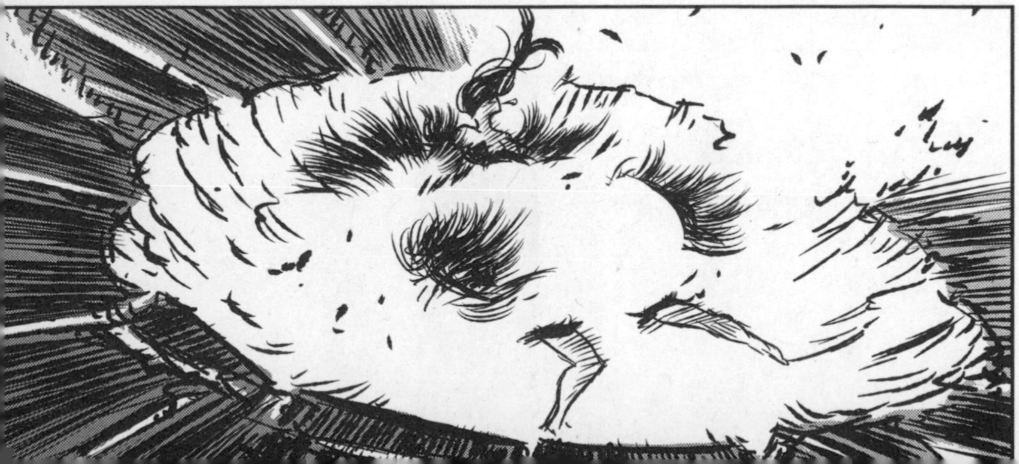

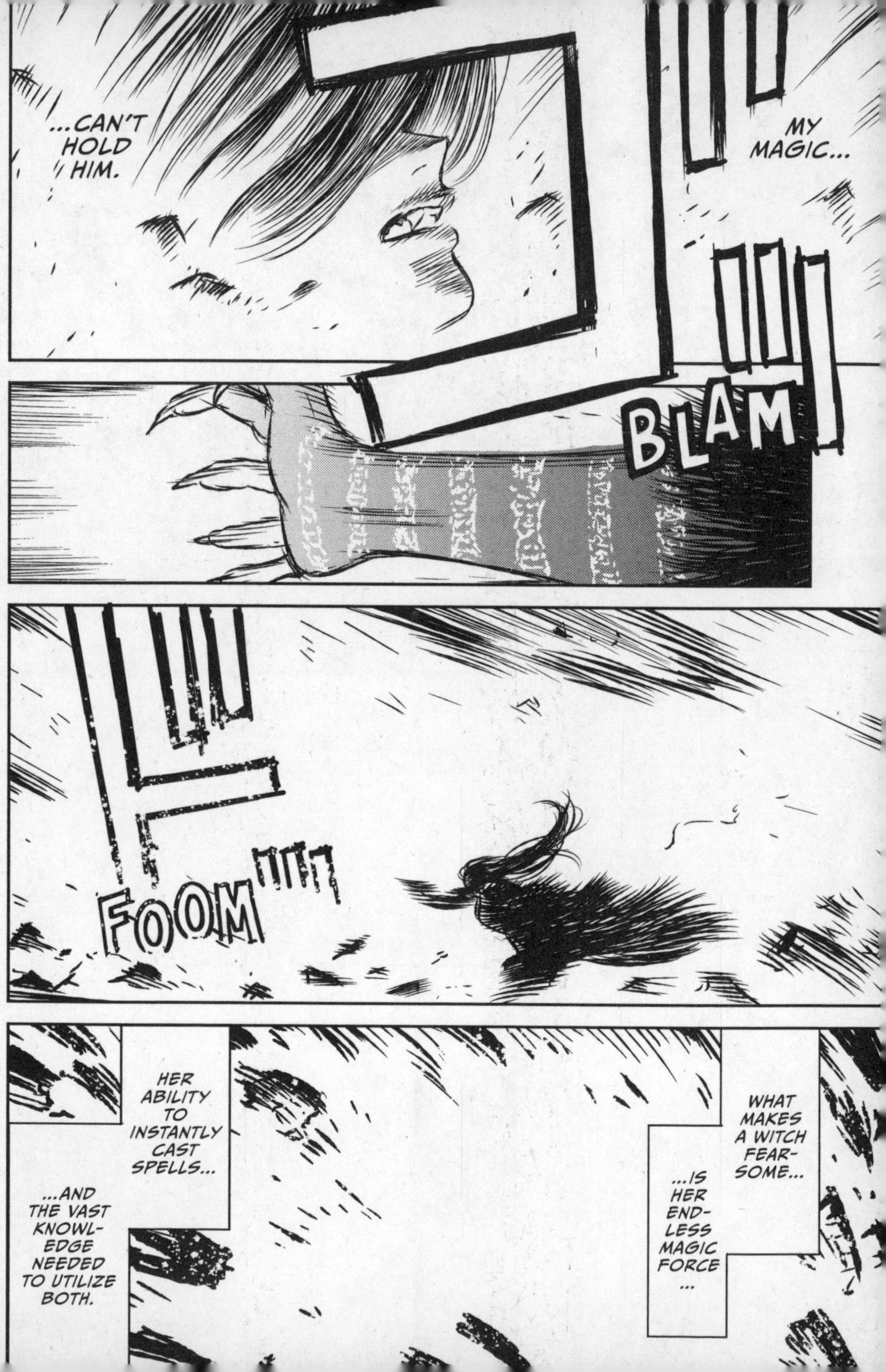
MY MAGIC...
...CAN'T HOLD HIM.
BLAM
FOOM
WHAT MAKES A WITCH FEARSOME...
...IS HER ENDLESS MAGIC FORCE...
HER ABILITY TO INSTANTLY CAST SPELLS...
...AND THE VAST KNOWLEDGE NEEDED TO UTILIZE BOTH.

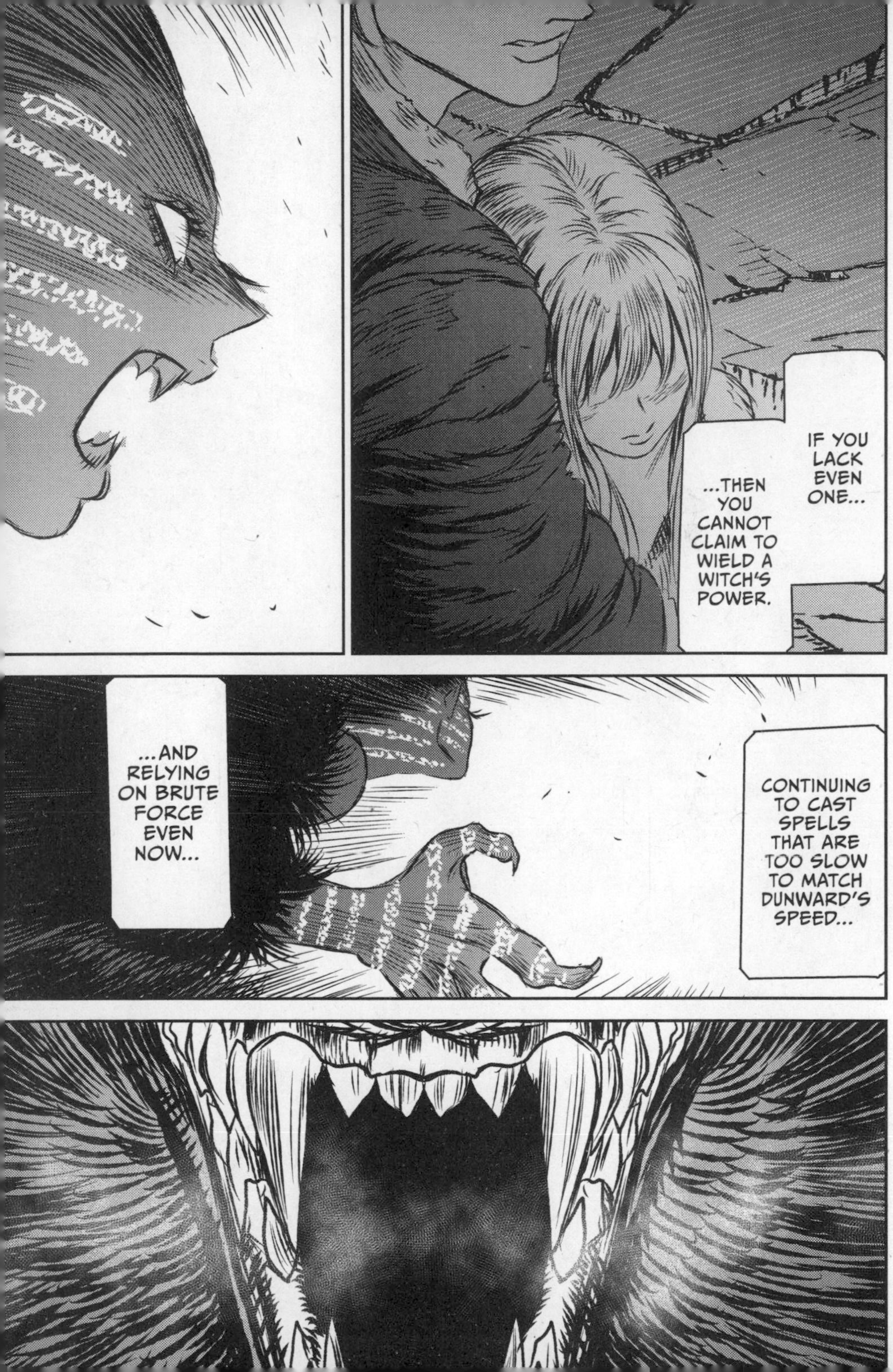
IF YOU LACK EVEN ONE...
...THEN YOU CANNOT CLAIM TO WIELD A WITCH'S POWER.
CONTINUING TO CAST SPELLS THAT ARE TOO SLOW TO MATCH DUNWARD'S SPEED...
...AND RELYING ON BRUTE FORCE EVEN NOW...

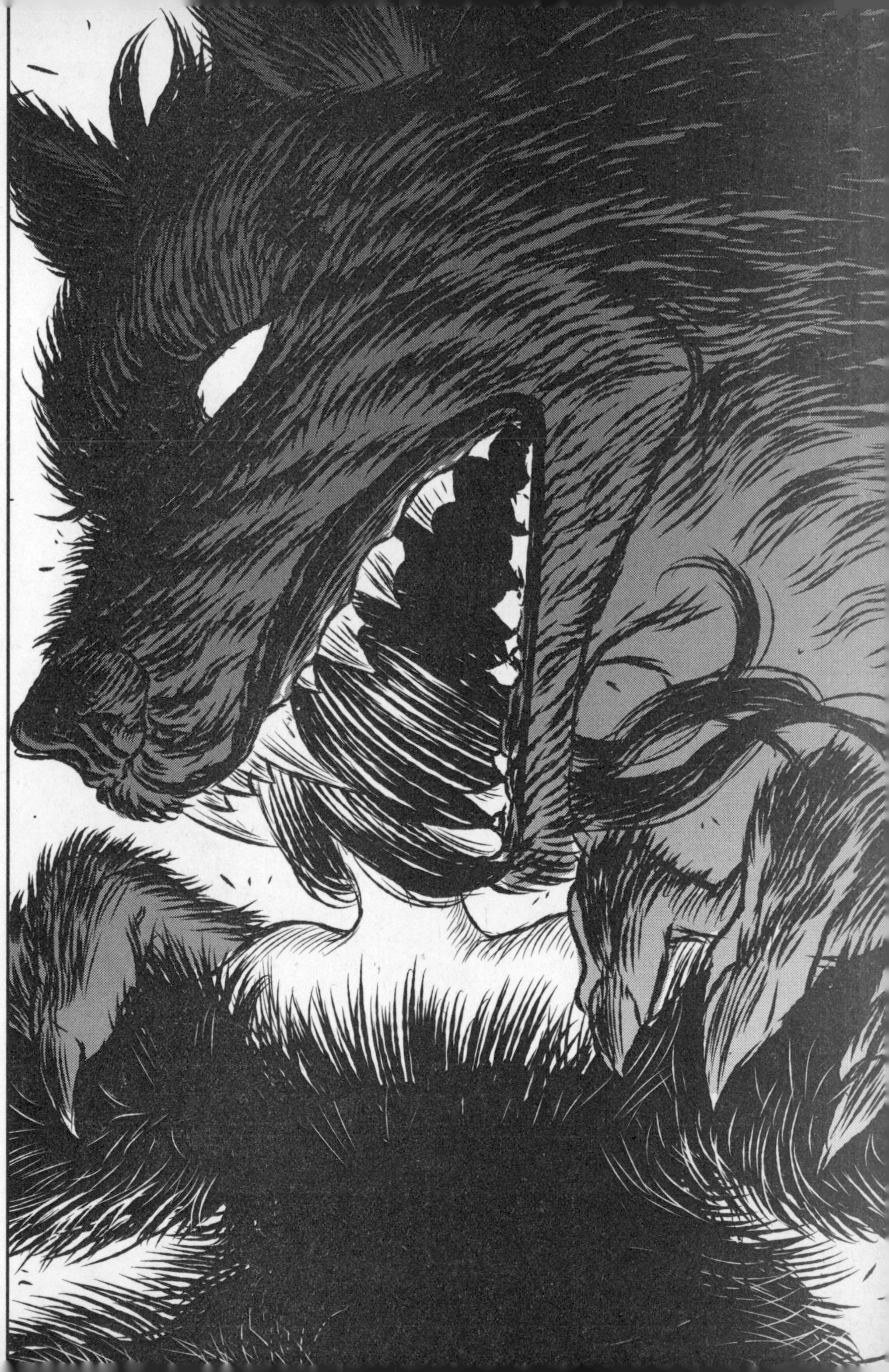

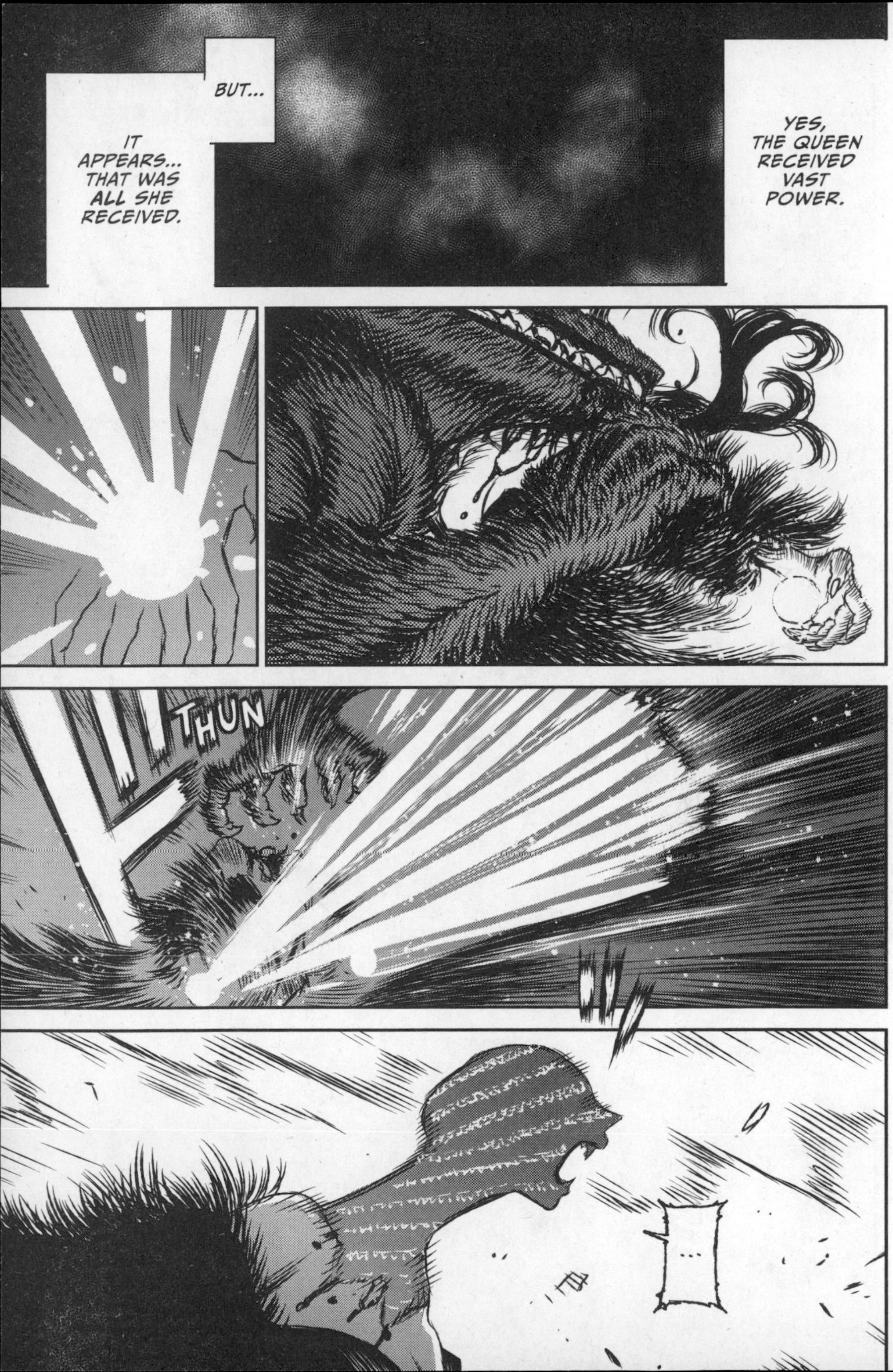
YES, THE QUEEN RECEIVED VAST POWER.
BUT...
IT APPEARS... THAT WAS ALL SHE RECEIVED.
THUN
...

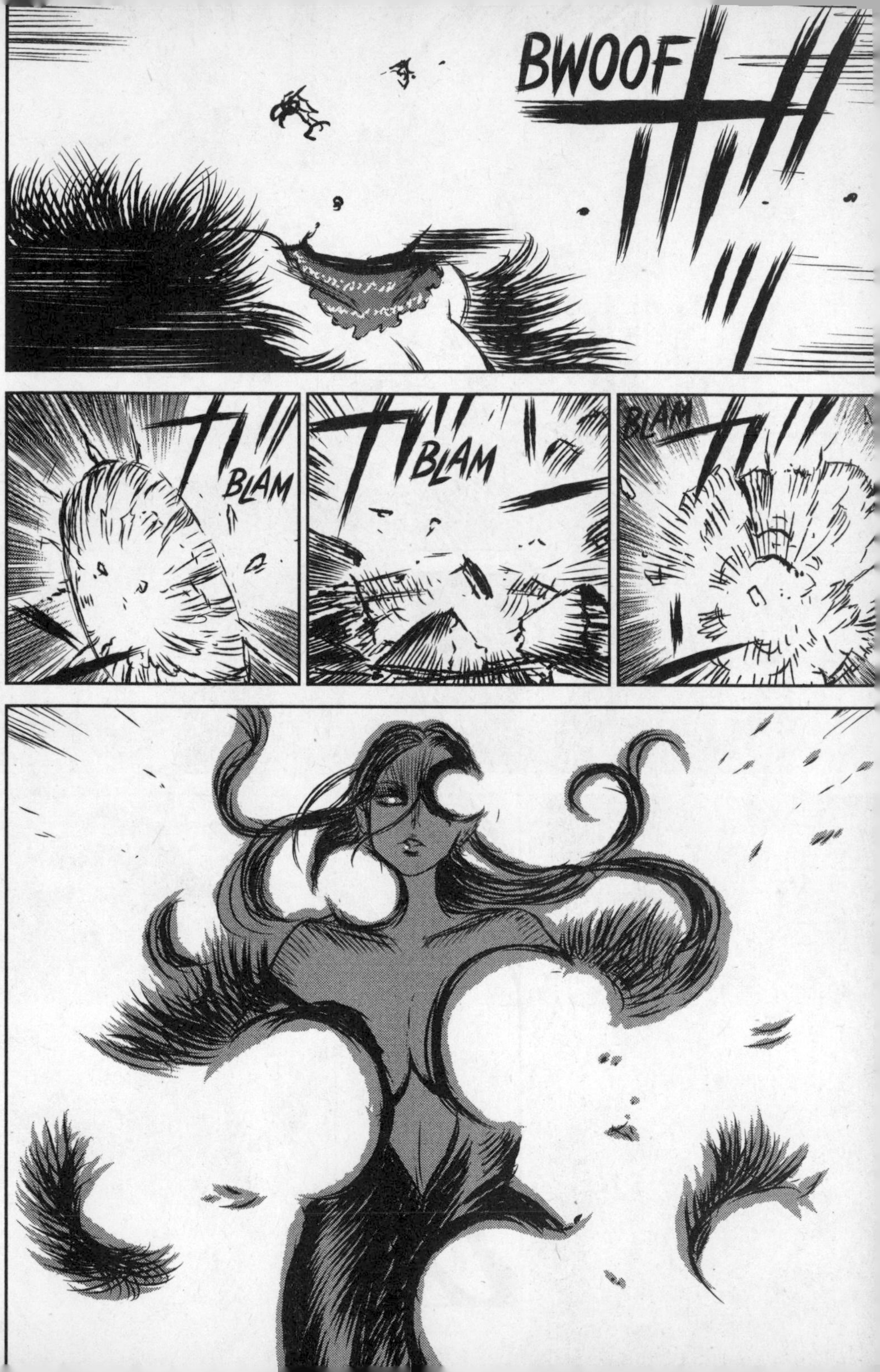
BWOOF
BLAM
BLAM
BLAM

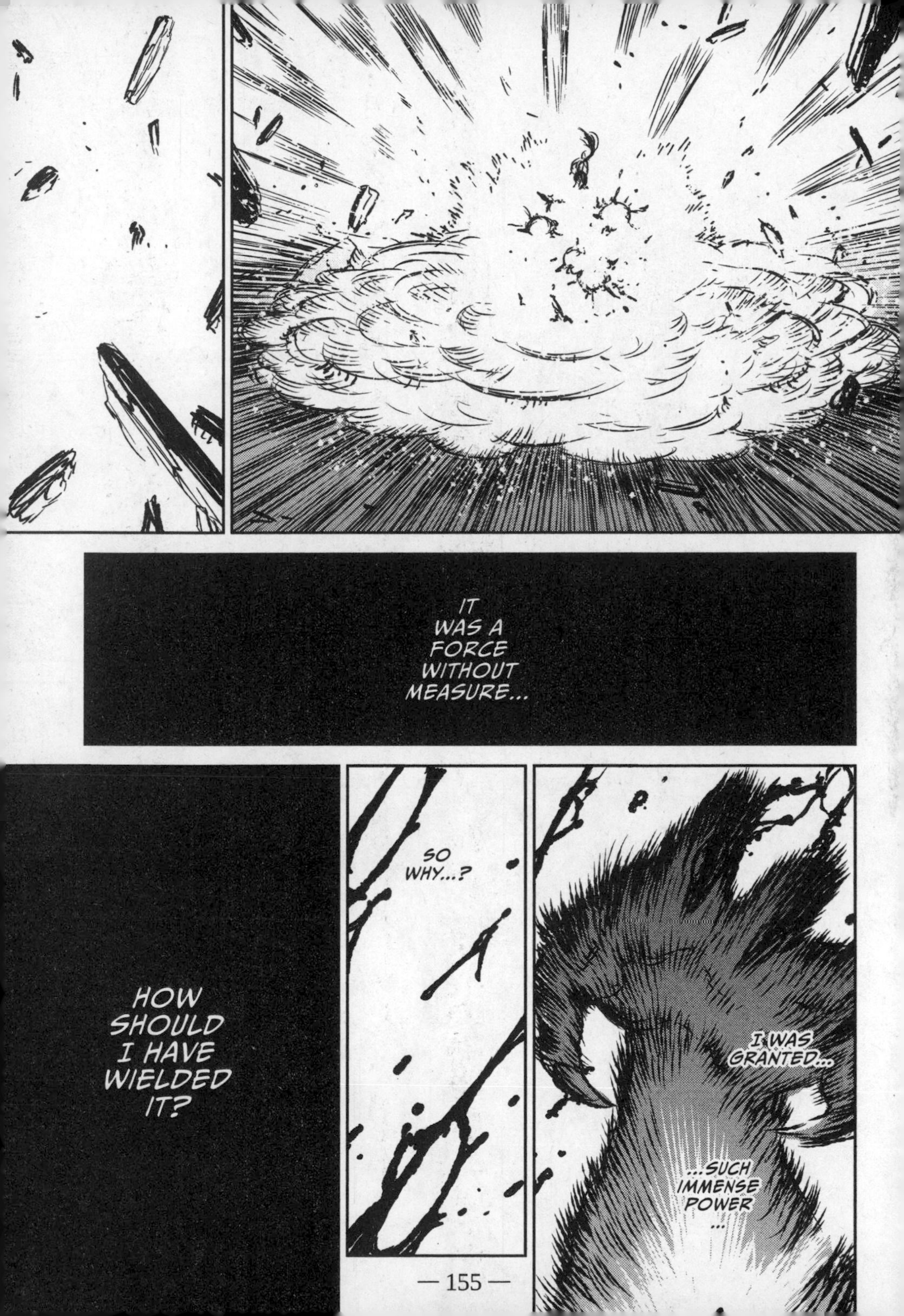
IT WAS A FORCE WITHOUT MEASURE...
I WAS GRANTED...
...SUCH IMMENSE POWER ...
SO WHY...?
HOW SHOULD I HAVE WIELDED IT?

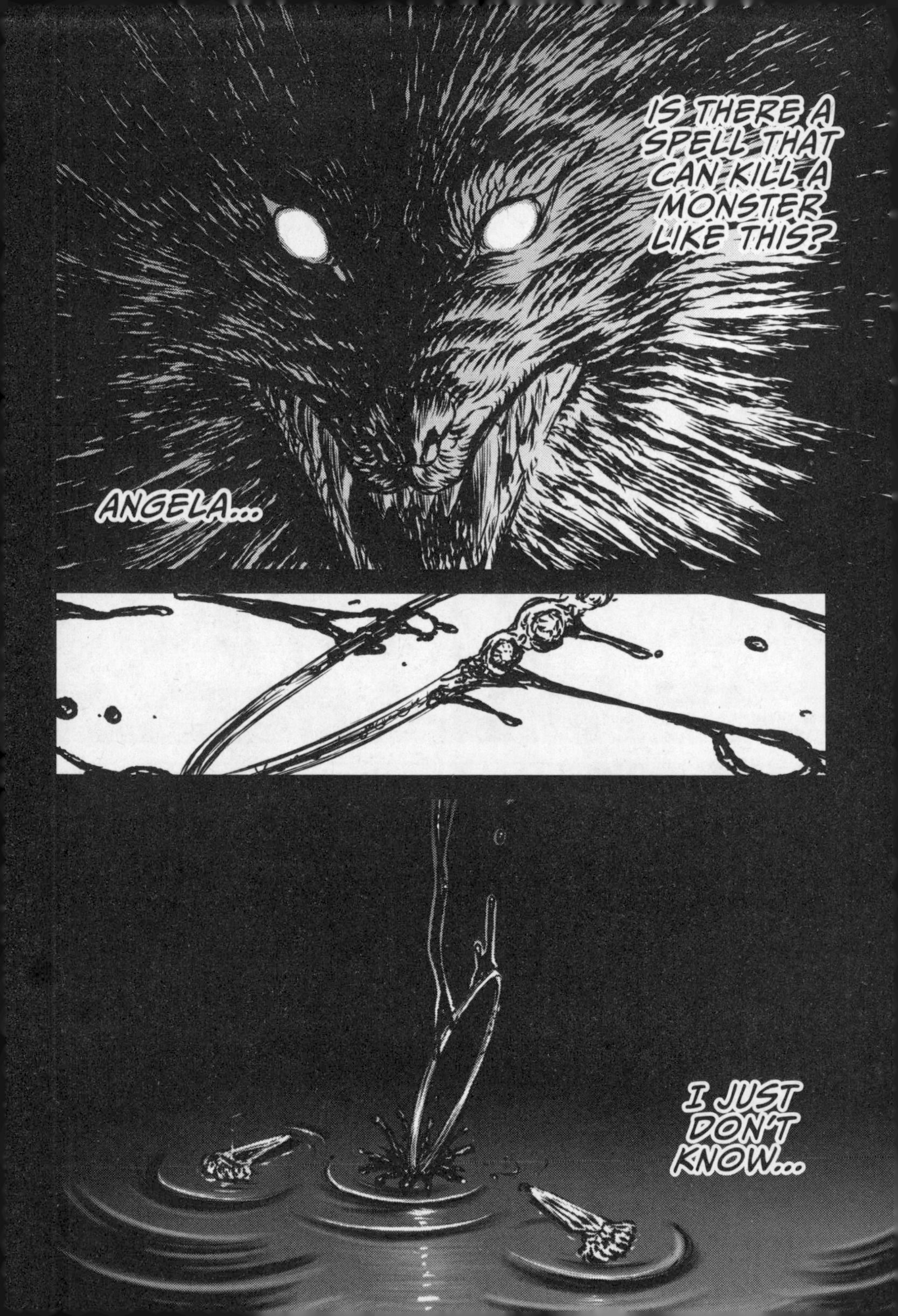
IS THERE A SPELL THAT CAN KILL A MONSTER LIKE THIS?
ANGELA...
I JUST DON'T KNOW...

THE WITCH AND THE BEAST

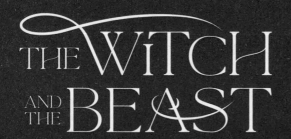

THE WITCH AND THE BEAST

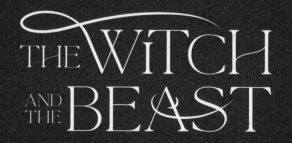

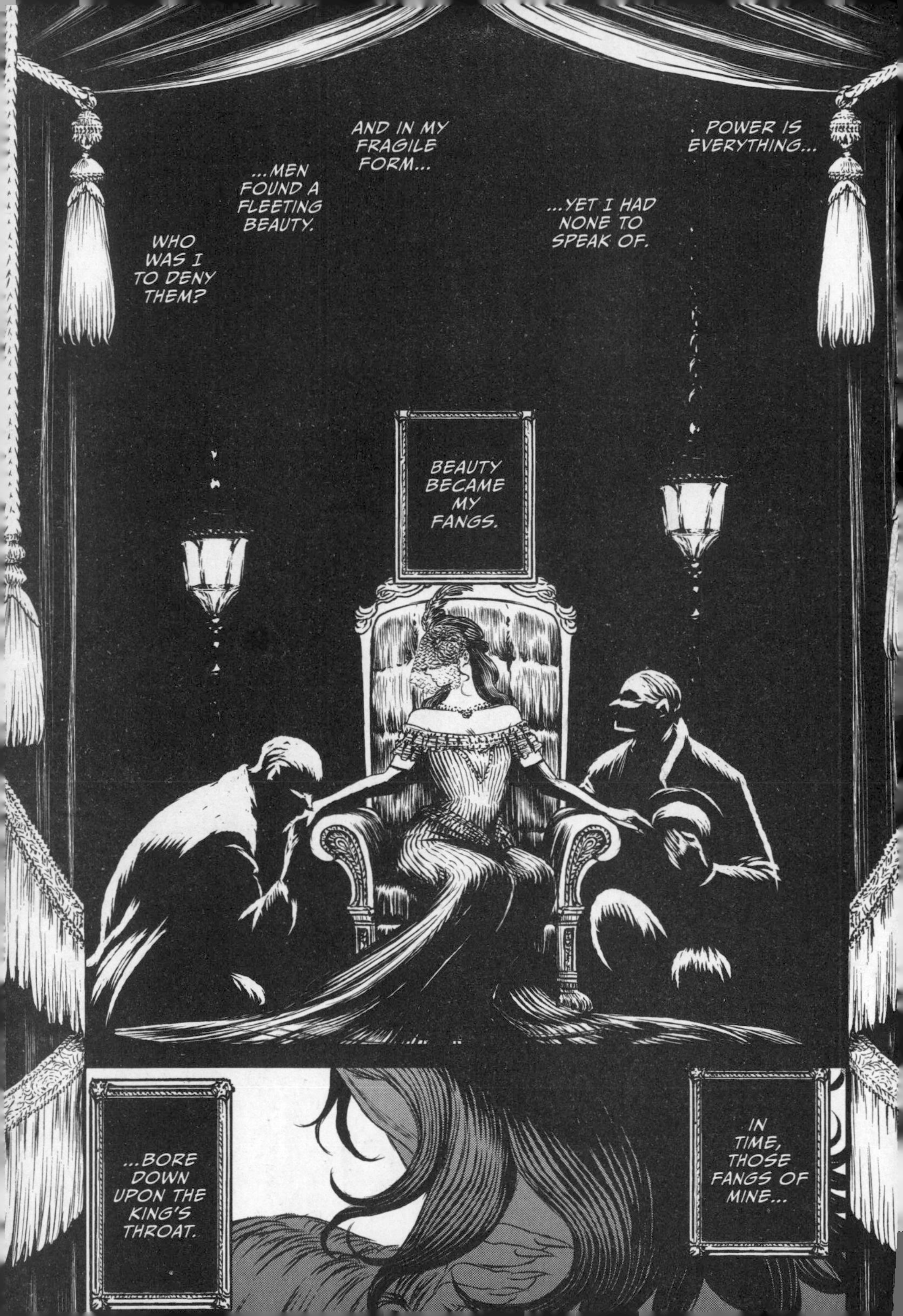
. POWER IS EVERYTHING...
...YET I HAD NONE TO SPEAK OF.
AND IN MY FRAGILE FORM...
...MEN FOUND A FLEETING BEAUTY.
WHO WAS I TO DENY THEM?
BEAUTY BECAME MY FANGS.
IN TIME, THOSE FANGS OF MINE...
...BORE DOWN UPON THE KING'S THROAT.

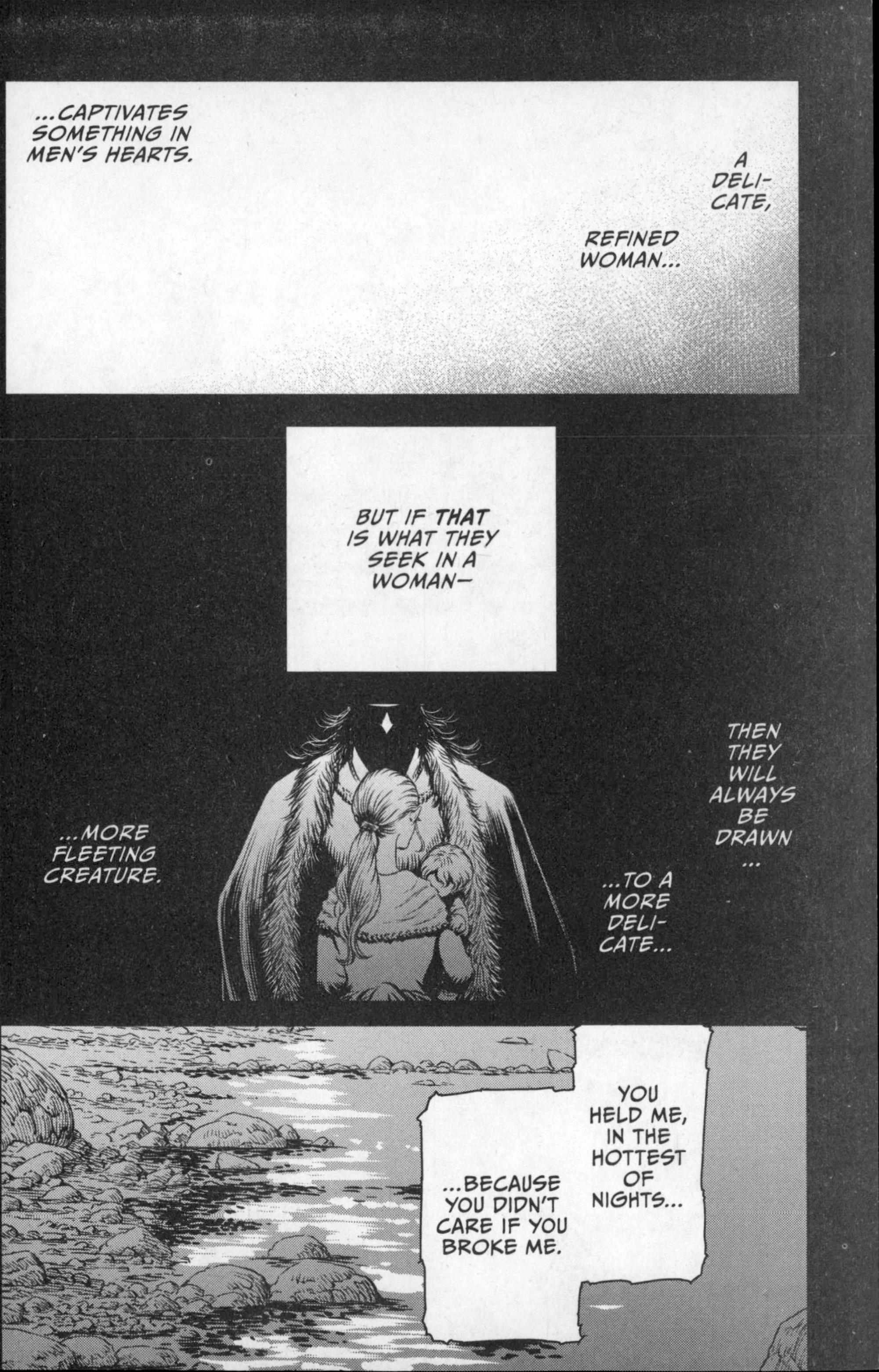
A DELI-CATE,
REFINED WOMAN...
...CAPTIVATES SOMETHING IN MEN'S HEARTS.
BUT IF THAT IS WHAT THEY SEEK IN A WOMAN—
THEN THEY WILL ALWAYS BE DRAWN ...
...TO A MORE DELI-CATE...
...MORE FLEETING CREATURE.
YOU HELD ME, IN THE HOTTEST OF NIGHTS...
...BECAUSE YOU DIDN'T CARE IF YOU BROKE ME.

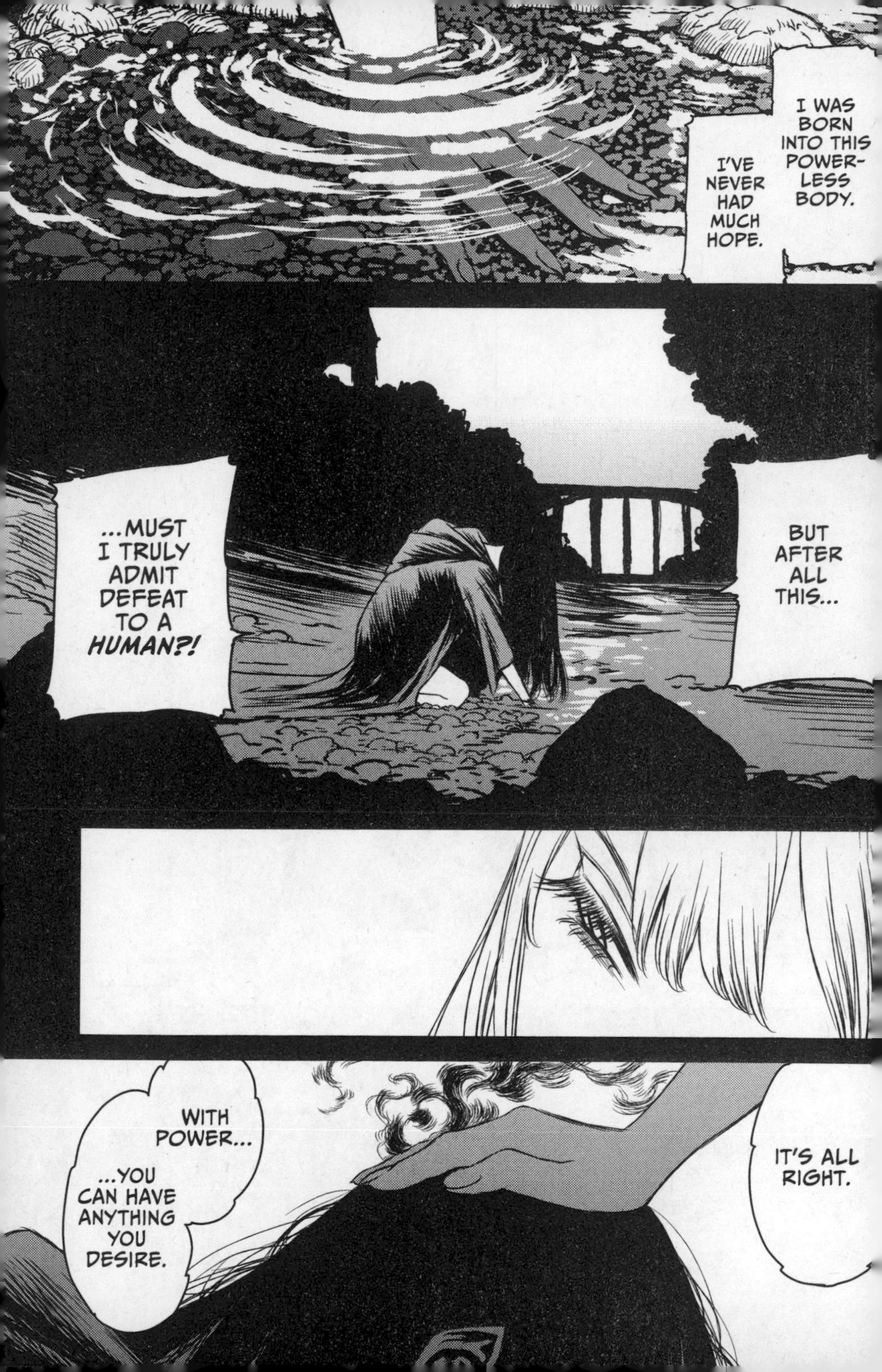
I WAS BORN INTO THIS POWERLESS BODY.
I'VE NEVER HAD MUCH HOPE.
BUT AFTER ALL THIS...
...MUST I TRULY ADMIT DEFEAT TO A *HUMAN?!*
IT'S ALL RIGHT.
WITH POWER...
...YOU CAN HAVE ANYTHING YOU DESIRE.

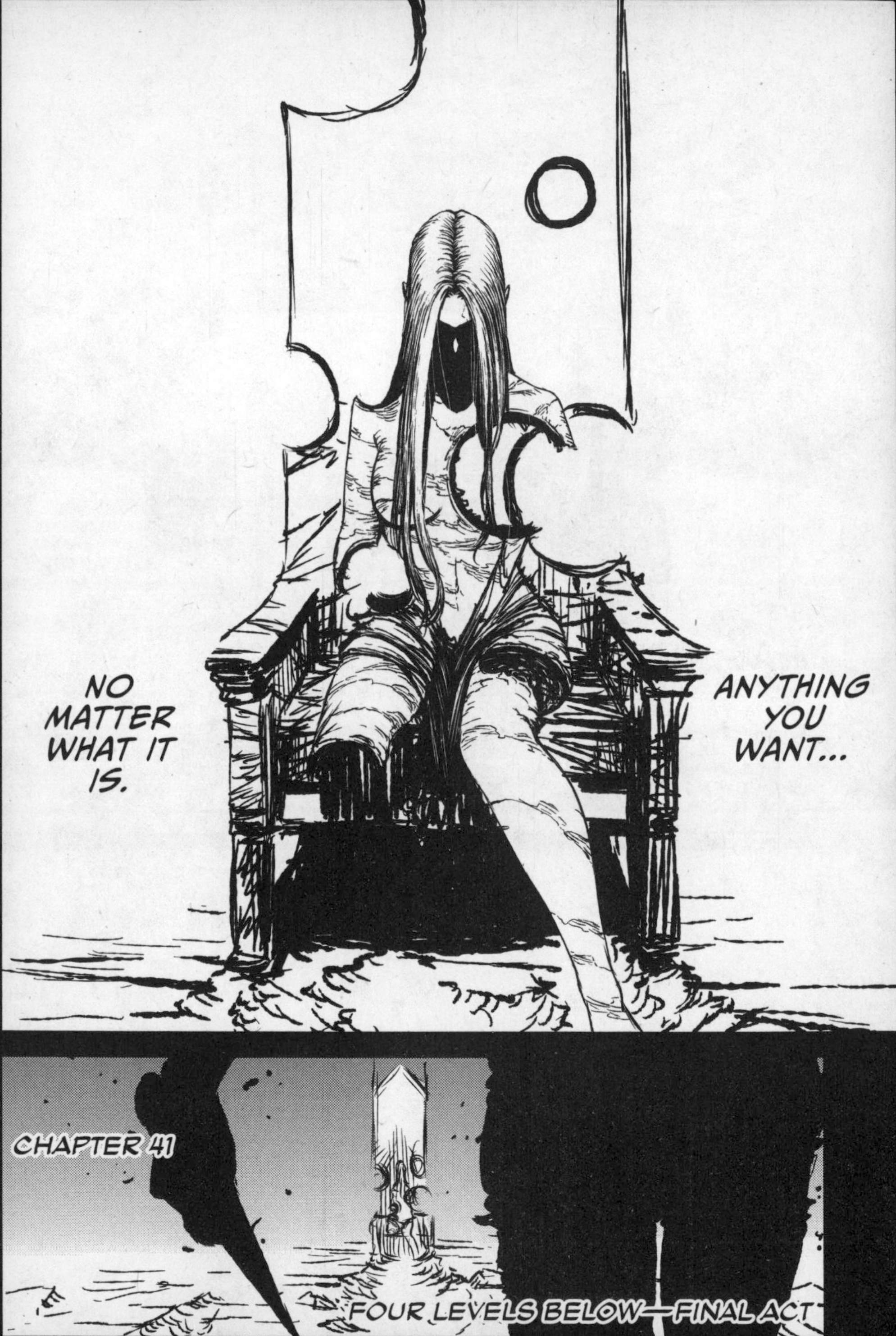
ANYTHING YOU WANT...
NO MATTER WHAT IT IS.
CHAPTER 41
FOUR LEVELS BELOW—FINAL ACT

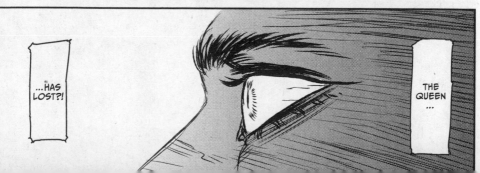

...HAS LOST?!

THE QUEEN ...

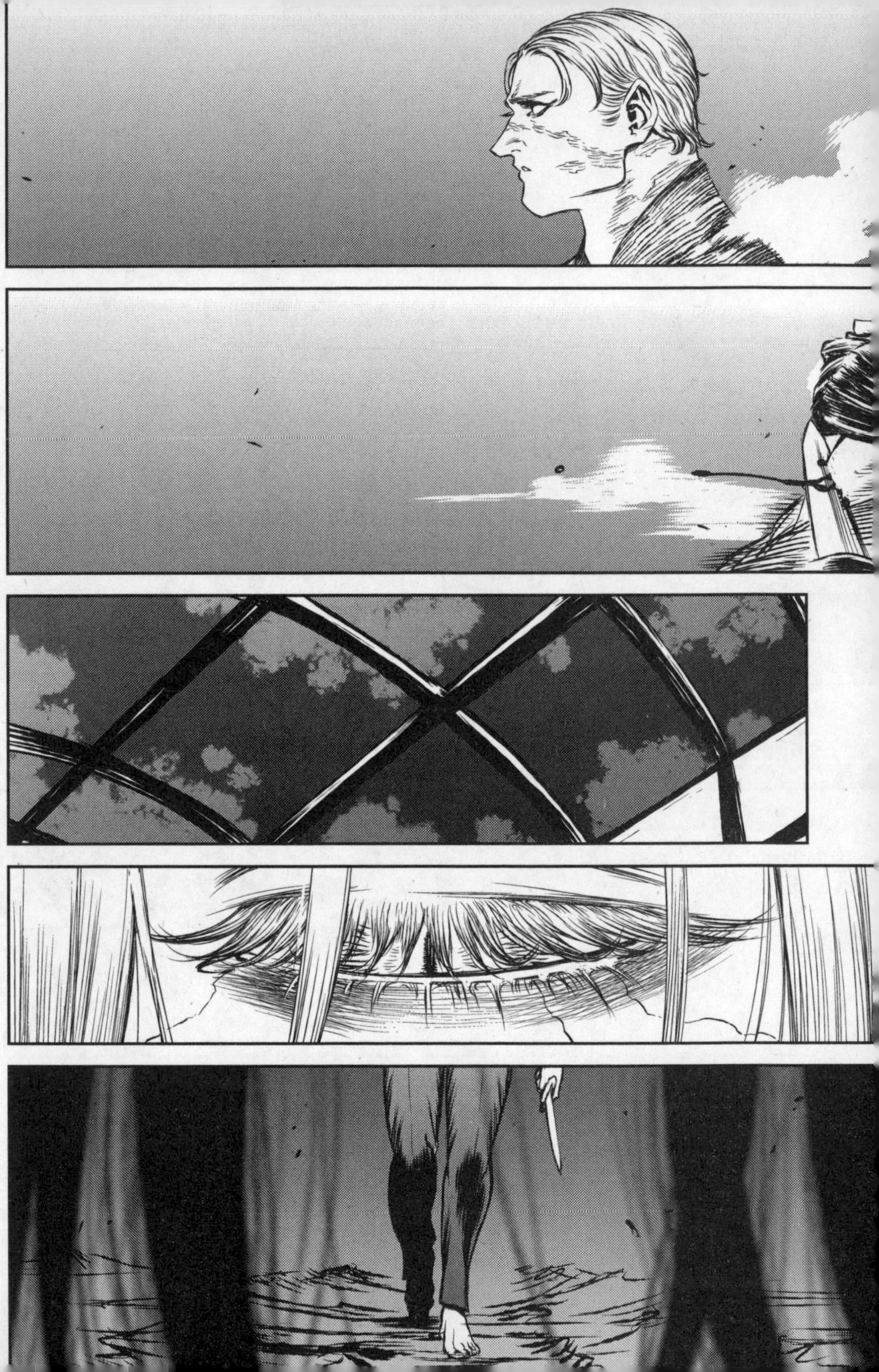

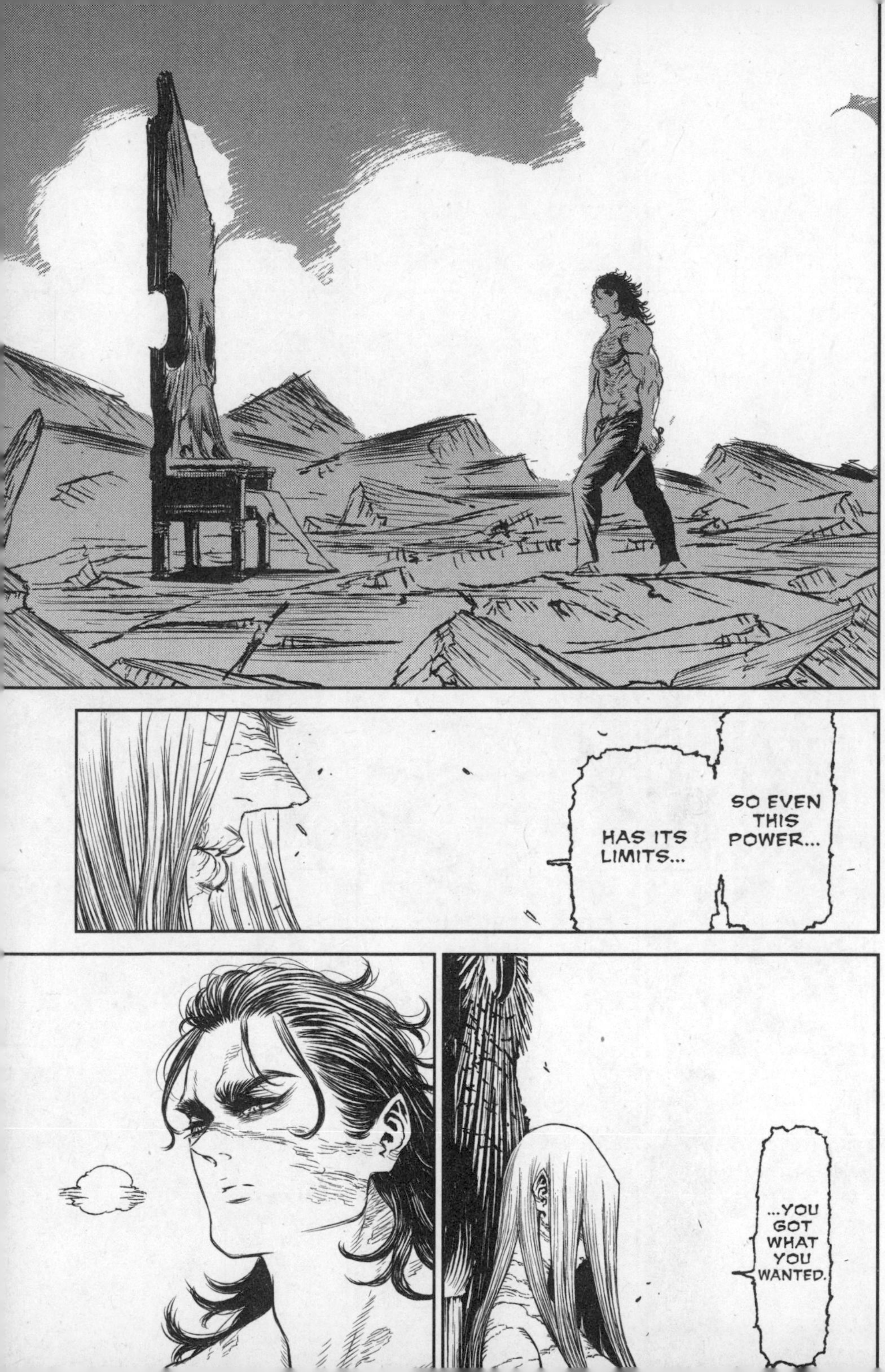
SO EVEN THIS POWER...
HAS ITS LIMITS...
...YOU GOT WHAT YOU WANTED.

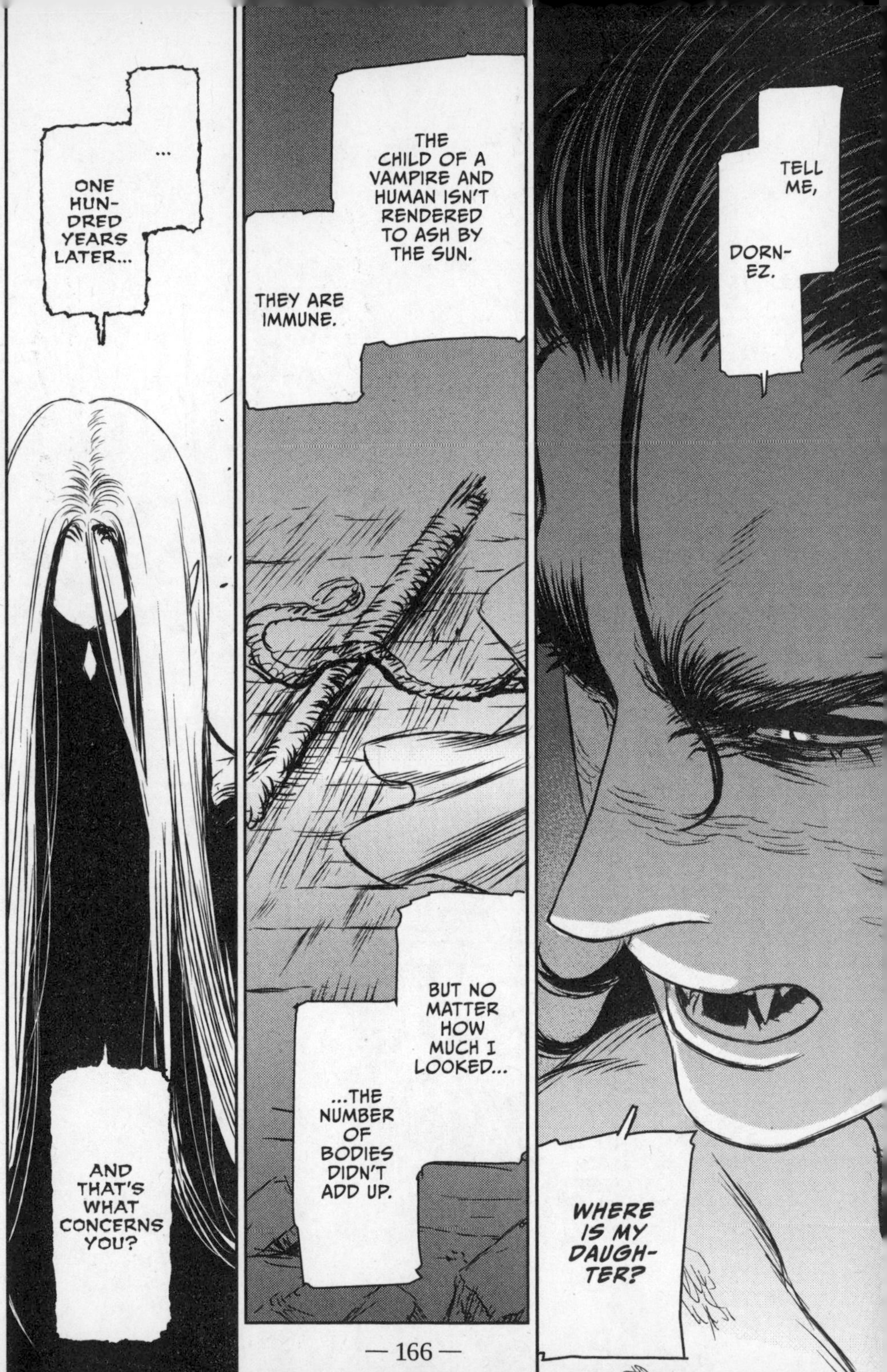
TELL ME, DORNEZ.
WHERE IS MY DAUGHTER?
THE CHILD OF A VAMPIRE AND HUMAN ISN'T RENDERED TO ASH BY THE SUN.
THEY ARE IMMUNE.
BUT NO MATTER HOW MUCH I LOOKED...
...THE NUMBER OF BODIES DIDN'T ADD UP.
... ONE HUNDRED YEARS LATER...
AND THAT'S WHAT CONCERNS YOU?

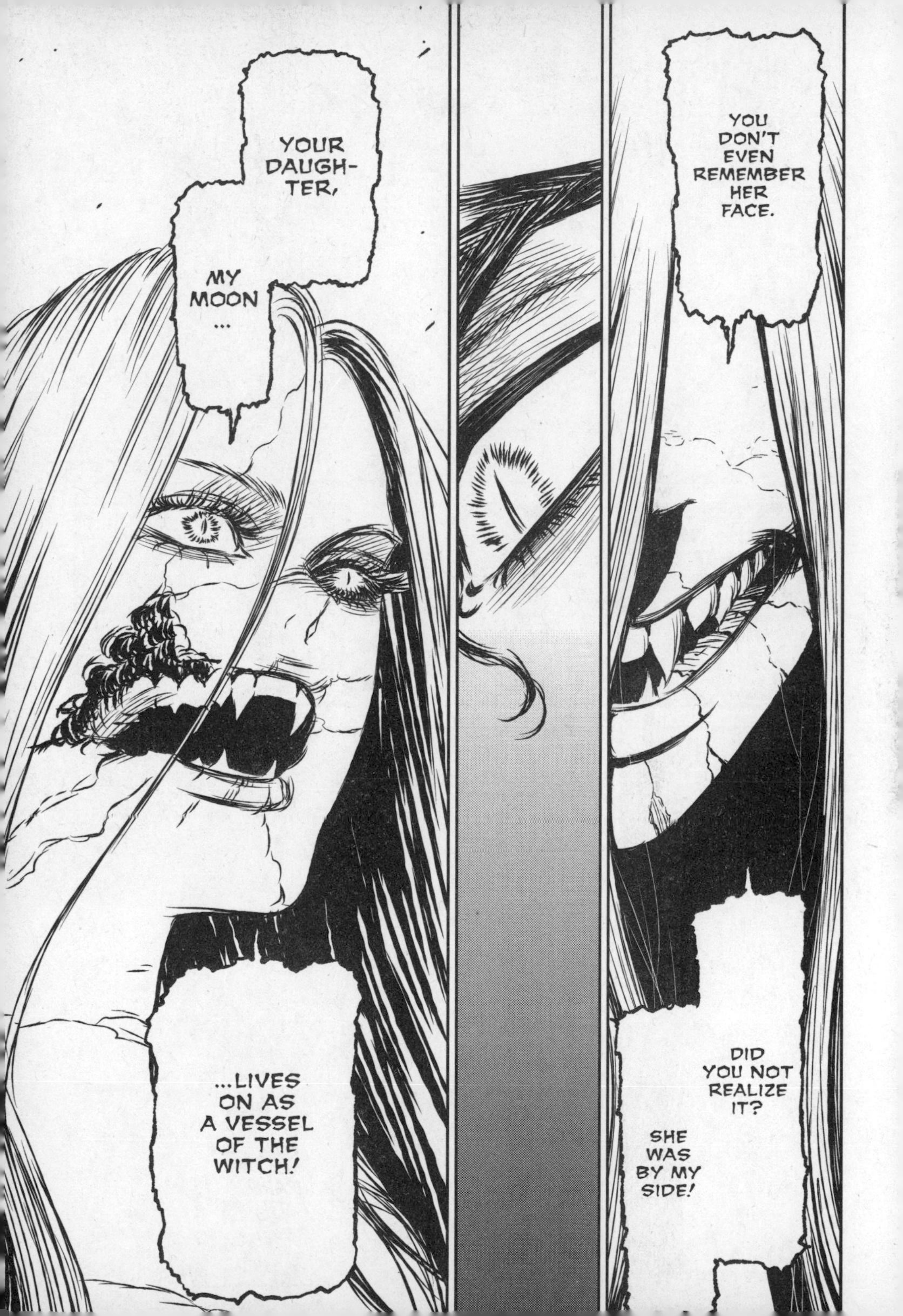
YOU DON'T EVEN REMEMBER HER FACE.
DID YOU NOT REALIZE IT?
SHE WAS BY MY SIDE!
YOUR DAUGHTER,
MY MOON ...
...LIVES ON AS A VESSEL OF THE WITCH!

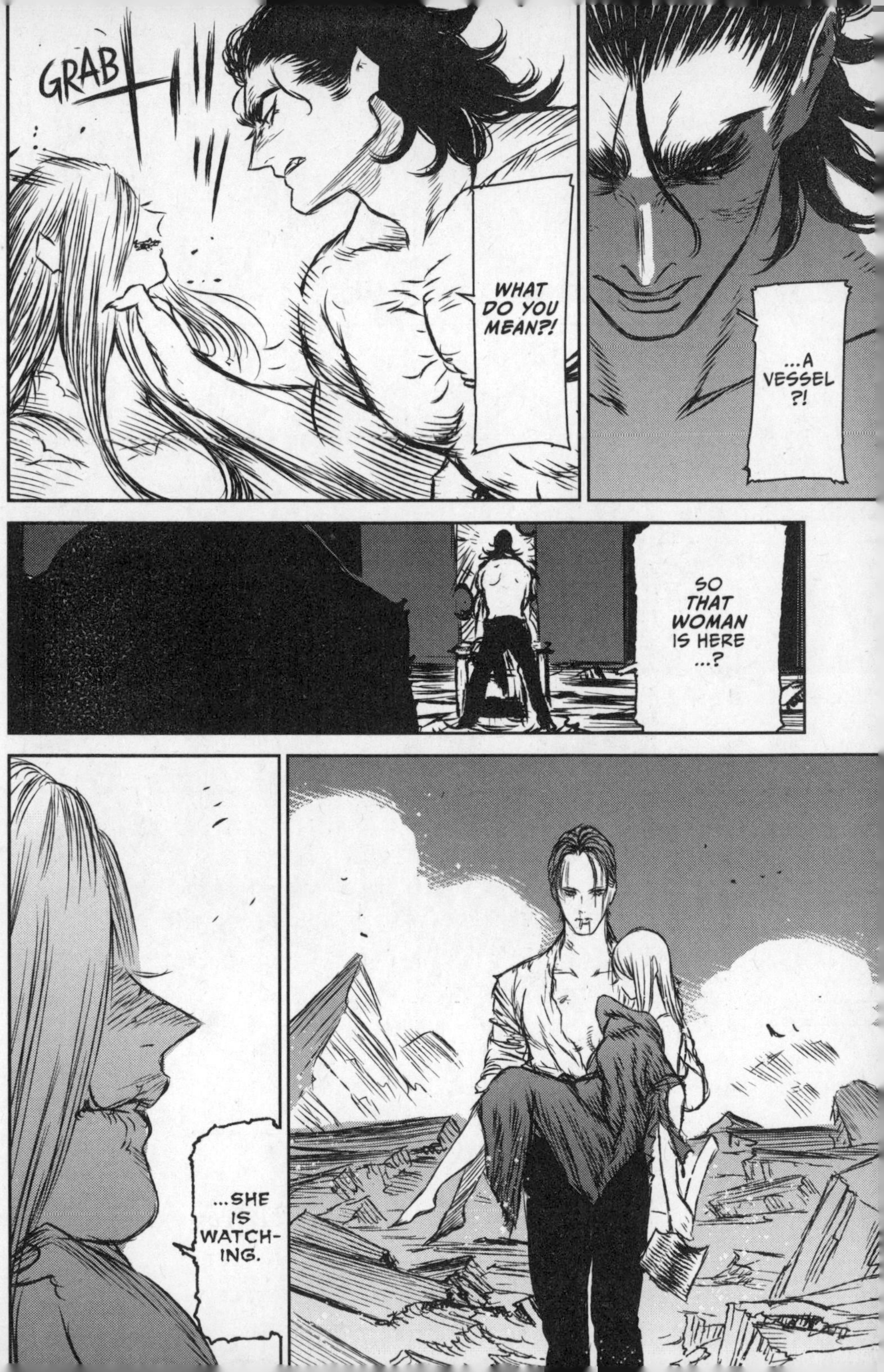
...A VESSEL ?!
GRAB
WHAT DO YOU MEAN?!
SO THAT WOMAN IS HERE ...?
...SHE IS WATCHING.

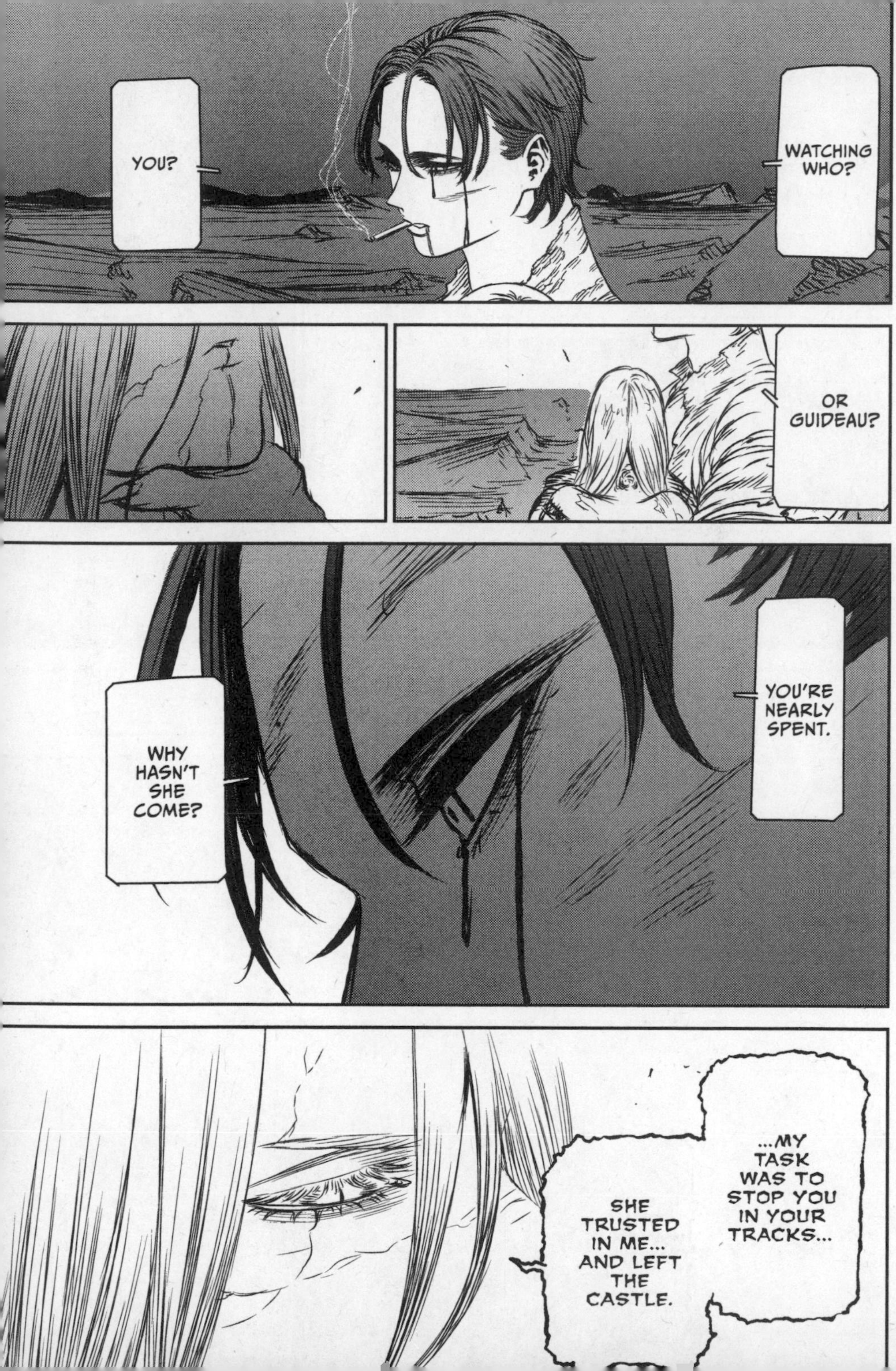
WATCHING WHO?
YOU?
OR GUIDEAU?
YOU'RE NEARLY SPENT.
WHY HASN'T SHE COME?
...MY TASK WAS TO STOP YOU IN YOUR TRACKS...
SHE TRUSTED IN ME... AND LEFT THE CASTLE.

IT'S HER *FAVOR,* ISN'T IT?

WHEN A WITCH BESTOWS HER FAVOR, SHE LOSES ACCESS TO WHATEVER GIFT SHE GIVES...

...AND SHE CAN ONLY SHARE IT ONCE IN HER LIFE.

ONE WOULD HAVE TO BE VERY IMPORTANT TO HER.

BUT YOU MUST HAVE REALIZED IT BY NOW...

ANGELA CAN SWITCH BETWEEN BODIES.

"ONCE IN A LIFETIME" DOESN'T QUITE APPLY TO HER.

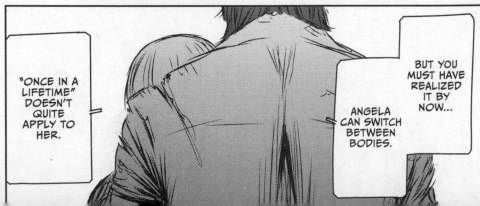

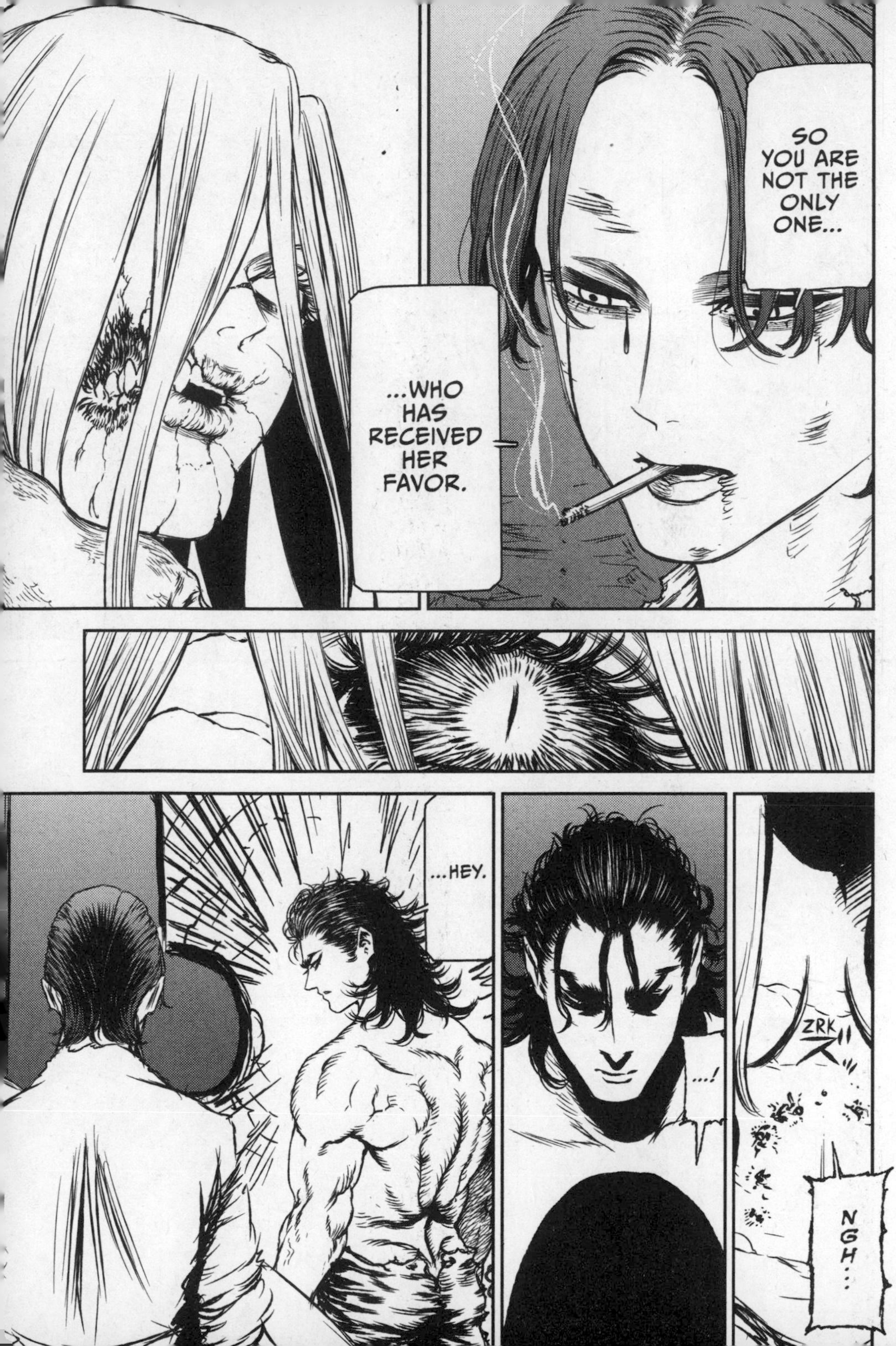
SO YOU ARE NOT THE ONLY ONE...
...WHO HAS RECEIVED HER FAVOR.
ZRK
NGH...
...!
...HEY.

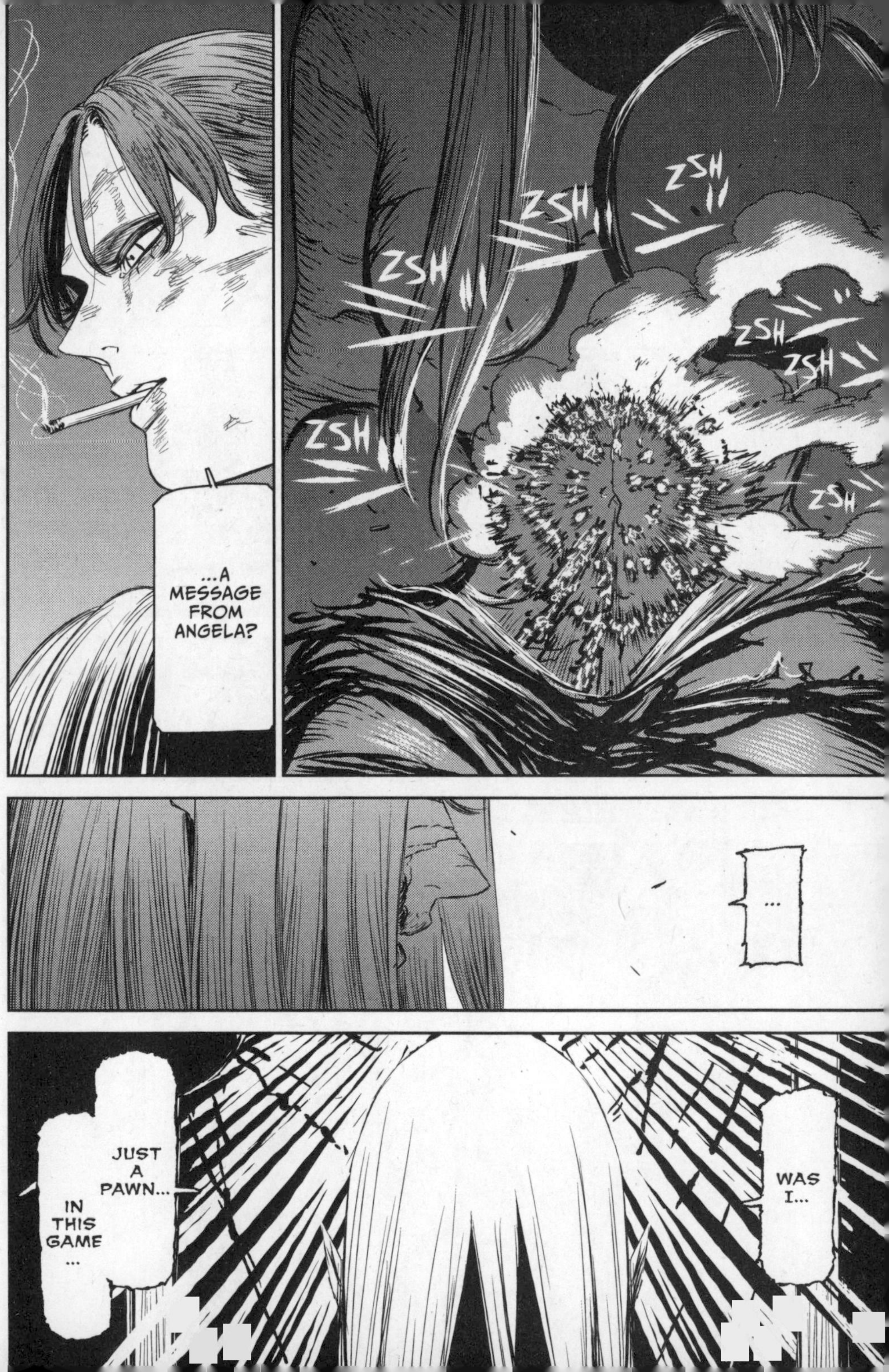
ZSH
ZSH
ZSH
ZSH
ZSH
ZSH
ZSH
...A MESSAGE FROM ANGELA?
...
WAS I...
JUST A PAWN...
IN THIS GAME ...

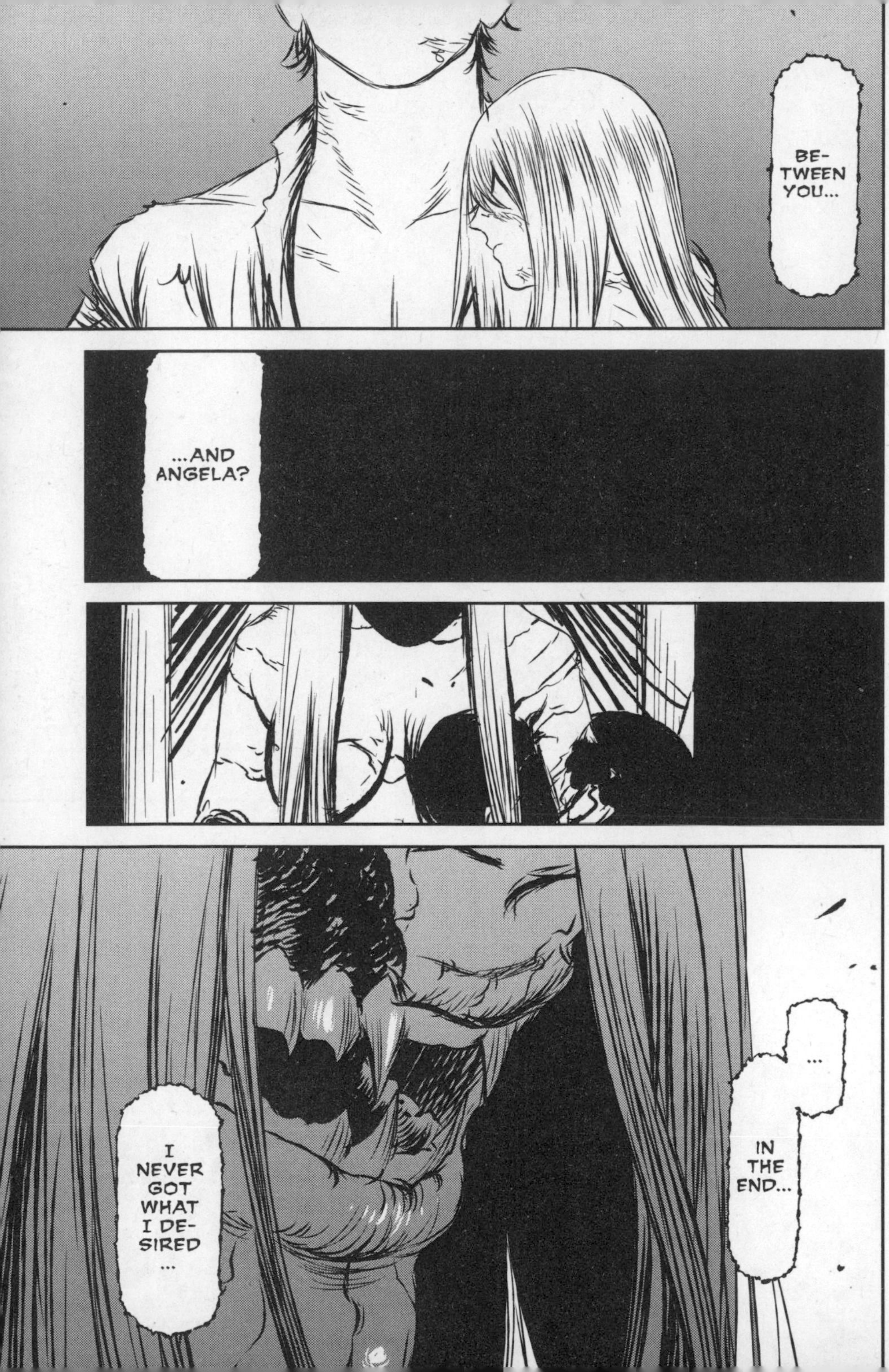
BE-TWEEN YOU...
...AND ANGELA?
... IN THE END...
I NEVER GOT WHAT I DE-SIRED ...

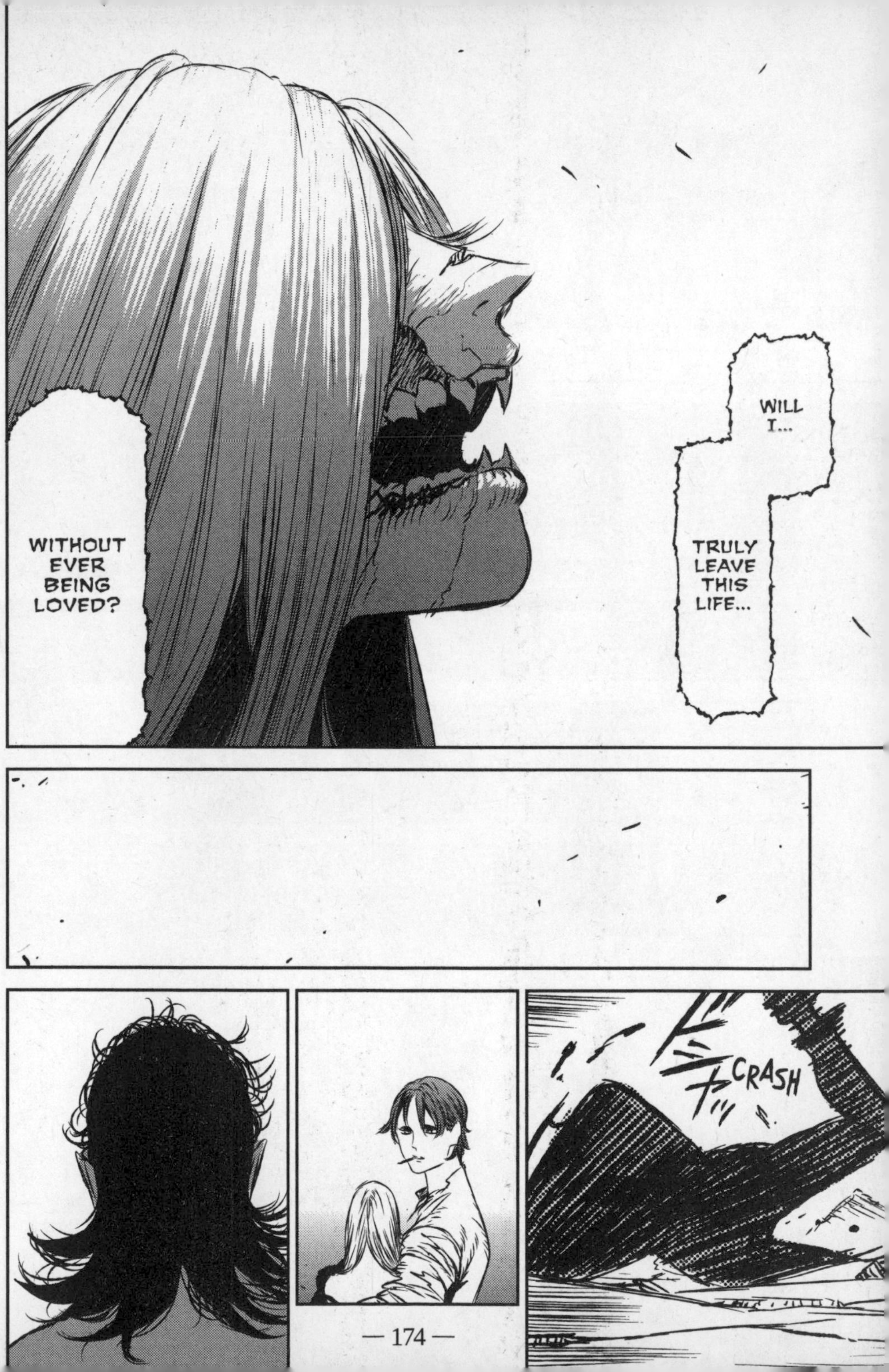
WILL I...
TRULY LEAVE THIS LIFE...
WITHOUT EVER BEING LOVED?
CRASH

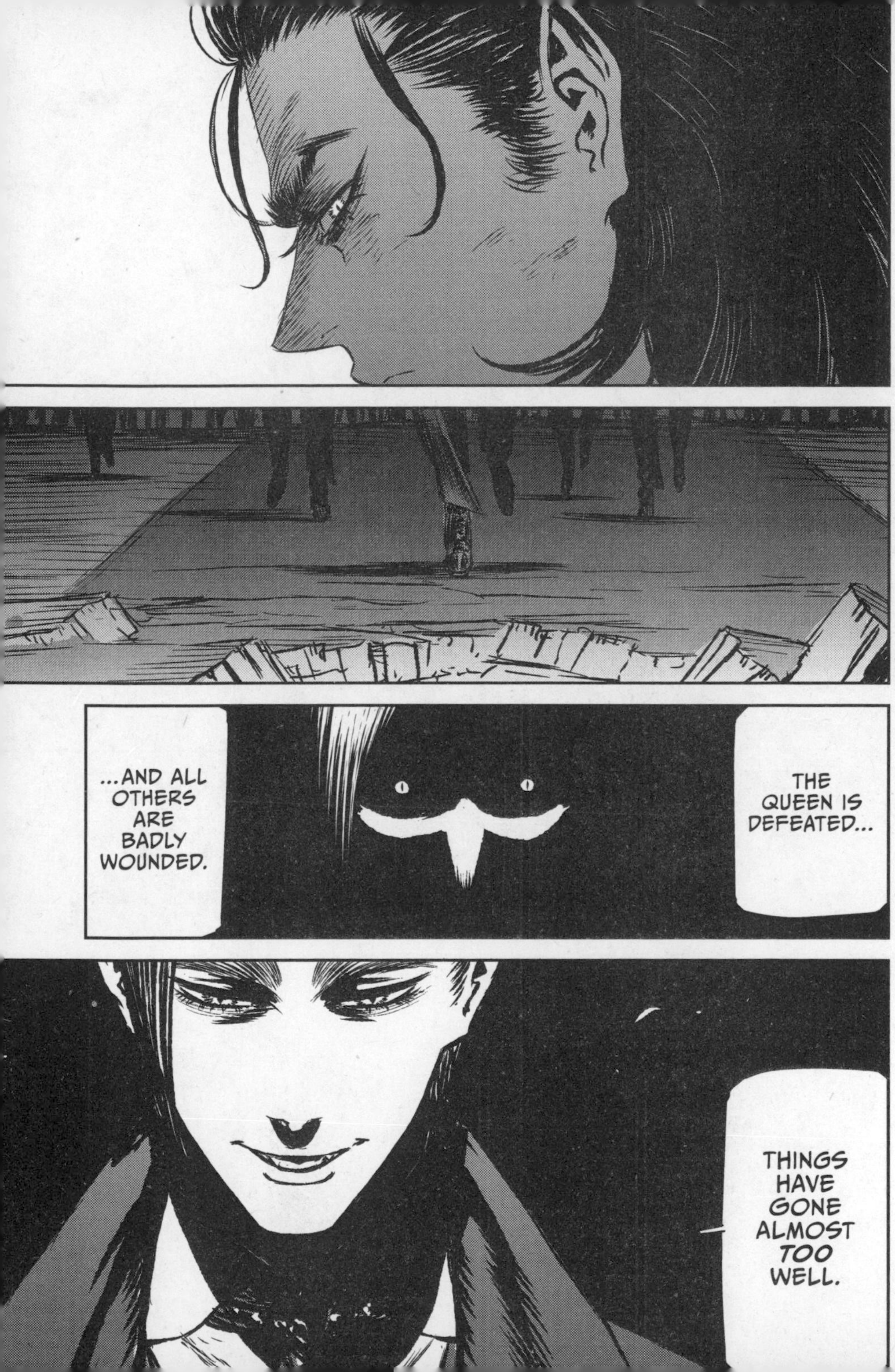
THE QUEEN IS DEFEATED...
...AND ALL OTHERS ARE BADLY WOUNDED.
THINGS HAVE GONE ALMOST *TOO* WELL.

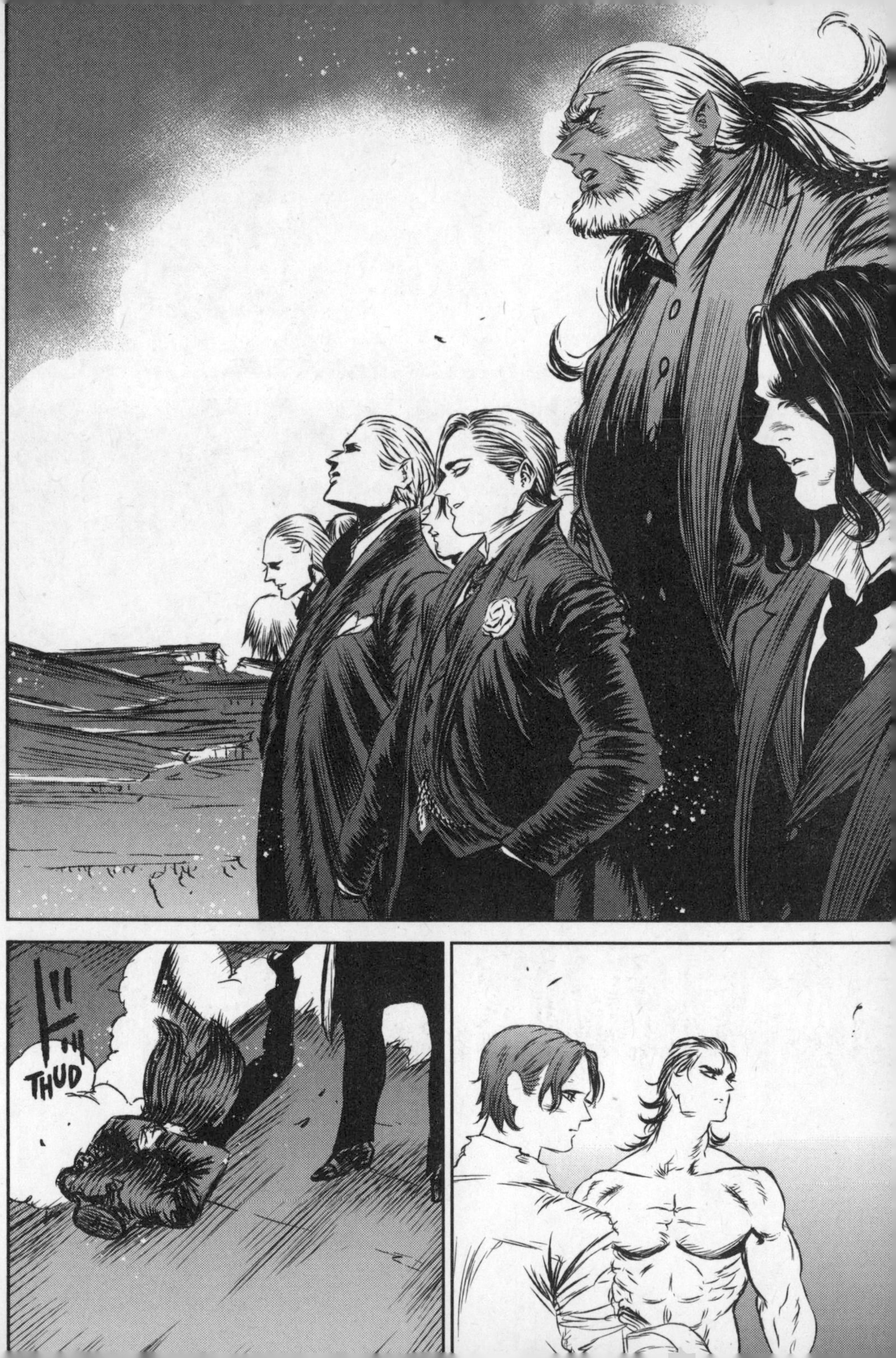
THUD

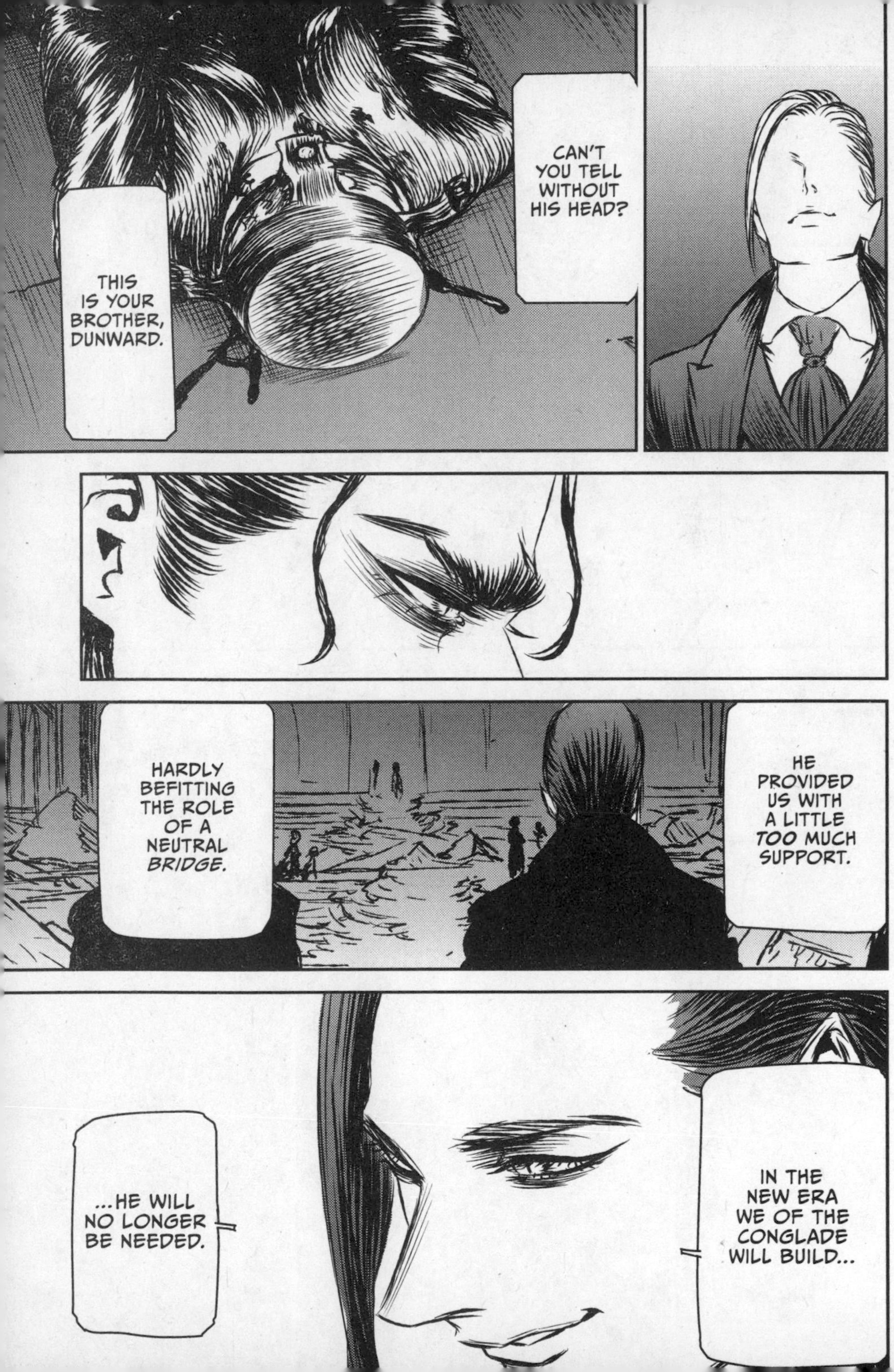
CAN'T YOU TELL WITHOUT HIS HEAD?
THIS IS YOUR BROTHER, DUNWARD.
HE PROVIDED US WITH A LITTLE *TOO* MUCH SUPPORT.
HARDLY BEFITTING THE ROLE OF A NEUTRAL *BRIDGE*.
IN THE NEW ERA WE OF THE CONGLADE WILL BUILD...
...HE WILL NO LONGER BE NEEDED.

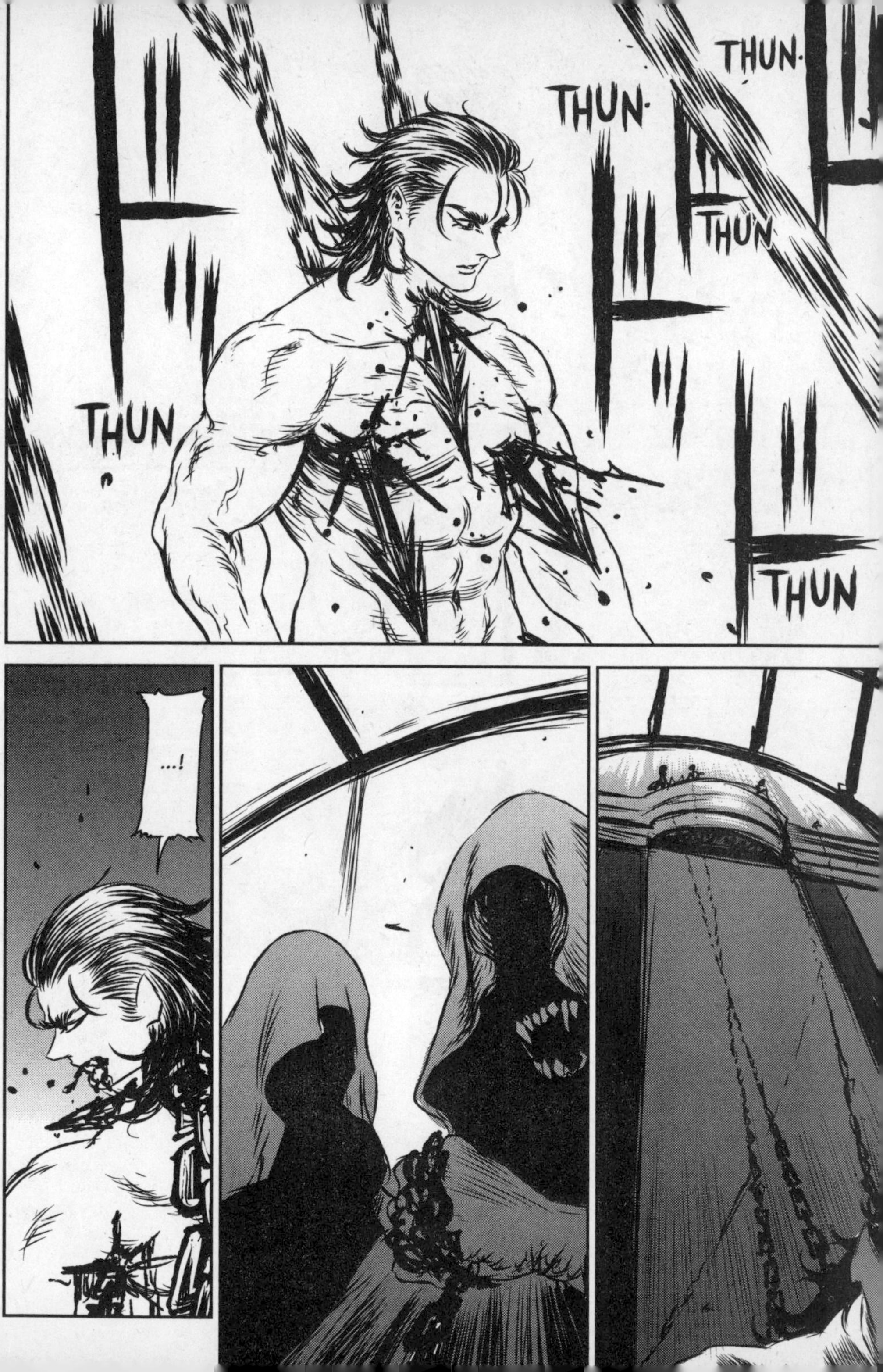
THUN-
THUN-
THUN
THUN
THUN
...!

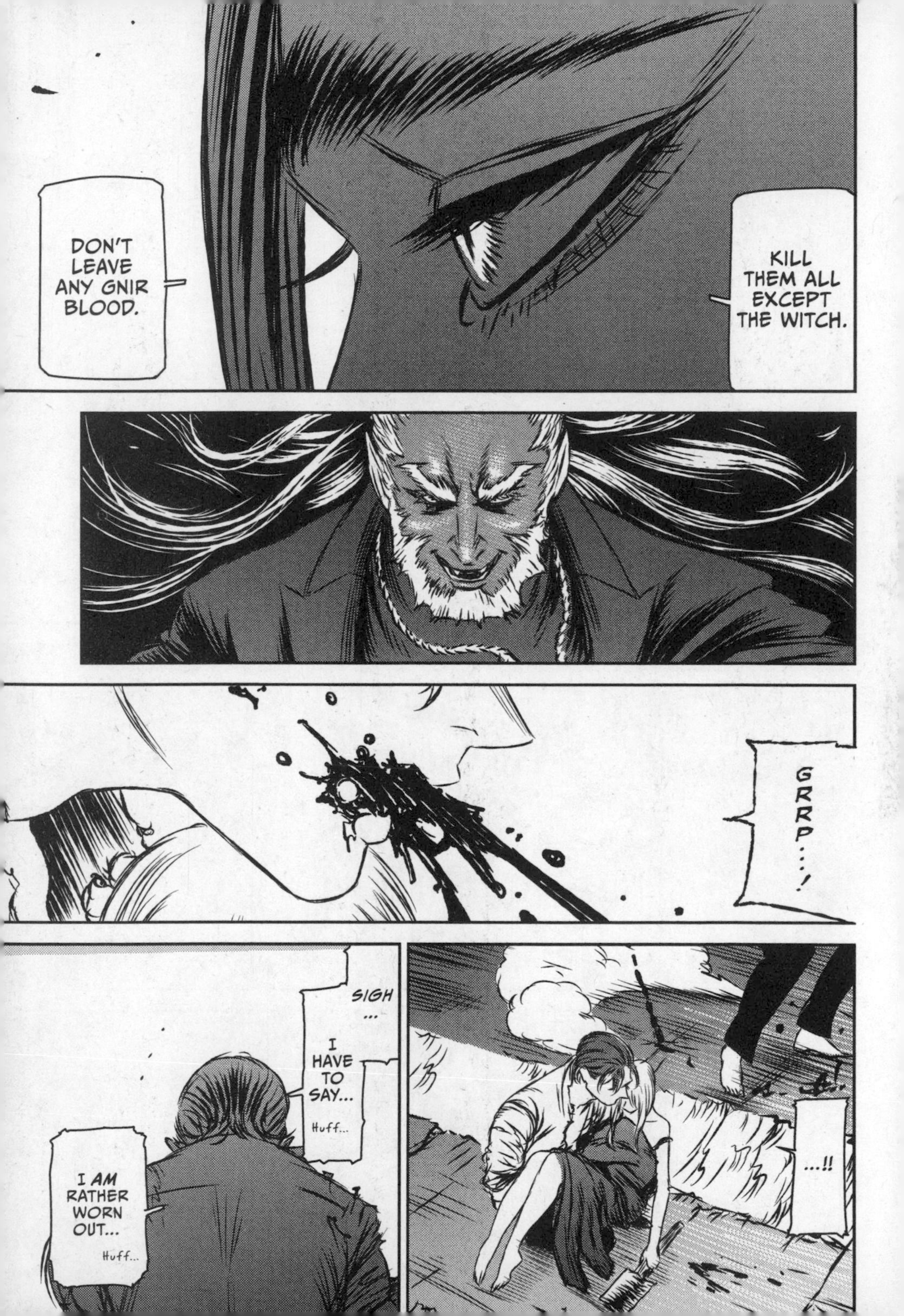
KILL THEM ALL EXCEPT THE WITCH.
DON'T LEAVE ANY GNIR BLOOD.
GRRP...!
...!!
SIGH ...
I HAVE TO SAY...
Huff...
I *AM* RATHER WORN OUT...
Huff...

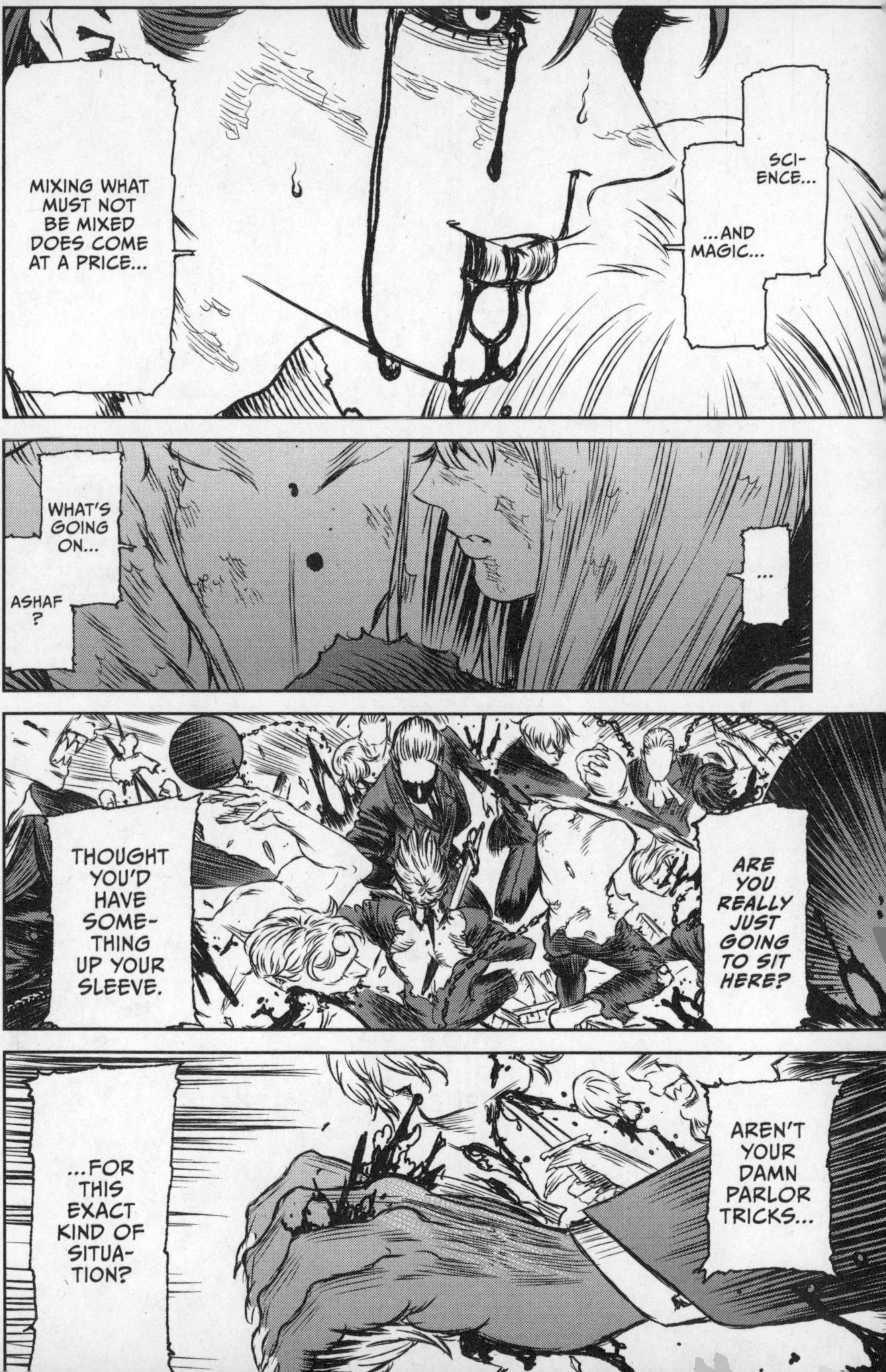
SCIENCE...
...AND MAGIC...
MIXING WHAT MUST NOT BE MIXED DOES COME AT A PRICE...
...
WHAT'S GOING ON...
ASHAF?
ARE YOU REALLY JUST GOING TO SIT HERE?
THOUGHT YOU'D HAVE SOMETHING UP YOUR SLEEVE.
AREN'T YOUR DAMN PARLOR TRICKS...
...FOR THIS EXACT KIND OF SITUATION?

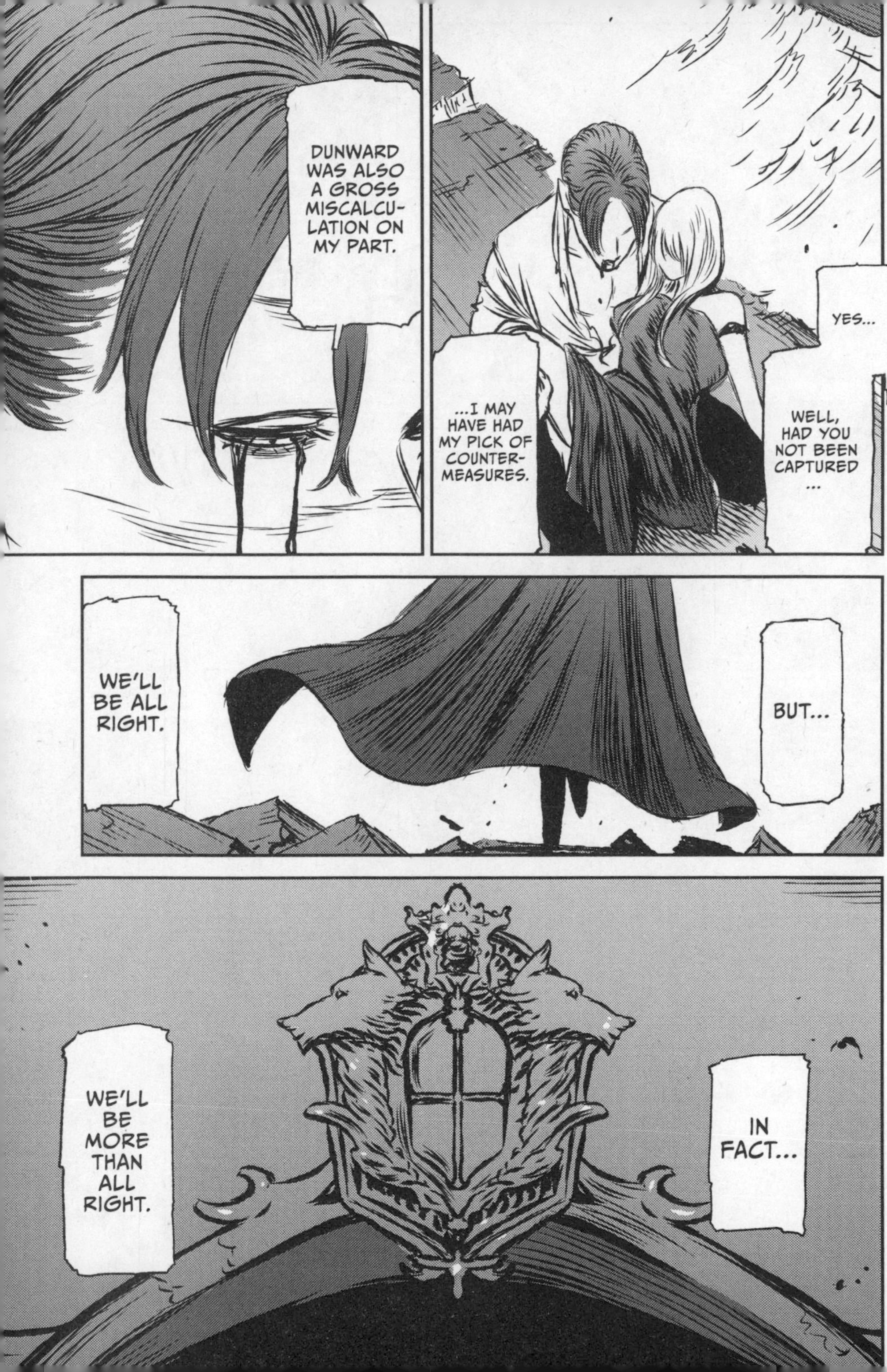
YES...
KOFF!
WELL, HAD YOU NOT BEEN CAPTURED...
...I MAY HAVE HAD MY PICK OF COUNTER-MEASURES.
DUNWARD WAS ALSO A GROSS MISCALCULATION ON MY PART.
BUT...
WE'LL BE ALL RIGHT.
IN FACT...
WE'LL BE MORE THAN ALL RIGHT.

FLASH

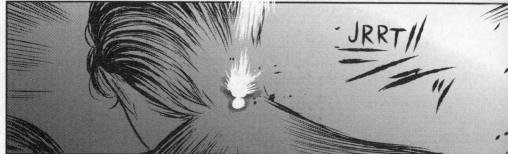

JRRT

THE SKY...

...HEY!

ジュウウウウ
FRIZZZZ

...!!

WHAT'S THAT?!

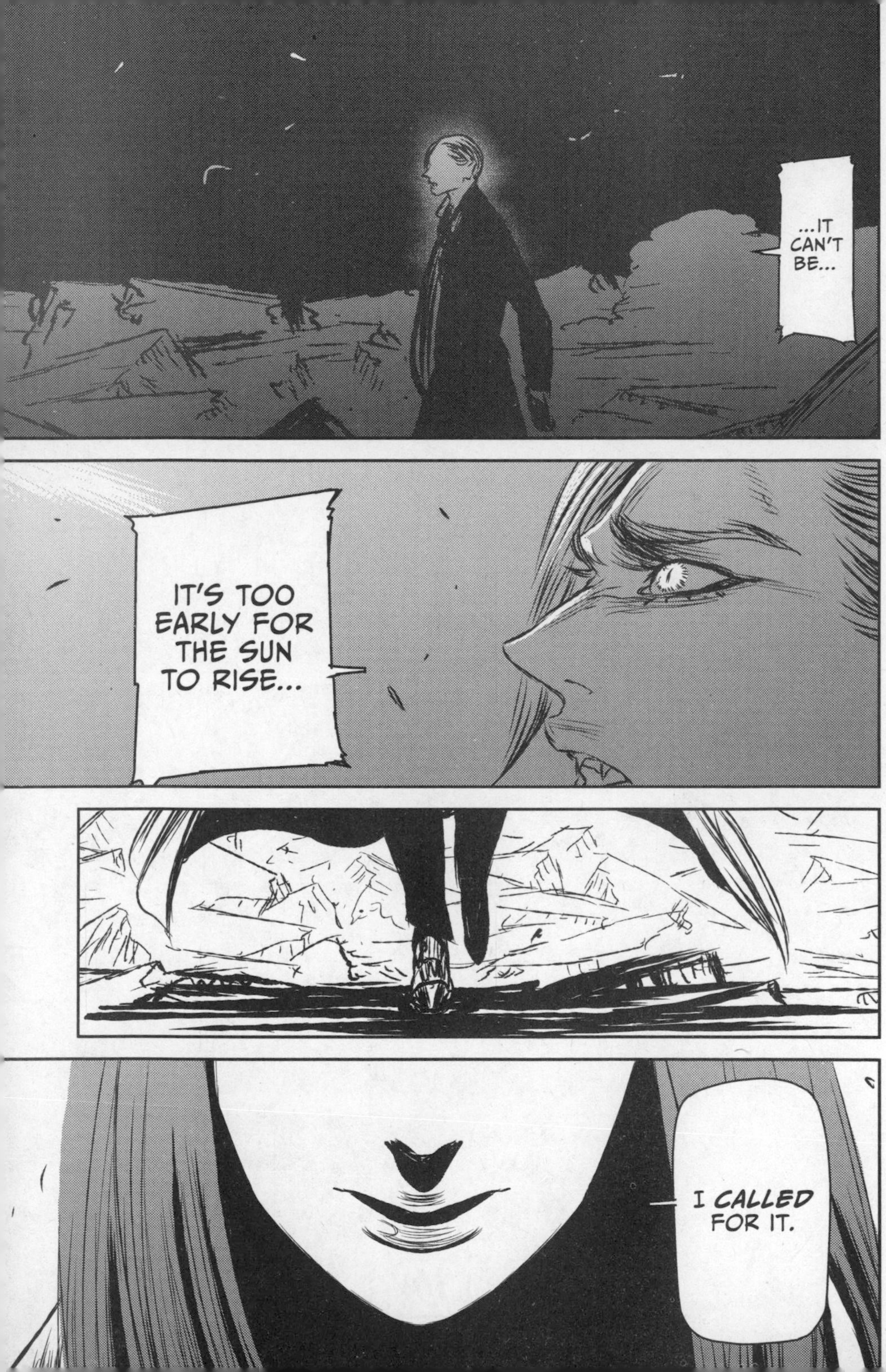
...IT CAN'T BE...
IT'S TOO EARLY FOR THE SUN TO RISE...
I CALLED FOR IT.

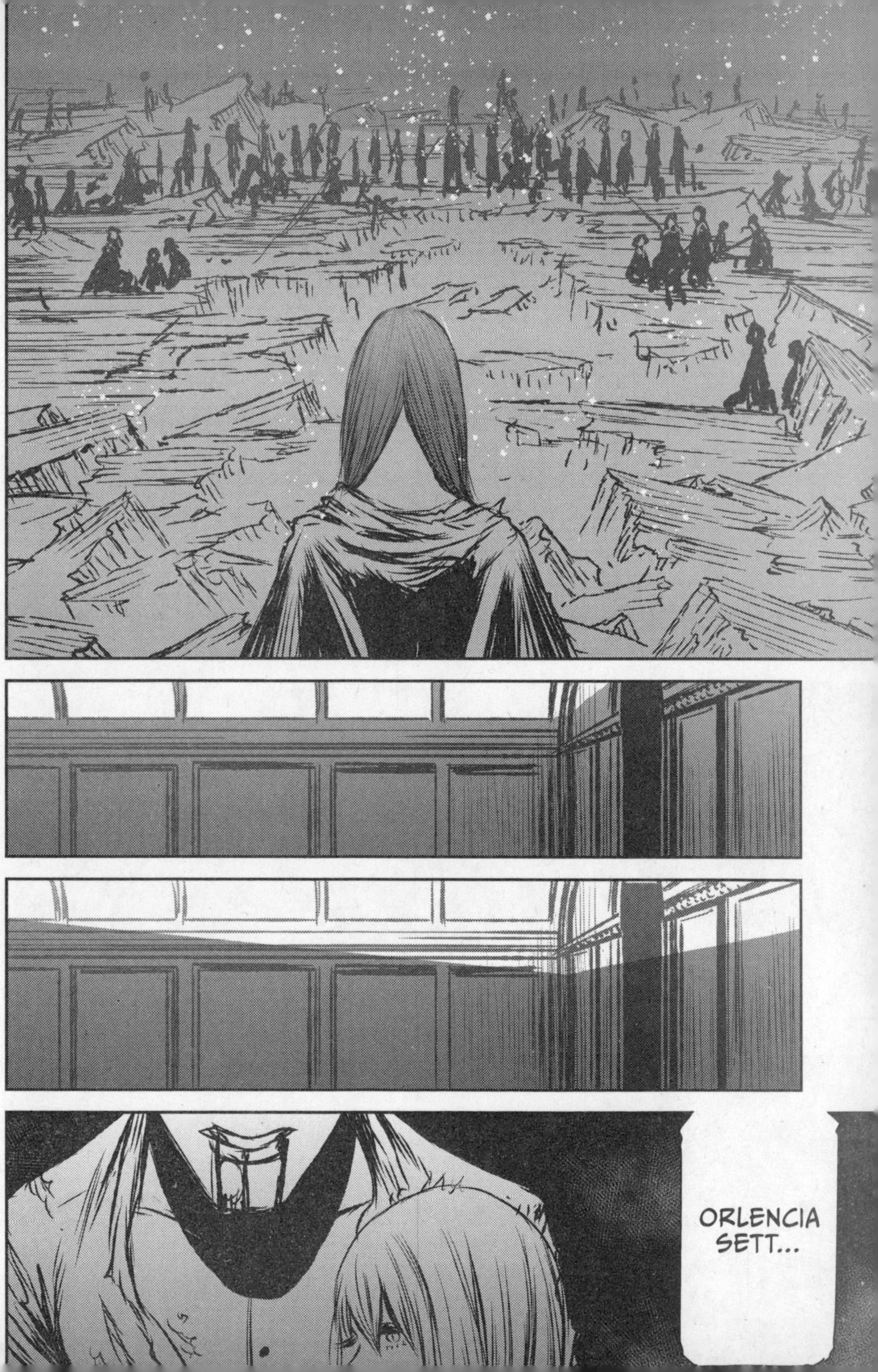
ORLENCIA
SETT...

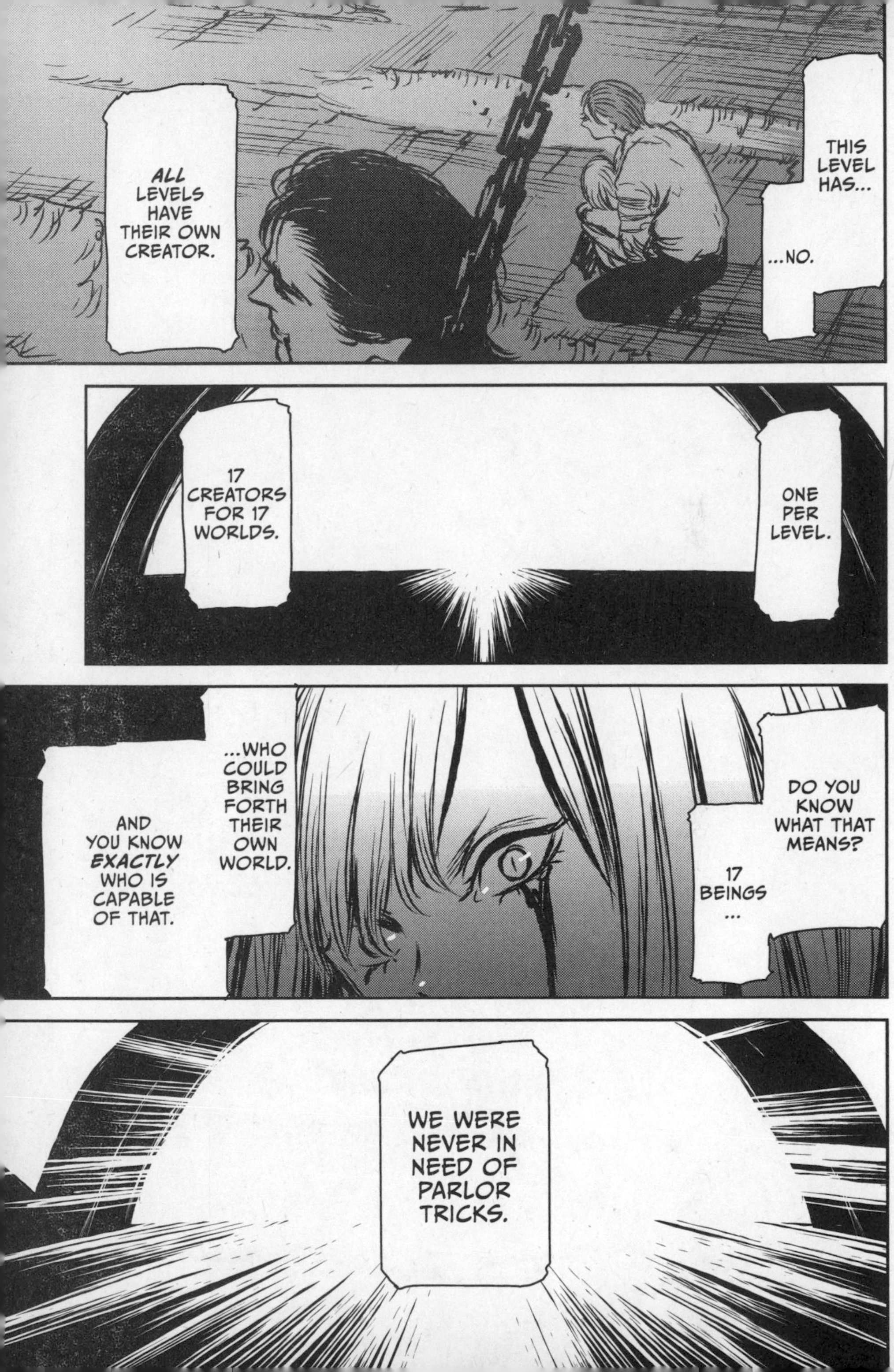
THIS LEVEL HAS...
...NO.
ALL LEVELS HAVE THEIR OWN CREATOR.
ONE PER LEVEL.
17 CREATORS FOR 17 WORLDS.
DO YOU KNOW WHAT THAT MEANS?
17 BEINGS ...
...WHO COULD BRING FORTH THEIR OWN WORLD.
AND YOU KNOW EXACTLY WHO IS CAPABLE OF THAT.
WE WERE NEVER IN NEED OF PARLOR TRICKS.

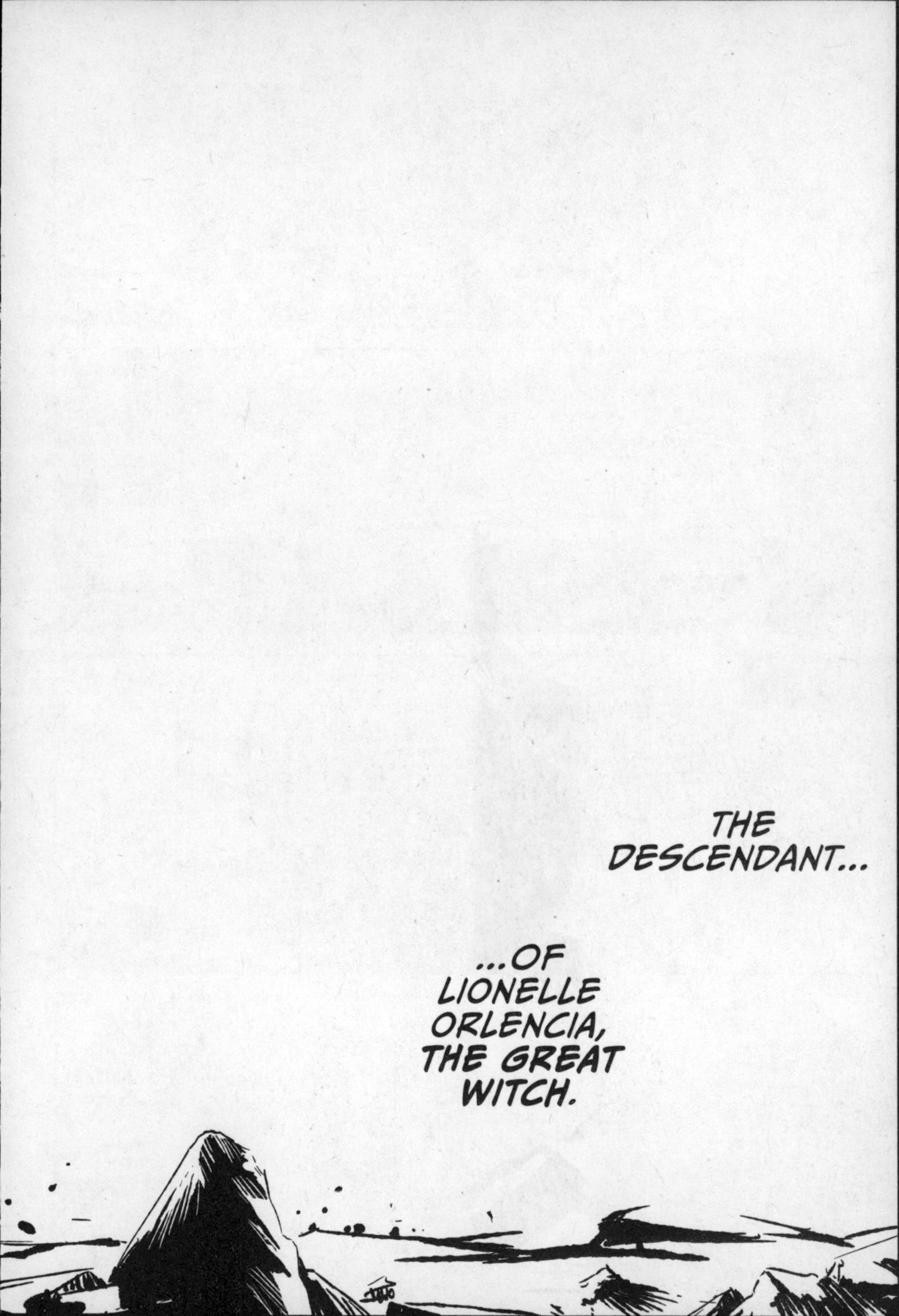
THE DESCENDANT...
...OF LIONELLE ORLENCIA, THE GREAT WITCH.

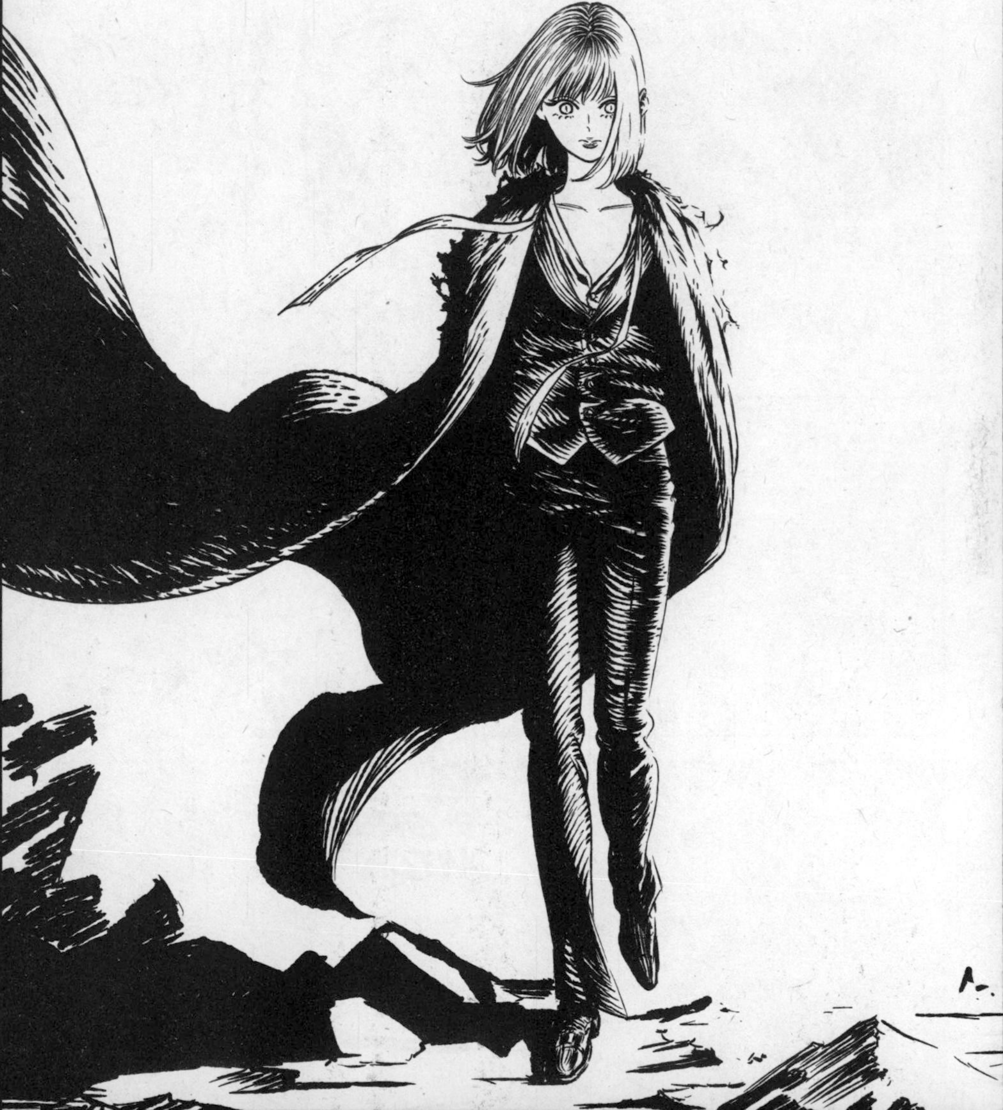

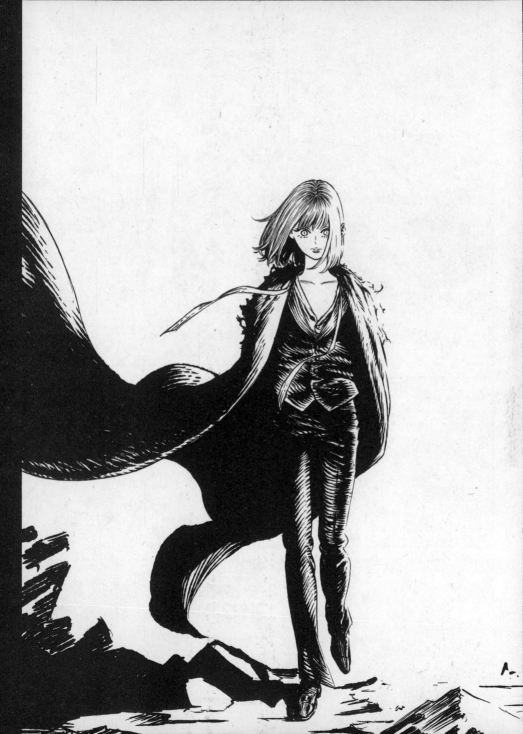

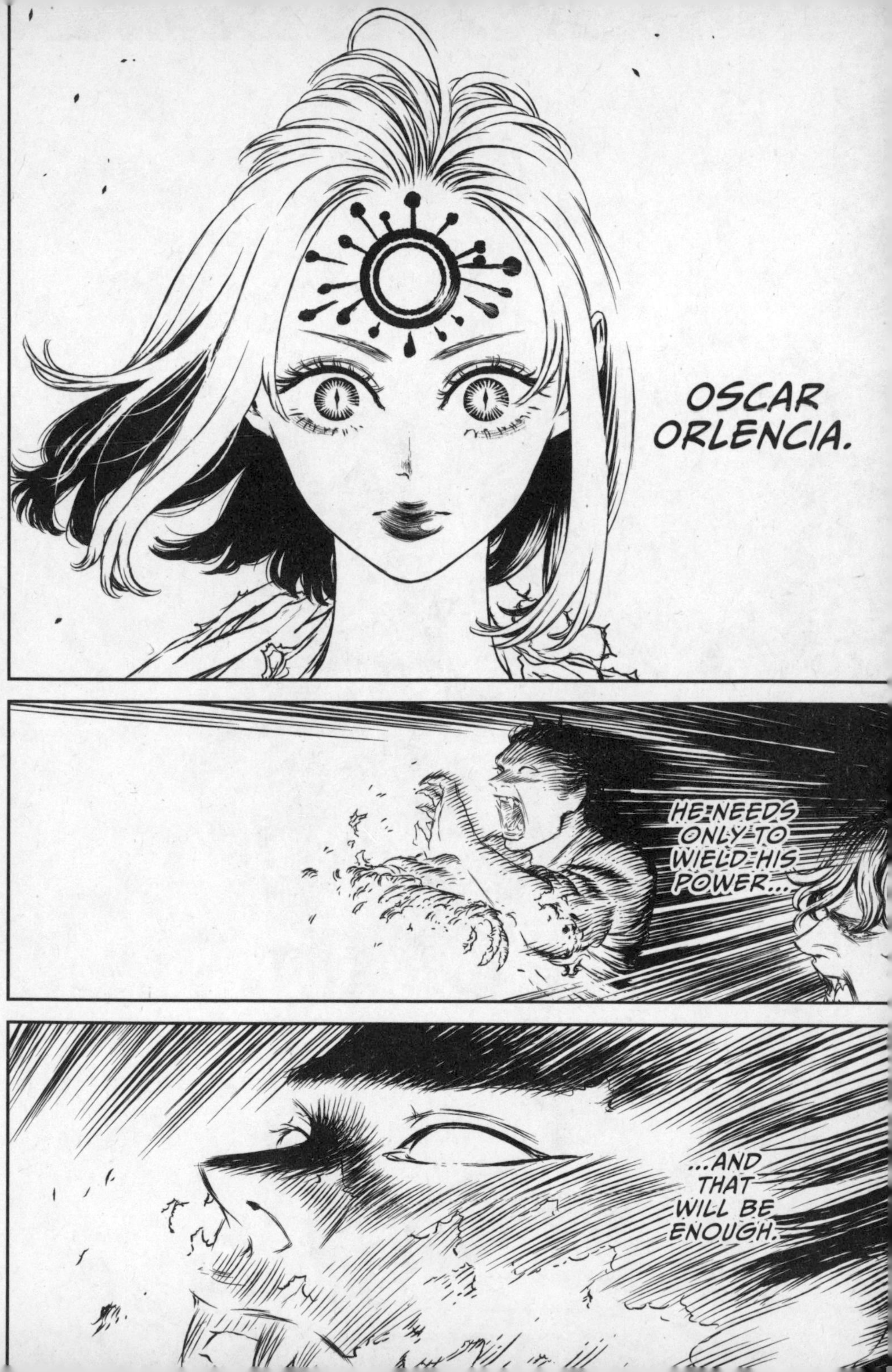
OSCAR ORLENCIA.
HE NEEDS ONLY TO WIELD HIS POWER...
...AND THAT WILL BE ENOUGH.

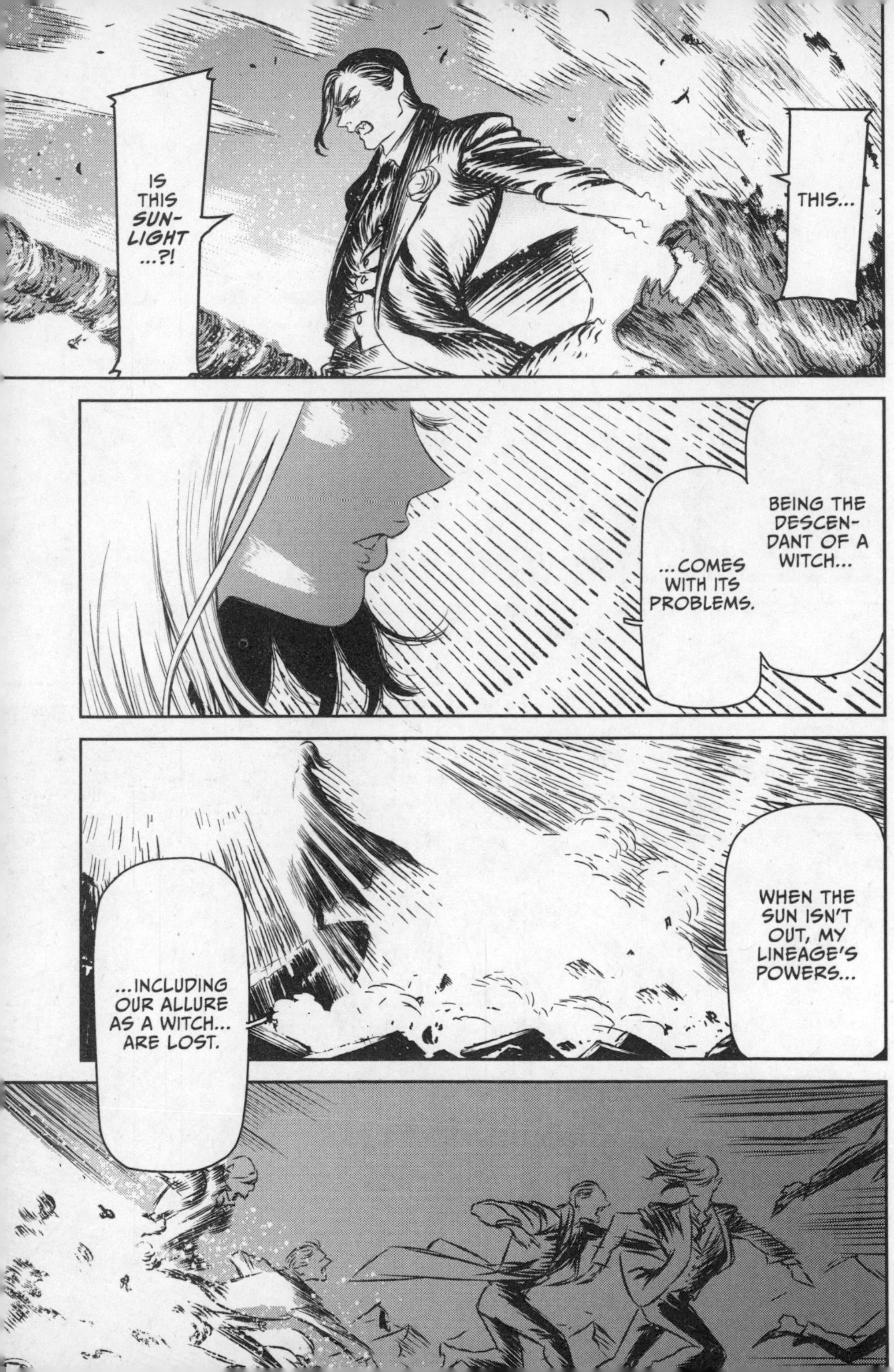
THIS...
IS THIS SUN-LIGHT ...?!
BEING THE DESCEN-DANT OF A WITCH...
...COMES WITH ITS PROBLEMS.
WHEN THE SUN ISN'T OUT, MY LINEAGE'S POWERS...
...INCLUDING OUR ALLURE AS A WITCH... ARE LOST.

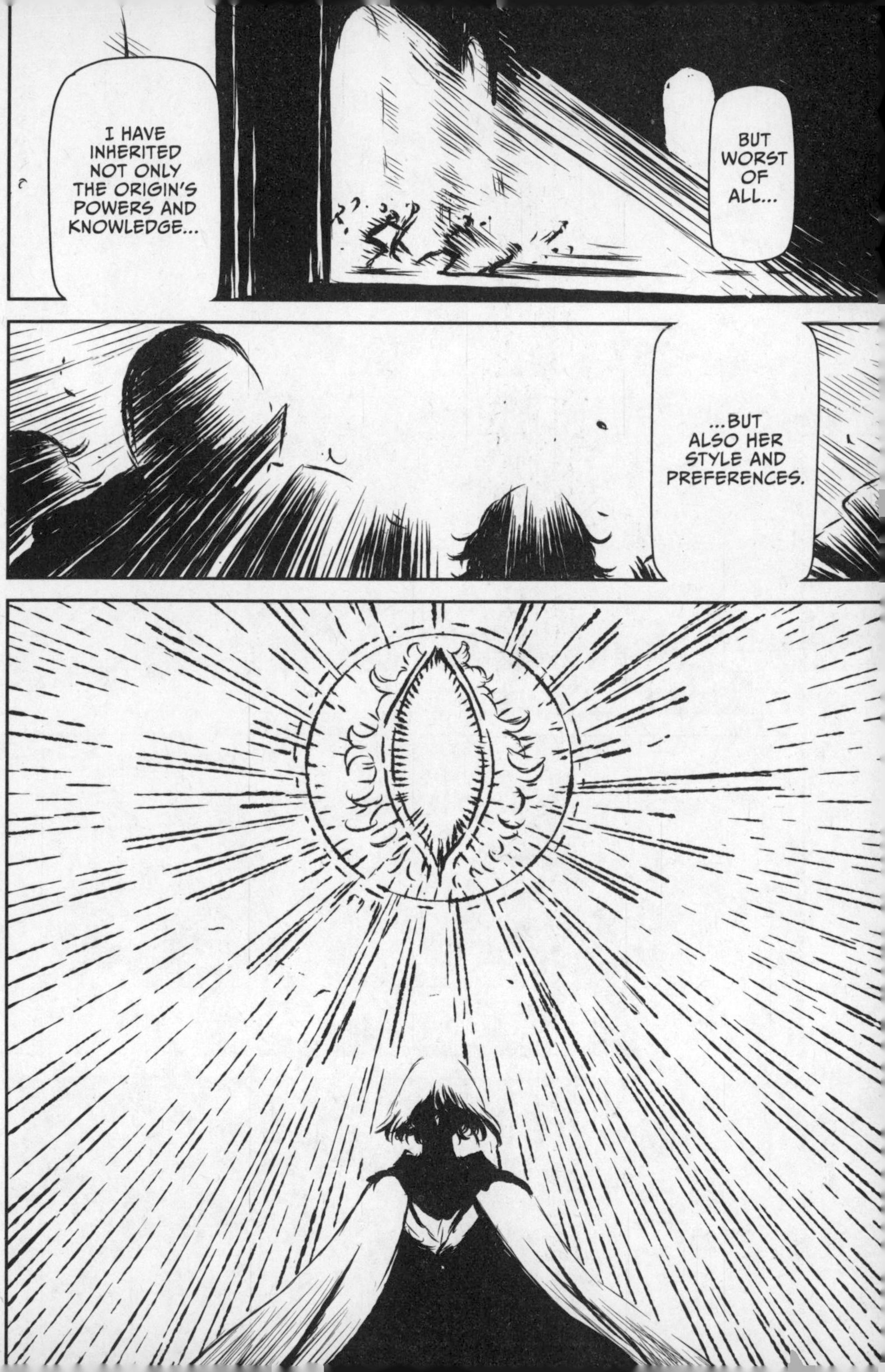
BUT WORST OF ALL...
I HAVE INHERITED NOT ONLY THE ORIGIN'S POWERS AND KNOWLEDGE...
...BUT ALSO HER STYLE AND PREFERENCES.

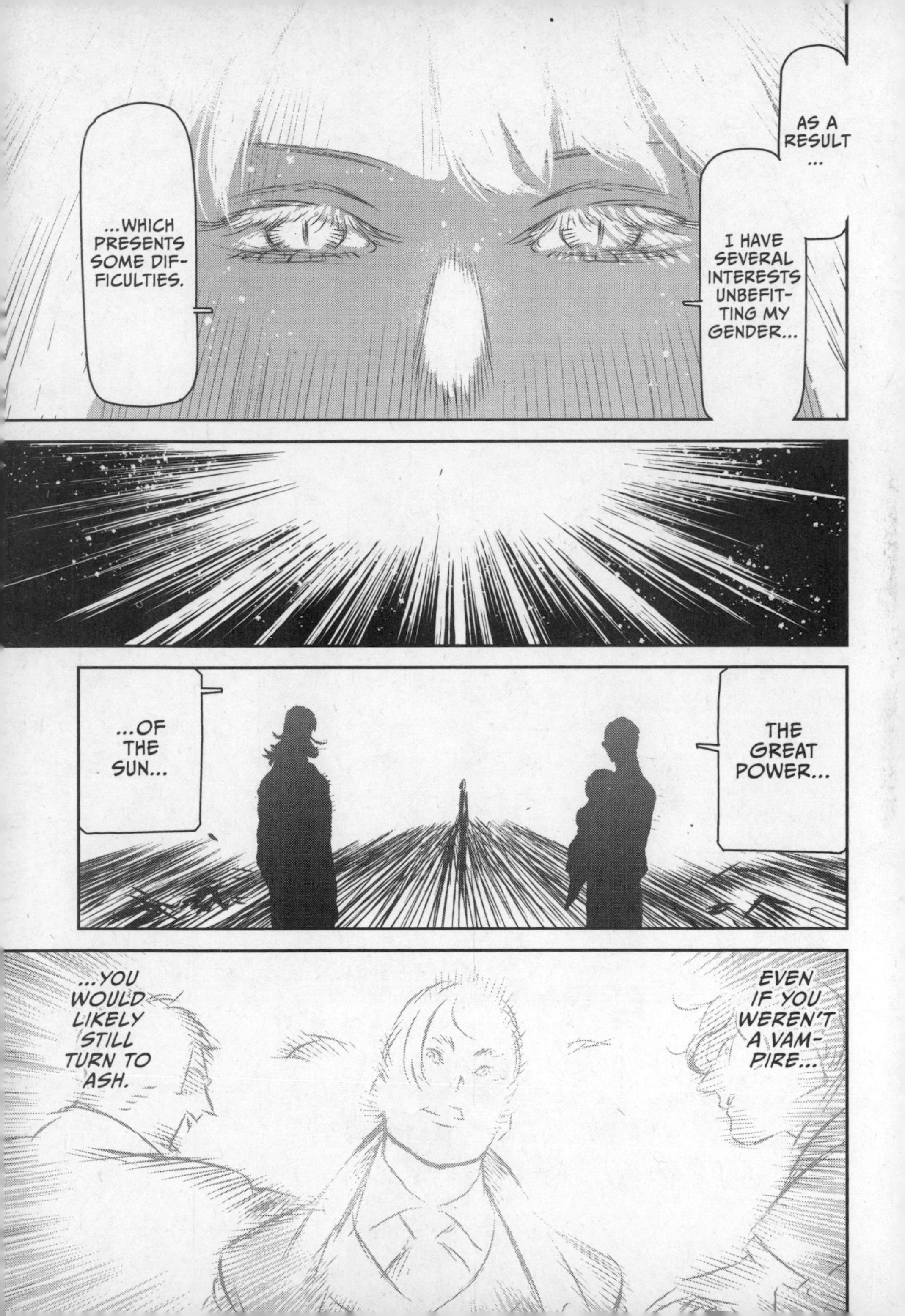
AS A RESULT...
I HAVE SEVERAL INTERESTS UNBEFITTING MY GENDER...
...WHICH PRESENTS SOME DIFFICULTIES.
THE GREAT POWER...
...OF THE SUN...
EVEN IF YOU WEREN'T A VAMPIRE...
...YOU WOULD LIKELY STILL TURN TO ASH.

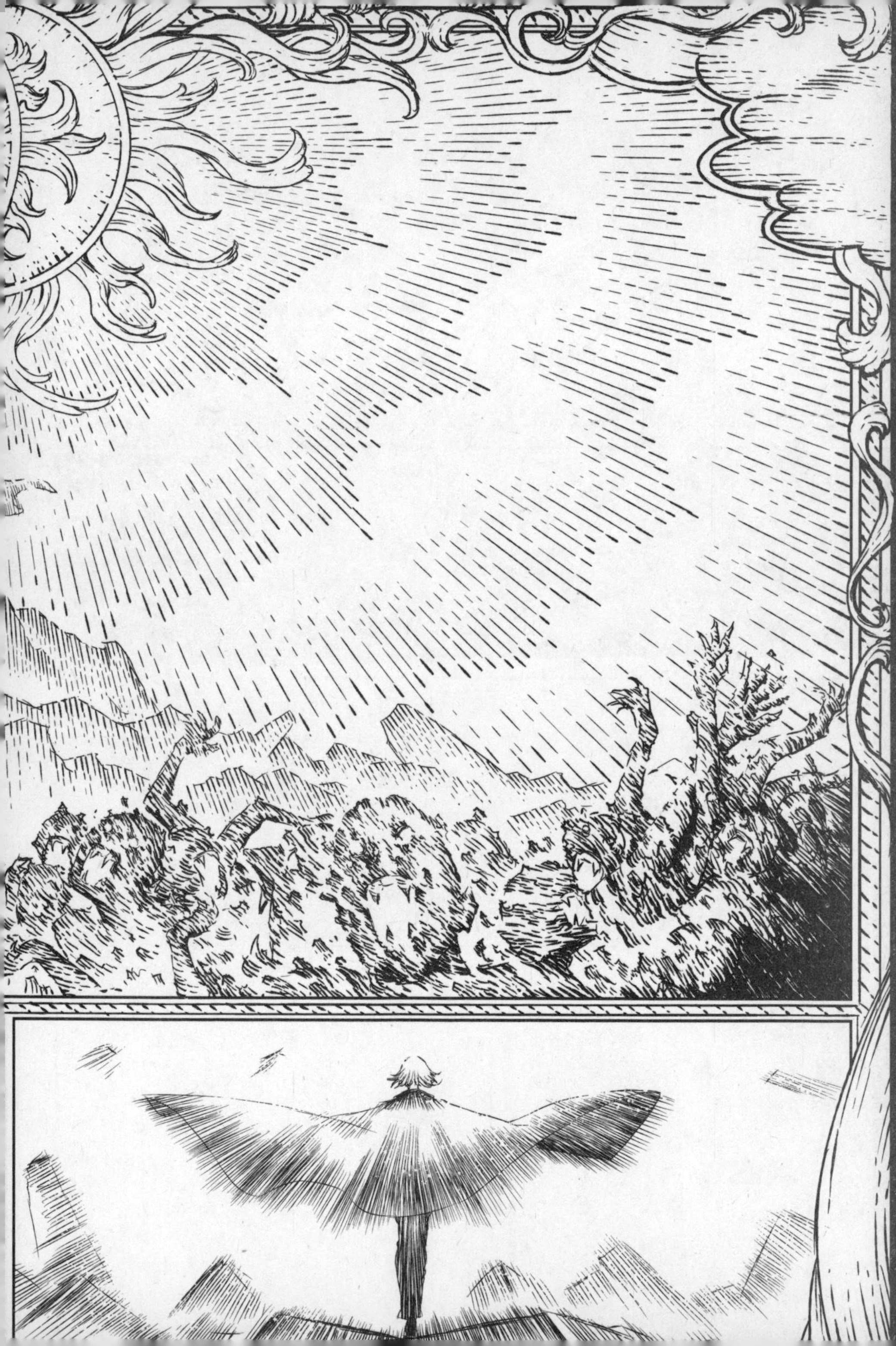

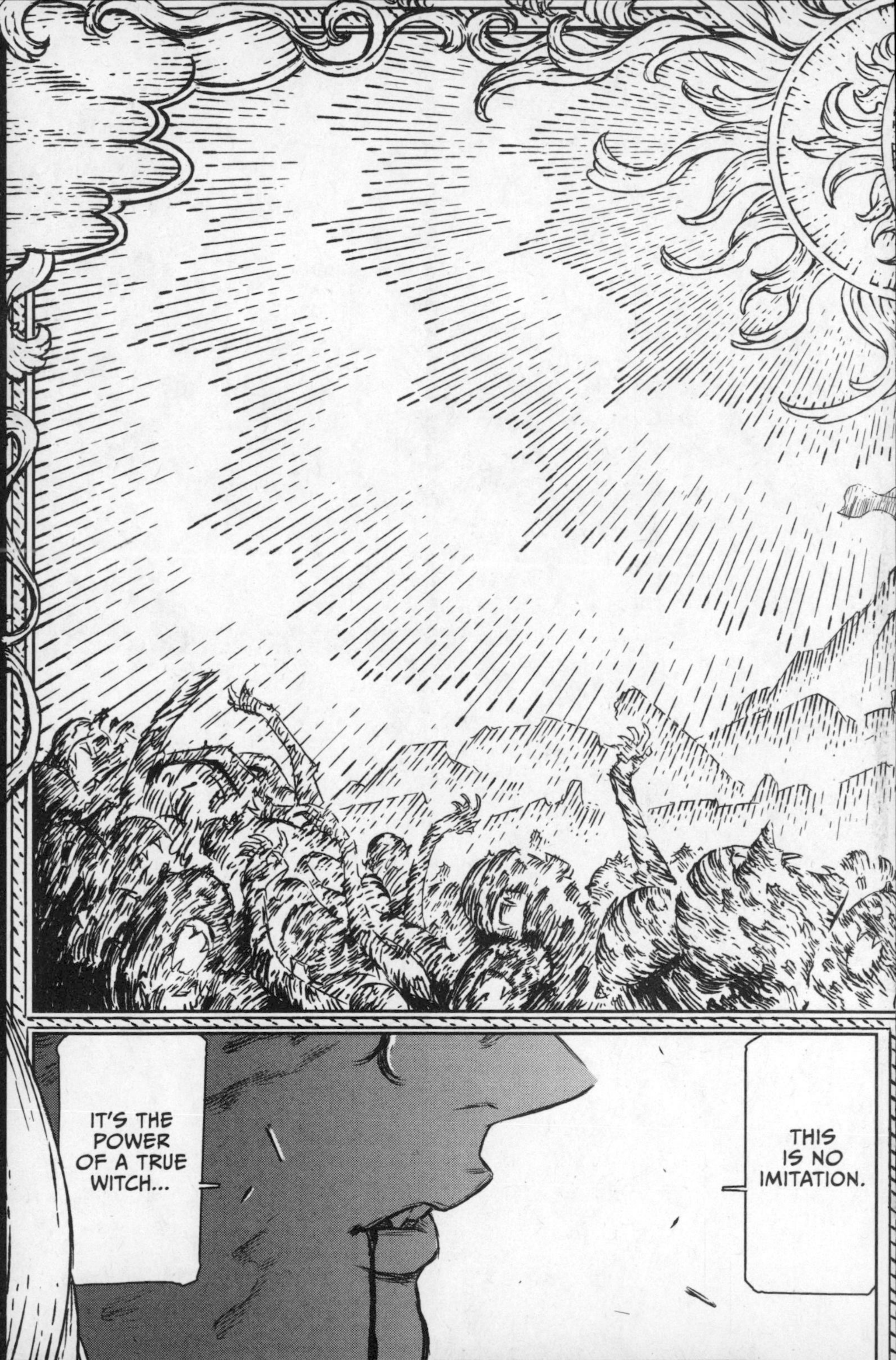
THIS IS NO IMITATION.
IT'S THE POWER OF A TRUE WITCH...

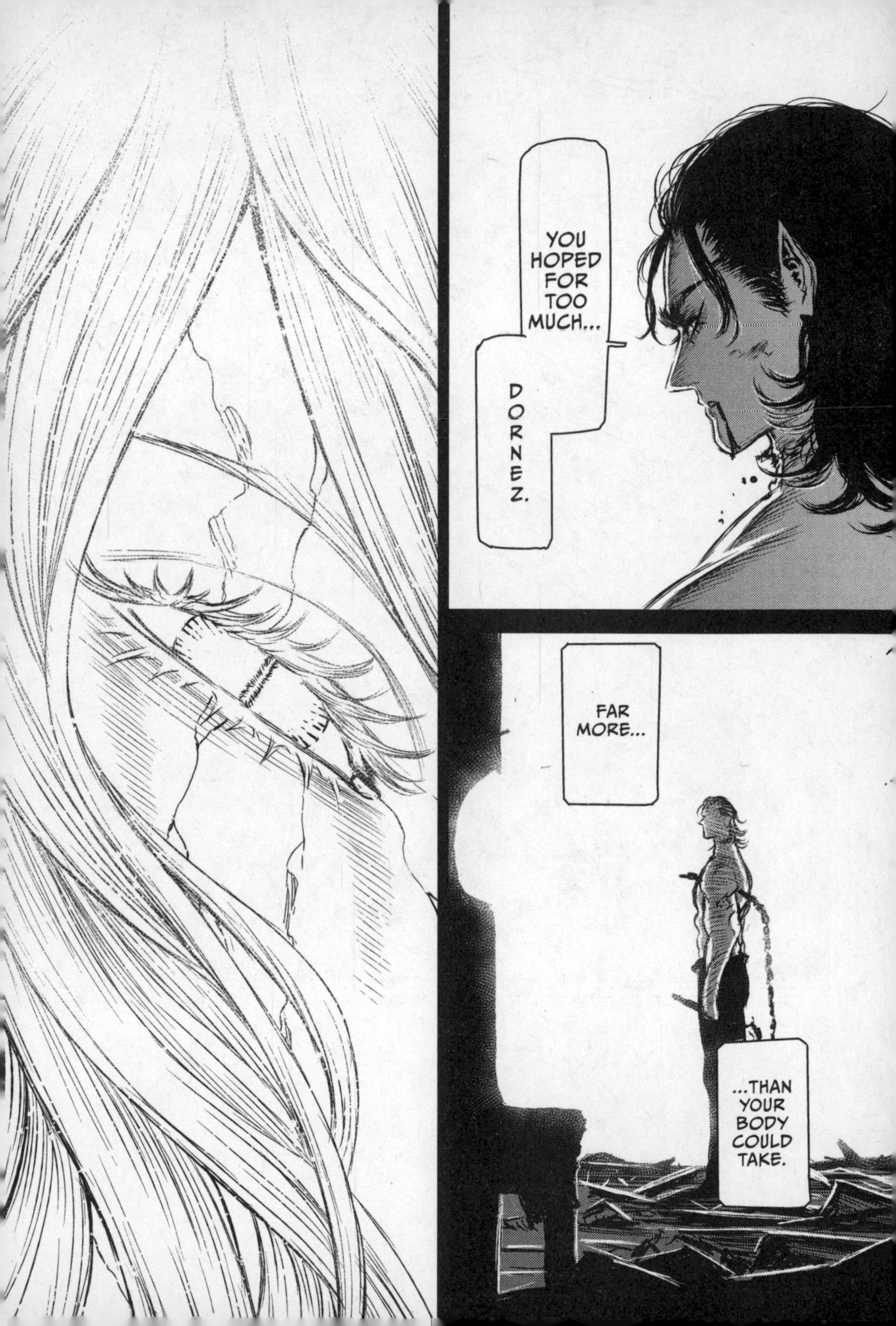
YOU HOPED FOR TOO MUCH...
DORNEZ.
FAR MORE...
...THAN YOUR BODY COULD TAKE.

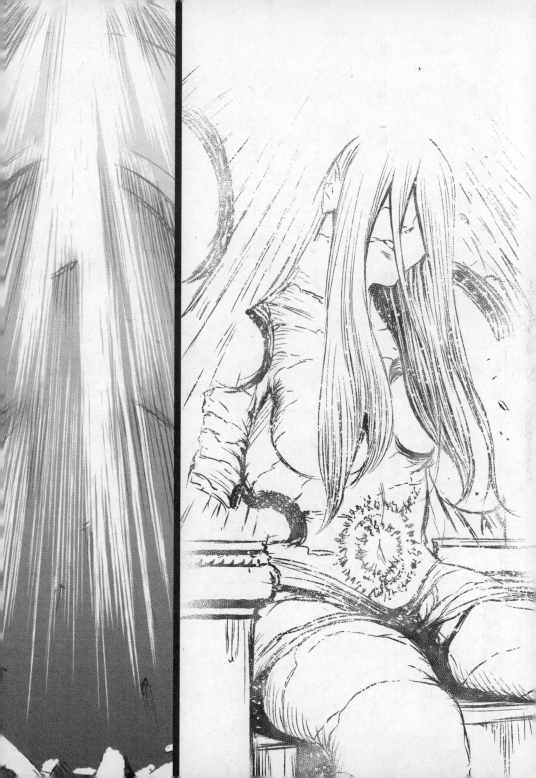

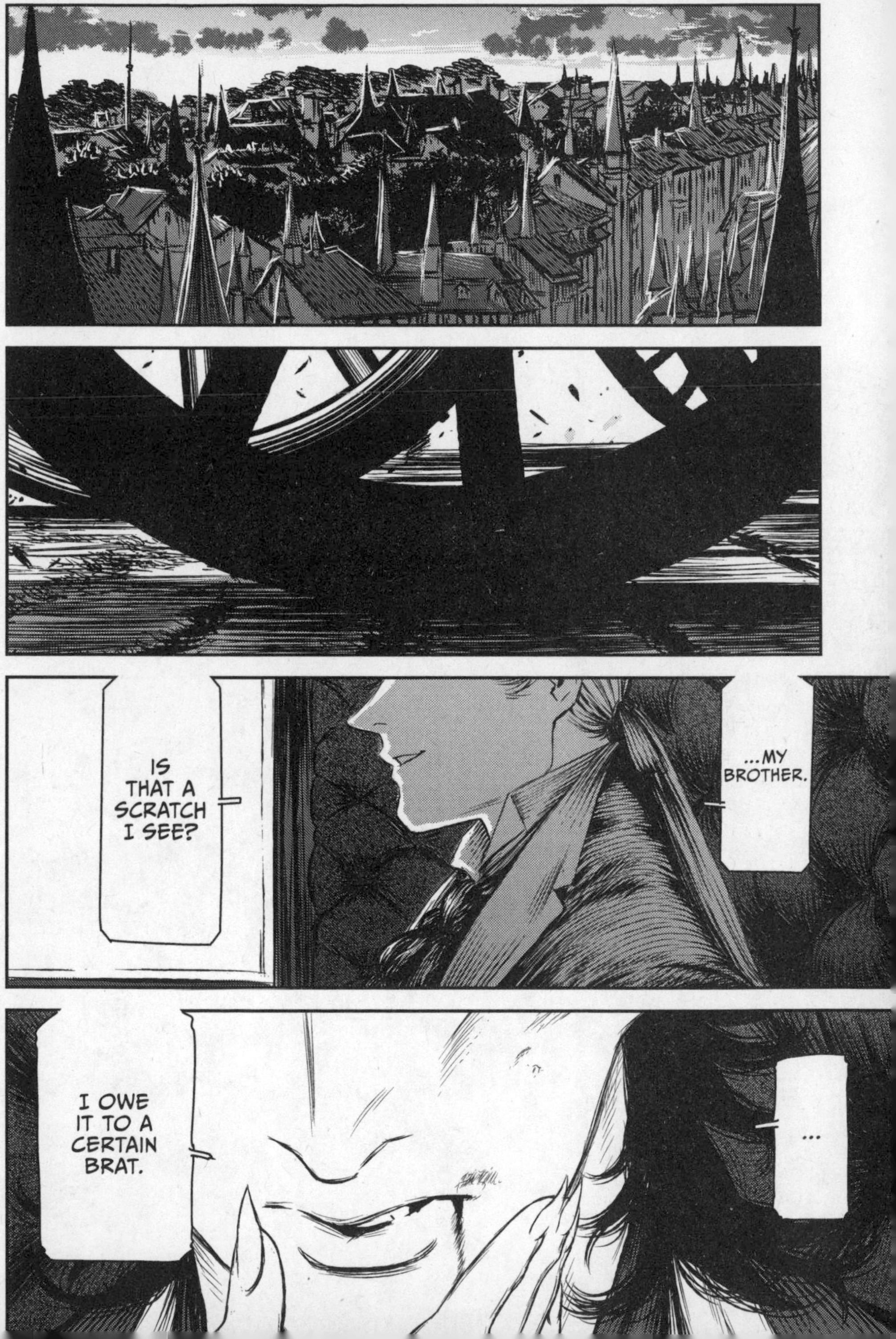
...MY BROTHER.
IS THAT A SCRATCH I SEE?
...
I OWE IT TO A CERTAIN BRAT.

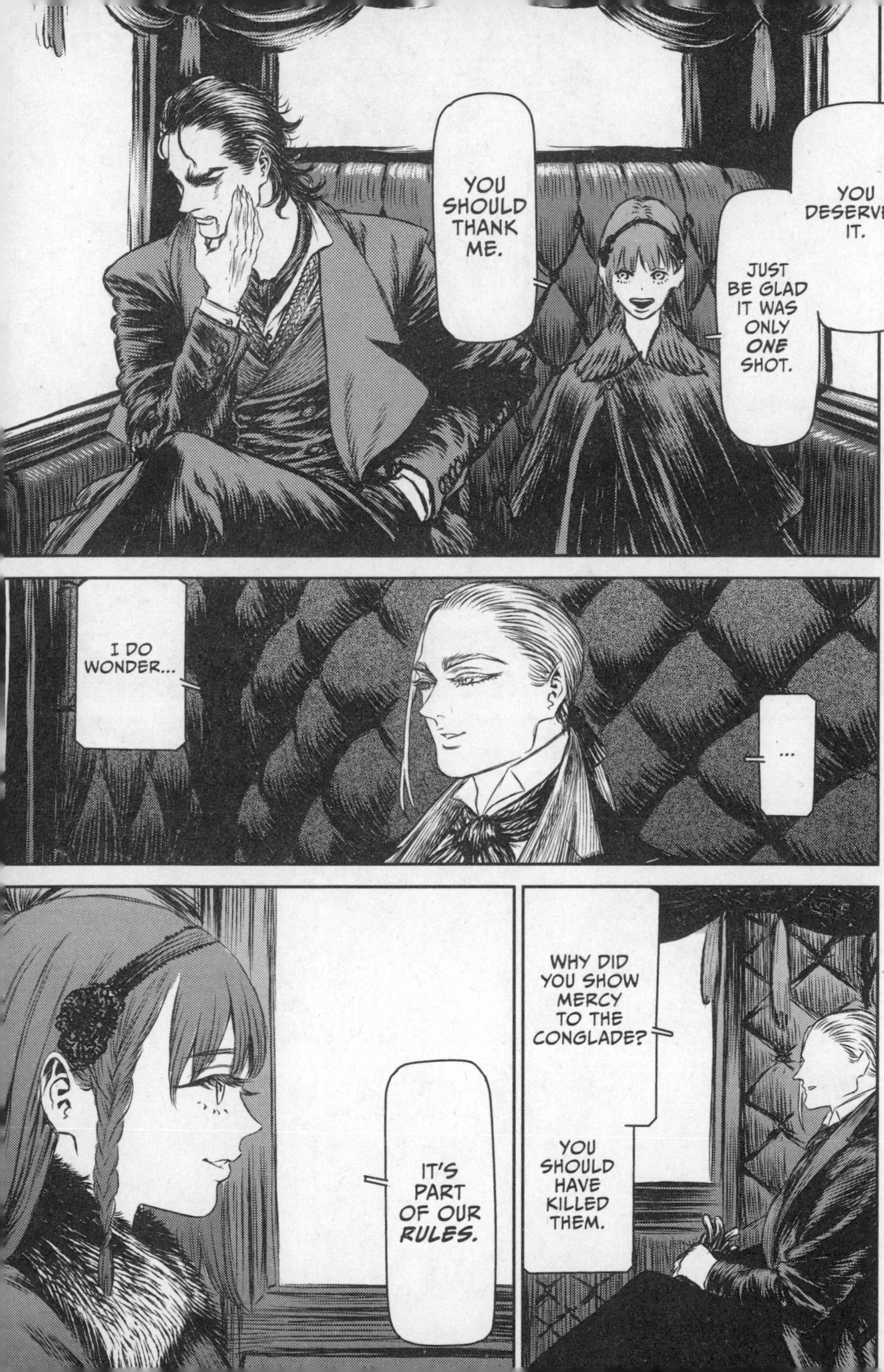
YOU DESERVED IT.
JUST BE GLAD IT WAS ONLY *ONE* SHOT.
YOU SHOULD THANK ME.
...
I DO WONDER...
WHY DID YOU SHOW MERCY TO THE CONGLADE?
YOU SHOULD HAVE KILLED THEM.
IT'S PART OF OUR *RULES.*

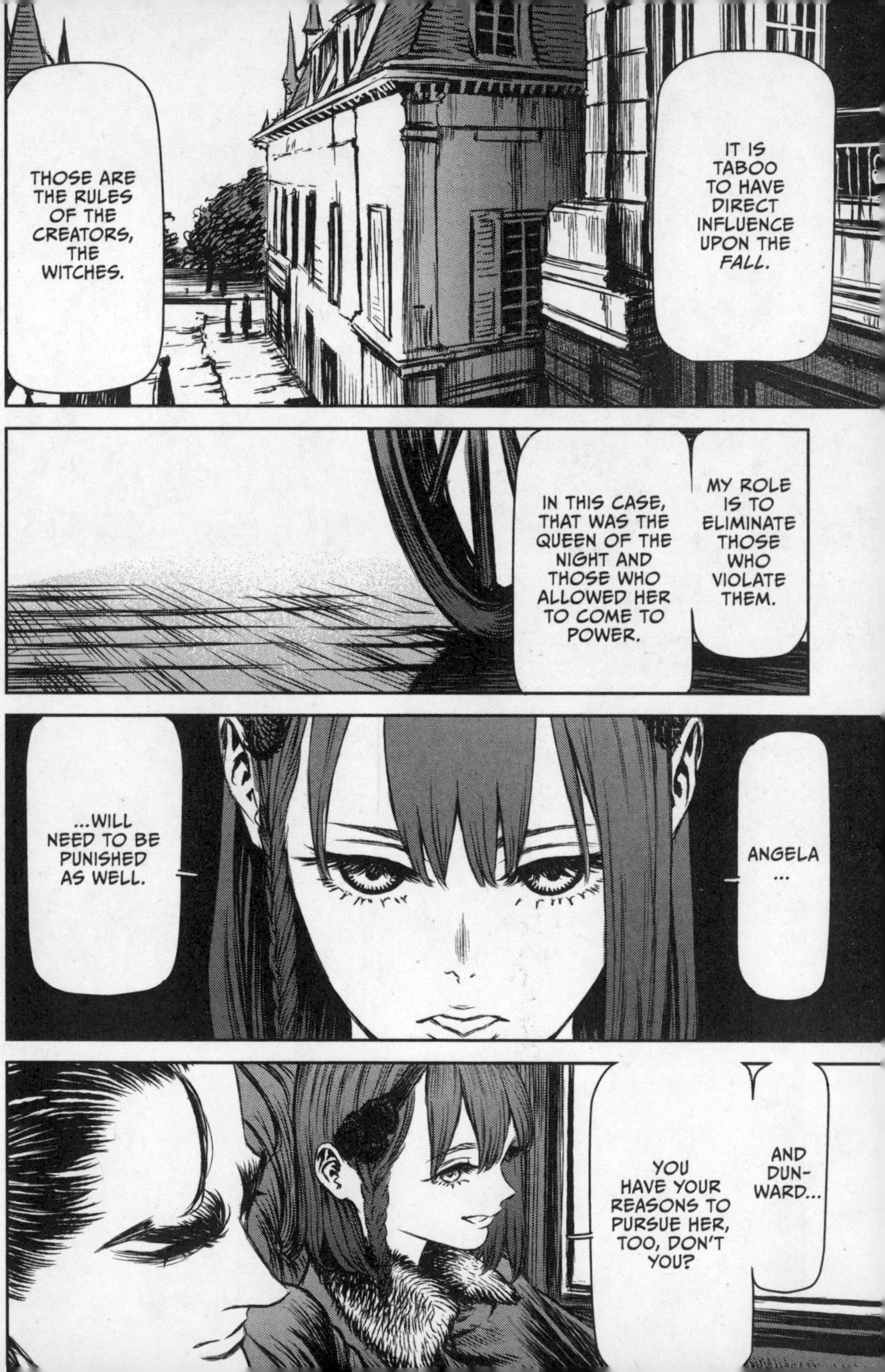
IT IS TABOO TO HAVE DIRECT INFLUENCE UPON THE FALL.
THOSE ARE THE RULES OF THE CREATORS, THE WITCHES.
MY ROLE IS TO ELIMINATE THOSE WHO VIOLATE THEM.
IN THIS CASE, THAT WAS THE QUEEN OF THE NIGHT AND THOSE WHO ALLOWED HER TO COME TO POWER.
ANGELA ...
...WILL NEED TO BE PUNISHED AS WELL.
AND DUN-WARD...
YOU HAVE YOUR REASONS TO PURSUE HER, TOO, DON'T YOU?

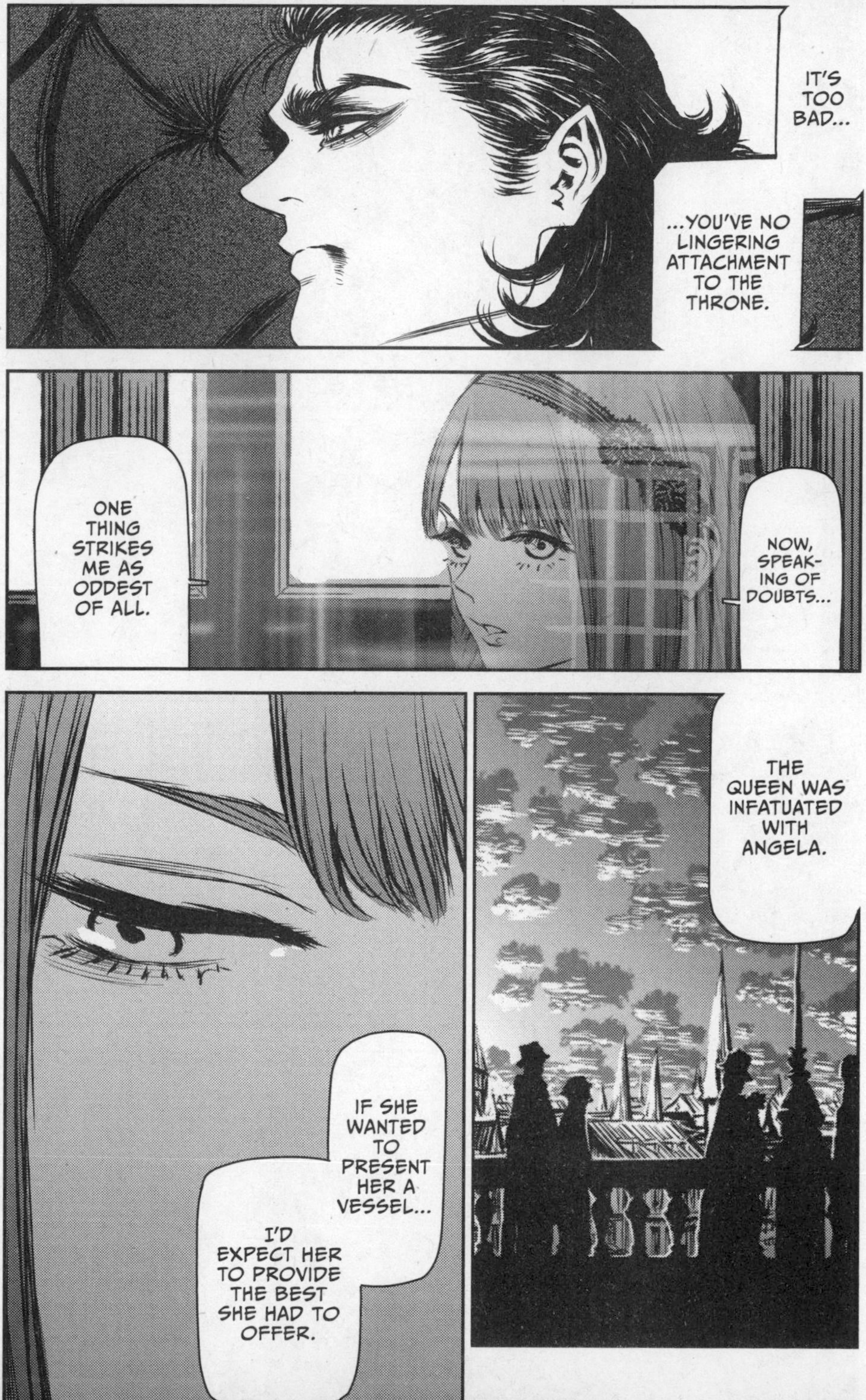
IT'S TOO BAD...
...YOU'VE NO LINGERING ATTACHMENT TO THE THRONE.
NOW, SPEAK-ING OF DOUBTS...
ONE THING STRIKES ME AS ODDEST OF ALL.
THE QUEEN WAS INFATUATED WITH ANGELA.
IF SHE WANTED TO PRESENT HER A VESSEL...
I'D EXPECT HER TO PROVIDE THE BEST SHE HAD TO OFFER.

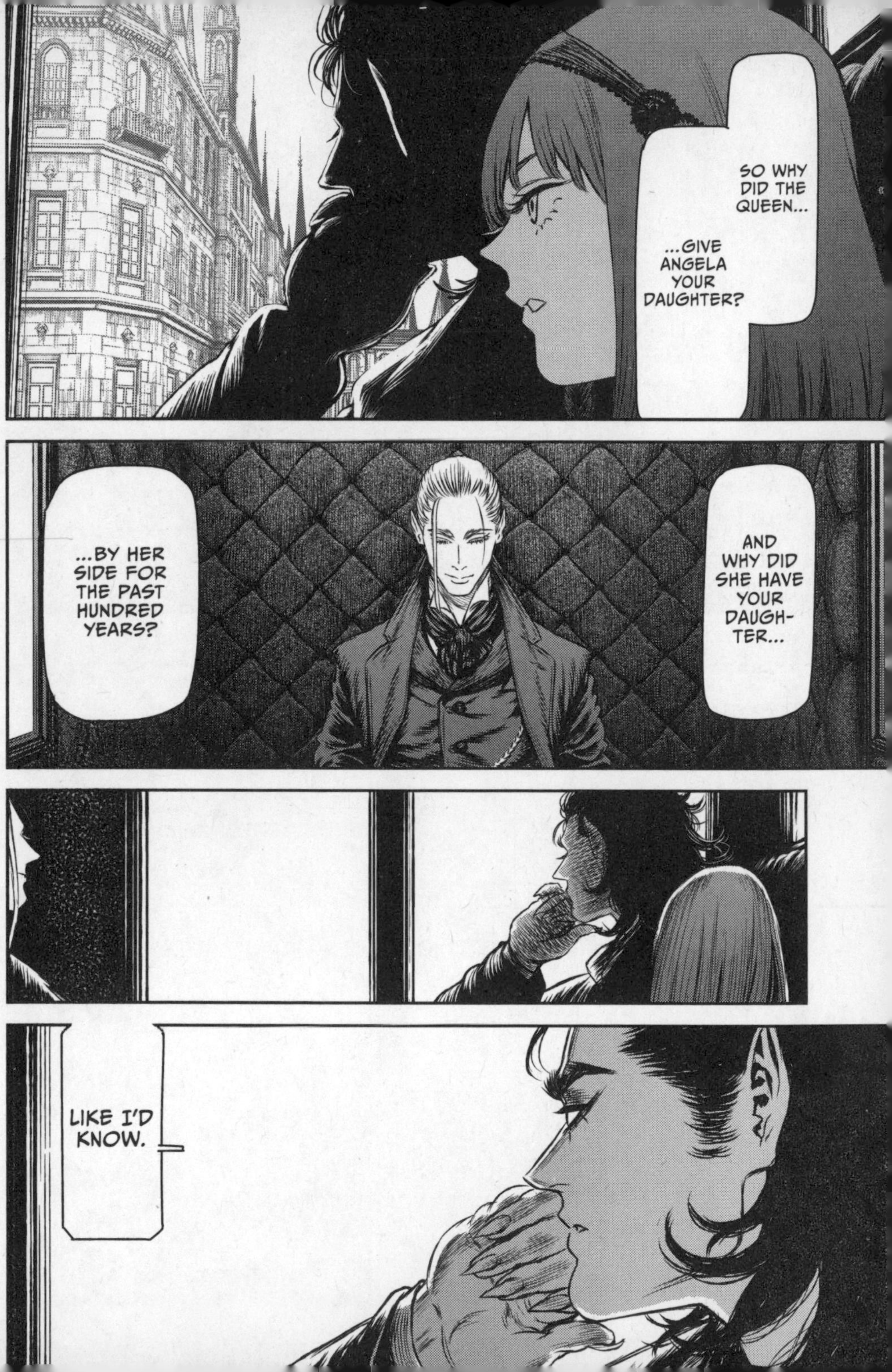
SO WHY DID THE QUEEN...
...GIVE ANGELA YOUR DAUGHTER?
AND WHY DID SHE HAVE YOUR DAUGH-TER...
...BY HER SIDE FOR THE PAST HUNDRED YEARS?
LIKE I'D KNOW.

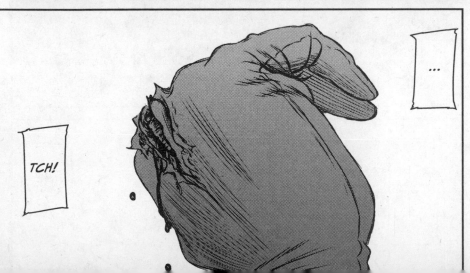

...

TCH!

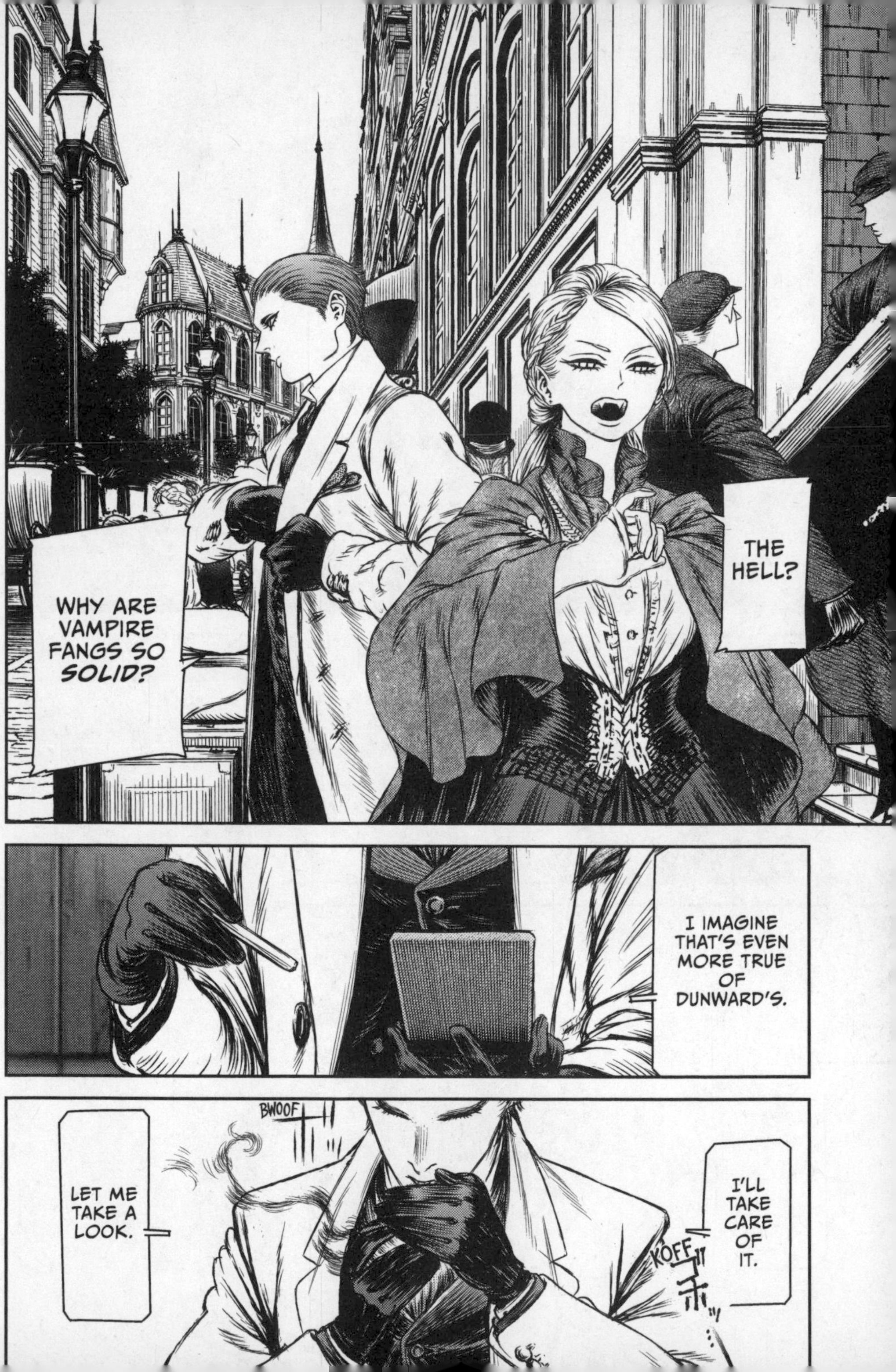
THE HELL?
WHY ARE VAMPIRE FANGS SO *SOLID?*
I IMAGINE THAT'S EVEN MORE TRUE OF DUNWARD'S.
BWOOF
I'LL TAKE CARE OF IT.
KOFF
LET ME TAKE A LOOK.

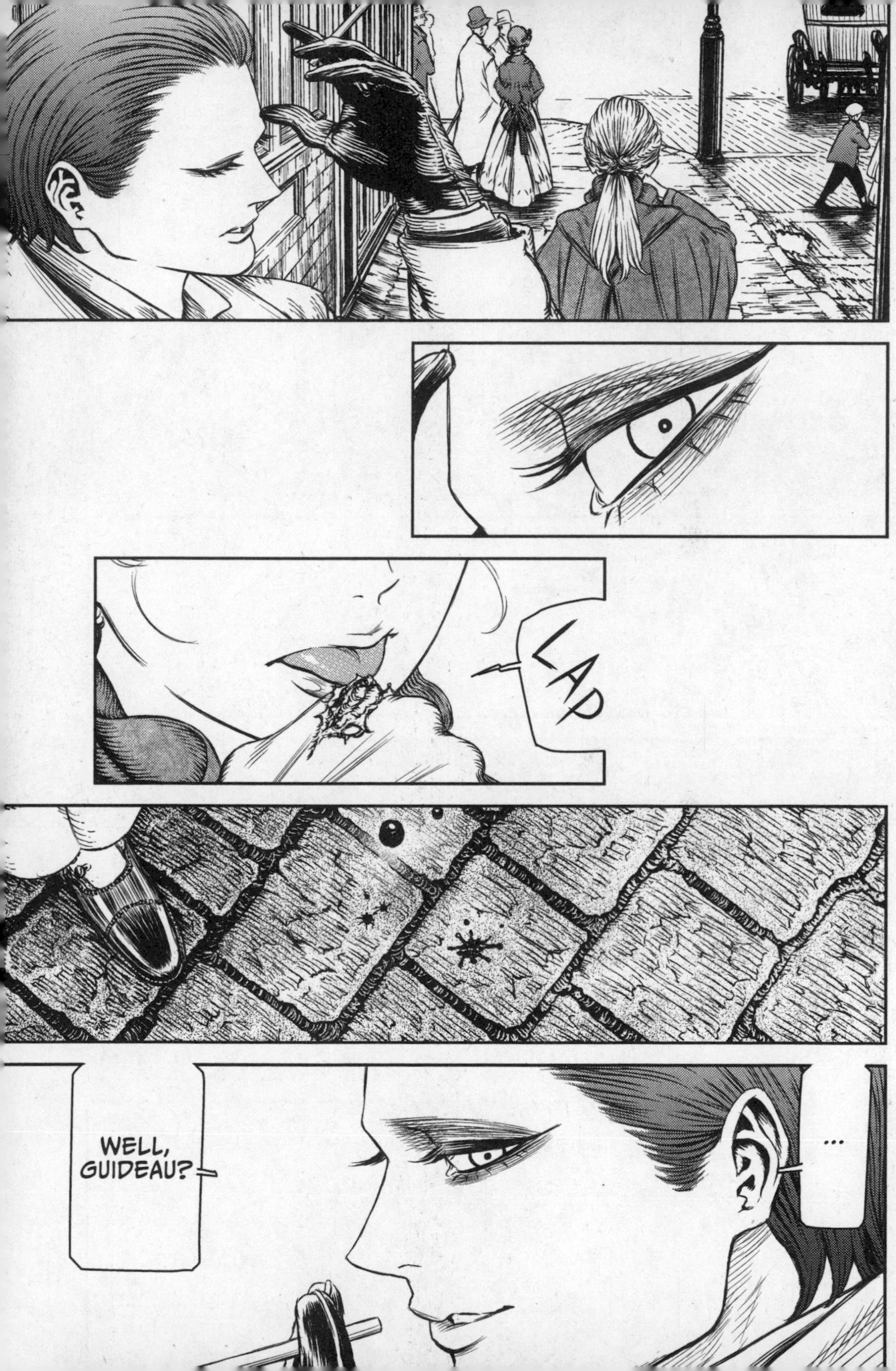
LAP
...
WELL, GUIDEAU?

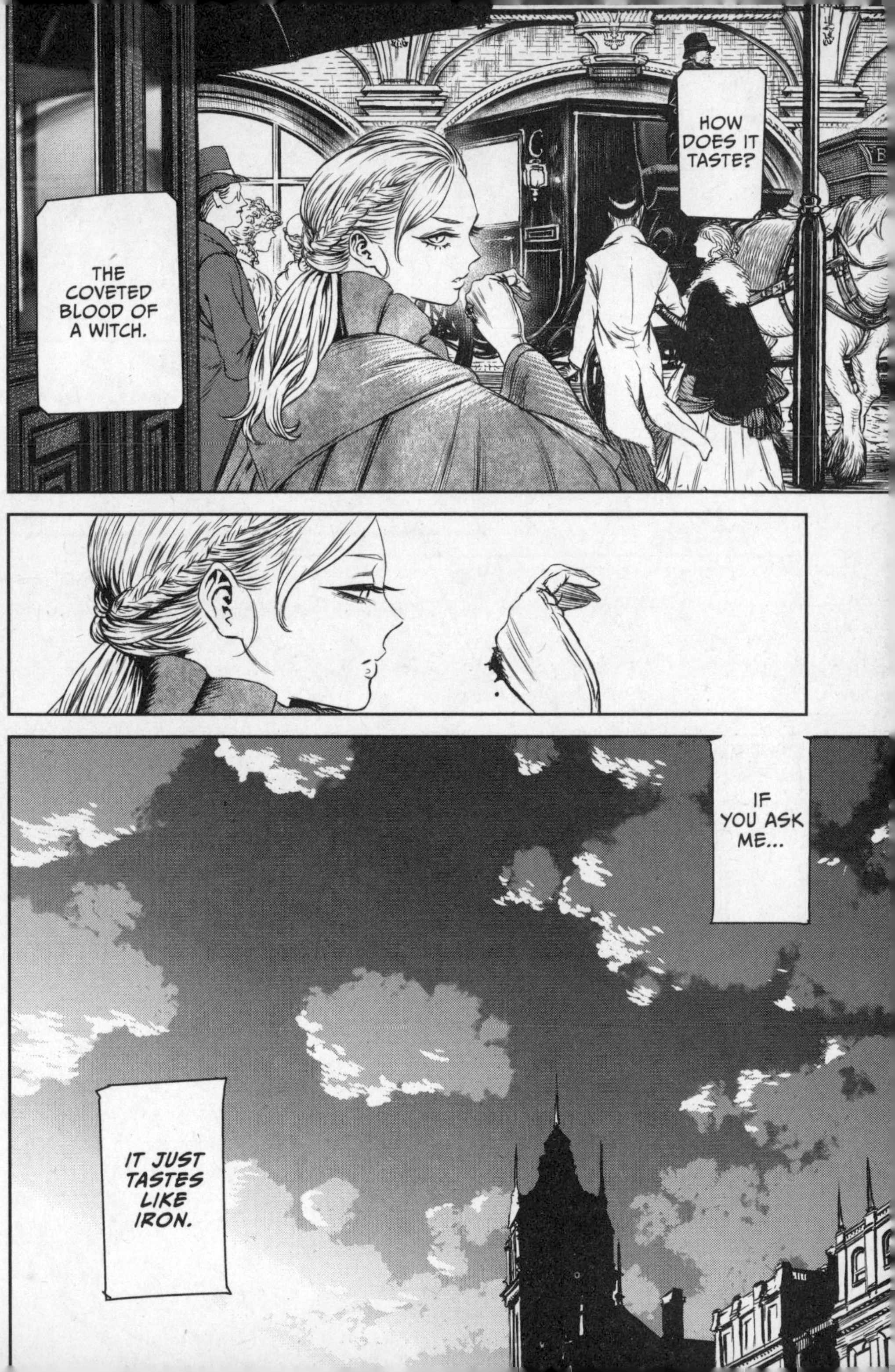
HOW DOES IT TASTE?
THE COVETED BLOOD OF A WITCH.
IF YOU ASK ME...
IT JUST TASTES LIKE IRON.

THE WITCH AND THE BEAST

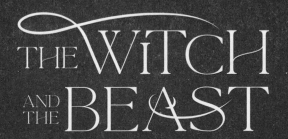

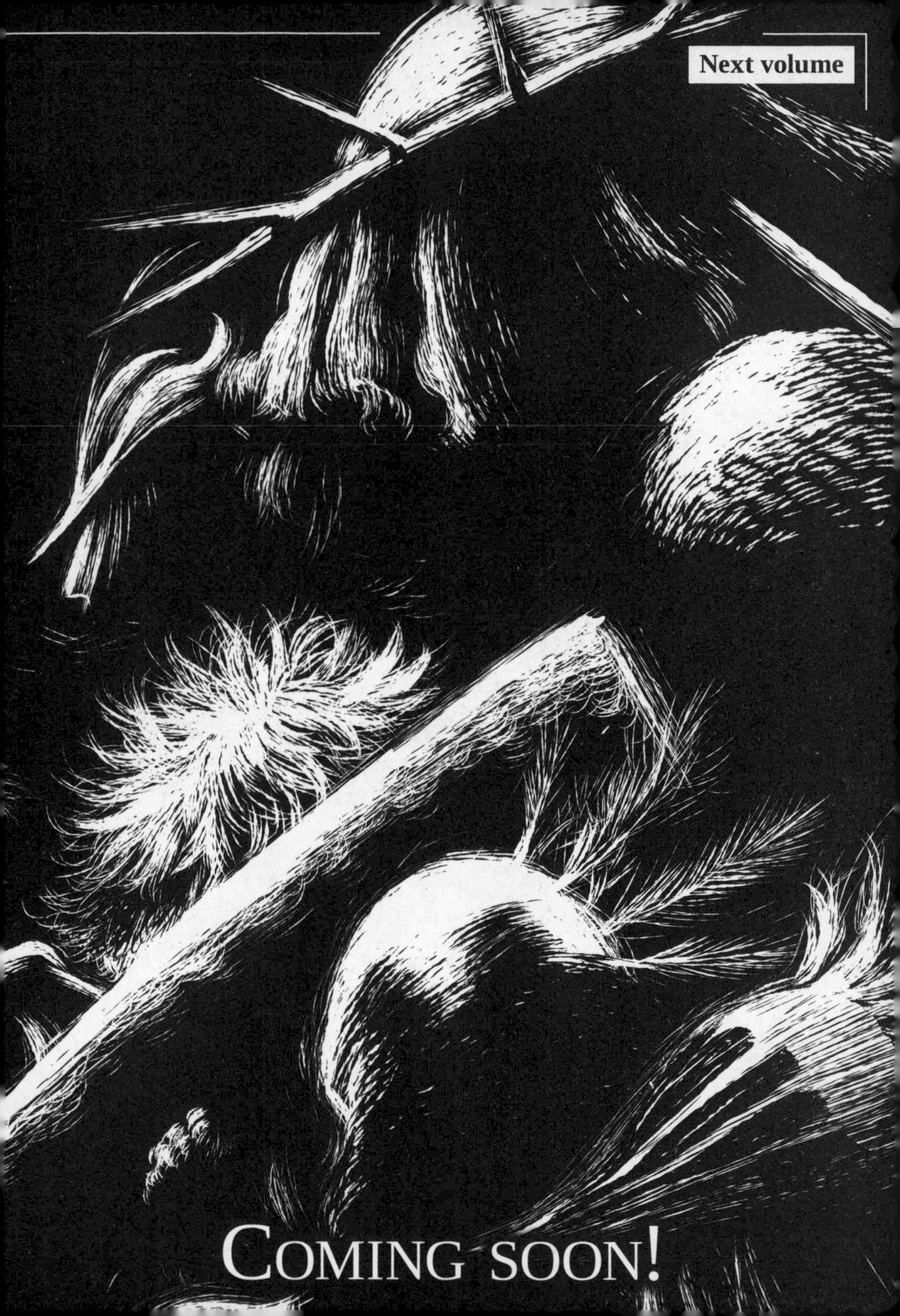
Next volume
Coming soon!

THE RETURN.

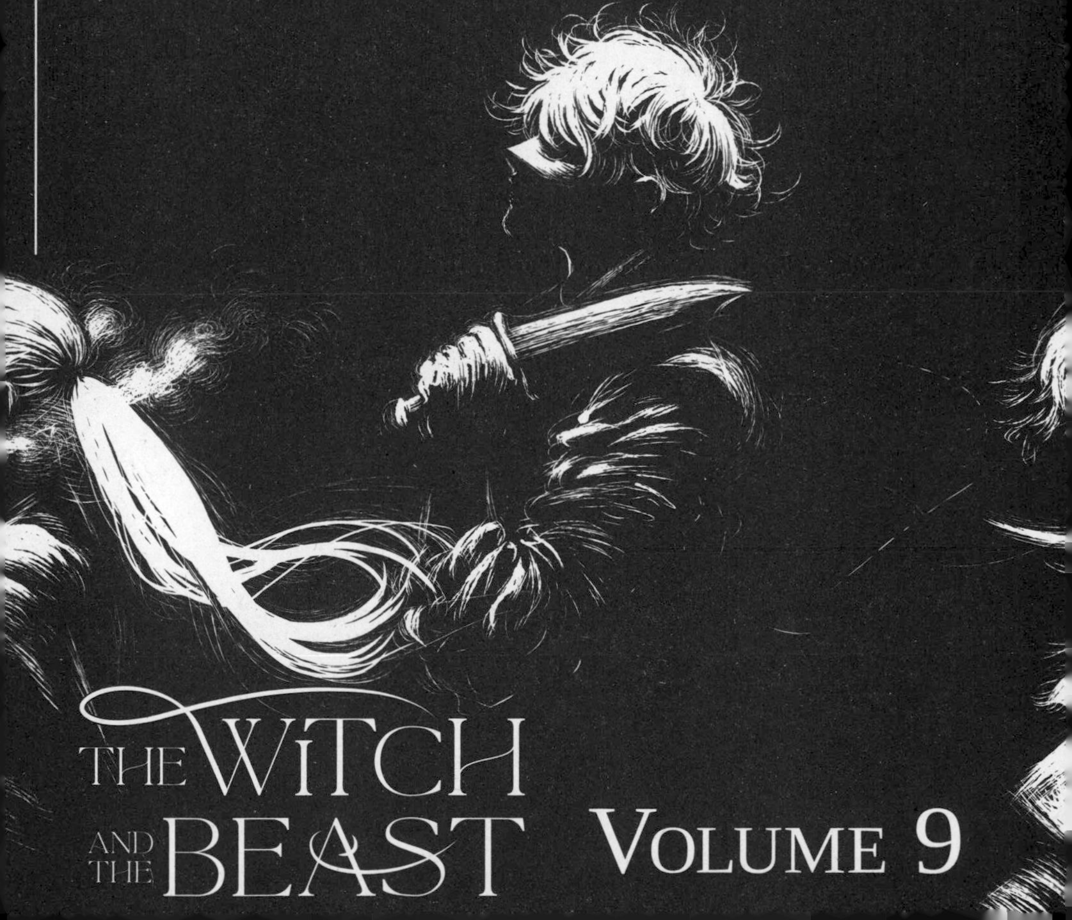

THE WITCH AND THE BEAST

VOLUME 9

A Kodansha Comics Trade Paperback Original
The Witch and the Beast 8 copyright © 2021 Kousuke Satake
English translation copyright © 2022 Kousuke Satake

Published in the United States by Kodansha Comics, an imprint of Kodansha USA Publishing, LLC, New York.

Publication rights for this English edition arranged through Kodansha Ltd., Tokyo.

First published in Japan in 2021 by Kodansha Ltd., Tokyo as *Majo to yaju*, volume 8.

ISBN 978-1-64651-302-4

Original cover design by Yusuke Kurachi (Astrorb)

Printed in the United States of America.

www.kodansha.us

1st Printing
Translation: Kevin Gifford
Lettering: Phil Christie
Editing: Vanessa Tenazas
Kodansha Comics edition cover design by My Truong

Publisher: Kiichiro Sugawara

Director of publishing services: Ben Applegate
Associate director of operations: Stephen Pakula
Publishing services managing editors: Alanna Ruse, Madison Salters
Production managers: Emi Lotto, Angela Zurlo
Logo and character art ©Kodansha USA Publishing, LLC